TRADIVOX
VOLUME IX

TRADIVOX

CATHOLIC CATECHISM INDEX

VOLUME IX

Peter Canisius

Edited by
Aaron Seng

SOPHIA INSTITUTE PRESS
MANCHESTER, NEW HAMPSHIRE

Sophia Institute Press
Box 5284, Manchester, NH 03108
1-800-888-9344

www.SophiaInstitute.com

Sophia Institute Press® is a registered trademark of Sophia Institute.

ISBN 978-1-64413-366-8

LCCN: 2022936274

The Manner of Execution at Tyburn.

Dedicated with love and deepest respect
to all the English Martyrs and Confessors.
Orate pro nobis.

CONTENTS

ACKNOWLEDGMENTS

THE publication of this series is due primarily to the generosity of countless volunteers and donors from several countries. Special thanks are owed to Mr. and Mrs. Phil Seng, Mr. and Mrs. Michael Over, Mr. and Mrs. Jim McElwee, Mr. and Mrs. John Brouillette, Mr. and Mrs. Thomas Scheibelhut, Mr. and Mrs. Kyle Barriger, as well the visionary priests and faithful of St. Stanislaus Bishop and Martyr parish in South Bend, Indiana, and St. Patrick's Oratory in Green Bay, Wisconsin. May God richly reward their commitment to handing on the Catholic faith.

FOREWORD

The Catholic faith remains always the same throughout the centuries and millennia until the coming of our Lord at the end of the time, likewise "Jesus Christ is the same yesterday, today and forever" (Heb 13:8). The Catholic faith is "the faith, which was once delivered unto the saints" (Jude 1:3). The Magisterium of the Church teaches us solemnly the same truth in the following words of the First Vatican Council: "The doctrine of the faith which God has revealed, is put forward not as some philosophical discovery capable of being perfected by human intelligence, but as a divine deposit committed to the spouse of Christ to be faithfully protected and infallibly promulgated. Hence, too, that meaning of the sacred dogmas is ever to be maintained, which has once been declared by holy mother Church, and there must never be any abandonment of this sense under the pretext or in the name of a more profound understanding. May understanding, knowledge and wisdom increase as ages and centuries roll along, and greatly and vigorously flourish, in each and all, in the individual and the whole Church: but this only in its own proper kind, that is to say, in the same doctrine, the same sense, and the same understanding (cf. Vincentius Lerinensis, *Commonitorium*, 28)."[1]

An authentically Catholic catechism has the function of learning and teaching the unchanging Catholic faith throughout all generations. The Roman Pontiffs indeed, taught: "There is nothing more effective than catechetical instruction to spread the glory of God and to secure the salvation of souls."[2] Saint Pius X said, that "the great loss of souls is due to ignorance

---

[1] Vatican I, Dogmatic Constitution *Dei Filius de fide catholica*, Ch. 4
[2] Pope Benedict XIV, Apostolic Constitution *Etsi minime*, n. 13

of divine things."[3] Therefore, the traditional catechisms have enduring value in our own day and age, which is marked by an enormous doctrinal confusion, which reigns in the life of the Church in the past six decades, and which reaches its peak in our days.

I welcome and bless the great project of the "Tradivox" in cataloguing and preserving the hundreds of long-lost Catholic catechisms issued with episcopal approval over the last millennium. This project will convincingly show the essentially unchanging nature of the apostolic doctrine across time and space, and so I invite the faithful of the entire world to support this historic effort, as we seek to restore the perennial catechism of the Church. The project of a catechism restoration on behalf of "Tradivox" will surely be of great benefit not only to many confused and disoriented Catholic faithful, but also to all people who are sincerely seeking the ultimate and authentic truth about God and man, which one can find only in the Catholic and apostolic faith, and which is the only religion and faith willed by God and to which God calls all men.

+Athanasius Schneider, O.R.C.,
Titular Bishop of Celerina
Auxiliary Bishop of the Archdiocese of Saint Mary in Astana

[3] Cf. Pope St. Pius X, Encyclical *Acerbo nimis*, n. 27

PREFACE

S OME are surprised to find that when a given Catholic is asked to "look something up in the catechism," he may well respond: "Which one?" The history of the Catholic Church across the last millennium is in fact filled with the publication of numerous catechisms, issued in every major language on earth; and for centuries, these concise "guidebooks" to Catholic doctrine have served countless men and women seeking a clear and concise presentation of that faith forever entrusted by Jesus Christ to his one, holy, Catholic, and apostolic Church.

Taken together, the many catechisms issued with episcopal approval can offer a kind of "window" on to the universal ordinary magisterium — a glimpse of those truths which have been held and taught in the Church *everywhere, always, and by all.* For, as St. Paul reminds us, the tenets of this Faith do not change from age to age: "Jesus Christ yesterday and today and the same for ever. Be not led away with various and strange doctrines" (Heb 13:8-9).

The catechisms included in our *Tradivox Catholic Catechism Index* are selected for their orthodoxy and historical significance, in the interest of demonstrating to contemporary readers the remarkable continuity of Catholic doctrine across time and space. Long regarded as reliable summaries of Church teaching on matters of faith and morals, we are proud to reproduce these works of centuries past, composed and endorsed by countless priests, bishops, and popes devoted to "giving voice to tradition."

In This Volume

The two works contained in this volume are among the most outstanding catechisms of the Catholic Reformation period, composed by the great catechist and doctor of the Church, St. Peter Canisius.

A NATIVE OF Nijmegen in the Netherlands, Peter Canisius entered the Society of Jesus in 1543 and immediately began a pattern of humble and diligent apostolic work for the good of souls. After years of weary wars and social turbulence, Germany was at that time no stranger to political and religious corruption. Because of this, the protestant revolutionaries had there been afforded what was perhaps the widest scope for action in all of Europe; and although even non-Catholic historians acknowledge that the heretical systems were never a truly popular movement of religious reform, the errors of Luther posed avaricious opportunity for the nobility and landed classes, who soon held vested interest in the public success of heresy. Into the midst of this social and religious turmoil went the young Canisius at the age of twenty-two, commissioned to establish the first Jesuit house in Germany. He quickly distinguished himself as a preacher and teacher, often despite the efforts of the local archbishop of Cologne, Hermann von Wied, who turned apostate and was deposed three years later in 1546, the year of Canisius's priestly ordination. Within the space of a few years, Canisius would serve as a consulting theologian, professor of theology, and university rector, all while maintaining a regular programme of popular preaching and local catechesis wherever he went.

While teaching at the new college in Vienna, the emperor Ferdinand I besought the faculty to compose a serviceable catechism for use in the kingdom – a task that eventually fell entirely to Canisius, as he would later describe in his spiritual testament:

> When I worked for the emperor Ferdinand in Vienna, and preached the holy doctrine at the university and in church, he desired that I not only work through the spoken word, but also with the pen, and compose for his Austrian subjects, whose faith had been damaged, a

catechism which could, with God's mercy, gently lift up the apostates and return those who had gone astray to the true path again.[1]

Although by no means "the first Catholic catechism" as is sometimes claimed, the result of Canisius's efforts was a landmark text in every respect. It preceded the momentous catechism of Trent[2] by more than a decade, and represents the crystallization of the genre into the form that remains familiar today: a highly distilled and systematic series of questions and answers, crafted to the understanding of a particular audience, and translated into the vernacular for the widest possible dissemination.

Canisius would in fact produce three catechisms in the late 1550s, although the latter two are often regarded merely as condensed iterations of the sizable original: the Large Catechism or *Summa Doctrina Christianae* (1555), a compendious and impressively annotated work intended for priests and scholars, which the author expanded from 211 to 222 questions over a rapid succession of editions to meet the needs of theological disputation at the time. This larger work was swiftly followed by *Catechismus Minimus* (1556), which was little more than a 59-question synopsis that fell into obscurity at a comparatively early date, inasmuch as it was first printed as an anonymous appendix to a Latin grammar book, and did not prove especially useful in subsequent decades. The third and most renowned text by far was the *Catechismus Minor* (1558) for students, the work most often referred to as "the Canisius catechism" and variously known as the Small Catechism, Little Catechism, Intermediate Catechism, the *Parvus Catechismus Catholicorum*, and even "the Canisius."

This third work quickly proved to be the most popular of the three. It was received not only as an excellent instruction in the faith, but as a pedagogical model of notable quality in its own right, reproducible in translation throughout the Jesuit mission territories. As the *Catholic Encyclopedia* observes: "The catechism of Canisius is remarkable for its ecclesiastically correct teachings, its clear, positive sentences, its mild and

---

[1] Paul Begheyn, SJ, "The Catechism (1555) of Peter Canisius, the Most Published Book by a Dutch Author in History," *Quaerendo* 36 (January 2006): 51–84.

[2] The *Catechism of the Council of Trent* is found in Volume VII of this series.

dignified form. It is today recognized as a masterpiece even by non-Catholics."[3] Appearing during major technical advances in printing, this catechism became one of the first international bestsellers: no fewer than three hundred editions across Austria, Bohemia, France, Slovenia, Hungary, Spain, Sweden, Ethiopia, India, China, and Japan appeared during the author's own lifetime, and it went into innumerable editions and translations after his death. There are presently over eleven hundred known editions of the work, securing its status as the most published book by a Dutch author in history. The great saint Robert Bellarmine, after publishing his own catechism,[4] admitted that if he had been aware of the *Parvus* at the time, "I would not have put so much effort into writing a new catechism. I would then have simply translated Peter Canisius's catechism from Latin into Italian."[5]

BELLARMINE WAS NOT the only Jesuit interested in translating Canisius's work. In the face of an increasingly oppressive protestant government, demand for Catholic books was driving a steady stream of translation work through the underground press and manuscript networks of England, in which Fr. Henry Garnett, SJ (d. 1606) featured prominently. He is believed to be the first translator if not also the printer of Canisius's two larger catechisms in the English vernacular, both of which are republished in this volume.

The text of the Large Catechism is extracted from the 1622 edition of St. Omer, itself a reprint of the secret press edition of ca. 1592 entitled *A Summe of Christian Doctrine*. This is the largest version of Canisius's original *Summa*, which included expanded treatments of apostolic tradition, the various sins, and the Catholic doctrine of justification. The number of references to scripture and the Church fathers grew from roughly 1,500 to nearly 4,000 in this edition in order that "either being assaulted by any

[3] Otto Braunsberger, "Blessed Peter Canisius," *The Catholic Encyclopedia*, special ed. (New York: The Encyclopedia Press Inc., 1911), 11:759.
[4] A copiously illustrated edition of Bellarmine's *Short Catechism* may be found in Volume II of this series.
[5] Begheyn, *The Catechism of Peter Canisius*, 60.

adversary, or by thyself seeking to rescue out of miserable captivity any soul, [thou] mayest have authorities to allege for whatsoever thou shalt say." In addition to sourcing and standardizing the thousands of references utilized in this edition, we have corrected several printer errors from the original and introduced a number of subheadings to render this large text more navigable.

The English translation of the Small Catechism is taken in turn from publisher John Cousturier's *An Introduction to the Catholick Faith* (1633), which served as a kind of doctrinal and devotional handbook for Catholics of the Stuart era by adding memorizable lists and a large devotional appendix to Canisius's *Parvus Catechismus Catholicorum*. The introductory material has been retained in its entirety, with its familiar lists for keeping the faith "imprinted and even rivetted in thy heart." The translator's opening exhortation to avoid the heresies of the day are matched by a resounding reminder to practicing Catholics that their religious profession alone is not sufficient for salvation: "Not all who are baptized according to the rites of the Catholic Church shall receive everlasting life, but only those who after baptism live righteously, that is, abstain from vices and desires of the flesh."

It would be impossible to overstate the lasting impact that Canisius effected through his catechisms, which come down to us still marked by a charity and humility uncommon to the period. On the third centenary of his death, Pope Leo XIII observed:

> There exist, in effect, certain analogies between our age and the period in which Canisius lived: a period when the spirit of revolution and looseness of doctrine resulted in a great loss of faith and decline in morals. To deliver youth especially from this double scourge was the goal of this man who, after Boniface, is the second apostle of Germany. ... [His catechisms] were used not only in the schools as a spiritual milk for the children, but they were also explained publicly in the churches to the benefit of all. Thus, during three centuries, Canisius has been regarded as the teacher of Catholics in Germany. In popular speech "knowing Canisius" was synonymous with "preserving the Christian faith."[6]

---

[6] Encyclical *Militantis Ecclesiae* (August 1, 1897), nos. 2, 8.

Pope Benedict XVI confirmed the enduring importance of the saint's work in our own century: "Still in my father's generation, people in Germany were calling the catechism simply 'the Canisius.' He really was the Catechist of Germany for centuries, he formed people's faith for centuries."[7] We are honored to once again place the catechisms of this estimable doctor of the Church into the hands of readers around the world.

EDITORIAL NOTE

Our *Catholic Catechism Index* series generally retains only the doctrinal content of those catechisms it seeks to reproduce, as well as that front matter most essential to establishing the credibility of each work as an authentic expression of the Church's common doctrine, e.g., any episcopal endorsement, *nihil obstat*, or *imprimatur*. However, it should be noted that especially prior to the eighteenth century, a number of catechisms were so immediately and universally received as reliably orthodox texts (often simply by the reputation of the author or publisher), that they received no such "official" approval; or if they did, it was often years later and in subsequent editions. We therefore include both the original printing date in our Table of Contents, and further edition information in the Preface above.

Our primary goal has been to bring these historical texts back into publication in readable English copy. Due to the wide range of time periods, cultures, and unique author styles represented in this series, we have made a number of editorial adjustments to allow for a less fatiguing read, more rapid cross-reference throughout the series, and greater research potential for the future. While not affecting the original content, these adjustments have included adopting a cleaner typesetting and simpler standard for capitalization and annotation, as well as remedying certain anachronisms in spelling or grammar.

At the same time, in deepest respect for the venerable age and subject matter of these works, we have been at pains to adhere as closely as possible to the original text: retaining archaisms such as "doth" and "hallowed,"

---

[7] *L'Osservatore Romano*, English Edition, February 16, 2011.

Woodcut depicting an early method used in the production of Catholic catechisms, circa 1568.

and avoiding any alterations that might affect the doctrinal content or authorial voice. We have painstakingly restored original artwork wherever possible, and where the rare explanatory note has been deemed necessary, it is not made in the text itself, but only in a marginal note. In some cases, our editorial refusal to "modernize" the content of these classical works may require a higher degree of attention from today's reader, who we trust will be richly rewarded by the effort.

We pray that our work continues to yield highly readable, faithful reproductions of these time-honored monuments to Catholic religious instruction: catechisms once penned, promulgated, and praised by bishops across the globe. May these texts that once served to guide and shape the faith and lives of millions now do so again; and may the scholars and saints once involved in their first publication now intercede for all who take them up anew. *Tolle lege!*

Sincerely in Christ,
Aaron Seng

TRADIVOX
VOLUME IX

SVMMA DOCTRINAE CHRISTIANAE.

CAPVT PRIMVM DE FIDE & Symbolo Fidei.

Quis dicendus est Christianus?

QVi IESV CHRISTI veri Dei *Acto. II*
& hominis salutarem doctrinam
in eius Ecclesia profitetur. Omnes
proinde leges & sectas, quæ extra
CHRISTI doctrinam & Ecclesiam
vbiuis gentium reperiuntur, vt est
Iudaica, Mahometica, hæretica,
damnat & detestatur penitus, qui
verè Christianus est, et in ipsa CHRI
STI doctrina firmiter acquiescit.

A QVO

A

SUMME

OF CHRISTIAN
DOCTRINE:

Composed in Latin, by the R. Father
PETRUS CANISIUS,
of the Society of Jesus.

2. *Thess.* 3. 6. We denounce unto you, Brethren, in the name of
our Lord Jesus Christ, that you withdrawe yourselves from
every brother walking inordinately, and not according
to the Tradition which they have received of us.

At S. OMERS
For JOHN HEIGHAM, with
permission of Superiors.

Against Those Which Are Ignorant of Things Necessary to Salvation

"No man must run to the darkness of ignorance, that in them he may seek an excuse. For one thing it is not to have known, and another thing to have refused to know. For the will is reprehended in him of whom it is said, 'He would not understand that he might do well.' Yea, that very ignorance which is not of those who will not know, but of those who simply do not know, doth excuse no man, so that he shall not burn with the everlasting fire, if therefore he did not believe because he never heard what he might believe, but perhaps that he may burn more tolerably. For not without cause was it said: 'Pour out thy anger upon the nations which have not known thee.'[1] And that which the apostle[2] hath saith: When he shall come 'in flame of fire to give revenge upon those which know not God.'"[3]

"Because thou hast rejected knowledge, I will also reject thee."[4]

"They said unto God: Depart from us, we will not have the knowledge of thy ways."[5]

"If any man know not, he shall not be known."[6]

"Be ye not made as the horse and mule, in whom there is no understanding."[7]

"Cease not my son to hear doctrine, neither be thou ignorant of the speeches of knowledge."[8]

"We must not think that ignorance will be a sufficient excuse: for there will come a time when, even for our ignorance, we will be punished, when not so much as our ignorance shall obtain pardon."[9]

---

[1] Ps 78:6
[2] 2 Thes 1:8
[3] Augustine, *On Grace and Free Will*, Ch. 5
[4] Os 4:6
[5] Jb 21:14
[6] 1 Cor 14:38
[7] Ps 31:9
[8] Prv 19:27
[9] Chrysostom, *Homily 26 on Romans*

The Preface to the Reader

The glorious apostle Saint Peter[10] very fitly compareth the word of God and the doctrine of the Holy Ghost unto a candle shining in a dark place, until the day dawn, and the daystar arise in our hearts. For although Christ our Savior, the true light of the world, hath by his most bitter passion and precious wounds given light unto our darkness; yea, and of darkness which we were before, made us a shining light: yet so long as we remain in the mist of this mortality, and that it appeareth not what we shall be, we are truly light in comparison of heretics and infidels, but in respect of heaven, we are in the night, and continually converse in obscurity and darkness. All honor then and glory be (as it is worthy) yielded unto him, who, lest we walking in darkness knowing not whither to go, hath provided us a candle of his holy doctrine even in the midst of Egypt, and set it upon a candlestick in the Catholic Church; and where those which are out of this house of God live in palpable darkness, the children of this light may safely expect the rising of this star, which never shall set, which is the clear vision of God's everlasting glory. This light, although by diverse persons who love darkness better than light, it hath by sundry means been assaulted, yet hath these assaults done nothing else but, by increasing the adverse darkness, made the light appear more glorious; and contrary to man's expectation (yet agreeably to God's disposition) not brought water to quench, but fuel to feed so lively flames. Hence may we in all places of our country to our own great comfort, and God's singular glory, out of prisons, out of judgments, out of all manner of public places, out of many persons and families, behold the beams of this light so vehemently issuing forth, that "coming out of the East," for to use our Savior's words, "it appeareth even to the West,"[11] and it shineth so generally abroad that it is renowned in the whole world, which feeling the beauty thereof, glorifieth our Father of light which is in heaven.

[10] Cf. 2 Pt 1:19
[11] Mt 24:27

Only thou (my dear Catholic brother) who being unlearned seekest to tread the steps of thy forefathers, and walking in the darkness of this mortal life, procurest to follow those which before thee have carried lights for thy direction, it sometimes cometh into my mind to fear, lest either thy torchbearers being taken from thee, or for over-long watching, the oil of the lamp which they may leave thee (I mean charity and a good conscience,[12] the tinder and fuel of that light of faith) beginning to fail, the light itself may little by little be extinguished, and so thou returning to thy former darkness, together with the children of darkness, mayest fall and perish. We are not ignorant of his cogitations, who, like a roaring lion, goeth about seeking whom he may devour; and amongst other sleights which he useth, transfiguring himself into an angel of light, with a counterfeit light of hypocrisy and heresy, seeketh to deprive thee of that which is true and sincere.

Wherefore I offer unto thee a torch or candle, containing in it, although in a small match, the whole light of Christian religion, which although it belighted at the candle of another man, yet thou knowest, that light is nevertheless, because it is received of another: and in this it is more free from all suspicion, whereas it is the same light which lighteth many other parts of the world. This when thou hast once received, and fully enjoyed thyself, think that thou hast not performed thy duty, if thou impart it not to thy children. O how they are deceived, and in how great danger of everlasting damnation do they live, who as though they had by carnal generation brought into this world brute beasts (whose only end is to live here, without any end of heavenly bliss) do not seek for their children the means of their salvation, only providing for them earthly riches, not caring for heavenly. Nor considering that besides the very bond of the law of nature, or of God himself, who hath given most strait charge of good education of children, Christ our Savior has consecrated Christian marriages into a sacrament, for this end amongst others, that they present unto our Savior sanctified children by baptism first, and afterward by all Christian and Catholic discipline. Marriage was instituted to propagate

---

[12] Cf. 1 Tm 1:19

the people of God, not to build up the confused walls of Babylon. The Turk or the Jew, if he should perceive his child to have been present at Christian ceremonies, would not stick to embrew his hands in that which he begot. And yet he which professeth himself a Catholic, be sending his child or permitting his child to be sent to such things as are indispensably forbidden by God himself, doth unnaturally deprive his innocent son of that which he could not give him. But true it is which our Savior said, that "wiser are the children of this world in their generation, than the children of light."[13] But thou dear brother, when thou fallest into any such prevarication, think assuredly that thy light has become darkness. And that in darkness thou shalt so long remain, until thou take away the bushel that thou hast set before others' eyes and permit the light to shine to all those of whom thou hast charge.

But to the intent that thou mayest not only perform this duty, which is necessarily and upon pain of utter darkness of thee, but also like unto a child of light, seek that which is perfect, and according to the nature of light, liberally endeavor to communicate unto all men that which thou hast thyself of God received, I have set down in the annotations of this book, which all those places of holy fathers and scriptures which are in the Latin: to the intent that thou either being assaulted by any adversary, or by thyself seeking to rescue out of miserable captivity any soul, mayest have authorities to allege for whatsoever thou shalt say. Of the places of scripture for the most part, I have quoted the very verse that suddenly thou mayest find wherein consisteth the force of the proof.

Finally, I have added certain little kindled fires to lighten some secret corners which might otherwise annoy thee. All which God grant that it may to his glory both maintain and increase the light of thy heart, and bring forth in many obscure minds such brightness of true belief, that we may all worthily walk by the same, conforming our lives thereunto. That so "being made worthy unto the part of the lot of the saints, in the light,"[14] we may, by him which hath delivered us from the power of darkness, be

[13] Lk 16:8
[14] Col 1:12

translated at the length into the everlasting kingdom of the Son of his love, where we shall not only need neither sun nor moon, but we shall receive that perfect light of the Lamb, by whom only as we have been redeemed, so must we also be glorified.

®f Faith and of the Creed

The Meaning of Christian and Christian Doctrine

1. **Who is to be called a Christian?**[15]
He which doth profess the wholesome doctrine of Jesus Christ, true God and man in his Church.[16] He, therefore, which is a true Christian doth utterly condemn and detest all other religions and sects that are elsewhere to be found in any nation or country out of the doctrine and Church of Christ, as the Jewish, heathenish, Turkish, or heretical sect. And doth firmly stay himself in the true doctrine of Christ.

2. **In what brief sum may Christian doctrine be comprehended?**
That a Christian do know and observe those things which do belong both to wisdom and justice.[17] Wisdom, as St. Austen showeth,[18] consisteth in the virtues theological, faith, hope, and charity,[19] which are both infused by God, and being purely and most fervently practiced in this life, they do make man blessed and divine. Justice standeth in two parts,[20] in declining

[15] Cf. Acts 11:26; 1 Pt 4:16
[16] Cf. Athanasius, *Apologia contra Arianos*, Pt. 2; Cyprian, Bk. 4, Epistle 2; *On the Unity of the Church*; Ignatius of Antioch, *Epistle to the Magnesians*; Augustine, *Tractate 113 on John*; *Sermon 181, De Temp.*, Ch. 12; *Enchiridion*, Ch. 5; Tertullian, *Prescription against Heretics*
[17] Cf. Ecclus 1:33
[18] Cf. Augustine, *Retractationes*, Bk. 2, Ch. 63; *Enchiridion*, Ch. 2-3
[19] Cf. 1 Cor 13:13
[20] Cf. Prosper, *Sententia ex Augustine*, n. 98

from evil and doing good. For hereunto belongeth that which the kingly prophet saith: "Turn from evil, and do good."[21] Now out of these fountains, to wit, wisdom and justice, other things are easily drawn and deduced, whatsoever do appertain to Christian instruction and discipline.

3. **What is first taught in Christian doctrine?**
Faith, that very gate and entrance to our salvation, without the which none in this life can find and call upon, serve and please Almighty God. For, "he that cometh to God must believe,"[22] saith the apostle. And, "he that believeth not, shall be condemned"[23] and "is already judged"[24] by the sentence of Christ.[25]

Of Faith

4. **What is understood by the name of faith?**
A gift of God and a light wherewith man, being illuminated, doth firmly assent and cleave unto those things which are revealed by God, and proposed unto us by the Church to be believed,[26] as are these that follow. That God is one in three Persons,[27] that the world was created of nothing,[28] that God was made man,[29] and suffered death for our sakes,[30] that Mary is both a Virgin and the Mother of God,[31] that all the dead are to be raised again to life,[32] that man is born again of water and the Holy Ghost,[33] that

[21] Ps 33:15; Cf. Ps 36:27; 1 Pt 3:10
[22] Heb 11:6
[23] Mk 16:16
[24] Jn 3:18
[25] Cf. Rom 11:14; Heb 11:6; Augustine, *Sermon 38, De Temp.*; *Sermon 1, De Verbis Apostoli*, Ch. 4; Leo the Great, *Sermon 4, De Nat. Dom.*
[26] Cf. Eph 2:8; Heb 11:1; Basil, *Sermon Concerning Faith*; Bernard, *Epistle 190*; Augustine, *Against the Fundamental Epistle of Manichaeus*, Ch. 5
[27] Cf. 1 Jn 5:7
[28] Cf. Gn 1:1
[29] Cf. Jn 1:14; Lk 2:7
[30] Cf. Rom 5:8-10
[31] Cf. Council of Ephesus; Lk 1:35
[32] Cf. 1 Cor 15:51
[33] Cf. Jn 3:5

Christ is wholly in the Blessed Sacrament;[34] and other such of like sort that are the reverend mysteries of our religion, which, being revealed by God, cannot be comprehended by man's capacity, but may be conceived only by faith.[35] Whereupon the prophet saith: "Unless ye will believe, ye shall not understand."[36] For faith respecteth not the order of nature, neither doth she trust to experience of senses, or rely upon the might or reason of man, but upon the power and authority of God, holding this as a most undoubted verity, that the most sovereign and eternal truth, which is God, cannot either deceive nor ever be deceived.[37]

Wherefore, it is the very condition and property of faith to "bring all understanding into captivity, unto the obedience of Christ,"[38] with whom there is no word that is hard to be done, much less impossible.[39] This faith is the light of the soul, the door or entrance to life, the foundation of eternal salvation.[40]

5. **Is there any brief comprehension of faith and sum of all those things that we must believe?**

There is that which the twelve apostles have delivered in their Creed, and which they have aptly distinguished into twelve sections and articles. A work doubtless worthy of such authors which, next unto Christ our Lord, were the principal and most holy founders of the Christian faith.[41] And this Creed surely is, as it were, a plain and evident mark whereby

[34] Cf. Councils of Constance, Florence, and Trent

[35] Cf. Ecclus 3:22; 2 Cor 10:5

[36] Is 7:9 (LXX version)

[37] Cf. Basil, *On Psalm 115*; *Moralia*, Rule 8; Gregory the Great, *Homily 26 on the Gospels*; Chrysostom, *On 1 Corinthians*, Homily 4

[38] 1 Cor 10:5

[39] Cf. Jer 32:27; Lk 1:37

[40] Cf. Eusebius of Emesa, *Homily 2, De Sym.*; Cyril of Jerusalem, *Catechetical Lecture 5*; *On John*, Bk. 4, Ch. 9; Chrysostom, *Sermon on Faith, Hope, and Charity*

[41] Cf. Clement of Rome, *Epistle 1 ad Jacobum Fratrem Domini*; Ambrose, *Epistle 81*; *Sermon 38*; Augustine, *Sermon 181, De Temp.*; Rufinus, *Commentary on the Apostles' Creed*; Irenaeus, *Against Heresies*, Bk. 1, Ch. 2; Bk. 3, Ch. 4; Jerome, *To Pammachius against John of Jerusalem*, Ch. 9; Leo the Great, *Semon 11 on the Passion*; *Epistle 13 to Pulcheria*; *Sermon against Eutychius*; Maximus, *Sermon De Traditione Symb.*

Christians are to be distinguished and discerned from whole wicked persons, which do profess either none at all, or not the right faith of Christ.

Of the Creed

6. **Which be the articles of this Creed?**
   1. I believe in God the Father Almighty, Maker of heaven and earth.
   2. And in Jesus Christ, his only Son our Lord.
   3. Which was conceived by the Holy Ghost, born of the Virgin Mary.
   4. Suffered under Pontius Pilate, was crucified, dead, and buried.
   5. He descended into hell, the third day he rose again from the dead.
   6. He ascended into heaven and sitteth at the right hand of God the Father Almighty.
   7. From thence he shall come to judge the quick and the dead.
   8. I believe in the Holy Ghost.
   9. The holy Catholic Church; the communion of saints.
   10. The forgiveness of sins.
   11. The resurrection of the flesh.
   12. And the life everlasting. Amen.[42]

7. **To what end specially are these words of the Creed?**
   To this end surely: that we may have comprehended in a brief sum the true knowledge of God and of heavenly things, which knowledge truly is necessary to every man that he may live well and happily. And in this Creed, the acknowledging and confessing of the most Holy Trinity hath the first and principal place, that it may in no wise be doubted, but that God, than whom nothing more mighty or better or wiser can be imagined,[43] is one and simple in essence, or divine nature, but is distinguished into

[42] The Creed is expounded by these authors following: Cyril of Jerusalem, *Catechetical Lectures*; Chrysostom, *Homilies 1 and 2 on the Creed*; Augustine, *Enchiridion*; *A Sermon to the Catechumens on the Creed*; *Of Faith and the Creed*; *Sermons 115, 119, 123, 125, 131, 181, 192, 193, 194, De Temp.*; Eusebius of Emesa, *Homilies 1 and 2 on the Creed*; Chrysologous, *Sermons 57, 58, 59, 60, 61, 62*; Maximus, *Homily 1 de Diversis*.

[43] Cf. Augustine, *Confessions*, Bk. 1, Ch. 4

three Persons,[44] so that before all things it be undoubtedly believed that one is the Father, another is the Son, another is the Holy Ghost.[45] The Father is he which begetteth his Son from all eternity: the fountain and framer of things. The Son being begotten of the substance of the Father, is the Redeemer and Savior of the world.[46] The Holy Ghost, which is also called the Paraclete, is the governor of the Church or of Christ's faithful people.[47] Now these three are one: that is to say, one, true, eternal, infinite, and incomprehensible God.[48] Therefore, to this most holy and indivisible Trinity, three principal parts of the Creed do very fitly answer. To wit: the first, of creation; the second, of redemption; the third, of sanctification.[49]

8. **What is the sense and meaning of the first article of the Creed: "I believe in God the Father"?**

It doth first of all show us one God, and the first Person in the Godhead to be the heavenly Father, eternal and most sovereign in might and majesty, to whom nothing is impossible or hard to be done, who hath all power of life and of death.[50]

This God the Father begot the Son from all eternity, and in this time of grace he made us also his children by adoption.[51] His power is so great, that with his only Word he made as well visible as invisible things of nothing, and being so made, doth from time to time preserve and govern them with most high and supreme goodness and wisdom, from whom and to whom are all things.[52] He is the Father of light, with whom there is no change or alteration, the Father of mercies, and God of all consolation;[53] finally, such a one and so puissant, that all things in heaven, in earth, and under the

---

[44] Cf. Augustine, *Of Faith and the Creed*, Ch. 9
[45] Cf. Mt 28:19; Athanasius, *Quicumque Vult*
[46] Cf. Ps 109:3; Heb 1:2; 1 Jn 4:10, 14
[47] Cf. Jn 15:26; 16:7; 14:16, 26
[48] Cf. 1 Jn 5:7; 1 Tm 1:17; 6:15; Jer 32:17-19
[49] Cf. Jer 9:23; Jn 17:3; 1 Cor 2:2; 1 Pt 1:8
[50] Cf. Ws 16:13; 1 Kgs 2:6
[51] Cf. Ps 2:7; Heb 1:2; Rom 8:14
[52] Cf. Ps 32:6; Col 1:16; Mt 6:26; Heb 13:5; 1 Tm 4:10; 6:15; Rom 11:36
[53] Cf. Jas 1:17; 2 Cor 1:3; Acts 14:14

earth do presently obey at his beck, who being our guide and protector, we are preserved safe and harmless, even in the greatest evils and dangers.[54]

9. **What hath the second article: "I believe in Jesus Christ"?**

It doth show the second Person in deity, Jesus Christ, very God and very man; called surely by the name of Jesus, that is to say, the Savior of his people; and Christ, to wit, anointed by the Holy Ghost and full of all grace and truth, our Messiah, King, and high priest that holdeth the principality and sovereignty in all things, and in whom doth corporally inhabit the whole fullness of the Godhead.[55]

Furthermore, it doth show him to be the only Son of God, born of his Father, begotten before all worlds, natural, consubstantial, and altogether equal unto him according to the Godhead;[56] also our Lord, and Lord of all those that believe in him, as having himself of his own accord delivered us when we were lost out of the bondage and thralldom of Satan, and most liberally redeemed us being subject to the yoke of sin and damnation.[57]

He also hath dominion over the wicked: for all things are made subject under his feet.[58] But then he will openly show himself Lord of lords, King of kings,[59] both to the wicked and to the whole world, when he shall bring in subjection all and every his enemies, whether they will or no,[60] and shall burn them as chaff in unquenchable fires.[61] This is that beloved Son, this is our Emmanuel and master whom we must hear;[62] neither is there "any other name under heaven given unto men, wherein we must be saved."[63]

---

[54] Cf. Lk 12:5; Gn 17:2; Ps 26:1; 90; 124:1; Jb 41:1; 1 Cor 10:13; Ecclus 33:1; Cf. also Dt 6:4; Mt 6:9; 1 Tm 1:17; Gn 1:1; Is 53:1; Jb 37:3, 23; Eccles 3:11; Lk 1:37; Jer 32:17

[55] Cf. Jn 1:14; Apoc 17:14; 19:16; Heb 3:1; 5:5; 1 Pt 2:25; Col 1:18; 2:9

[56] Cf. Eph 1:3; Jn 10:36; Heb 1:1ff; Apoc 1:17; Mt 28:18; Dn 7:2ff; Phil 2:6

[57] Cf. Lk 15:6, 24; Rom 8:1ff; 1 Cor 6:20; 1 Pt 1:19

[58] Cf. Ps 8:8; Rom 14:9

[59] Cf. Apoc 19:16; 17:14

[60] Cf. Mt 25:30; 1 Cor 15:24; Ps 109:1

[61] Cf. Lk 3:17, 22; Mt 3:12

[62] Cf. Lk 20:13; Mt 3:17; 17:5; Is 7:14

[63] Acts 4:12; Cf. 1 Jn 5:20; Lk 1:32; 2:10ff; Mt 1:21; Is 9:6; 61:1; Lk 4:18; Ps 44:8; 88:21; Acts 4:27; 10:38; 1 Kgs 10:1; 16:13

10. **What is set before us to believe in the third article: "Conceived by the Holy Ghost"?**

It doth testify unto us that the same Lord that was begotten even from all eternity of God the Father without a mother, for our sakes descended from heaven and took upon him the nature of man, in which he was temporally conceived in Nazareth and in Bethlehem under the emperor Augustus, born without a father of the most pure and undefiled Virgin, the power of the Holy Ghost thus working in her,[64] so that (which exceedeth all admiration) the Word was made flesh, and God became man, and Mary was both the Mother of God and a Virgin.[65]

This temporal conception and generation of the Son of God doth contain the original of man's salvation and redemption, and it is the form of our regeneration,[66] whereby it cometh to pass that we, the cursed children of Adam being conceived of an unclean seed and born the children of wrath, are purified and made clean;[67] also, that of carnal we are made spiritual, and the very sons of God in Christ, to whom the eternal Father would have the elect to be made conformable,[68] "that he might be," saith St. Paul, "the firstborn in many brethren."[69]

11. **What doth the fourth article contain: "Suffered under Pontius Pilate"?**

It showeth that Christ, when he had made an end of his most excellent teaching and working of miracles, did at last accomplish his conflict and agony for the redemption of us that were perished. Therefore, although he were a most innocent and unspotted Lamb, yea and God, also immortal, yet to show his passing great charity toward us, he suffered willingly of most wicked persons all manner of extreme and bitter torments:[70] whereupon he neither eschewed the most unjust judgment of the wicked judge Pilate, nor yet the most shameful and opprobrious punishment of the cross, undertaking a

---

[64] Cf. Gal 4:4; Rom 1:3; Mt 1:18, 20; Lk 1:26; 2:1; Is 7:1ff; Jer 31:22
[65] Cf. Council of Ephesus; Jerome, *Against Helvidius*; Ambrose, *Epistle 81*; Ez 44:2
[66] Cf. Jn 3:5; 1 Pt 2:1ff; 3:21; Heb 2:3; 7:25; Ti 3:5
[67] Cf. Jb 14:4; Eph 2:3; Rom 6:3
[68] Cf. Rom 8
[69] Rom 8:29; Cf. Mi 5:2; Jn 1:1; 16:28; Is 53:8; Jn 6:39; 4:6-51
[70] Cf. Jn 18:4; 19:11; 3:14; 12:32; Mt 27:27; Mk 15:16; Lk 23:14; Jn 19:16; Acts 13:28

most cruel death for us, and not refusing to be buried in another man's monument: to the intent that both living and dying, he might give and employ himself wholly for the behoof of mortal men.[71] Which passion of Christ, blood, cross, wounds, and death do continually yield comfort, health, virtue, and life unto sinners yet,[72] so that we obey and suffer together with our head, that so we may also be glorified with him.[73] "For he being consummate was made to all that obey him cause of eternal salvation."[74]

12. **What use and profit is there in that we frame the cross of Christ with our fingers and do sign our forehead there withal?**

This ceremony surely both the piety of men of ancient time passed, and the constant custom of the Church doth commend unto us. And first of all, we are hereby stirred up to a thankful remembrance of the most high mystery and benefit, which was for our sakes accomplished upon the cross and most bountifully bestowed upon us.

Then we are provoked to fix and settle the true and whole glory, and the anchor of our salvation, in the cross of our Lord.

Furthermore, this is a testimony, that we have no communication with the enemies of Christ's cross, Jews or heathen, but do freely profess against all such him whom we serve, our Lord Jesus, and him crucified.[75]

By this sign also we are moved to the study of patience, that if we be desirous of eternal glory (as surely we ought all to be) we do not think much to embrace that cross which we honor, and the way of the same cross, with Christ our captain.[76]

---

[71] Cf. Ws 2:12; Heb 12:3; Phil 2:8; Rom 5:6; Mt 27:60; Ti 2:14; Gal 1:4; Is 53:12

[72] Cf. 1 Pt 1:18; 1 Jn 1:7; Apoc 1:5; Eph 1:7

[73] Cf. Rom 8:17; 2 Cor 1:7; 1 Tm 2:11

[74] Heb 5:9; Cf. Acts 10:37; Mt 27:50; Mk 15:24; Is 50:6; 53:1; Jb 1:29; Heb 7:26; 1 Pt 1:19; 2:22; Apoc 1:18; 1 Tm 6:13; Rom 5:6; Jn 15:13

[75] Cf. Tertullian, *De Corona Militis*, Ch. 3; Basil, *De Spiritu Sancto*, Ch. 27; Augustine, *On the Catechizing of the Uninstructed*, Ch. 20; *Tractate 118 on John*; Gregory Nazianzen, *Oration 3*; Jerome, *Letter 22*, Ch. 37; *Letter 64*; *On Ezechiel*, Ch. 9; Chrysostom, *Homily 55 on Matthew*; Hist. trip., Bk. 6, Ch. 1; Ephrem, *De Vera Paen.*, Ch. 3; Nicephorus, *Church History*, Bk. 18, Ch. 20; Cyril of Jerusalem, *Catechetical Lectures 4 and 13*; Chrysostom, *Quod Christus Sit Deus*

[76] Cf. Mt 16:24; Lk 9:23; 1 Pt 3:14; 2:19

Moreover, we fetch from hence victorious armor against Satan, long since subdued by the virtue of the cross: yea, and so we are fenced against all the adversaries of our welfare.[77]

Finally, that we may the more happily take anything in hand, and find more prosperous success in all our actions, we take unto us this noble and triumphant ensign of the cross;[78] and expecting in this sign to get the victory, we do not doubt oftentimes to say: "In the name of the Father and of the Son and of the Holy Ghost."[79]

13. **What would the fifth article have us to believe: "He descended into hell, and then rose again"?**

It teacheth us that Christ, after he was dead upon the cross, did penetrate in soul even down to hell, that he might both show himself conqueror of death and of the devil and also a deliverer of the fathers that were detained in limbo; but according to his body wherein he had lain in the sepulcher, the third day after, when it pleased him to return triumphantly from hell, he, by his own power, arose again unto life, being immortal and glorious and the firstborn of the dead.

By which wonderful work he doth comfort and instruct us, that the elect are delivered out of the power of death, hell, and the devil, and he doth offer and commend unto all men such grace and favor of rising again, that those which believe truly in Christ may rise from vice to virtue, from the death of sin unto the life of grace,[80] and finally in the end of the world, from the death of the body to an immortal life.[81] "For he which raiseth up Jesus, will raise up us also with Jesus."[82]

---

[77] Cf. Athanasius, *Life of St. Anthony*; Jerome, *Life of St. Hilarion*; Ignatius of Antioch, *Epistle to the Philadelphians*

[78] Cf. Ambrose, *Sermon 43*

[79] Cf. Eusebius, *Life of Constantine*, Bk. 1 and 2; Nicephorus, *Church History*, Bk. 8, Ch. 3; Bk. 7, Ch. 47 and 49

[80] Cf. Rom 6:4; Col 3:1; Phil 3:20; Eph 4:22; 1 Pt 1:3

[81] Cf. 1 Cor 15:22

[82] 2 Cor 4:14; Cf. 1 Thes 4:14; Cf. also Ps 15:10; Zac 9:11; 1 Pt 3:19; Col 2:15; Ecclus 24:45; Acts 2:24; Os 13:14; Irenaeus, *Against Heresies*, Bk. 5, Ch. 31; Augustine, *Epistle 99*; *Epistle 57*, q. 1; *City of God*, Bk. 20, Ch. 15; *Sermon 137, De Temp.*; Jerome, *On Ephesians*,

14. **What signifieth the sixth article: "He ascended into heaven"?**

It showeth that our Lord Jesus, after that he had finished the work of man's redemption, and appeared alive again unto his disciples, and confirmed with many arguments the truth of his resurrection, at the last, on the forty day after, ascended into heaven, that, according to his human nature, he might be exalted above all things, and himself alone above all others, renowned and honored of all men.

Therefore, our Lord Jesus sitteth in heaven on the right hand of the power of God, exercising equal power with the Father, governing all things; and wholly shining with divine majesty;[83] which is indeed to sit at the right hand of his Father.[84] This joyful ascension of Christ is the assurance of our faith and hope, so that whither the head hath gone before, (when once his enemies are vanquished) thither the members also, so that they obey and cleave to their head, may have great hope to attain.[85] "I go, (saith he), to prepare you a place."[86]

15. **What doth the seventh article insinuate: "From thence he shall come to judge"?**

It setteth before our eyes the latter day of judgment, when Christ shall descend in human flesh from the highest heaven, and shall sit in dreadful doom and judgment over the whole world, and in the open face thereof, shall render unto every one according to his works. Therefore, in the seat and throne of his majesty, he shall judge all without exception, good and bad, as well those that shall be alive when the day of judgment shall come, as those that were before departed out of the world.[87]

Ch. 4; *On Osee*, Ch. 13; Tertullian, *Against Marcion*, Bk. 2, Ch. 4; Mt 12:29; Heb 2:14; Mk 16:9; Apoc 1:5, 18; Jn 2:19; Col 1:18; 1 Cor 15:5

[83] Cf. Ps 109; Acts 7:55; Lk 22:69; 1 Cor 15:25; Eph 1:20; Mt 28:18

[84] Cf. Augustine, *Of Faith and the Creed*, Ch. 7

[85] Cf. Heb 5:9; Rom 8:17; 2 Tm 2:11; Jn 15:6

[86] Jn 14:2; Cf. Ps 67:19, 33ff; 46:6; 8:2; Mk 16:19; Jn 3:13; Acts 1:1; Eph 4:8; 2:6; 1:20; Col 3:1; Heb 1:3; 1 Pt 2:4; 1 Jn 2:1; Jn 20:17

[87] Cf. Mt 25:31; 24:11; Lk 21:25; Acts 10:42; 1 Thes 4:15; 5:2; 1 Cor 15:51; 2 Thes 2:1; 2 Pt 3:3

Whereby we are admonished to live so much more warily and up-rightly, by how much more certainly we are persuaded that all the actions, thoughts, and designments of our life are always apparent before the presence of Almighty God, that seeth all things and judgeth them most righteously.[88] For he is a righteous and just searcher of hearts and revenger of iniquities, before whose tribunal we must all be presented, that every one may receive at his hand accordingly as he hath behaved himself in his body, be it well or evil.[89] Who will neither defraud anything well done in this life of due reward, nor let any evil deeds escape unpunished.[90]

16. What is the sum of the articles of the second Person in deity?
This: that Christ is true God and man, who began and brought to pass the wonderful work of man's redemption, so that he is unto us the way, truth, and life, by whom only when we had all perished, we were saved and restored, and reconciled unto God the Father.[91]

Of the benefit and true use of which redemption we find thus written: "The grace of God our Savior hath appeared to all men instructing us, that, denying impiety and worldly desires, we live soberly, justly, and godly in this world, expecting the blessed hope and advent of the glory of the great God and our Savior Jesus Christ, who gave himself for us that he might redeem us from all iniquity, and might cleanse to himself a people acceptable, a pursuer of good works."[92] These be the words of the apostle St. Paul; and in another place: "We are the work of God, created in Christ Jesus in good works, which God hath prepared that we should walk in them."[93] And again, "Christ died for all: that they also which live may not now live to themselves, but to him that died for them and rose again."[94]

[88] Cf. Mt 12:36; Ws 1:8; Is 66:18; Eccles 12:14; Rom 2:14; Apoc 20:11; Basil, *Epistle 46 to a Fallen Virgin*
[89] Cf. Jer 17:9; Heb 4:12; Gal 6:5; 1 Thes 4:6; Eccles 12:14; 2 Cor 5:10; Rom 14:10
[90] Cf. Mt 16:4; Jb 24:12; Cf. also Ps 96:2; Is 3:13; 66:13; Jn 5:22, 26; Soph 1:14; Mal 4:1; Jl 3:1
[91] Cf. Jn 14:6; Rom 5:6; Apoc 1:5; 1 Tm 2:5; Rom 3:24
[92] Ti 2:11-14
[93] Eph 2:10
[94] 2 Cor 5:15

Wherefore we must take diligent heed of the erroneous opinion of those that do confess Christ not wholly and perfectly but, as it were, lame and maimed, whilst they do only acknowledge him as a mediator and Redeemer, in whom we may trust,[95] but do not withal admit him for a law-maker, whose commandments we must obey; and a pattern of all virtue, which we must imitate;[96] and a just judge, who surely is to repay the due reward or punishment to the works of everyone.[97]

17. **What doth the eighth article teach us: "I believe in the Holy Ghost"?**
It specifieth the Holy Ghost, the third Person in deity; who, proceeding from the Father and the Son, is true God, coeternal, coequal, and consubstantial to both, and to be worshipped with the same faith, and with equal honor and adoration.

This is that Paraclete and teacher of truth, that doth lighten, purify, and sanctify the hearts of believers with his grace and gifts, and confirm them in all holiness. This is the pledge of our inheritance, who helpeth our infirmity and divideth to every one according as he will his diverse gifts.[98]

18. **What addeth the ninth article: "I believe the holy Catholic Church"?**
It doth show and declare unto us the Church, that is to say, the visible congregation of Christ's faithful people, for which the Son of God, taking upon him the nature of man, did and suffered all things.[99]

And first it teacheth that the same Church is one, and uniform in faith, and in the doctrine of faith, and administration of sacraments;[100] which,

---

[95] Cf. 1 Tm 2:5; Rom 3:24
[96] Cf. Is 33:22; Jas 4:12; Jn 13:15, 34; 1 Jn 2:6; 1 Pt 2:21
[97] Cf. 2 Tm 4:7; Rom 2:5; Creed of Constantinople; Council of Florence; Gn 1:2; Ps 103:30; Jb 24:13; Mt 28:19; Jn 1:32; 14:16; 16:7; 1 Jn 5:7; Rom 8:9; 2 Cor 3:17; 1 Cor 6:15; 3:16; Ps 40:12; Is 11:1; Gal 5:22; Rom 5:5; Cf. also Jn 1:1, 14, 34; 1 Jn 5:20; Eph 1:7
[98] Cf. Eph 1:13; Rom 8:26; 1 Cor 12:11
[99] Cf. Mt 5:15; Is 60:1; 2:2; Ps 18:5; Augustine, *Tractate 1 on John*; *Epistle to Catholics of the Donatist Sect*, Ch. 16; *On Psalm 30*, conc. 2; Chrysostom, *Homily 4 de Verb. Esaiae*
[100] Cf. Jn 11:52; 10:16; 17:11; Cant 6:8; 1 Cor 1:10; 12:12, 25; Eph 4:3; Cyprian, *On the Unity of the Church*; Irenaeus, *Against Heresies*, Bk. 1, Ch. 3; Jerome, *Epistle 123 to Ageruchia*, Ch. 4; Chrysostom, *Homily 1 on 1 Corinthians*

under one only head Christ Jesus, and one vicegerent upon earth, the chief bishop, is governed and kept in unity.[101]

Then, it giveth us to understand that she is holy. Because Christ doth always sanctify her by the Holy Ghost, so that she is never destitute or void of holy men and holy laws. Neither can any man be partaker of any holiness and sanctification that is not of her society and congregation.[102]

Thirdly, that she is catholic, that is to say, universal, so that she, being dispersed throughout the world, in her motherly bosom receiveth, embraceth, and safely keepeth all persons of all times, places, and nations, so that they be of one mind and consent in the faith and doctrine of Christ.[103]

Fourthly, that there is in the same Church a communion of saints, so that those which live in the Church, as in the house and family of Almighty God, do hold an inseparable society and unity amongst themselves, and as members of one and the selfsame body, help and assist one another, with mutual benefits, merits, and prayers. Amongst them there is unity of faith, consent of doctrine, conformable use of sacraments;[104] and notwithstanding the dissentions and errors, whatever they be, that, by means of some few, may spring and grow up, yet are they always "careful to keep the unity of the Spirit in the band of peace."[105] And in this communion, undoubtedly not only the saints of the Church militant, that do travail as pilgrims upon earth, but also all the blessed saints of the Church most happily triumphant with Christ in heaven, as also the souls of the

[101] Cf. Cyprian, *On the Unity of the Church*; *Epistle 55*; *Epistle 69*; Irenaeus, *Against Heresies*, Bk. 3, Ch. 3; Jerome, *Epistle 15 to Damasus*; *Epistle 16 to Damasus*; Leo the Great, *Epistle 89 ad Vien.*

[102] Cf. Eph 5:27; Can 4:7; 1 Pt 2:9; Augustine, *Enchiridion*, Ch. 56; *On Psalm 85*; Bernard, *Sermon 3 in Virg. Nat.*; Gregory the Great, *Moralia in Job*, Bk. 35, Ch. 6; Irenaeus, *Against Heresies*, Bk. 3, Ch. 40

[103] Cf. Acts 1:8; Gn 22:18; Mk 16:15, 20; Lk 24:47; Mt 28:19; 16:18; Augustine, *Epistle 170*; *Epistle 166*; *Against the Fundamental Epistle of Manichaeus*, Ch. 4; *De Vera Religione*, Ch. 7; Pacian, *Epistle 1 ad Simpron.*; Vincent of Lerins; Jerome, *Dialogue against the Luciferians*, Ch. 9; Bede, *On Canticle of Canticles*, Ch. 6

[104] Cf. Eph 4:11, 16; Ps 118:63; Col 1:12; Phil 1:4; 2 Cor 8:14; 1 Jn 1:3; Rom 12:4; 1 Cor 12:4; Augustine, *Tractate 32 on John*

[105] Eph 4:3

godly, which, having departed this life, are not yet come to that happy estate of the blessed saints, are altogether jointly comprehended.[106]

Out of this communion of saints (like as out of the ark of Noah) there is certainly undoubted destruction, but no salvation for mortal men:[107] not for the Jews or heathens that never received the faith of the Church; not for heretics that have forsaken the faith once received, or any way corrupted the same; not for schismatics that have divided themselves from the peace and unity of the Church; finally, not for excommunicate persons that, for any grievous crime or cause, have deserved to be cut off as hurtful, pernicious members from the body of the Church.[108]

And all and every of these because they do not appertain unto the Church and to her holy communion, they cannot be partakers of the grace of God and eternal salvation, except they be first reconciled and restored unto the same Church, from which they, through their own default, have once been separated.[109] For most certain is the rule of Saint Cyprian[110] and St. Augustine,[111] that: he shall not have God to be his Father, that will not have the Church to be his mother.

19. **What doth the tenth article set before us?**

Remission of sins, without the which none can be just or obtain salvation. And this most rich treasure Christ hath purchased for us, by his bitter

---

[106] Cf. Eusebius, *Ecclesiastical History*, Bk. 7, Ch. 19; Augustine, *Epistle to Catholics of the Donatist Sect*, Ch. 6; *Epistle 19*; *De Vera Religione*, Ch. 6; *Sermon 181, De Temp.*, Ch. 13; *Enchiridion*, Ch. 56; *City of God*, Bk. 20, Ch. 9; Gregory the Great, *Dialogues*, Bk. 4, Ch. 39

[107] Cf. Gn 7:23; 1 Pt 3:20; Is 60:12; Augustine, *Epistle 50*; *Epistle 152*; *Epistle to Catholics of the Donatist Sect*, Ch. 4 and 19; Fulgentius, *Letter to Peter on the Faith*, Ch. 37-39; Pacian, *Epistle 2 ad Simpro.*; Irenaeus, *Against Heresies*, Bk. 4, Ch. 43; Gregory the Great, *Moralia in Job*, Bk. 14, Ch. 2; Chrysostom, *Homily 11 on Ephesians*; Fourth Lateran Council, Const. 1; Alcimus Avitus, *De Spiritualis Historiae Gestis*, Bk. 4, Ch. 19; 1 Jn 2:19; Jn 6:66; Jude 1:18

[108] Cf. 1 Cor 5:4; 1 Tm 1:20; Nm 12:14; Mt 18:17; 2 Jn 1:10; 2 Thes 3:6, 14; Cyprian, *Epistle 62*; Augustine, *Contra Adversarium Legis et Prophetarum*, Bk. 1, Ch. 17; Eusebius apud John Damascene, *Sacra Parallela*, Bk. 3, Ch. 45

[109] Cf. Augustine, *Sermon 181, De Temp.*; *On Psalm 88*, conc. 2; *Epistle 204*; Cyprian, *Epistle 57*; *Epistle 52*

[110] Cf. Cyprian, *On the Unity of the Church*, n. 6

[111] Cf. Augustine, *A Sermon to Catechumens on the Creed*, Ch. 1

death and most precious blood, that the whole world might be exempted from sin and from the perpetual punishments due unto the same.[112]

Of which treasure certes, they only are made partakers by the grace of Christ that do unite themselves by faith and baptism to the Church of Christ, and do abide in the unity and obedience of the same.[113] Then afterward, they also that have diligently done penance for their sin committed after baptism, and do conveniently use those medicines and remedies against sin that Christ hath ordained, to wit, the holy sacraments of the Church.[114] And hereunto belongeth the power of the keys, as they call it, which Christ for the remission of sins hath committed unto the ministers of the Church,[115] and especially to the apostle St. Peter, and his lawful successors, as to the supreme guides and rulers of the Church.[116]

20. **What hath the eleventh article?**

It declareth the resurrection of the flesh, which at the latter day shall be common to good and bad. For this frail brittle body of ours that we bear about with us, pestered with so many diseases, and subject to such continual griefs and miseries, that must after our death become a prey for worms, shall then revive: when at that last day, all the dead at the voice of Christ the judge shall be raised both to life and judgment. All therefore shall appear in flesh before the tribunal of Christ, that everyone without exception, accordingly as he hath behaved himself in his body, which then shall be restored unto him whole again, so may receive either good or evil.[117] "And they that have done good things, shall come forth into the

---

[112] Cf. Is 33:22; Mt 1:21; 9:6; Apoc 1:5; Lk 24:47; Acts 10:42; Heb 9:13; 1 Jn 1:7; Eph 1:7; Col 1:13; Heb 1:3

[113] Cf. Acts 2:38; 8:12, 36; Mk 16:16; Jn 3:5; Augustine, *Enchiridion*, Ch. 65; *Sermon 11, De Verbis Domini*, Ch. 20 and 22

[114] Cf. 2 Cor 12:21; Acts 8:22; Jn 20:23; Apoc 2:5

[115] Cf. Jerome, *Epistle 14 to Heliodorus*, Ch. 8; Augustine, *Homily 49*, Ch. 3; *Homily 50*, Ch. 4 and 5; *inter quinquag. hom.*; Chrysostom, *On the Priesthood*, Bk. 3; Cyprian, *Epistle 54*; Lk 10:35; Mt 18:18; Jn 20:22

[116] Cf. Mt 16; Hilary, *On Matthew*, Ch. 16; Bernard, *De Consideratione*, Bk. 2, Ch. 8; Council of Florence; Jn 21:15

[117] Cf. 2 Cor 5:10; Rom 14:10

resurrection of life: but they that have done evil, into the resurrection of judgment and punishment everlasting."[118]

In the faith and belief hereof, a good and patient man doth take solace and comfort in the greatest miseries that may befall, so that at the very last gasp of life, he will say, "I know that my Redeemer doth live, and in the last day I shall rise from the earth, and again be compassed about with my skin, and in my flesh I shall see God."[119] Wise therefore certes, and most wise are those that do bring into the servitude of justice and virtue these earthly dying members, and do prepare this body as a pure vessel for the happy immortality that is to come.[120]

21. **What is the last article?**

Of life everlasting,[121] which we may nothing doubt to remain unto the elect after their death. And this is the fruit and final end of faith, hope, patience, and Christian-like exercise. For the obtaining of which life, to a true believer, no work of piety ought to seem difficult, no labor painful, no grief bitter, no time long or tedious in well working or suffering. And if this life, notwithstanding that it is replete with all manner of calamities, be accompted a thing most choice and delightful, how much more is that life to be had in great price and estimation which is so far off from any feeling and fear of evil, and is replenished on every side with heavenly and unspeakable joys, pleasure, and delights, that never shall have end?[122] Of which life Christ saith thus: "Fear not little flock, for it hath pleased your Father to give you a kingdom."[123] And at the latter day of judgment he will say unto the elect:

[118] Jn 5:29; Cf. Mt 13:10, 40; 25:46; Athanasius, *Quicumque Vult*
[119] Jb 19:25-26
[120] Cf. Col 3:5; 1 Pt 3:18; 1 Cor 9:27; Rom 6:12; 1 Cor 15:42; Cf. also Is 26:19; Jb 19:25; Ez 37; 1 Cor 15:51; 1 Thes 4:16; Jn 11:24; 5:25; Mt 22:23; Dn 12:2; Phil 3:21; Jerome, *Epistle 119 to Minervius and Alexander; Epistle 61; On John*, Ch. 9ff; Gregory the Great, *Moralia in Job*, Bk. 14, Ch. 30ff; Augustine, *Enchiridion*, Ch. 84ff; *City of God*, Bk. 22, Ch. 12ff
[121] Cf. 1 Cor 2:9; Jn 17:3; Mt 19:12, 14, 17, 23, 29; 25:34, 46; Apoc 2:7, 10, 17, 26; 3:11, 21; 7:14; 21:2, 10, 23; 22:1, 12; Rom 2:6; Ti 1:1; 2:13; 3:7; 2 Tm 4:7; 1 Jn 2:25; 3:2; 1 Pt 1:3; Rom 6:22
[122] Cf. Augustine, *City of God*, Bk. 22, Ch. 29-30; *De Libero Arbitrio*, Bk. 3, Ch. 25; *Sermon 64, De Verbis Domini*, Ch. 1ff; *A Sermon to Catechumens on the Creed*, Ch. 12
[123] Lk 12:32

"Come ye blessed of my Father, possess you the kingdom prepared for you, from the foundation of the world."[124] But unto the wicked he will speak in this manner: "Get ye away from me you cursed, into fire everlasting, which was prepared for the devil and his angels."[125] Which sentence doth not only touch heathens, heretics, schismatics, and public sinners;[126] but appertaineth also to all those Christians that end their lives in mortal sin.[127]

Last of all, this clause, *Amen*, is added in the end, that it may plainly appear how firmly and surely grounded we stand in the profession and testimony of this Christian faith and confession.[128]

22. **Is it sufficient for a Christian to believe those things only that are contained in the Creed?**

First and specially, no doubt, those things that are taught us in the Creed of the Apostles are to be believed, and openly professed of everyone.[129] Which also are made more plain, being conferred with the Creed of the fathers and with that of Athanasius.[130]

Secondly, a Christian must of necessity believe whatsoever the divine and canonical scripture doth contain.[131] But the certain and legitimate books of scripture no man may discern by any other means than by the judgment and authority of the Church.[132]

Thirdly, hereunto do belong those things that are necessarily drawn and deduced, partly out of the articles of the Creed, and partly out of holy scriptures.[133]

---

[124] Mt 25:34

[125] Mt 25:41

[126] Cf. Fulgentius, *Letter to Peter on the Faith*, Ch. 8, 40

[127] Cf. Ez 18:4; 33:8; Rom 6:23; Ws 1:16; 1 Cor 6:9

[128] Cf. Jerome, *Epistle 26 to Marcella*

[129] Cf. Ambrose, *Concerning Virginity*, Bk. 3; Augustine, *A Sermon to Catechumens on the Creed*

[130] Editor's note: The Athanasian Creed, *Quicumque Vult*, is included in full in Volume VI of this series.

[131] Cf. 2 Pt 1:19; Rom 15:4; 2 Tm 3:15

[132] Cf. Conc. Tol. I. c. 21; Augustine, *Sermon 129, De Temp.*; *Sermon 191, De Temp.*; Jerome, *Epistle 15 to Damasus*; Augustine, *Against the Fundamental Epistle of Manichaeus*, Ch. 5; Council of Trent, Session 4

[133] Cf. Mt 22:29

Fourthly and lastly, are all such documents to be holden as most holy and to be firmly believed which the Holy Ghost revealeth unto us, and pronounceth by the Church, whether they be commended unto us by writing, or delivered by tradition and word of mouth.[134] Which point we will touch more at large hereafter.

These therefore are the things in which the true Catholic faith doth consist, without the which all sectaries do in vain promise to themselves and others grace and salvation in Christ.[135]

𝔒𝔣 𝔥𝔬𝔭𝔢, 𝔱𝔥𝔢 𝔏𝔬𝔯𝔡'𝔰 𝔓𝔯𝔞𝔶𝔢𝔯, 𝔞𝔫𝔡 𝔱𝔥𝔢 𝔄𝔫𝔤𝔢𝔩𝔦𝔠𝔞𝔩 𝔖𝔞𝔩𝔲𝔱𝔞𝔱𝔦𝔬𝔫

Of Hope

23. What is hope?

Hope is a virtue infused by God, whereby we do with assured trust and confidence expect at God's hand the good of our salvation and life everlasting.

To small purpose it is to believe in God, and the word of God, and to profess the divine doctrine of holy Church, unless a Christian, having once understood the goodness of Almighty God, do conceive hope and confidence of obtaining grace and eternal salvation. Which hope doth so fortify and uphold the just man in the greatest miseries,[136] that although he be destitute of all worldly helps, yet will he confidently say: "Although he kill me, yet will I hope in him."[137] And, "In God I have hoped, I will

---

[134] Cf. Cyril of Alexandria, *Epistle 10 to Nestorius*; Irenaeus, *Against Heresies*, Bk. 3, Ch. 4; Bk. 4, Ch. 4, 5, 33; Jerome, *Dialogue against the Luciferians*, Ch. 4; Vincent of Lerins, *Contra Novat.*

[135] Cf. Leo the Great, *Sermon 4, De Nativ. Dom.*; Cf. also Heb 5:12; 6:1; 1 Pt 3:15

[136] Cf. Ecclus 34:15; Rom 8:35; Ps 30:25; Prv 28:1

[137] Jb 13:15

not fear what flesh may do onto me."[138] "My God, I trust in thee, I will not be ashamed."[139]

24. **By what means may a man come to have this hope?**

First of all, one great help hereunto is to pray fervently and often to Almighty God.[140] Also hope is to be nourished and stirred up with daily meditation of the goodness and benefits of God, those especially which Christ our Lord, for his infinite charity toward us, performed and promised even to the undeserving.[141] Last of all, there must be annexed purity and cleanness of conscience[142] which must ever show itself by good works, and invincible patience in all adversity.[143] For they that want the testimony of a good conscience, or have not a purpose to amend their life, they, I say, have not that hope which they should, but do rather rashly vaunt of presumption, and a very vain and unfruitful confidence, howsoever they boast of God's grace and of the merits of Christ.[144]

"Hope in our Lord," saith the prophet, "and do goodness."[145] And again: "Be thou subject to our Lord and pray to him."[146] And another prophet: "Our Lord is good to those that hope in him, to the soul that seeketh him."[147] And that this hope must not be altogether void of fear,[148] it appeareth by this place of the psalm: "Our Lord is well pleased over them that fear him, and in them that hope and trust in his mercy."[149]

---

[138] Ps 55:5

[139] Ps 24:2; Cf. Augustine, *Enchiridion*, Ch. 8; 1 Cor 13:13; Rom 5:2; 8:24; Ti 2:13; 3:7; 1 Pt 1:3; 1 Jn 5:14; Jas 1:3, 5; Jn 14:13; 15:7, 16; 16:23; Mk 11:24; Ps 26:13-14; 129:6; 72:28; 61:8, 11; 1 Tm 4:10; 1 Thes 5:8; Eph 6:17; Heb 10:35; 6:18

[140] Cf. 1 Thes 5:16; Lk 11:9; 18:1; Mt 7:7; Ecclus 18:22

[141] Cf. Eph 2:4; Ti 3:3; Rom 8:29; Jn 3:16; 1 Cor 4:9; Heb 10:23; Ti 1:2; Rom 4:8, 17, 20; 8:18

[142] Cf. Prv 15:15; 1 Jn 3:21; Augustine, *On Christian Doctrine*, Bk. 1, Ch. 37, 40; Bk. 3, Ch. 10; *In Praefat., On Psalm 31*

[143] Cf. 2 Cor 1:7; Heb 3:6; 10:24; 1 Jn 3:3; Col 1:21; 2 Pt 1:10

[144] Cf. 2 Pt 2:18; Ecclus 5:4, 6; Gregory the Great, *Moralia in Job*, Bk. 33, Ch. 15

[145] Ps 36:3

[146] Ps 36:7

[147] Lam 3:25

[148] Cf. Gregory the Great, Bk. 6, *Epistle 22 ad Gregorian.*; Bernard, *De Fest. Magdal.*

[149] Ps 146:11

25. **What good things are those which a Christian must hope for?**

First and especially those good things of the kingdom of heaven, which do make men blessed and happy, and exempteth them from all manner of misery.[150] Then, all such things as serving for the necessary uses of mortal men in this life, which are rightly desired and prayed for at God's hands, ought to be reputed in the number of those good things which are to be hoped for and expected. All which are specially expressed in our Lord's Prayer,[151] as which Christ our Lord with his own most sacred mouth delivered, and with wonderful wisdom prescribed to all those that would gladly by prayer lay open their hope and good desires before God.[152]

Of Our Lord's Prayer

26. **What is the form of our Lord's Prayer?**

This that followeth: Our Father which art in heaven.

1. Hallowed be they name.
2. Thy kingdom come.
3. Thy will be done in earth, as it is in heaven.
4. Give us this day our daily bread.
5. And forgive us our trespasses, as we forgive them that trespass against us.
6. And lead us not into temptation.
7. But deliver us from evil. Amen.[153]

---

[150] Cf. Ti 2:13; 3:7
[151] Cf. Heb 4:16; Augustine, *Enchiridion*, Ch. 114
[152] Cf. Mt 6:9-13; Lk 11:2-4
[153] The *Pater Noster* is expounded by these: Tertullian, *De Oratione*; Gregory of Nyssa, *Sermons on the Lord's Prayer*; Cyprian, *Sermon 6 on the Lord's Prayer*; Cyril of Jerusalem, *Catechetical Lecture 23*, n. 11-18; Chrysostom, *Homily on the Lord's Prayer*; *On Matthew*, Ch. 6; Jerome, *On Matthew*; Theophilus, *On Matthew*; Eut., *On Matthew*; Ambrose, *On the Sacraments*, Bk. 5, Ch. 4; Augustine, *Epistle 130 ad Probam*, Ch. 11; *On the Sermon on the Mount*, Bk. 2, Ch. 4ff; *Homily 42 ex 50*; *Sermon 126, 135, 182, De Temp.*; *Sermon 9, Ex Div.*; Chrysostom, *Sermon 67ff*; Innocent III, *De Mist. Missae*, Ch. 17ff; Petrus Laod. German. Patriarcha Const.; John Cassian, *Conferences of the Desert Fathers*, Col. 9, Ch. 18ff.

27. What is the sum of our Lord's Prayer?

There are seven petitions contained therein,[154] unto which all manners and forms of prayers whatsoever may and ought to be referred, whether we treat with Almighty God for the obtaining of some good things, or for the wiping away of sin, or for the turning away of any evil whatsoever. And in the three first petitions, those things are in order demanded which are properly eternal and everlasting; in the four others we do ask even temporal things, as being necessary for us, to the getting of the eternal.[155]

28. What is meant by the beginning of this prayer: "Our Father which art," etc.?

It is a little preface, and it putteth us in mind of that great and inestimable benefit whereby God the Father, that eternal Majesty, reigning most happily in heaven, received us into his favor, and for Christ, his Son's sake, adopted us by the Holy Ghost to be his sons and heirs unto his heavenly kingdom.

And this remembrance of so great benefits doth not only stir up attention, but provoke also the sons to render love again to their Father and to obey him,[156] and it doth in like manner encourage them to pray and afford them confidence to obtain.[157]

29. What is the sense of the first petition: "Hallowed be thy name"?

We desire that as well in ourselves as in all others, that may always be preferred and advanced which standeth most with the glory and honor of our sovereign and most excellent Father.

And this indeed we do perform, when the confession of the true faith, hope, and charity, and holy conversation of Christian life do show forth their light and force in us,[158] that others also beholding the same may take occasion to glorify our Father.[159]

---

[154] Cf. Augustine, *Enchiridion*, Ch. 115; *On the Sermon on the Mount*, Bk. 2, Ch. 10
[155] Cf. Augustine, *Epistle 130 ad Probam*, Ch. 12
[156] Cf. Cyprian, *Sermon on the Lord's Prayer*
[157] Cf. Lk 11:13; Jas 1:6; Cf. also Ex 15:11; Is 42:5; 63:15; Mal 1:6; 2 Cor 1:3; Phil 4:20; Apoc 4:10; Rom 8:15; Gal 4:5; 1 Pt 3:22; Leo the Great, *Sermon 6 Nat. Dom.*
[158] Cf. Lk 1:72; 1 Pt 1:15; 3:16; Phil 2:15
[159] Cf. Mt 5:17; Cf. also 1 Pt 2:12; 4:11; 1 Cor 10:31; Col 3:17; Rom 15:6; Ecclus 36:1

30. **What is contained in the second petition: "Thy kingdom come"?**

We do ask that God by his grace and justice may reign in his Church, yea, and in the whole world, all adversary powers and evil affections being once abandoned and rooted out.

Then we do wish and pray that, being once called out of this world as out of a troublesome pilgrimage and warfare, we may be speedily transported into the kingdom of glory and everlasting felicity, to reign with Christ and his saints forever.[160]

31. **What importeth the third petition: "Thy will be done"?**

We do wish in this petition that, as the angels and blessed saints in heaven, so we also upon earth, though weak and of small force, may exhibit unto Almighty God exact obedience, desiring or coveting nothing so much as that we may willingly submit ourselves to the will of God, both in prosperity and adversity; and, renouncing our own will, which is prone unto evil,[161] we may rest and settle our minds in the will of God.[162]

32. **What hath the fourth petition: "Give us this day our daily bread"?**

We do, like poor folks and beggars, crave of the author and fountain of all goodness those things that be sufficient for the daily maintenance of our corporal life, to wit, food and clothing; also those things that do serve to better the life of the soul, as: the word of God, the spiritual food of the soul;[163] the most holy and Blessed Sacrament of the Altar, that heavenly bread; and other most wholesome sacraments and gifts of God, which do feed, cure, and confirm the inward man to a well ordered and happy kind of life.[164]

---

[160] Cf. Phil 1:23; Heb 11:13; 1 Pt 2:11; Jb 7:1; 2 Cor 5:6; Ws 5:16; Apoc 22:4; Mt 8:11; Cf. also Mt 6:33; Rom 14:17; Ps 22:1; 79:2; Lk 1:33; 17:20; 1 Cor 3:10; 4:20; Eph 1:18, 23; Mt 13:41; 1 Cor 15:24; Col 1:13; Ps 67:2

[161] Cf. Gn 8:21; Mt 26:41; Bernard, *Sermon 3, De Resur.*

[162] Cf. Jn 4:34; 5:30; 6:38; 1 Kgs 3:18; Cf. also Ps 102:20; Rom 1:10; Acts 9:6; 21:14; Dt 12:8; Heb 13:21; Jas 4:15; Lk 22:42; 1 Pt 4:2; Acts 5:29; Jb 1:21; 1 Pt 5:6

[163] Cf. Mt 4:4; Am 8:11; Ecclus 15:3; Prv 9:5

[164] Cf. Mt 26:26; 6:11; Jn 6:51; Jerome, *On Matthew*, Ch. 6; Cyprian, *Sermon on the Lord's Prayer*; Ambrose, *On the Sacraments*, Bk. 5, Ch. 4; Augustine, *On the Sermon on the Mount*, Bk. 2, Ch. 7; Cf. also Jas 1:5, 17; Ps 39:18; Dt 10:18; Gn 28:20; 1 Tm 6:8; Prv 30:8; Ps 144:15

33. **How is the fifth petition understood: "Forgive us our trespasses"?**

In this we crave that God will mercifully purge us from the spot of sin, which above all things is most foul and pestilent unto the soul; and that he will also remit those very debts which we have contracted by sinning.

And lest our prayer should not be available by reason that we are evil-affected toward our neighbor, we add this besides: that all secret hate and desire of revenge being laid aside, we are at atonement with our neighbor, and have forgiven everyone that hath offended us, even from the bottom of our hearts.[165] For this is that which Christ signified in another place when he said: "Forgive and ye shall be forgiven."[166] And again: "If you will not forgive men, neither will your Father forgive you your offenses."[167]

34. **What is the sense of the sixth petition: "Lead us not into temptation"?**

Because this present life is a very warfare upon earth, whilst we are always assaulted with divers temptations and in a hard and continual conflict with the world, the flesh, and the devil, therefore, being devoutly careful of our own estate, we sue for help at the hands of Almighty God, that we do not yield to such assaults of our adversaries, and, by yielding, incur damnation; but that standing always in this continual combat, relying upon the might and hand of God, we may valiantly resist the power of the devil, have the world in contempt, chastise the flesh, and so finally, as invincible soldiers of Christ, be crowned after the victory: "For no man is crowned," as witnesseth the apostle, "unless he strive lawfully."[168]

35. **What is the seventh and last petition: "Deliver us from evil"?**

We pray at the last, that God will not suffer us to be overthrown and cast away with the wicked by the calamities of this world, wherewith even the

---

[165] Cf. Rom 12:17, 19; Col 3:12; Lk 23:34; Acts 7:60; Mk 11:25; Eph 4:32
[166] Lk 6:37
[167] Mt 6:15; Cf. Mt 18:22, 33; Ecclus 22:1; Augustine, *Enchiridion*, Ch. 74; Cf. also Lam 4:8; 1 Cor 10:6; Lv 26:14; Nm 5:6, 20; Ex 32:27; Lk 7:47; Tb 12:10; Ws 16:14; Ps 50:3-4, 9, 11
[168] 2 Tm 2:5; Cf. Jb 7:1; Jdt 8:21; Tb 3:21; 12:13; Mt 4:1; 26:41; Heb 2:18; 2 Thes 3:3; 1 Jn 2:14, 16; 5:4; Mt 16:24; 1 Cor 9:25, 27; 10:12; Jas 4:4; 1:12; 1 Pt 5:8, 10; 2 Pt 2:9; Eph 6:11; Col 3:5; Apoc 2:7, 10, 11, 17, 26; 2 Tm 4:7

godly also are exercised; but that by his benignity he deliver us so far forth as is expedient for our salvation, and mercifully defend us from all evil, both of body and soul, as well in this life as in the life to come. For so hath himself promised: "Call upon me in the day of tribulation, I will deliver thee and thou shalt honor me."[169]

Last of all, we conclude the whole prayer with this one word, *Amen*, that we may show our confidence in praying and hope of obtaining, in regard as well of Christ's promise that never faileth,[170] "Ask, (saith he) and it shall be given you,"[171] as also of the infinite clemency and ready mercy of God the Father, insomuch that hereupon, St. John hath said, "Whatsoever we shall ask, according to his will, he heareth us."[172]

36. What is the sum of our Lord's Prayer?

It containeth a perfect and absolute form, not only of asking that which is good, but also of praying to be delivered from whatsoever is evil.

And amongst the things that be good, this is first to be wished and prayed for: that all men may glorify our heavenly Father at all times and in all places; then, that we may be partakers of his kingdom; afterward, that we may not want those helps that are convenient for the attaining unto the same kingdom, as is: on the behalf of our soul, to be comfortable to the will of God; and as touching our body, to have necessary living and maintenance.

But those things that are added in the second place, and do continue to the end of the prayer, do express the affect of one that craveth delivery from evils, which by the grace and power of Almighty God, he desireth to have either utterly taken away, to wit, sin, the contagion of all goodness and the sink and puddle of all evils; or else, that they be so tempered that by their violence they hinder us not in the way to salvation. Such are divers temptations that invade us in this world and all calamities both

---

[169] Ps 49:15

[170] Cf. 2 Cor 1:20; Ambrose, *On Psalm 40*; Jerome, *On Matthew*, Ch. 6

[171] Mt 7:7; Lk 11:9; Cf. Lk 11:10, 16, 23

[172] 1 Jn 5:14; Cf. 3 Kgs 8:33; Prv 10:25, 28, 30; Ecclus 23:4; Jer 2:14; Tb 1:22; 2:10; Ecclus 27:1, 4, 6; Apoc 3:10; Ps 24:15; 30:3, 5, 8-9, 16; 33:5, 7-8, 18

present and to come. All other things that are to be said touching prayer shall be reserved for that place where the three kinds of good works shall be expounded.

Of the Angelical Salutation

37. **Which is commonly called the Angelical Salutation?**

That which was pronounced unto the most holy Virgin, the Mother of God in these words: "Hail Mary full of grace, our Lord is with thee; blessed art thou among women, and blessed is the fruit of thy womb, Jesus. Holy Mary, Mother of God, pray for us sinners now and in the hour of our death. Amen."[173]

38. **Whereupon came this manner of saluting the Mother of God?**

First, of the words and examples of the gospel, whereas the great archangel Gabriel and Elizabeth, the holy mother of the forerunner of our Lord, both inspired by the Holy Ghost, do so teach and instruct us.[174]

Then we have this form of salutation confirmed and ratified by the continual custom and consent of the Church, which the holy ancient fathers and men of old time have religiously observed, even to this day, and would have also of us to be observed.[175]

39. **What doth it profit us to use this manner of salutation?**

By those excellent words, we are first of all admonished of that exceeding great benefit, that the eternal Father would begin in Christ, by Mary the Mother of God, and mercifully bestow upon mankind by redeeming it.[176]

---

[173] Cf. Lk 1:28, 42; Liturgies of Chrysostom and James; Augustine, *Sermon 2 on the Annunciation*; Ambrose, *On Luke*, Ch. 1; Chrysostom, *Sermon 140ff*; Bernard, *Homily 3, Super Missus Est*; Fulgentius, *Sermon De Laud. B. Virg.*

[174] Cf. Lk 1:28, 42

[175] Cf. John Damascene, *In Cant. de Annunc.*; Athanasius, *In Evang. de SS. De para*; and many more as appeareth in the answers and accompanying footnotes to Questions 40 and 41, below.

[176] Cf. Gal 4:4; Lk 11:27; 1:30

This is also a singular commendation of the most holy and wonderful Virgin, which God hath determined to be the finder forth of grace, and mother of life unto us all.

Wherefore no marvel, if after those godly petitions which we offered unto God in our Lord's Prayer, being here mindful of the grace that we received by Christ, we do not only praise the Mother of Christ, but also God the Father in the same Virgin Mother of God, and rejoicing together with the angels with great reverence, and often salute her.

40. **What is the sense of this salutation?**

In the first words thereof, we do justly rejoice with and, in rejoicing, praise and renown her that was to us the second, and that a most happy, Eve. For that woe of malediction that the first Eve brought into the world, this other by her wholesome fruit hath taken away and hath exchanged the very curse of the children of Adam with a perpetual blessing.

Most worthy no doubt to be called "full of grace," as who, being full of God, full of virtues, alone (for I will use St. Ambrose his words) obtained that grace which no other had ever deserved before, that she might be replenished with the author of grace. And what place could there be in her soul or body for any vice, when she was made the temple of the holy of all holies?[177]

There is added besides, "our Lord is with thee," because both the power of the Father did singularly overshadow her; and the Holy Ghost came plentifully upon her;[178] and the Word being made flesh, from her did proceed in most wonderful wise, as a bridegroom from his chamber.[179]

Then it followeth, "blessed art thou among women," because she was together a spouse by virginity and a mother by fruitfulness.[180] And therefore with great right all generations do and shall always call her blessed.[181] A woman all fair and immaculate;[182] a Virgin before her

---

[177] Cf. Ambrose, *On Luke*, Ch. 1; Cf. also Bernard, *Sermon 9, Ex Parvis*
[178] Cf. Lk 1:35
[179] Cf. Jn 1:14; Ps 18:6
[180] Cf. Is 7:14; Ez 44:3
[181] Cf. Lk 1:48
[182] Cf. Cant 4:7

delivery, at her delivery, and after her delivery; always uncorrupted, free from all spot of sin;[183] exalted above all heavens, who no less by giving life was profitable, than unhappy Eve by killing was hurtful, unto all mankind.[184]

"And blessed is the fruit of thy womb, Jesus," as he, that springing up like a flower from Mary the root, hath both showed himself, after a sort, fruit of the earth;[185] and doth in such manner yield the fruit of life and salvation to his members, as a vine doth juice and life unto the branches.[186] O blessed womb indeed that bare and brought forth a Savior to the world; O blessed paps without doubt, that being filled from heaven, suckled the Son of Almighty God.[187]

Finally, the Church hath added in the end, "Holy Mary, Mother of God, pray for us sinners now and in the hour of our death."[188] For we, following the steps of the holy fathers,[189] do not only salute that wonderful Virgin, worthy of all commendation, which is as a lily amongst thorns;[190] but do also believe and profess that she is endowed with so great power and ability from God, that she is able to profit, favor, and pleasure miserable mortal men, especially when they do commend themselves and their desires unto her, and do humbly sue for the grace of God, by the Mother's intercession.

[183] Cf. Ambrose, *Epistle 81*; Jerome, *The Perpetual Virginity of Blessed Mary*; *Against Jovinianus*

[184] Cf. Augustine, *On Nature and Grace*, Ch. 36; Council of Trent, Session 5; Session 6, Can. 23

[185] Cf. Is 11:1

[186] Cf. Jn 15:5

[187] Cf. Lk 11:27

[188] Antiquum Breviarium et Novum

[189] Cf. Ephrem, *De Laud. Mar.*; *in orat. ad eandem*; *in lament. B. Virg.*; Irenaeus, *Against Heresies*, Bk. 5, Ch. 19; Gregory Nazianzen, *Oration 18 on Cyprian*; *Christus Patiens*; Fulgentius, *Sermon De Laud. B. Virg.*, Ch. 12; Bernard, *Sermon 2, Dom. I post octa. Epiph.*; *Sermon 1 and 4 on the Assumption*; John Damascene, *Oration 1 De Natvi. B. Mariae*; *in carmine ad eandem*

[190] Cf. Cant 2:1-2; Cf. also Andrew of Crete, *On the Angelical Salutation*; Irenaeus, *Against Heresies*, Bk. 3, Ch. 31, 33; Jerome, *Epistle 22 to Eustochium*; Innocent III, *Sermon 2 on the Assumption*; Bernard, *Homily 2 in Missus Est*; Augustine, *Sermon 2 on the Annunciation*; Ambrose, *On Luke*, Ch. 1; Bernard, *Sermon 9, Ex Parvis*

41. Testimonies of the fathers touching the Virgin.

Irenaeus: As Eve was seduced to swerve from Almighty God, so Mary was persuaded to obey God; so that Mary a Virgin was made the advocate of Eve a virgin; and as mankind was made subject to death by a virgin, so it is loosened by a Virgin; a virgin's disobedience being counterpeased by a Virgin's obedience.[191]

Saint Chrysostom in his *Liturgia*: It is very meet and just to glory thee, the Mother of our God, ever most blessed and altogether undefiled, more honorable than the cherubims, and more glorious incomparably than the seraphims, which without all corruption hast brought forth God. We do magnify thee, the very Mother of God. "Hail Mary full of grace, our Lord is with thee; blessed art thou among women, and blessed is the fruit of thy womb"; because thou hast brought forth the Savior of our souls.

St. Ambrose: Let the virginity and life of blessed Mary be set forth unto us as it were in an image, from whom, as from a glass, there shineth out bright the beauty of chastity and fairness of virtue. What is more noble than the Mother of God? What is more bright than she whom brightness did choose? What is more chaste than she that brought forth a body without contagion of the body? Such a one was Mary, that her only life might be a document to all men.[192]

Saint Athanasius: Forasmuch as he is King that was born of the Virgin, and the same also Lord and God: for that cause, she that bare him is truly and properly judged to be a Queen, a Lady, and the Mother of God. This new Eve is called the mother of life, and she remaineth replenished with the first fruits of immortal life above all living creatures. We do call her therefore, again and again, and evermore, and every way most blessed. To thee we cry, be mindful of us, O most holy Virgin, which even after thy delivery remainedst a Virgin. "Hail Mary full of grace, our Lord is with thee": the holy orders of all angels and men do call thee blessed. "Blessed art thou among women and blessed is the fruit of thy womb": make intercession for us O Mistress, and Lady, and Queen, and Mother of God.[193]

[191] Cf. Irenaeus, *Against Heresies*, Bk. 5, Ch. 19
[192] Cf. Ambrose, *Concerning Virginity*, Bk. 2
[193] Cf. Athanasius, *In Evang. de Sancta Nostra Dei-para*

St. Gregory Nazianzen:
O ter beata Mater, O lux virginum
Quae templa caeli lucidissima incolis,
Mortalitatis liberata sordibus,
Ornata iam immortalitatis es stola:
Meis benignam ab alto aurem exhibe verbis,
Measque, Virgo, suscipe, obsecro, preces.
O Mother thrice happy, and light of virgins pure,
Inhabiting the temples bright of heavenly globe,
Thou now from mortal filth exempted, and secure
Of immortality, art decked with the robe.
Yield courteous audiences from on high to what I say,
And entertain my suits, O Virgin, I thee pray.[194]

Saint Augustine: Holy Mary succor the miserable, help the faint-hearted, cherish the sorrowful, pray for the people, be a mean for the clergy, and make intercession for the devout womankind. Let all feel thy help, whosoever do celebrate thy commemoration.[195]

Fulgentius: Mary was made the window of heaven, because by her God gave the true light unto the world. Mary was made the ladder of heaven, because, by her, God descended down to earth, that by her also men may ascend into heaven. Mary was made the restorer of women, because by her they are known to be exempted from the ruin of the first curse.[196]

St. Bernard: The kingly Virgin is the very way by which our Savior came unto us, proceeding out of her womb, as a bridegroom out of his chamber. By thee let us have access to thy Son, O blessed finder forth of grace, bringer forth of life, and mother of salvation, that by thee he receive us, who by thee was given unto us.[197]

[194] Gregory Nazianzen, *Christus Patiens*
[195] Cf. Augustine, *Sermon 2 on the Annunciation*
[196] Cf. Fulgentius, *Sermon, De Laud. Mariae*
[197] Cf. Bernard, *Sermon 2, De Adv.*; *Homily 2, Super Missus Est: et in illud Apoc. Signum magnum apparuit.*; *Sermon, De Nat. Virg.*

Of Charity, the Church, and Commandments

Of Charity

42. Is it sufficient for a Christian to be instructed in the doctrine of faith and hope?

It is very necessary that he which hath attained unto faith and hope be indued with charity also. For of these three virtues, St. Paul teacheth jointly thus: "Now there remaineth," saith he, "faith, hope, charity, these three, but the greater of these is charity."[198]

Great undoubtedly is faith, which may suffice to move mountains, and work miracles.[199] Great also is hope, a certain helmet, and anchor of salvation, which, setting before us the goodness of God and the greatness of reward, doth afford both effectual comfort to them that labor and a singular confidence to them that pray.[200] But greatest of all is charity, the prince of all virtues, which knoweth neither measure nor end, nor forsaketh them that die, being stronger than death itself,[201] without which in a Christian there may be indeed both faith and hope, but they cannot be sufficient to the leading of a good and happy life.[202] For which cause St. John saith: "He that doth not love, abideth in death,"[203] although in the mean season he believe and hope, as the example of the foolish virgins in the gospel doth plainly declare unto us.[204]

---

[198] 1 Cor 13:13

[199] Cf. 1 Cor 13:2; Mk 11:23; Mt 7:22

[200] Cf. 1 Thes 5:8; Eph 6:17; Heb 6:19

[201] Cf. Prosper, *De Vita Contemplativa*, Bk. 3, Ch. 13, 15; Augustine, *On Psalm 47*; *Tractate 5 on John*; *Enchiridion*, Ch. 17; *Sermon 53, De Temp.*

[202] Cf. Augustine, *On the Trinity*, Bk. 15, Ch. 18

[203] 1 Jn 3:14

[204] Cf. Mt 25:11; Augustine, *Sermon 23, De Verbis Domini*, Ch. 4, 8

43. What then is charity?

A virtue infused by God, by which God is sincerely loved for himself, and our neighbor for God.

For God is chiefly to be loved in all things, and above all things, and for himself alone, as alone being the most sovereign and eternal good which only satisfieth our minds;[205] whose love and honor ought to be the beginning and final end, both of our will and of all our works.[206] Then, for God's sake must we love our neighbor,[207] that is to say, every man without exception. Forasmuch as we be all neighbors amongst ourselves, and linked together with a great affinity, both in regard of the same human nature common to all the children of Adam, and also by reason of God's grace and everlasting glory, whereof all that will may be partakers.[208]

44. How many precepts of charity be there?

In substance, two; whereof the first of loving God is thus propounded in the old and new law: "Thou shalt love the Lord thy God, from thy whole heart, and with thy whole soul, and with all thy strength. This is the greatest and the first commandment. And the second is like to this: Thou shalt love thy neighbor as thyself. On these two commandments dependeth the whole law and the prophets."[209]

This charity is the fullness of the law, and sum of justice,[210] that is to say, the band of perfection.[211] Charity, I say from a pure hart, and a good conscience, and a faith not feigned.[212]

---

[205] Cf. Bernard, *De Diligendo Deo*
[206] Cf. 1 Cor 10:31; Col 3:17
[207] Cf. Augustine, *Homily 38 ex 50*, Ch. 2ff
[208] Cf. Augustine, *On Psalm 118*, conc. 8; *Sermon 52, De Temp.*; *Sermon 59, De Temp.*; Cf. also Mt 22:36; Lk 10:27; Mk 12:30; Augustine, *On Christian Doctrine*, Bk. 3, Ch. 10
[209] Dt 6:5; Mt 22:37-40; Cf. Mk 12:30-31; Lk 10:27; Gregory the Great, *Moralia in Job*, Bk. 10, Ch. 6, 7
[210] Cf. Rom 13:10
[211] Cf. Col 3:14
[212] Cf. 1 Tm 1:5

45. How doth true charity show itself?

The proof of love and charity is to perform the same in deeds and to observe God's commandments.[213] Whereupon, St. John, also the beloved of Christ, saith: "This is the charity of God, that we keep his commandments; and his commandments are not heavy."[214] And again, "He that saith he knoweth God, and keepeth not his commandments is a liar, and the truth is not in him. But he that keepeth his word, in him in very deed, the charity of God is perfected. In this we know that we be in him."[215]

And Christ himself teacheth: "If you love me, keep my commandments...He that hath my commandments and keepeth them, he it is that loveth me. And he that loveth me shall be loved of my Father: And I will love him, and will manifest myself unto him...He that loveth me not, keepeth not my words."[216]

Of the Ten Commandments

46. Which are the commandments of God specially belonging to charity?

The ten words of God first delivered by Moses to the Jews, and afterward commended by Christ and his apostles to all Christians, which are commonly called the decalogue or the ten commandments,[217] and are thus set down:

"I am thy Lord God.

1. Thou shalt not have any strange gods before me. Thou shalt not make to thyself any graven thing to worship it.[218]

2. Thou shalt not take the name of thy Lord God in vain.

3. Remember thou keep holy the sabbath-day.

[213] Cf. Gregory the Great, *Homily 30 on the Gospels*
[214] 1 Jn 5:3
[215] 1 Jn 2:4-5
[216] Jn 14:15, 21, 24
[217] Cf. Mt 19:17; 5:18; 22:37; Mk 10:19; 12:31; Lk 18:19; 10:25; Rom 2:13; 13:8; 7:12; Gal 5:14; Jas 2:8; 1:25; 4:11; 1 Tm 1:5; Council of Trent, Session 6, Can. 19-21
[218] Cf. Lv 26:1. The commandments are expounded by: Origen, *Homily 8 on Exodus*; Augustine, *Quaestiones in Exodum*, q. 71; *Sermon, De Decem Plagis*; *Sermon 9, De Decem Chordis*

4. Honor thy father and thy mother, that thou mayest live long in the land which thy Lord God will give thee.

5. Thou shalt not kill.

6. Thou shalt not commit adultery.

7. Thou shalt not steal.

8. Thou shalt not bear false witness against thy neighbor.

9. Thou shalt not covet thy neighbor's wife.[219]

10. Thou shalt not covet his house, nor his field, nor his handmaid, nor his ox, nor his ass, nor anything that is his."[220]

47. **What meaneth this beginning, "I am thy Lord God"?**

Almighty God beginneth the ten commandments with the knowledge of himself, and with the insinuation of his majesty. That the lawmaker being once known, we may fear and reverence him the more, and the commandments which he hath set down may be of greater authority amongst all men. For we are so seriously dealt withal, that if ever we mean to be saved, we must first, as in a most bright glass, here assuredly behold the will of the Divine Majesty and the whole and perfect manner of living well;[221] and then this most holy law being once known by the help of Christ's Spirit, exactly keep and observe the same.[222]

Neither truly doth our lawmaker only give commandments, but doth withal promise his blessing, and assisteth with his helping hand.[223] "I will put," saith he, "my spirit in the midst of you, and I will cause that you may walk in my commandments, and that you may keep my judgments, and that you may work."[224] For which cause when Christ also had commanded, "Take up my yoke upon you,"[225] lest any man should allege the difficulty

[219] Cf. Dt 5:21

[220] The commandments are thus distinguished by: Augustine, *Quaestiones in Exodum*, q. 71; *Epistle 119*, Ch. 11; Clement of Alexandria, *The Stromata*, Bk. 6, Ch. 16; Jerome, *On Psalm 32*; Ex 20:1; 34:28; Lv 19; Dt 4:13; 5:6; 10:4

[221] Cf. Mt 5:18; 19:17; 28:20; Heb 5:9; Ps 118:1, 4; 1 Jn 3:24; Augustine, *Quaestiones in Exodum*, q. 140

[222] Cf. Rom 8:26; Jn 1:17; Phil 4:13

[223] Cf. Ps 83:8; Dt 28:1; Lv 26:3

[224] Ez 36:27; Cf. Ez 11:19-20

[225] Mt 11:29

thereof as an excuse, he added, "for my yoke is sweet and my burden light";[226] unto those undoubtedly that, being induced with the spirit of grace, do walk in charity not feigned.[227]

48. What importeth the first commandment?

It forbiddeth and condemneth idolatry, superstitious observations, and the use of art magic and divination.

It teacheth also and requireth that we account no creature at all for God, though it be never so excellent; but that we believe and confess one only true, eternal, and infinite God, and that to him only we offer sacrifice,[228] and give that singular and sovereign honor which the Grecians call *latria*.[229]

And by means hereof it cometh to pass that above all things we honor, call upon, and adore that sovereign and eternal good, the most excellent, mighty, Maker, Redeemer, Savior, one immortal God,[230] who is blessed above all things, the giver of all grace and glory.[231]

49. How and in what sort do we, besides Almighty God, honor and call upon the saints also?

Of saints, to wit, of all those that are sanctified and born again in Christ, our meaning is not to speak in this place, as St. Paul doth often apply this name to all Christians;[232] but those we mean that have obtained the true rewards of their holiness in heaven.[233] Of whom the same St. Paul doth

---

[226] Mt 11:30

[227] Cf. 1 Jn 5:3; Council of Trent, Session 6, Can. 11; Can. 18; Chrysostom, *De Comp. Cor.*, Bk. 1; Basil, *The Shorter Rules*, q. 176; Augustine, *On Nature and Grace*, Ch. 43, 69; *Sermon 61, De Temp.*; *Sermon 191, De Temp.*; Jerome, *Epistle 15 to Damasus*; Cf. also Dt 6:1, 15, 24; 4:23, 40; 10:16; Mal 1:5, 14; Jer 32:17; Ps 46:3

[228] Cf. Augustine, *City of God*, Bk. 10, Ch. 1; *Epistle 49*, q. 3

[229] Cf. Augustine, *City of God*, Bk. 10, Ch. 1, 4; *Contra Faustum*, Bk. 15, Ch. 9; Bk. 20, Ch. 21

[230] Cf. Jn 4:23; Rom 10:11; 1 Jn 4:8; Mt 4:10; Lk 4:8; Is 43:1; 1 Tm 6:13

[231] Cf. Rom 9:5; Ps 83:12; Cf. also Dt 12:2; 4:15; 18:9; 1 Kgs 28:3; Ps 113:12; Lv 19:26, 31; 20:6, 27; Ecclus 34:4

[232] Cf. Rom 1:7; 2 Cor 1:1; Phil 4:22; Col 1:1; Phlm 1:7

[233] Cf. Apoc 7:9

testify that "by faith they overcame kingdoms, wrought justice, obtained promises."[234] And these in very deed are saints, immaculate, without spot and wrinkle; these are the most excellent members of the Church, and very choice instruments of God's Holy Spirit, unto whom no sin or evil can ever have access. Which saints do consist partly of angelical, partly of human nature; creatures certes of all most noble and blessed, to whom it is granted to be replenished with those most excellent and eternal good things that are in heaven,[235] and to live always in most perfect love and friendship with Christ our Lord.[236]

Therefore, by his favor, both they are able to understand what things are done amongst us upon earth, and, because they are inflamed with an exceeding charity toward their brethren, though far absent from them,[237] they are careful of our salvation, they favor us, and do with us all manner of good. And they deal so much more fervently in our behalf, by how much less cause they have to be careful for themselves;[238] and by how much greater perfection of sincere charity, and of all kind of virtue agreeable unto blessed saints, they continually do exercise.[239]

Not without great cause, therefore, do we reverence these lights of heaven, and next unto God, the fortresses and principal ornaments of the Church. Not without great cause do we esteem, praise, imitate, and love exceedingly these saints above all mortal men, though never so excellent. Not without great cause, according to our power, do we exhibit great honor unto them, being now advanced to such and so great dignity. Finally, not without great cause do we, according to Christian piety, make suit onto them, not that they may give anything as of themselves, but that

---

[234] Heb 11:33

[235] Cf. Eph 5:27; Apoc 5:8; 7:9; 21:2; 22:3; Eph 4:30; 1 Cor 6:19

[236] Cf. Phil 1:23; 2 Cor 5:16; Gregory the Great, *Moralia in Job*, Bk. 4, Ch. 32; Gregory of Nyssa, *Life of St. Ephrem*; Ephrem, *Comp.*, Bk. 1, last chapter

[237] Cf. Gregory the Great, *Moralia in Job*, Bk. 12, Ch. 13; *Dialogues*, Bk. 4, Ch. 33; Augustine, *On the Care of the Dead*, Ch. 15-16; Origen, *Contra Celsum*, Bk. 8; 4 Kgs 5:26; 6:9; 1 Cor 14:25

[238] Cf. Dn 10:12; Mt 18:10; Heb 1:14; Tb 12:12; Lk 15:7; Acts 5:19; 12:7; Apoc 5:8; 8:3; Cyprian, *Treatise 7*; Gregory of Nazianzen, *Oration 19*

[239] Cf. Jerome, *Against Vigilantius*, Ch. 2-3; Bernard, *In Vigilia Petri et Pauli*; *Sermon 2, In Feste Corundem*; *Sermon 2, De S. Victoris*

they may pray with us to God, the giver of all goodness, and that they may be favorable and effectual intercessors, even in their behalf that have delivered no good at all.[240]

Which kind of worship and invocation, if it be done rightly as it should, to wit, so as that supreme worship and honor due unto Almighty God, which we called *latria*, may stand whole and perfect, there is doubtless no inconvenience therein;[241] neither is it repugnant to holy scripture, but is approved by many firm testimonies of the Church and is very profitable.[242]

And in that we do in this manner, with the Church, honor and call upon the saints, it is so far off from obscuring the glory of Christ our Lord and Savior, that it doth more set forth and advance the same. For herein doth the most excellent virtue and glory of Christ our Redeemer shine and show itself,[243] in that he doth not only in himself, but in his saints also, appear mighty, glorious, and marvelous,[244] in that he honoreth them himself,[245] and will have them exceedingly honored in heaven and in earth;[246] also in that, that by them and for their sakes, he giveth many things and spareth oftentimes the undeserving.[247] For it is well known that Abraham,

---

[240] Cf. John Damascene, *An Exposition of the Orthodox Faith*, Bk. 4, Ch. 15; Basil, *Homily, In Sanctos Quadraginta Martyres*; *Homily, In Mamantem Martyrem*; Gregory Nazianzen, *Oration 18 on Cyprian*; *Oration 21 on Athanasius*; *Oration 20 on Basil*; Gregory of Nyssa, *Life of St. Ephrem*; Chrysostom, *Sermon on St. Peter in Chains*; Ambrose, *Concerning Widows*; *De Fid. Resur.*; *On Luke*, Ch. 22; Chrysostom, *Homily 66, ad pop.*; Ephrem, *De Laud. Mart.*; Jerome, *Epistle 108*, "Epitaph for Paula," Ch. 1, 7, 14; Augustine, *On the Care of the Dead*, Ch. 4; *On Baptism, against the Donatists*, Bk. 7, Ch. 1; Bernard, *Sermon 66 on Canticle of Canticles*; Theod., Bk. 8; Greg. aff. et in Philoth. Prud. in lib. peri Steph.; Second Council of Nicea, Act 6; *vide etiam supra in salutationem Angelicam*; Gn 48:16; Jb 5:1; Gn 32:26; Os 12:4; Zac 1:12; Jer 15:1

[241] Cf. Augustine, *City of God*, Bk. 10, Ch. 1; *Contra Faustum*, Bk. 20, Ch. 21; *City of God*, Bk. 8, Ch. 27

[242] Cf. Rom 15:30; Heb 13:18; Eph 6:18; Col 4:2; 1 Thes 5:25; 2 Thes 3:1; Lk 7:3; Jb 42:8

[243] Cf. Council of Trent, Session 25

[244] Cf. Ps 67:36; Jn 14:12

[245] Cf. Jn 12:26; Mt 19:28; Lk 19:17; Apoc 2:26; 3:21; 5:10

[246] Cf. Ps 138:17

[247] Cf. Chrysostom, *Homily 2 on Psalm 50*; *Homily 27 on Matthew*; *Homily 42 on Genesis*; *Sermon, De Virt. et Vit.*

Isaac, Jacob, David, Jeremiah are read to have profited the living, though they themselves were departed before.[248]

Whereupon, the fathers, when they speak of the saints, they often call them our favorers, intercessors, and patrons. And not without cause doubtless: forasmuch as the faithful suffrages of the saints, when they are humbly and devoutly desired in the name of Christ, are known by experience to have done good to many.[249]

For which cause the Vigilantians were long since condemned,[250] who defraud the saints and their holy relics of their honors, which the true Catholic Church hath always given unto them.[251]

Neither must we give ear unto malicious cavilers, who do falsely affirm that the honor due unto God is by this means translated unto men: that saints are adored for gods; that creatures are by Catholics made equal unto the Creator. For, that it is nothing so, both many other things do convince, and amongst the rest, that old and solemn supplication, called the litany, doth testify,[252] where God and the divine Persons are worshipped and invocated first of all, and in a far more high and excellent manner than the saints or all the orders of saints together.[253]

Hereupon also were those feasts of saints instituted, which Saint Augustine, writing against Faustus the Manichee, defendeth in this manner: "The Christian people," saith he, "doth celebrate the memories of

[248] Cf. Gn 26:3, 24; Ex 32:13; 3 Kgs 11:12, 32, 34, 36; 15:4; Is 37:35; 4 Kgs 8:19; 19:34; 20:6; 2 Mc 5:12

[249] Cf. Ambrose, *Concerning Widows*; *On Luke*, Ch. 21; Leo the Great, *Sermon 1 and 2 de Pet. et Pau.*; *Sermon, De Annivers.*; Paulinus, *Ad Cyth.*; *De B. Faelice*; Maximus, *De Tau. Mar.*; Basil, *Homily, In Sanctos Quadraginta Martyres*; Augustine, *Quaestiones in Exodum*, q. 108; Eusebius, *Praeparatio Evangelica*, Bk. 13, Ch. 7

[250] Cf. Jerome, *Against Vigilantius*, Ch. 2ff; *Epistle 109 to Riparius*; *On Isaias*, Ch. 65; Second Council of Nicea; Council of Gangra

[251] Cf. 4 Kgs 13:21; Ecclus 48:14; Augustine, *City of God*, Bk. 22, Ch. 8; John Damascene, *An Exposition of the Orthodox Faith*, Bk. 4, Ch. 16; Basil, *On Psalm 115*; Chrysostom, *Homily on St. Juventius and Maximus*; *Homily on St. Babylas*; *Sermon on St. Peter in Chains*; Ambrose, *Epistle 85*; *Sermon 91*; *Sermon 93*; Gregory Nazianzen, *Iamb. 18*; Council of Trent, Session 25; Acts 19:12; 5:15; Lk 8:44; Mt 14:36

[252] Cf. Gn 19:1; 23:7; 33:3, 6; 42:7; Jo 5:14; 1 Kgs 20:41; 25:23; 4 Kgs 2:15; 1 Par 29:20

[253] Cf. Bernard, *Sermon, Concerning Four Types of Prayer*; Victor., *De Persecutione Wandalica*

martyrs with a religious solemnity, that they may both stir themselves up to the following of their steps, and also be made partakers of their merits, and helped by their prayers."[254]

50. **Is the received use of the images of Christ and his saints contrary to this first commandment?**

No, surely; for we do not, as the heathens are wont, worship images, stocks, and stones, as if they were certain gods (for that is specially prohibited in this commandment), but after a Christian manner, and with a devout mind, we do there honor Christ himself and his saints,[255] where they are represented unto us by their images set before us.[256]

So doth the Church, both of old and of this present time, teach with one consent, commending unto us the devout and reverend images: the use of which we have received as commended unto us by apostolical tradition; and we retain as approved by a most holy general council of fathers.[257] Yea, God himself appointed to the ancient synagogue their peculiar images.[258]

For which cause was condemned the error of the iconoclasts, or image breakers, as they that made no difference between the likeness of the gods and the images of Christ and his saints,[259] nor had any consideration of the time of grace, or the new law, wherein God himself, being made man,

[254] Augustine, *Contra Faustum*, Bk. 20, Ch. 21; Cf. Augustine, *On Psalm 88*, conc. 3; *Sermon 47, De Sanctis*; Bernard, *In Vigilia Petri et Pauli*; Isidore, *De Ecclesiasticis Officiis*, Bk. 1, Ch. 34-35

[255] Cf. Lv 26:1; Tertullian, *Against Marcion*, Bk. 2, Ch. 22

[256] Cf. Basil, *De Spiritu Sancto*, Ch. 18; John Damascene, *An Exposition of the Orthodox Faith*, Bk. 4, Ch. 17; Athanasius, *Sermon 4, Contra Arianos*

[257] Cf. Second Council of Nicea; Fourth Council of Constantinople, Can. 3; Augustine, *Harmony of the Gospels*, Bk. 1, Ch. 10; John Damascene, *In Vita Silv.*; Athanasius, *De Pass. Imag.*, Ch. 4; Gregory the Great, Bk. 9, Epistle 9; Bk. 7, indict. 2, Epistle 53 and 109; John Damascene, *An Exposition of the Orthodox Faith*, Bk. 4, Ch. 17; Eusebius, *Ecclesiastical History*, Bk. 7, Ch. 14; Sozomen, *Church History*, Bk. 5, Ch. 20; Nicephorus, *Church History*, Bk. 2, Ch. 7, 43; Bk. 6; Ch. 16; Nicetas, *De Imperio Mannuelis*, Bk. 5; Jonas of Orleans, *De Imag. Cultu.*; John Damascene, *In Tribus Orationibus de Imagi*

[258] Cf. Ex 25:24; 37:8; Nm 7:89; 21:8; 3 Kgs 6:23

[259] Cf. Second Council of Nicea, Act 7; Fourth Council of Constantinople, Can. 7; Nicephorus, *Church History*, Bk. 16, Ch. 27; Gregory the Great, Bk. 9, Epistle 9; Council of Trent, Session 25

hath put on upon himself his own image and likeness, which he created in the beginning and hath represented himself unto us in the same.[260] And it is not only an absurd error, but also a most wicked madness of those that do cast out of sacred places the holy images, and amongst them also the cross of our Lord, and with sacrilegious hands pull down in a manner all the holy things they can.[261]

51. What is prescribed unto us by the second commandment?

It forbiddeth the abuse and irreverence of God's holy name, which is committed by perjurers, blasphemers, and those that rashly swear by God, by the saints, or other holy things,[262] against that saying, "Do not swear...let your talk be yea, yea, and no, no."[263]

Then it requireth that, according to the right use of the tongue: we exhibit great reverence to God's holy name; we keep our oaths; we break not our vows made to God and his Church;[264] finally, that we handle the holy word of God with reverence.[265]

52. What are we bound unto by the third commandment?

It requireth that we spend in good works the sabbath or festival day observed in the Church. And therefore, it willeth that our minds be then present and void of cares, freely disposing itself to yield interior and exterior honor unto God, in faith, hope, and charity. It willeth us that without all lets and encumbrances, we meditate of God's benefits, we be occupied about holy things, we pray and honor Almighty God, both privately and publicly with others "in spirit and truth."[266]

[260] Cf. Gn 1:26; Phil 2:7
[261] Cf. Paulinus, *De Gestis Longobard.*, Bk. 6, Ch. 14; *De Gestis Roman.*, last book; in fine Ioan. Patr. Hier. in vita Damasc.; Cf. also Bar 6:25, 38; Dt 4:15; 5:8; Ps 113:12; 134:15; Ws 14:1, 21; 1 Cor 10:7; 8:4
[262] Cf. Eighth Council of Toledo, Can. 2
[263] Jas 5:12; Cf. Mt 5:37
[264] Cf. Ps 33:2; Jer 4:1; Ps 14:5; 49:14; 75:12; Eccles 5:3; 1 Tm 5:12; Dt 23:21
[265] Cf. Ps 49:16; 2 Cor 2:17; 4:2; Council of Trent, Session 4; Cf. also Ex 20:7; Lv 9:12; 5:1; Ecclus 23:8; 27:15; Zac 5:2; 8:17; Lv 24:14; Mt 5:34
[266] Jn 4:23; Cf. Dt 5:12; Nm 15:32; Lv 23:2; Ignatius of Antioch, *Epistle to the Philadelphians*; Leo the Great, *Sermon 3, De Quadrag.*; Gregory the Great, Bk. 11, Epistle 3;

It forbiddeth to labor on holy days, to spend any time in handicrafts, and to use profane occupations, to the intent certes that we may attend to a holy repose in going to Church and hearing Mass, the public sacrifice of the Church, and the ordinary sermon, accordingly as godly devout persons have always accustomed to keep this commandment.

53. What is the sum of these three commandments?

These three first commandments which appertain to the first table do instruct and teach us how we may give true honor unto God, to wit, interior and exterior, with heart and deed, in private and in public.

The other seven, hereafter following, are called precepts of the second table, added to this end: to explicate our duty toward our neighbor.[267]

54. What is proposed and enjoined in the fourth commandment?

Here are children taught what duty they owe to their parents, by whose means they came into this world, and by whose labor they are honestly brought up. Also, subjects are taught to perform their duty to their superiors, that is to say, to all that are supereminent in some dignity and power, whether it be in civil or ecclesiastical government.[268]

And both they unto their parents, and these unto their superiors, do owe both interior and exterior reverence and observance,[269] succor also and obedience.[270]

Furthermore, we are forbidden any kind of way to offend or grieve any such persons of high calling or authority, be it by word, deed, or any manner of sign.[271]

Jerome, *On Galatians*, Ch. 4; Augustine, *Contra Adimantum Manichaei Discipulum*, Ch. 16; *Sermon 251, De Temp.*; Council of Mainz, Can. 36; Second Council of Macon, Can. 1; Council of Agde, Can. 21, 47; Cf. also Ex 20:8; 31:13; Dt 5:12; Lv 23:2; Jer 17:21; Is 56:4; Apoc 1:10; Acts 20:7; 1 Cor 16:2; Augustine, *Ad Iam. Epistle 119*, Ch. 12, 13; *Epistle 181*, Ch. 1; *Sermon 154, De Temp.*; Leo the Great, *Epistle 81*, Ch. 1

[267] Cf. Augustine, *Quaestiones in Exodum*, q. 71; *On Psalm 32*, conc. 2. See also the annotation accompanying the answer to Question 46, above.

[268] Cf. Rom 13:1; Heb 13:7; Ti 3:1; 2:9; 1 Tm 2:1; 6:1; 1 Pt 2:13; 5:5; Eph 6:5; Col 3:22

[269] Cf. Lv 19:32; 1 Pt 2:13; Gn 43:26; 1 Tm 6:1; Ecclus 4:7; Acts 10:25

[270] Cf. 1 Tm 5:17; 1 Cor 9:7; Mt 10:9; 22:21; Lk 10:7; Ambrose, *Hexameron*, Bk. 5, Ch. 16

[271] Cf. Mt 15:3; Heb 13:17; Ex 21:15; 22:28; Lv 20:9; Dt 21:18; 27:16; Prv 20:20; 28:24; 30:11, 17; Ecclus 3:14; Cf. also Dt 5:16; Col 3:20; Eph 6:1; Ecclus 3:15; Prv 23:23; Tb 4:3

55. What importeth the fifth commandment?

It doth not only prohibit all external slaughter and violence that may prejudice the body and life of our neighbor, but also cutteth off anger, hatred, rancor, indignation, desire of revenge, and all other internal affects, tending any ways toward the hurt of our neighbor.

It requireth meekness of mind, civility, clemency, courtesy, and beneficence, that is to say, that we do easily forget injuries, and do not covet revengement, but that we pardon one another all offenses,[272] as God in Christ hath pardoned us.[273]

56. What hath the sixth commandment?

It forbiddeth fornication, adultery, and all unlawful copulation, and unclean voluptuousness whatsoever.

Moreover, it will have occasions eschewed and cut off which do provoke and cherish the lusts of the flesh, as filthy speeches, dishonest tongues, and unchaste gestures.[274]

Contrariwise, it requireth fidelity in wedlock,[275] also all manner of purity, both of mind, in our thoughts and desires,[276] and of body, in the tongue, face, eyes, ears, and touching, finally, in all exterior show and behavior: that whether we live in private or abroad with others, we not only avoid all sign of riot, voluptuousness, and intemperancy, but also diligently practice modesty, frugality, and continency.[277]

---

[272] Cf. Eph 4:1; Col 3:12; Rom 12:14, 17; 1 Pt 3:8; Eph 6:9; Phil 4:7; Mt 6:14; 5:38; 18:21, 33; Lk 6:37; Mk 11:25; Prv 24:29

[273] Cf. Eph 4:23; Cf. also Gn 9:5; Lv 24:17; 19:16; Dt 5:17; Ex 20:13; 21:12; Mt 5:21; Jas 2:11; 1 Jn 3:15; Eph 4:26, 31; Col 3:8; Ps 4:5; Rom 12:17, 19; Dt 32:35; Ecclus 28:1; Heb 10:30; 12:15

[274] Cf. Col 3:5, 8; Eph 5:3; 2 Pt 2:6, 10, 12

[275] Cf. 1 Thes 4:4; Heb 13:4; Tb 4:6; 1 Cor 7:3, 10

[276] Cf. Tb 3:16; Mt 15:18; Dn 13:8, 56

[277] Cf. 1 Tm 5:11; Ecclus 9:3; Jb 31:1, 11; Prv 6:24; Gn 9:22; Dt 25:11; Gn 38:9; 1 Tm 2:8; 1 Pt 3:1; Is 3:16; Am 6:4; Jas 5:15; Rom 13:12; Ez 16:48; 1 Tm 5:6, 22; Cf. also Lv 20:10, 22; 19:29; Dt 22:20; 23:17; Mt 5:28; Ecclus 41:21, 27; 1 Cor 6:9; 15; Eph 4:18; 5:3; Prv 6:24; Jdt 4:7, 32

57. What are we taught in the seventh commandment?

It forbiddeth all unlawful handling and usurpation of another man's goods by theft, robbery, simony, usury, unjust lucre, cozenage, and any other contracts whereby brotherly charity is hurt, and our neighbor by craft circumvented. On the contrary part, this precept requireth that in all business and traffic whatsoever, justice be kept inviolate, and that the profit of our neighbor when occasion serveth, by all manner of means or help of our part, be advanced.[278]

58. What is comprehended in the eighth commandment?

We are by it prohibited to bear false and deceitful witness against any man, and any way to subvert in judgment the cause of our neighbor, yea, or out of judgment to hurt his good name: which doubtless is done by all whisperers, detractors, railers, false accusers, and flatterers. Briefly, all lying and abuse of the tongue against our neighbor is here forbidden.

We are withal taught to speak well and favorably of our neighbor, to wit, for his defense and profit, without any color, dissimulation, or deceit.[279]

59. The two last commandments, what do they contain?

They forbid all concupiscence of another man's wife or goods: that we do not only abstain from other men's wives, unlawful traffic, and open manifest wrong, but also that we do not, so much as in will or desire, hurt or deliberate to hurt any man.

These two precepts, therefore, require the sincerity and benevolence of our heart toward all men to be sound and perfect, that whatsoever is for the commodity and health of our neighbor, we do wish from our heart, and do not at any time consent to covetousness, with the least injury that may be to another man.[280]

[278] Cf. Ps 14:1; Lk 6:30; Ez 18:5, 7-8, 12, 17; Rom 13:7; Mt 5:40; Cf. also Lv 19:11, 13, 35; Eph 4:28; 1 Cor 6:7; Lk 6:34; Acts 8:18; 4 Kgs 5:20; Dt 25:13; Prv 11:1; 20:10; Ecclus 10:6, 8; 1 Thes 4:6

[279] Cf. Lv 19:11, 13; Ex 23:16; Dt 5:19; 16:18; 19:15; 27:19; Prv 12:17; 4:24; 24:21; 25:18; Jas 4:11; 1 Pt 2:1; Eph 4:25; Prv 17:4, 7, 9, 15; 18:6; 19:5; Rom 1:29; Ps 5:7, 10; Apoc 21:8, 27; 22:15; Jas 3:2, 14; Mt 12:35; Col 3:8, 16; Eph 4:29; Prv 15:1, 4, 7; Ecclus 6:1, 5

[280] Cf. Dt 5:20; Ecclus 25:28; Mt 5:28; Rom 13:9; 1 Thes 4:3; Jas 1:14; Is 1:23; Ecclus 5:1; 18:30; Ps 25; 61:11; Acts 20:33; Jb 31:1, 11; 1 Cor 10:24; Tb 9:9; 10:11; Gn 24:59; 1 Tm 6:9

60. To what end are all the ten commandments to be referred?

To charity, two sorts whereof those two tables, wherein by the finger of God these commandments were engraven, do commend unto us.[281] For the commandments of the first table do teach us that which belongeth to the love of God; and those of the second, that which appertaineth to the love of our neighbor.

Therefore, of these ten, the two first do cause thus much: that we do specially avoid those vices which are most repugnant to the service and honor of God, as idolatry and perjury.

Then doth the third commandment admonish us that we yield unto him the most faithful manner true and pure service, and honor in heart, word, and deed. Which surely when it is well observed, no doubt but that God only is in all things, and above all things, loved and honored.

Now, the sum of the precepts that belong to the love of our neighbor standeth even in this one point: "That which of another thou hatest to be done unto thee, see that not at any time thou do it to another."[282] To which doth answer that speech of Christ: "All things whatsoever you will that men do to you, do you also to them: for this is the law and the prophets."[283]

61. Which are the duties and arguments of brotherly charity?

Of these Saint Paul discourseth in this manner: "Charity is patient, is benign: charity envieth not, dealeth not perversely; is not puffed up; is not ambitious, seeketh not her own, is not provoked to anger, thinketh not evil; rejoiceth not upon iniquity, but rejoiceth with the truth; suffereth all things, believeth all things, hopeth all things, beareth all things."[284]

And Christ, to the intent he might exhibit himself unto us a pattern of true and perfect charity, in that last supper, which he wonderfully seasoned with excellent tokens of his charity, said very earnestly: "A new commandment I give you, that you love one another, as I have loved you,

---

[281] Cf. Ex 32:15; 34:1
[282] Tb 4:16
[283] Mt 7:12; Cf. Lk 6:31
[284] 1 Cor 13:4-7

that you also love one another."[285] And again: "This is my precept, that you love one another, as I have loved you."[286] Which surely is of so great importance that Saint Paul affirmeth that "he that loveth his neighbor hath fulfilled the law."[287]

Therefore, that we may conclude this place of charity with an oracle of God himself, it is thus written: "Choose life, that both thou mayest live and thy seed. And love thy Lord thy God. And obey his voice and cleave unto him. For he is thy life and the length of thy days."[288] Then that no man may doubt but that the evangelical doctrine of Christ doth herein accord with the law, let us remember that Christ himself did say: "If thou wilt enter into life, keep the commandments."[289] And in another place, having commended unto us the precepts and works of charity, he also annexeth these words: "This do and thou shalt live."[290] "For not the hearers of the law are just with God, but the doers of the law shall be justified."[291]

Of these doers were Abel, Noah, Abraham, Zechariah, whom the scripture testifieth to have been just before God, as those that loved God and their neighbor in work and in truth.[292]

Wherefore, David, not the least amongst them, glorying after a holy manner, singeth thus: "I have run the way of thy commandments, when thou hast dilated my heart."[293] I have loved, I have observed, I have kept thy commandments, and thy testimonies;[294] "in keeping them much retribution";[295] "accursed are they that decline from thy commandments."[296]

---

[285] Jn 13:34

[286] Jn 15:12

[287] Rom 13:8

[288] Dt 30:19-20

[289] Mt 19:17

[290] Lk 10:28

[291] Rom 2:13

[292] Cf. Gn 6:9; 7:1; in oratione Manassis.; Ws 10:4; Mt 23:35; 1:19; Jb 13:18; Lk 1:6; 2:25; Jas 2:21

[293] Ps 118:32

[294] Cf. Ps 118:47-48, 51, 55, 101-102, 110, 113, 127-128, 157, 159, 163, 167-168

[295] Ps 18:12

[296] Ps 118:21; Cf. 1 Cor 13:4; Gregory the Great, *Moralia in Job*, Bk. 10, Ch. 8; Jn 13:1; Lk 22:15

Of Tradition, and Precepts in General

62. **Are there any other commandments to be observed by Christians besides these ten?**

There are doubtless: forasmuch as our lawmaker[297] and master[298] Christ hath not only taught the ten commandments of the law,[299] but hath also commanded in general all those things that do concern the yielding of obedience unto apostolical and ecclesiastical commandments. To this end are those speeches of the gospel: "As my Father hath sent me, I also do send you."[300] "He that heareth you, heareth me: and he that despiseth you, despiseth me."[301] "If he will not hear them, tell the church: and if he will not hear the church, let him be to thee as the heathen and the publican";[302] in which places Christ attributeth, and willeth to be attributed, the chief and last judgment unto the Church, that is to say, to the prelates and governors of the Church,[303] as St. Chrysostom doth interpret, and the words of the gospel immediately following do declare and convince.[304]

For which cause, it is not in vain written of the apostle Saint Paul: "He walked through Syria and Cilicia, confirming the churches: commanding them to keep the precepts of the apostles and the ancients."[305]

63. **What then are the precepts of the apostles and ancients which St. Paul would have us to keep?**

Saint Denis Areopagite, scholar of St. Paul, affirmeth that they are of two sorts, to wit, partly written and partly unwritten.[306] To both kinds doth

---

[297] Cf. Jas 4:12

[298] Cf. Mt 23:8

[299] Cf. Mt 19:17

[300] Jn 20:21; Cf. Jn 17:18

[301] Lk 10:16

[302] Mt 18:17

[303] Cf. 3 Kgs 8:14

[304] Cf. Chrysostom, *Homily 61 on Matthew*; Basil, *Consist. Monast. Theophyl.*, Ch. 30; Eutim., *On Matthew*, Ch. 18

[305] Acts 15:41; Cf. Acts 16:4

[306] Cf. Dionysius, *Ecclesiastical Hierarchy*, Ch. 1; Basil, *De Spiritu Sancto*, Ch. 27; Eusebius, *Demonstratio Evangelica*, Bk. 1, Ch. 8; Epiphanius, *Adversus Haeresus*, n. 61 contra Apostolicos; Tertullian, *De Corona Militis*, Ch. 3-4

belong that which St. John the Evangelist saith: "He that knoweth God, heareth us. He that is not of God heareth us not. In this we know the spirit of truth and the spirit of error."[307]

And surely the first kind, which is committed to letters and standeth in written laws, is apparent enough: for that it consisteth of those books that are canonical.

But the latter consisteth in those precepts and ordinances which are comprehended under this one name of *traditions*, and usually so called by the fathers. For they are not kept in writing, as the former, but delivered by word of mouth, and, as it were, by hand from our ancestors surrendered over unto us, and commended unto the Church.[308]

64. **Are both these kinds of precepts necessary to be observed?**
They are doubtless, if we will follow the doctrine of Saint Paul giving us this charge: "Stand and hold the traditions which you have learned, whether it be by word, or by our epistle."[309] Whereupon he in this respect commendeth the Corinthians, because they did diligently keep the precepts of the apostles, which they had already by word of mouth received.[310] Then he warneth the Thessalonians that they withdraw themselves from every brother walking inordinately, and not according to the tradition received from the apostles.[311]

And this is that which the holy Council of Nice, consonant to divine scripture, hath expressed in so plain terms: "It behooveth us to observe with one consent and inviolably ecclesiastical traditions; whether they by writing or by custom be retained in the Church."[312] And we read in St. Cyprian that, that is of no less force which the apostles by the inspiration of the Holy Ghost have delivered, than that which Christ himself hath delivered.[313] For

[307] 1 Jn 4:6
[308] Cf. Cyprian, *Sermon, De Ablutione Pedum*; Jerome, *Dialogue against the Luciferians*, Ch. 4; Chrysostom, *Homily 4 on 2 Thessalonians*
[309] 2 Thes 2:14; Cf. Chrysostom, *Homily 4 on 2 Thessalonians*; Theophylactus
[310] Cf. 1 Cor 11:2
[311] Cf. 2 Thes 3:6
[312] Second Council of Nicea, Act 7; Cf. Fourth Council of Constantinople, Can. 1
[313] Cf. Cyprian, *Sermon, De Ablutione Pedum*

as the Holy Ghost and Christ have one and the same Godhead, so is the authority and power of them both equal in their sacred ordinances.[314]

65. How may we know which are apostolical and approved traditions in the Church?

Of these St. Austen hath prescribed us a rule worthy to be noted, saying: "Those things that we keep not written, but delivered, which are certainly observed all the world over, it is understood that they are holden as commended and ordained, either by the apostles themselves, or by general councils whose authority in the Church is most wholesome."[315] So the same holy Doctor discoursing against the Donatists, yea even against all heretics, admonisheth this very seriously: "Look what the universal Church holdeth, which by counsels hath not been decreed, and yet ever hath been used, it is very well believed that, by no other means than by the authority of the apostles themselves, it hath been delivered."[316]

And Leo the Great agreeing hereunto, saith: "It is not at all to be doubted, but that whatsoever is holden in the Church as a custom of devotion, it proceedeth from apostolical tradition and of the doctrine of the Holy Ghost."[317]

66. What are those apostolical traditions which Christians must observe?

There are sufficient store of examples, extant amongst the fathers, and such of the fathers as above a thousand years since deserved public credit. By tradition, Origen and St. Austen do teach that infants are to be baptized.[318] St. Denis and Tertullian do show that prayers and oblations ought to be made at the altar for them that are departed.[319]

---

[314] Cf. Ibid.

[315] Augustine, *Epistle 54 to Januarius*, Ch. 1

[316] Augustine, *On Baptism, against the Donatists*, Bk. 4, Ch. 24; Cf. Augustine, *On Baptism, against the Donatists*, Bk. 2, Ch. 7; Bk. 5, Ch. 23

[317] Leo the Great, *Sermon 2, De Jejunio Pentecostes*

[318] Cf. Origen, *On Romans*, Ch. 6; Augustine, *De Genesi ad Litteram*, Bk. 10, Ch. 23; *On Baptism, against the Donatists*, Bk. 4, Ch. 24

[319] Cf. Dionysius, *Ecclesiastical Hierarchy*, Ch. 7; Tertullian, *De Exhortatione Castitatis*, Ch. 11; *De Corona Militis*, Ch. 3; *On Monogamy*, Ch. 10

Hereupon St. Jerome and Epiphanius do plainly affirm that the set fasts of the Church, especially that of Lent, are to be observed.[320] So in like manner doth Saint Ambrose and Saint Chrysostom avouch the dignity of those things that are solemnly prosecuted in the holy office of the Mass.[321]

Then, besides Damascene,[322] the fathers that the Second Nicene Council doth cite do witness by the same reason that the images of Christ and his saints are to be reverenced.[323]

Finally, to omit all others, that great and holy doctor Saint Basil affirmeth that the sacred chrism and other solemn ceremonies used in the most holy sacraments are holden upon tradition.[324]

And the same saint addeth further: "If we do once attempt to refuse the ordinances and customs that are not written as things of small moment and importance, we shall covertly, and by little and little, fall to disprove the very ratified sentences of the gospel, or rather, we shall bring the preaching thereof to a bare name."[325] "But I," saith he, "do think it apostolical to stick to those traditions also that are not written."[326]

67. **How much at this day do men err and go astray about apostolical and ecclesiastical traditions?**

Very much no doubt; whilst many do despise them, others neglect them or, at the least, make no more account of them than of the statutes of civil magistrates, and feign them to be decrees of men, which may be observed and broken at a man's pleasure, as being too very little or no profit at all: calling them things indifferent.[327] Some there are who will have all manner of traditions of like moment, and so they do shamefully confound certain places of scripture, as though there were no difference between Pharisaical

[320] Cf. Jerome, *Epistle 41 to Marcella*; Epiphanius, *Adversus Haeresus*, n. 75
[321] Cf. Ambrose, *in officio Mediolan.*; Chrysostom, *in Liturgia*
[322] Cf. John Damascene, *An Exposition of the Orthodox Faith*, Bk. 4, Ch. 17; *Oration, De Imag.*
[323] Cf. Second Council of Nicea, Act 6, Bk. 4; Act 7
[324] Cf. Basil, *De Spiritu Sancto*, Ch. 27
[325] Ibid.
[326] Basil, *De Spiritu Sancto*, Ch. 19
[327] Cf. Rom 13:1

traditions and apostolical;[328] between Judaical[329] and ecclesiastical;[330] between private and particular traditions and those which being received by the consent of the whole Church, and approved so many ages together, by the common custom of devout persons, and, as it were, by hand delivered over unto us, are found in a manner all the world over.[331]

68. **What is to be thought of such as reject and make no account of the traditions of the Church?**

These doth the word of God reprove and condemn when it appointeth traditions to be observed;[332] and commandeth us to hear the Church;[333] and to keep the precepts of the apostles and ancients.[334] It is the word of God that maketh us subject to magistrates, both civil[335] and ecclesiastical,[336] to the modest and also to the wayward,[337] for conscience sake:[338] it will have us give both great reverence and obedience unto their laws:[339] "Obey," saith it, "your prelates and be subject unto them."[340] "All things that they shall say to you, observe ye and do ye, but according to their works do ye not."[341] Wherefore, these fellows do not only despise men, but God himself, most gracious and mighty, whom they should hear and reverence[342] in the apostles[343] and their successors.[344] Therefore, they do manifestly resist the word

---

[328] Cf. Mt 15:9
[329] Cf. Col 2:8, 20
[330] Cf. 2 Thes 2:14; Acts 15:41; 16:4
[331] Cf. Augustine, *Epistle 54 to Januarius*, Ch. 1-2; *Epistle 82 ad Casul.*
[332] Cf. 2 Thes 2:14; 1 Cor 11:2
[333] Cf. Mt 18:27
[334] Cf. Acts 15:41; 16:4
[335] Cf. Rom 13:1; Mt 22:21
[336] Cf. Mt 23:2; Lk 10:16
[337] Cf. 1 Pt 2:13
[338] Cf. Rom 13:5
[339] Cf. Ti 3:1
[340] Heb 13:17
[341] Mt 23:3
[342] Cf. 1 Thes 4:8; 1 Cor 14:37
[343] Cf. Jn 20:21; 17:18; Lk 10:16
[344] Cf. Cyprian, *Epistle 69 ad Flor.*; Basil, *Constitu. Mon.*, Ch. 23

of God, whilst they resist the power and ordinance of God, and purchase damnation unto themselves thereby, if we believe St. Paul.[345]

Undoubtedly, this is the very ordinance of God himself, which cannot be abolished by any authority of man, that by certain laws, and those partly written, which the tradition of the apostles commendeth unto us: the Church be governed, true doctrine preserved, religion defended, concord nourished, discipline kept and observed.[346]

69. **What hath the judgment of the fathers been about this matter?**

Origen, a famous and very ancient author, hath written in these words: "Every such one is of us to be accounted a heretic that professeth himself to believe Christ, and believeth other ways of the truth of Christian faith than hath the definition of the Church's tradition."[347] And the same in another place: "That only is to be thought the truth," saith he, "which in no point disagreeth from the tradition of the Church."[348] And it is the speech of St. Jerome: "I do think it good to admonish thee, that the customs of the Church, especially those that are not against faith, are so to be observed, as they were delivered from our ancestors."[349]

And St. Augustine teacheth in this manner: "If the authority of divine scripture do prescribe anything, there is no doubt but that we ought so to do as we have read; and so, in like manner, if the Church do use anything throughout the world, for to dispute that a man ought not so to do were a part of most insolent madness."[350] And again the same: "In those matters wherein the word of God hath set down no certainty, the custom of God's people, or the decrees of our ancestors are to be holden as a law."[351] And

---

[345] Cf. Rom 13:2

[346] Cf. Basil, *De Spiritu Sancto*, Ch. 27; Augustine, *On Baptism, against the Donatists*, Bk. 4, Ch. 24; Bk. 2, Ch. 7; Bk. 5, Ch. 23, 26; Epiphanius, *Adversus Haeresus*, n. 55; Eusebius, *Ecclesiastical History*, Bk. 3, Ch. 30

[347] Origen, *On Titus*, Ch. 3; Cf. Pamphilus, *Apologia pro Origen*; Irenaeus, *Against Heresies*, Bk. 4, Ch. 43

[348] Origen, *De Principiis*, Preface, n. 2

[349] Jerome, *Epistle 71 to Lucinius*

[350] Augustine, *Epistle 54 to Januarius*, Ch. 5

[351] Augustine, *Epistle 36 to Casulanus*, Ch. 1

as the transgressors of divine laws, so also the contemners of the Church's customs are to be restrained.[352]

Finally, Tertullian, a most learned and ancient writer of the Church, in one whole book together disputeth against those that do admit nothing that is not expressly set down in the scripture, and he contendeth very earnestly that there be certain unwritten traditions and observations of the Church, which none can take exceptions against, but heretics only.[353] But, "if any man seem to be contentious," that we may use St. Paul's words, "we have no such custom, nor the church of God."[354]

Of the Church

70. **I pray you then, what is the Church?**

The Church is the whole multitude of all those that profess the faith and doctrine of Christ, which Christ the Prince of pastors committed both unto St. Peter the apostle and also to his successors, to be fed and governed.[355]

And therefore, all heretics and schismatics do not deserve the name of a *Church*, but do falsely arrogate the same unto themselves:[356] who although they seem to profess the faith and doctrine of Christ, yet they refuse to be the sheep of the high pastor and bishop which Christ hath made chief governor over the sheepfold of the Church in his own stead, and hath by the perpetual succession in the Roman Church continually preserved.[357]

This chair of St. Peter, this primacy of the Church, whosoever doth deny and oppugn: first, they do not understand the large promises of Christ, made unto St. Peter, and the mystical keys of the kingdom of heaven delivered to him only,[358] and many other things written of Saint Peter, the

[352] Cf. *Distinct. 11*, Ch. "In his."
[353] Cf. Tertullian, *Prescription against Heretics*
[354] 1 Cor 11:16
[355] Cf. Chrysostom, *On the Priesthood*; Council of Florence; Bernard, *De Consideratione*, Bk. 2, Ch. 8
[356] Cf. Jerome, *Dialogue against the Luciferians*, Ch. 9; Cyprian, *Epistle 69*
[357] Cf. Irenaeus, *Against Heresies*, Bk. 3, Ch. 3; Tertullian, *Against Marcion*, Ch. 9; Optatus of Milevis, *Against the Donatists*, Bk. 2; Augustine, *Epistle 165*; *Epistle 42*; *Psalmus contra Partem Donati*; *Answer to Petilian the Donatist*, Bk. 2, Ch. 51
[358] Cf. Mt 16:18; Jn 21:15; Lk 22:31; Mt 10:2; Jn 1:42; Mt 17:24; Acts 1:15

prince, the mouth, and head of the apostles; then, they do manifestly break the peace and certain order of the Church, which, without a high bishop and his supereminent authority, can neither be well-governed nor kept long in unity, nor hold that sound strength that is necessary to bear out the violence of hell's gates;[359] lastly, they do impudently discredit the fathers, and their councils and writings, consenting all together about this manifest note of the Church, yea, and the consonant voice of all Christianity.[360]

This Church and her dignity acknowledge Saint Jerome, whose words are these: "He that is joined to Peter's chair, is mine."[361] Optatus of Africa hath acknowledged her, who witnesseth that among the true notes of the Church, the chair of Saint Peter is the principal.[362] St. Augustine hath acknowledged her, who writeth expressly that, in the Church of Rome, the sovereignty of the see apostolic hath always flourished.[363] Saint Cyprian hath acknowledged her, who imputeth the cause of all heresies and schisms that do grow to this alone: that men do not obey one high priest and judge in Christ his room.[364] Saint Ambrose hath acknowledged her, insomuch that he hath said that in all things he did covet to follow the Roman Church.[365]

And more ancient than all these, and near unto the apostles' time, that very apostolical man Irenaeus giveth such a testimonial of commendation to the Church of Rome: "To this Church," saith he, "because of the chiefer principality, it is necessary that all the Church have recourse,"[366] that is to say, all the faithful that are dispersed in all places: in which Church by

[359] Cf. Cyprian, *On the Unity of the Church*; Hilary, *On Matthew*, Ch. 16; Jerome, *On Matthew*, Ch. 16; *Against Jovinianus*, Bk. 1, Ch. 14; Cyril of Alexandria, *On John*, Bk. 2, Ch. 12; Augustine, *Tractate 56 on John*; *Tractate 124 on John*; Origen, *Homily 2 in Divers.*; *Tractate 6 on Matthew*; Basil, *De Paenit.*; Chrysostom, *Homily 87 on John*; *Homily 55 on Matthew*; *Homily 9 de Paenit.*; *Sermon de Caten et Gladio S. Pet.*; *Homily in SS. Petrum et Eliam*; Leo the Great, *Sermon 3 de Annivers.*; *Epistle 89 ad Epis. Vien.*

[360] Cf. Augustine, *Against the Fundamental Epistle of Manichaeus*, Ch. 4; *De Utilitate Credendi ad Honoratum*, Ch. 17; *Contra Faustum*, Bk. 11, Ch. 2

[361] Jerome, *Epistle 16 to Damasus*; Cf. Jerome, *Epistle 15 to Damasus*

[362] Cf. Optatus of Milevis, *Against the Donatists*, Bk. 2

[363] Cf. Augustine, *Epistles 162, 9, 92, 93, 165*

[364] Cf. Cyprian, *Epistle 55*; *Epistle 69*; Jerome, *Dialogue against the Luciferians*, Ch. 4; Leo the Great, *Epistle 84 ad Anast.*, Ch. 11

[365] Cf. Ambrose, *On the Sacraments*, Bk. 3, Ch. 1; *On the Death of Satyrus*

[366] Irenaeus, *Against Heresies*, Bk. 3, Ch. 2

those that are in all places of the world hath always been conserved the apostolical tradition.[367]

71. What dignity and authority hath the Church?

Almighty God doth advance his Church (of all things upon earth the most dearest unto him) with many and most excellent dowries, promises, and benefits. Her, he doth always adorn, preserve, defend, and maintain.

Her also he hath appointed to be his house wherein all the sons of God may be cherished, taught, and exercised.[368]

His pleasure was to make her the pillar and ground of truth, that we may not doubt any wit of her doctrine, which as a mistress, keeper, and interpreter of the truth, obtaineth credit and authority inviolable.[369]

Moreover, he hath determined that she should be builded upon a sure rock; that we might assuredly know how she is unmovable and steadfast;[370] and how she prevaileth as unvanquishable against the very gates of hell,[371] to wit, the most sharp and grievous assaults of all adversaries.

Finally, he will have her to be a certain city most holy set upon a hill, apparent to all men, and easy to go unto:[372] lest any man forsaking her, might betake himself to the pestiferous dens and dungeons of heretics;[373] and being seduced with those false speeches, "Behold here is Christ, behold there,"[374] might depart and be withdrawn from her.

This is the lover, sister, and only spouse of Christ, which holy scripture proposeth and commendeth unto us;[375] for whose redemption, cleansing,

---

[367] Cf. Tertullian, *Prescription against Heretics*, Ch. 36; Cyprian, *Epistle 45*; *Epistle 46*; Theodoret, *Ecclesiastical History*, Bk. 2, Ch. 4; Bernard, *Epistle 190 ad Innoc.*; *De Consideratione*, Bk. 2, Ch. 8; Council of Chalcedon, Act 3; Anacletus, *Epistle 1*; *Epistle 3*; Marcell., *Epistle 1*; Synod of Alexandria ad Faelicem; Cf. also Rom 12:4; 1 Cor 12:12; 1 Pt 5:4; Jn 21:15; Mt 16:18

[368] Cf. 1 Tm 3:15; Ps 22:2; Jn 10:16

[369] Cf. 1 Tm 3:15; Augustine, *Contra Cresconium*, Bk. 1, Ch. 33; Bk. 2, Ch. 32

[370] Cf. Mt 16:18; 7:25; Eph 2:20; Ps 86:2; 47:9; Augustine, *On Psalm 47*; Alcimus Avitus, *De Spiritualis Historiae Gestis*, Bk. 4, Ch. 14

[371] Cf. Mt 16:18

[372] Cf. Apoc 21:2; Mt 5:15; Is 2:2; Mi 4:1; Mal 1:11; Acts 1:8; Ps 21:26, 28

[373] Cf. 1 Jn 2:19

[374] Mt 24:23; Cf. Origen, *Tractate 29 on Matthew*; *Tractate 30 on Matthew*

[375] Cf. Cant 4:7; 6:8

sanctification,[376] gathering together, and wholly uniting unto himself, the Son of God did and suffered all things, insomuch as he doubted not to give his most holy body and blood for the love of her.[377]

For her he asked and obtained that her faith, unity, and steadfastness might never fail.[378]

To her he hath promised,[379] and faithfully sent down and left a teacher, president, and governor, the Holy Ghost:[380] "He," saith he, "shall teach you all things and suggest unto you all things, whatsoever I shall say to you."[381] "He shall abide with you forever."[382] "He shall teach you all truth,"[383] to wit, whatsoever is necessary to be known and believed.[384]

72. **By whom, I pray you, doth the Holy Ghost teach us the truth in the Church?**

By those, undoubtedly, whom the apostle witnesseth to be ordained by the Holy Ghost to govern the Church: whom he calleth bishops, prelates, pastors also, and doctors. And these after the apostles have been ever, and yet are the chief ministers of God and of the Church,[385] and high stewards and dispensers of the mysteries of Almighty God.[386]

The authority of whom both in many other things, and especially in the sacred synods,[387] may evidently be seen where they have not only power to determine certain things of faith and religion, but also by their

[376] Cf. Eph 5:26
[377] Cf. Jn 11:52; Col 1:8, 24; Eph 4:12; 1:22
[378] Cf. Jn 17:21; Lk 22:31; Mt 16:18
[379] Cf. Jn 14:15, 26; 15:26; 16:12
[380] Cf. Acts 2:4
[381] Jn 14:26
[382] Jn 14:16
[383] Jn 16:13
[384] Cf. Augustine, *Tractate 97 on John*; Cf. also 1 Cor 12:28; Eph 5:25; Jn 14:15, 26; 16:12; 17:11, 17; Mt 28:20; 16:18; Ps 120:4
[385] Cf. Augustine, *On Psalm 44*
[386] Cf. 1 Cor 4:1
[387] Cf. *Apostolic Canons*, Can. 38; First Council of Nicea; Sozomen, *Church History*, Bk. 6, Ch. 7; Emperor Theodosius apud Cyrillum ep.; Emperor Basil in the Fourth Council of Constantinople, Act 10; Athanasius, *Epistle, ad Solitariam Vitam Agentes*; Rufinus, *Ecclesiastical History*, Bk. 1, Ch. 5

own right and apostolic authority, to protest and say: "It hath seemed good to the Holy Ghost, and us,"[388] as it appeareth by the acts of the first council holden at Jerusalem. It was certes of old a very heinous crime, and such a one as was punished by death,[389] if any man had not obeyed the judgment of the high priest that governed the chair of Moses.[390] And yet the Church hath now authority in governing, judging, and decreeing, no wit inferior to that which then the synagogue had.[391] That law of obedience that was amongst the Jews standeth also in force amongst the Christians: that the judgments of the high priests, whose dignity and authority is most excellent, about all such matters as do belong unto religion, be received, approved, and observed.[392]

And therefore, they do incur the guilt of an enormous crime who are so far off yielding any authority and obedience unto the magistrates of the Church, that they presume, even openly, to oppugn and abolish sometimes the holy laws of the high bishops,[393] who have always had supreme power and authority to determine of holy things,[394] and sometimes the reverend decrees of general councils, whose authority in the Church, as St. Augustine speaketh, is most wholesome.[395] Finally, sometimes, the undoubted sentence of the fathers about matters of faith, whose general judgment and consent in one matter is a firm testimony of Christian verity.[396] It was very notably spoken of good and devout emperors: "He doth injury to the judgment of the Council, whosoever goeth about to call into question and public disputation those things that are once judged and rightly disposed."[397]

[388] Acts 15:28
[389] Cf. Dt 17:12
[390] Cf. Mt 23:2
[391] Cf. Cyprian, *Epistle 55 to Cornelius*; *Epistle 62 to Pomponius*
[392] Cf. Gregory the Great, Bk. 1, *Epistle 24 ad Patriar.*; Bk. 2, indict. 11, *Epistle 10 ad Savin.*; Nicephorus, *Church History*, Bk. 16, Ch. 23
[393] Cf. Third Council of Toledo, Can. 1, Dist. 19, 9, q. 1f. Patet
[394] Cf. Jerome, *Epistle 15 to Damasus*; *Epistle 16 to Damasus*; Council of Chalcedon, Act 3, in epi. ad Leon.; Third Council of Constantinople, Act 4
[395] Cf. Augustine, *Epistle 54 to Januarius*, Ch. 1; *On Baptism, against the Donatists*, Bk. 1, Ch. 18; Gregory the Great, Bk. 1, *Epistle 24 ad Patriar.*; Bk. 2, indict. 11, *Epistle 10 ad Savin.*
[396] Cf. Vincent of Lerins, *Contra Novat.*; Augustine, *Contra Julianum*, Bk. 1-2; Pacian, *Epistle 1 ad Simpron.*
[397] Council of Chalcedon, Act 3; Cf. Gelas., *in ep. ad Epi. Dar.*; Leo the Great, *Epistle*

73. To what end is this divine ordinance and appointment, that there be always pastors and doctors in the Church?

This ordinance of God is not a little profitable and wholesome for us, by which the power and holy government of the Church doth far excel all civil authority. For this is a spiritual power, by which the Christian people are singularly furthered in the achieving of spiritual and external good things.[398]

And first, it profiteth that we may use the words of St. Paul "to the consummation of the saints":[399] that is to say, that they which do exercise that power may exhibit every man perfect in Christ, as the same apostle speaketh in another place,[400] and by their diligence, bring the faithful to that perfection of holiness, to which they have been called.[401]

It profiteth also, "to the work of the ministry,"[402] that they, which are called and are indeed the chief ministers of the Church, may be always vigilant and careful, according to the great and high function committed unto their charge.[403]

It profiteth besides, "unto the edifying of the body of Christ,"[404] that these spiritual and wise architects may know[405] that about the mystical body of Christ, which requireth a singular industry in the building, they must be continually occupied; sometimes to lay and fortify the foundations of true faith;[406] sometimes to build up other things neccessary to the perfect righteousness of the faithful.[407]

---

53 ad Mart.; Epistle 50 ad Mart.; Epistle 78 ad Leonem Augustum; Cf. also Acts 20:28; 1 Tm 3:2; Heb 13:17; Eph 4:12; 1 Cor 12:28

[398] Cf. Chrysostom, On the Priesthood, Bk. 3; Homily 4 de Verb. Isa.; Homily 5 de Verb. Isa.; Ignatius of Antioch, Epistle to the Smyrnaeans; Ambrose, Concerning Virgins; On the Duties of the Clergy, Bk. 2, Ch. 2

[399] Eph 4:12

[400] Cf. Col 1:28

[401] Cf. 1 Thes 3:7; 2 Tm 3:17; 2 Cor 13:11

[402] Eph 4:12

[403] Cf. Acts 20:28; Heb 13:17; Cyprian, Epistle 66 ad Furn.

[404] Eph 4:12

[405] Cf. 1 Cor 3:1

[406] Cf. Eph 1:23; Col 1:18, 24; Eph 2:21

[407] Cf. 1 Cor 3:12

It profiteth finally, "that we be not children wavering and carried about with every wind of doctrine, in the wickedness of men,"[408] that is to say: for the weaker sort (which are always in the Church very many in number) the function of ecclesiastical prelates is very necessary,[409] especially at such time as the tempests of heresies and the storms of persecutions do bear into the house of the Church.[410] For then there is need of the present help of those who, according to their authority, both will and can keep off the wolves, defend the sheep, root out the cockle, and confirm sound doctrine, lest otherwise the simple be seduced by the words, writings, and examples of deceitful and wicked persons, from the kingly roadway of truth, but rather that all, not only knowing the truth, but practicing the same, may grow and go forward in him that is the head, Christ our Lord,[411] as the same apostle St. Paul hath also spoken.[412]

74. By what means may we obtain these so singular commodities?

By this no doubt: if we be not too highly, but soberly wise;[413] always careful to keep the unity of spirit in the band of peace, that so we may show ourselves the humble and obedient sheep of Christ.[414] Of which sheep certes it is the property to fly the wolves, and not to follow aliens, but their own pastors:[415] to submit themselves to them, as to the ordinary prefects of our Lord's fold;[416] and in them to hear the Spirit of truth.[417]

That Spirit it is which vouchsafeth even by evil prelates, to teach, feed, and preserve our Lord's flock; and which by them commendeth unto us the precepts both of God our Father and the Church our mother,[418] in these words: "Hear my son the discipline of thy father, and do not let go the law

[408] Eph 4:14
[409] Cf. 1 Cor 14:20; Rom 15:1; Acts 14:21; 1 Thes 3:2; 4:1; Ez 34:2
[410] Cf. Mt 7:25
[411] Cf. Acts 20:29; Ez 33:6; 2 Tm 2:23, 25; 4:2; Ti 1:9-11; 2 Pt 2:1; 3:3; Rom 16:17; Jude 1:17, 4, 10; Mt 7:15
[412] Cf. Eph 4:15
[413] Cf. Rom 12:3
[414] Cf. Eph 4:3; Jn 10:2; 21:17
[415] Cf. Jn 10:2; Ti 3:1; Heb 13:17; Mt 10:20
[416] Cf. Bernard, *De Praecepto et Dispensatione*, Ch. 12
[417] Cf. Jn 15:26; 14:7; 16:13
[418] Cf. Mt 23:2; Phil 1:15; Jn 11:51; Mt 18:17; Dt 17:12

of thy mother."[419] And again the same doth inculcate "Keep," saith he, "my son the precepts of thy father, and do not let go the law of thy mother."[420]

Of the Precepts of the Church

75. **Which are the precepts of the Church?**

There are five principal, necessary doubtless to be known and observed of every Christian.

1. The appointed holy days of the Church do thou celebrate.[421]
2. The holy office of the Mass, upon holy days, do thou hear with reverence.[422]
3. The fasts on certain days and times appointed, do thou observe.[423] For example, as the Lent, Ember days, and the next days before certain solemn feasts, which our forefathers have called vigils or eves, because they did use at such times all night to watch in the churches.[424]
4. Thy sins to thy proper priest do thou every year confess.[425]
5. The Holy Eucharist, at the least once in the year and that about the feast of Easter, do thou receive.[426]

76. **What profit doth the observation of these precepts bring?**

These and other like customs and precepts of the Church so many ages received, and with great consent and practice of devout Christians,

---

[419] Prv 1:8; Cf. Epiphanius, *Adversus Haeresus*, n. 75

[420] Prv 6:20

[421] Cf. Council of Lyons, apud Ivonem. p. 4, Can. 14; Second Council of Macon, Can. 1; Council of Mainz, Can. 36, 37; Council of Tribur, Can. 35; Ignatius of Antioch, *Epistle to the Philadelphians*

[422] Cf. Council of Agde, Can. 47 and 21; Council of Tribur, Can. 35; First Council of Orleans, Can. 28

[423] Cf. *Apostolic Canons*, Can. 68; Council of Gangra, Can. 19; Ignatius of Antioch, *Epistle to the Philadelphians*; Council of Mainz, Can. 34-35; Council of Selingstad, Can. 1-2; Bernard, *In Vigilia S. Andreae*; see the places cited in the treatise of good works, Question 182, below.

[424] Cf. Tertullian, *Ad Uxorem*, Bk. 2; *Apology*

[425] Cf. Fourth Lateran Council, Const. 21; Council of Trent, Session 14, Can. 6, 8

[426] Cf. Fourth Lateran Council, Const. 21; Council of Trent, Session 13, Can. 9

confirmed and very agreeable to piety and reason, do bring with them very notable and excellent commodities.

For they are wholesome exercises of faith, humility, and Christian obedience; they do advance honest discipline and concord among the people; they are goodly signs and badges of religion;[427] finally, they give marks and tokens of our inward piety, by which we ought jointly to shine with the good, and to show our light to the evil for their edification.[428]

Briefly, they do help us to this: that we may exactly observe that rule of the apostle: "Let all things be done honestly, and according to order among you."[429]

77. **Wherein is the authority of the Church necessary unto us?**

First of all, surely in this: that we may certainly discern the true and canonical scripture from that which is counterfeit and apocryphal.[430] Whereupon Saint Jerome doth testify: "We receive," saith he, "the old and new testament, in that number of books which the authority of the holy Catholic Church doth deliver."[431] And Saint Augustine: "I truly would not believe the gospel, except the authority of the Catholic Church did move me thereunto."[432]

It is also necessary that we may be assured of the true sense and apt interpretation of the scripture; lest that otherwise we never make an end of doubting and disputing about the sense of words.[433] "For all heretics," as the same holy saint hath written, "do labor to defend their false and deceitful opinions by the holy scriptures";[434] and yet, "the scriptures do

---

[427] Cf. Phil 4:8; 1 Cor 14:26, 40

[428] Cf. Mt 5:17; Rom 15:2; Phil 2:3, 14

[429] 1 Cor 14:40

[430] Cf. Gal 2:2; First Council of Toledo, Can. 25; Augustine, *Sermon 129, De Temp.*; *Contra Faustum*, Bk. 13, Ch. 4-5; Bk. 28, Ch. 2, 4

[431] Creed of Damasus; Cf. Augustine, *Sermon 19.1, De Temp.*; Council of Laodicea, Can. 59; Third Council of Carthage, Can. 47; Council of Trent, Session 4

[432] Augustine, *Against the Fundamental Epistle of Manichaeus*, Ch. 5

[433] Cf. Is 59:21; Augustine, *Contra Cresconium*, Bk. 1, Ch. 33; *Epistola ad Catholicos contra Donatistas*, Ch. 22; Council of Trent, Session 4; Vincent of Lerins, *Contra Nonatores*

[434] Augustine, *On the Trinity*, Bk. 1, Ch. 3; Cf. Hilary, *Ad Constantium Imperatorem*, Bk. 2; Vincent of Lerins

not consist in reading, but in understanding," as witnesseth St. Jerome.[435] Thirdly, that in the weightier questions and controversies of faith that may fall out,[436] there may be some judge by whose authority matters may be moderated.[437] For as that is most true that Epiphanius teacheth against heresies, that all things cannot be had out of the scriptures;[438] so doth Saint Augustine most rightly affirm that the authority of the Catholic Church is of special weight and value for our faith and assurance in a doubtful case.[439] Neither can the Holy Ghost be wanting to the Church, to lead her (as Christ hath promised) into all truth.[440]

Again, that for the diversity of persons, places, and times, canons may be ordained, perfect discipline preserved, and judgments pronounced.[441] For to the Church hath God given this power to edification, and not to destruction.[442] Moreover, to the intent that the stubborn and rebellious persons may feel that power of chastising and excommunication, which Christ hath ordained,[443] and Saint Paul exercised; and by the same may be corrected and repressed.[444] Hereupon St. Augustine: "They," saith he, "that govern in the Church may exercise discipline, so it be without tumult and in peaceable manner, against the wicked and outrageous."[445]

Wherefore in all these things, to omit many others, it is manifest that the Church's authority is not only profitable, but also necessary: so that, without the same, doubtless, the Christian commonwealth might be

[435] Jerome, *Dialogue against the Luciferians*, Ch. 9; Cf. Jerome, *On Galatians*, Ch. 1; Hilary, *On the Trinity*, Bk. 2

[436] Cf. Dt 17:8

[437] Cf. Acts 15:2

[438] Cf. Epiphanius, *Adversus Haeresus*, n. 61 contra Apostolicos

[439] Cf. Augustine, *Contra Faustum*, Bk. 11, Ch. 2; *On Baptism, against the Donatists*, Bk. 7, Ch. 53; *On Psalm 57*

[440] Cf. Jn 14:16; 16:13

[441] Cf. *Apostolic Canons*, Can. 38; First Council of Nicea, Can. 5; Fourth Lateran Council, Const. 6

[442] Cf. 2 Cor 10:8; 13:10

[443] Cf. Mt 18:17; Jerome, *On Matthew*, Ch. 17, 18

[444] Cf. 1 Cor 5:3; 1 Tm 1:20

[445] Augustine, *De Fide et Operibus*, Ch. 5; Cf. Augustine, *De Fide et Operibus*, Ch. 3; *Contra Epistolam Parmeniani*, Bk. 3, Ch. 2; Gregory the Great, *Homily 26 on the Gospels*; Chrysostom, *On the Priesthood*, Bk. 3

thought nothing else but a very Babylonical confusion. And therefore, as we do believe the scripture, and rely upon it, and attribute unto it special authority, for the testimony of the Holy Ghost speaking within it; so also do we owe faith, reverence, and obedience to the Church;[446] for that by Christ her head and spouse, she is informed, endowed, and confirmed with the same Spirit,[447] so that it is not possible but that she be as she is called: the "pillar and ground of truth."[448]

78. **What is the fruit and commodity of the whole doctrine touching the precepts and traditions of the Church?**
It is certes very great and full of variety. And surely the first is that we may know that we are not tied to letters only, or to divine scriptures. For, to use the words of Saint Irenaeus: "What if the apostles had left us no scriptures? Must we not have followed the order of tradition, which they delivered unto them, to whom they committed the churches?"[449] Therefore hath St. Basil said very well: "The verities which are held and taught in the Church: some we have out of the doctrine set forth in writing; some we have received from the tradition of the apostles, in mystery, that is, in hidden and secret manner. Both which have equal force and authority to the furtherance of piety. And these no man will gainsay, that hath been but even meanly experienced; what the laws of the Church are."[450] And it cannot be doubted, but that Christ and his apostles both did and taught many things, which although they are not written, yet they do very much appertain unto us and all posterity.[451] Of which St. Paul, warning us in general, saith: "For the rest, brethren, what things soever be true, whatsoever honest, whatsoever just, whatsoever holy, whatsoever amiable, whatsoever of good name: if there be any virtue, if any praise of discipline: these things

[446] Cf. 2 Pt 1:19; 2 Tm 3:16; Mt 18:17; Jn 14:16, 26; 16:12
[447] Cf. Acts 2:4; Eph 4:4
[448] 1 Tm 3:15
[449] Irenaeus, *Against Heresies*, Bk. 3, Ch. 4, n. 1; Cf. Epiphanius, *Adversus Haeresus*, n. 61
[450] Basil, *De Spiritu Sancto*, Ch. 27
[451] Cf. Jn 20:30; 21:25; Augustine, *Epistle 108*, ad Selencianam

think upon, which you have both learned, and received, and heard, and seen in me: these things do you, and the God of peace be with you."[452]

The next commodity of them is that we may rightly use Christian liberty: which men given to idleness and riot, if ever at any time, now most of all do make an occasion to the flesh, as the apostle speaketh, under pretense thereof they serve their filthy pleasures: and whatsoever in a manner they have a fancy unto, though it concern even the alteration of the decrees of religion, they think it lawful for them to do.[453] But from this profane novelty and rashness, the apostolical and ecclesiastical doctrines and decrees do call away, defend, and terrify us: bridling man's licentiousness, and teaching us to use Christian liberty in a convenient sort, to wit: so that being made free by Christ, from the yoke of sin and bondage of the old law,[454] we may willingly and of our own accord perform Christian duty; we may serve God in holiness and justice; we may follow the Holy Ghost as our guide in the law of charity, being the servants of justice, the sons of obedience, the practicers of humility, the keepers of patience, and lovers of penance and of the cross.[455] "You," saith the apostle, "are called into liberty: only, make not this liberty an occasion to the flesh, but by charity of spirit serve one another."[456] To the nourishing and maintenance of which charity of spirit, in the dutifulness of a holy servitude, both all honest things are profitable and the devout observation of the tradition of the Church is undoubtedly most available.

The last use and commodity is that we may truly discern between the lawful and bastard children of the Church, or between Catholics and heretics. For the first do simply stay themselves in the doctrine of the Church, whether the same be delivered unto them in writing as in the Bible, or approved by the traditions of the fathers.[457] For they do follow the word

---

[452] Phil 4:8

[453] Cf. Gal 5:13; 2 Pt 2:19; Augustine, *Epistle 54 to Januarius*, Ch. 1, 5

[454] Cf. 1 Pt 1:18; Rom 6:18, 20; Gal 3:13; 4:31; Rom 8:2

[455] Cf. Ps 53:8; Col 3:23; Lk 1:71; 2 Cor 3:17; Rom 6:22; 1 Cor 9:10; 1 Pt 1:22; 2:20; Lk 21:19; Mt 4:17; 16:24

[456] Gal 5:13

[457] Cf. Vincent of Lerins

of God: "Do not go beyond the ancient bounds, which thy fathers have set."[458] But, the other which are heretics, do swerve from this simplicity of faith, and from the approved sentence of our reverend mother the Church, and of the holy fathers; and they trust too much, either unto themselves, or to those that have revolted from the Church, insomuch as even being warned they do not come and amend their error. And therefore, of them hath Saint Paul so severely decreed when he saith: "A man that is a heretic, after the first and second admonition, avoid: knowing that he that is such a one, is subverted."[459] And to conclude with St. Cyprian: "Whosoever hath revolted from the unity of the Church, he must needs be found in the company of heretics."[460]

79. **What finally is the sum of all the premises?**

Those things that from the beginning hitherto have been handled, touching the sum of Christian doctrine, do tend to this end: that the true wisdom of a Christian man might be described and set before us; which is comprehended in these three virtues:[461] faith, hope, and charity.[462] By faith, the soul doth firmly consent unto God's truth and rely upon the same.[463] By hope, she doth yet more nearly apprehend the goodness of Almighty God; known now and conceived by faith.[464] Finally, by charity, she is joined and united unto God; and for God, to her neighbor.[465]

Now as concerning faith, the Creed of the Apostles doth instruct us, in that it setteth before us those things that are especially to be believed and professed of every Christian. And of those things that are to be hoped and prayed for, our Lord's Prayer hath informed us. Then, unto charity do those things belong which in the two tables of the ten commandments are exhibited unto us.

[458] Prv 22:28; Cf. Ecclus 8:11; Dt 32:7; Jer 16
[459] Ti 3:10
[460] Cyprian, *Epistle 73 to Pompey*, n. 11
[461] Cf. Augustine, *Retractions*, Bk. 2, Ch. 63
[462] Cf. 1 Cor 13:13; 2 Tm 2:22
[463] Cf. Heb 11:1
[464] Cf. Gal 5:5
[465] Cf. Rom 8:38; Jn 14:21, 23; Rom 13:8; Augustine, *Enchiridion*, Ch. 7

It is therefore a very notable saying of Origen: "I do think," saith he, "that faith is the first beginning, and the very foundation of salvation; and hope is the advancement and increase of the building; but that charity is the perfection and top of the whole work."[466]

Happy then are they which hear and keep the word of God; and they that know the will of the Father, and do fulfill the same: walking and persevering in faith, hope, and charity, by the government and protection of Christ our Lord.[467]

And this truly for the scope of our intention is sufficient, touching those chief and principal virtues which, because they are infused by God, and do make mortal men become divine, are worthily called virtues theological, and are rightly referred to Christian wisdom.

80. **Is there any other thing that belongeth unto Christian doctrine?**
Yea verily; for the doctrine of the sacraments doth expressly appertain thereunto: that Christians may know what instruments, as it were, they have need of, ordained by God, for the obtaining, exercising, increasing, preserving, yea and also repairing of faith, and hope, and especially charity.[468]

Yea, and moreover, true it is that neither Christian wisdom nor Christian justice can be established or holden without sacraments: as without the which all religion must needs be extinguished.[469]

They therefore are of very great importance in Christian doctrine, and very requisite it is that we handle them in particular.

[466] Origen, *On Romans*, Ch. 4
[467] Cf. Lk 11:28; Rom 2:13; Lk 6:46; Mt 7:21, 24; 19:17; 25:35; Jn 15:2; Mt 10:22; 24:13
[468] Cf. Augustine, *Tractate 120 on John*
[469] Cf. Augustine, *Contra Faustum*, Bk. 19, Ch. 11; *De Vera Religione*, Ch. 17; *Epistle 54 to Januarius*, Ch. 1

₫f the Sacraments

Of the Sacraments in General

81. Why are Christians to be instructed about the sacraments?

Because the knowledge and use of the sacraments doth bring to pass that Christians, having by the merits of Jesus Christ received grace, which is given by the sacraments, may be rightly exercised, and preserved, and set forward in divine worship.[470]

82. What and of how many sorts is this divine worship?

That is called divine worship which a Christian oweth and yieldeth as the highest and chiefest service to God his Creator and Savior.[471]

For there is no doubt, but that for this cause especially was man at the first made, and afterward redeemed; and unto this wholly designed and appointed, that he might purely and perfectly serve and worship Almighty God.[472]

Now divine worship is of two sorts: interior and exterior. The interior, by which we are in understanding and in will joined unto God, is accomplished by faith, hope, and charity, as hath been said before.[473] The exterior is a certain profession of the interior, which we declare by certain outward and visible signs and ceremonies.[474] For God, that hath no need of any good of ours, as being of himself blessed and wholly perfect, yet as his pleasure was that the whole man should consist both of a body and a soul,[475] so doth he require the same again wholly, to wit, according to all and every part of him, that he may by him be worshipped studiously and sincerely: first in

[470] Cf. Ti 3:5; Jn 3:5; 6:51, 55; 20:23
[471] Cf. Augustine, *City of God*, Bk. 10, Ch. 21
[472] Cf. Prv 16:4; Gn 1:26; 2 Cor 5:15; 1 Thes 5:9; 1 Pt 3:4
[473] Cf. Augustine, *Enchiridion*, Ch. 2-3
[474] Cf. Mt 5:17; Rom 12:17; 2 Cor 8:21; 1 Cor 14:40
[475] Cf. Ps 15:2; 1 Tm 6:15; Mt 5:48; Gn 2:7

soul, according to the interior worship as we have declared;[476] and in body, according to the exterior joined with the interior: which is done many ways, but principally and most profitably by the use of sacraments.[477]

For so it hath seemed good to the wisdom of God, to coapt itself to the imbecility of mortal men, and to exercise his might and power by certain external things and signs that may be perceived by the senses.[478] For our mind and soul immortal, being enclosed in this obscure and brittle body as in a prison, doth very much use the service of the senses, and without the help of them, she doth not commonly mount to the conception of heavenly things. Therefore, both in the old and new law, sacraments, and many other things appertaining unto exterior worship, have been by God ordained, and always by the people of God observed.[479]

83. What is a sacrament?

It is an external and visible sign of divine and invisible grace, instituted by Christ, that by it every man may receive the grace of God and sanctification.[480]

And therefore, they are not every manner of signs that are called the sacraments of the Church; but they are most certain holy and effectual signs commended unto Christians, by God's own institution and promise.

Signs they are, in that, by a certain external form and similitude, they do represent and declare unto us that which God by them worketh in us, invisibly and spiritually.[481]

Certain they are, and most holy and effectual signs: because that look what grace they signify, they do also infallibly contain and cause the same

[476] Cf. Prv 16:14; Lk 10:27; Mt 22:37; Dt 6:5
[477] Cf. 1 Cor 6:19; Ps 83:3
[478] Cf. Augustine, On Psalm 73; Contra Faustum, Bk. 18, Ch. 11; On Christian Doctrine, Bk. 3, Ch. 9; Quaestiones in Leviticum, q. 84; Quaestiones in Numeros, q. 33; Tertullian, On the Resurrection of the Flesh, Ch. 8; Gregory the Great, On 1 Kings, Bk. 6, Ch. 3
[479] Cf. Chrysostom, Homily 60, to the People of Antioch; Homily 83 on Matthew
[480] Cf. Bernard, De Coena Domini; Augustine, City of God, Bk. 10, Ch. 5; On Christian Doctrine, Bk. 3, Ch. 9; Ambrose, On the Sacraments, Bk. 4, Ch. 4; Council of Florence; Council of Trent, Session 7
[481] Cf. Augustine, Epistle 23; On the Catechizing of the Uninstructed, Ch. 26

to our sanctification.[482] For the sacraments for their own parts (as St. Cyprian speaketh) cannot be void of that force and virtue that is proper unto them;[483] neither doth the majesty of God by any means absent itself from the mysteries, though they be ministered even by wicked people and unworthy persons.[484]

As, for example, in the sacrament of baptism, the exterior washing, that cleanseth the filth of the body, is an effectual sign and token of the interior washing; as giving an infallible testimony that the soul is spiritually purified and cleansed. So also, other visible and external things, as oil and the forms of bread and wine, the use whereof is necessary in the sacraments, are fitly appointed unto us, both to signify and also to yield unto man the grace of God and the health of his soul;[485] so that he come not unworthily thereunto.[486]

For by baptism, we are regenerated and renewed; by confirmation, we are increased and strengthened; by the Holy Eucharist, we are nourished and refreshed; by penance, we are restored and healed in the spiritual life, in which we are by the rest of the sacraments in like manner according to the nature and quality of each of them, helped and bettered, as we will show hereafter in their due places.[487]

84. **Of what parts doth every sacrament consist?**

Of the word and the element. By *the word* in this place, understand some certain determinate words, wherein the very form, as they call it, of the sacrament doth consist. And by *the element*, conceive such external things, as are the very matter of the sacraments, as water, oil, bread, wine, and the like.[488]

---

[482] Cf. Augustine, *On Psalm 73; On Psalm 77; Contra Faustum*, Bk. 19, Ch. 11, 13, 16
[483] Cf. Cyprian, *Sermon, De Coena Domini*
[484] Cf. Augustine, *On Baptism, against the Donatists*, Bk. 3, Ch. 10; Bk. 5, Ch. 20
[485] Cf. Ti 3:5; Rom 3:7; 1 Cor 6:11; Tertullian, *On the Resurrection of the Flesh*, Ch. 8
[486] Cf. Prosper, *Sententia ex Augustine*, On Psalm 142
[487] Cf. Council of Florence; Jn 3:5; Ti 3:5; Acts 8:17; 1:8; Lk 24:49; Jn 6:51, 55, 58; 20:23
[488] Cf. Council of Florence; Augustine, *Tractate 80 on John*

Now, to these parts exactly taken are the rest of those things annexed which do belong to the fit ministering and worthy receiving of every sacrament, to wit: the institution of God; a convenient minister; a right intention in the minister; faith in the receiver; and whatsoever else of like sort.[489]

85. How many sacraments be there?

Seven;[490] which the Church, being the spouse of Christ and pillar of truth, having by the apostles received them from Christ himself, hath always hitherto kept and faithfully dispensed.[491] And they are these: baptism, confirmation, the Blessed Sacrament of the Eucharist, penance, extreme unction, order, and matrimony. Neither truly forceth it at all, if such names be not all of them extant in the scriptures; so that the matter itself be evident, and the verity and virtue of the sacraments be approved by divine testimony.[492] Albeit such things as by the apostles' tradition the universal Church holdeth and commendeth to be kept and observed, though they be not to be found in scripture, yet do they deserve of us full and perfect credit, as hath been already declared.[493] And touching the institution of every sacrament in particular, we will speak hereafter in their proper places.

But the force and virtue of them (as the most faithful interpreter of the scripture, Saint Augustine, saith:) "is of unspeakable value, and therefore, the contemnors of it are sacrilegious. For impiously certes is that despised, without the which no piety can be perfected."[494] And as the same holy father teacheth in another place: "The contemnor of the visible sacrament can never be invisibly sanctified."[495]

---

[489] Cf. Council of Trent, Session 7, "On the Sacraments in General," Can. 10-11; Council of Florence

[490] Cf. Council of Florence; Council of Constance, Session 15; Council of Trent, Session 7, "On the Sacraments in General," Can.1

[491] Cf. Cant 4:9; 1 Tm 3:15

[492] Cf. Mt 28:19; Acts 8:17; Mt 26:26; Jn 20:23; Jas 5:14; 1 Tm 4:14; Eph 5:32

[493] Cf. Augustine, On Baptism, against the Donatists, Bk. 4, Ch. 24; Bk. 2, Ch. 7; Bk. 5, Ch. 23; Epistle 54 to Januarius, Ch. 1; Chrysostom, Homily 4 on 2 Thessalonians

[494] Augustine, Contra Faustum, Bk. 19, Ch. 11; Cf. Augustine, Contra Faustum, Bk. 19, Ch. 16; Tractate 80 on John

[495] Augustine, Quaestiones in Leviticum, q. 84; Cf. Augustine, Contra Faustum, Bk. 32, Ch. 4

86. **Why were the sacraments instituted?**

First, that they may be very present remedies against sin, which is a pestilent disease of the soul, and except it be cured in this life, bringeth everlasting damnation.[496] And therefore, these do far excel the sacraments of the old law,[497] as being in virtue, greater; in commodity, more profitable; in number, fewer; in the conceiving of them, more honorable; in observation, more excellent: which besides their signification, do also sanctify and give salvation, as St. Augustine hath very well gathered out of the scriptures.[498]

Secondly, that we may have some certain and effectual signs of God's grace and good will toward us, which signs, whilst they represent themselves to the outward senses, they do not only stir up our faith in Christ and in the mercy and goodness of Almighty God,[499] but are moreover lively instruments, by which it hath seemed good unto Almighty God effectually to work our salvation.[500] So that it was notably said of an ancient father, that a sacrament even by itself alone is of an inestimable value.[501]

Thirdly, that there may be some tokens and, as it were, external marks of Christian profession, whereby the children of God and of the Church may mutually know one another, and that they may fruitfully exercise and keep themselves in unity, humility, and obedience, and so remain linked amongst themselves with the necessary bond and league of one religion. Otherwise, without sacraments cannot any sort of religion either stand or be sufficiently discerned.[502]

---

[496] Cf. Ws 16:14; Ecclus 21:2; Rom 6:23

[497] Cf. Council of Florence; Council of Trent, Session 7, "On the Sacraments in General," Can. 2, 4

[498] Cf. Augustine, *Contra Faustum*, Bk. 19, Ch. 13; *On Christian Doctrine*, Bk. 3, Ch. 19; *Epistle 54 to Januarius*, Ch. 1

[499] Cf. Rom 9:23

[500] Cf. Ti 3:5; Jn 6:58; 20:23

[501] Cf. Augustine, *On Baptism, against the Donatists*, Bk. 4, Ch. 24

[502] Cf. Augustine, *Contra Faustum*, Bk. 19, Ch. 11, 17; *De Vera Religione*; Basil, *Homily 13 in exhort. ad Bapt.*

87. And what is to be thought of the ministers of the sacraments?

We must so esteem them, "as the ministers of Christ, and the dispensers of the mysteries of God,"[503] that do bear the vessels of our Lord, and serve the tabernacle, and that by profession have authority in holy things, and with a certain right and title do minister the same.[504] For not to all indifferently, but to priests and bishops doth it belong, and it was by God himself enjoined, to consecrate, dispense, and minister the holy sacraments.[505]

And that we may not think that the sacraments do any wit depend upon the life and honesty of those that do minister them,[506] St. Augustine hath prescribed us this rule: "Sacraments," saith he, "are not therefore more true and more holy because they are ministered by a better man: for they of themselves are true and holy, by means of the true and holy God whose sacraments they are."[507] And again: "Remember that the manners of evil men do nothing hinder the sacraments of God, to make them either nothing at all or ever the less holy."[508] To which accordeth that sentence of St. Ambrose: "Do thou not regard the merits of the persons, but the offices of the priests: I mean in the administration of the sacraments."[509] "For even by the unworthy, God accustometh to work,[510] and by the life of the priest, there can be no prejudice to the grace of the sacraments," as witnesseth St. Chrysostom.[511]

---

[503] 1 Cor 4:1

[504] Cf. Is 52:11; Nm 1:50-51; 3 Kgs 8:4

[505] Cf. Nm 16:39; 2 Kgs 6:6; 2 Par 26:16; Second Council of Nicea, Can. 14; Council of Trent, Session 7, "On the Sacraments in General," Can. 10

[506] Cf. 1 Cor 1:13; 3:4; Council of Trent, Session 7, "On the Sacraments in General," Can. 12; Gregory Nazianzen, *Oration 40, On Holy Baptism*

[507] Augustine, *Contra Cresconium*, Bk. 4, Ch. 20; Cf. Augustine, *On Baptism, against the Donatists*, Bk. 4, Ch. 4

[508] Augustine, *Answer to Petilian the Donatist*, Bk. 2, Ch. 47; Cf. Augustine, *Tractate 5 on John*

[509] Ambrose, *On the Mysteries*, Ch. 5

[510] Cf. Jn 11:50; Mt 23:2

[511] Chrysostom, *Homily 8 on 1 Corinthians*

88. **What conception ought we to have of ceremonies, those especially that are ordinarily and solemnly used in the sacraments?**

Ceremonies approved by the Church are certain external rites, religiously and decently instituted: first, that they may be signs, testimonies, and exercises of the interior worship,[512] which God principally requireth at our hands.[513]

Then, that there may be some lively and fortible provocations unto religion, whereby the frailty of man may be fortified and underpropped, and, as it were, trained with the hand both to receive and also to retain holy mysteries.

Lastly, that those things which do appertain to the advancement of God's service, and to the preservation of public discipline and concord, may be prosecuted in the Church,[514] after an honest, comely, and decent order, as the apostle willeth.[515]

But those ceremonies specially which are used in the administration of the sacraments, and which we have received of the fathers,[516] delivered and commended unto us, as it were, by hand, ought with great diligence to be kept and observed.[517] For besides that they bring a decency unto the sacraments, and engender a certain reverence, they are also venerable unto us by a singular commendation of antiquity.[518]

Then besides their institution (most ancient and apostolical), they have plenty of mysteries full of gravity and dignity; as most holy and learned fathers have noted.[519] Finally, concerning these things and others of the like tenor, it is an excellent saying of Damascene: "Those things which Christian religion, most free from all error, doth admit and embrace, and so

[512] Cf. Jn 9:6; 11:33, 43; 20:22; Lk 24:50; Mk 7:33; 8:23; 10:16; Mt 8:3; 14:19

[513] Cf. Jn 4:23; Mt 15:8; Is 1:14

[514] Cf. Leo the Great, *Epistle 81 ad Dios.*; Innocent, *Epistle 1 ad Decent.*; Fourth Council of Toledo, Can. 2

[515] Cf. 1 Cor 14:40; Phil 4:5, 8

[516] Cf. Jer 6:16; Prv 22:28

[517] Cf. Basil, *De Spiritu Sancto*, Ch. 27; Council of Trent, Session 7, "On the Sacraments in General," Can. 13

[518] Cf. Tertullian, *De Corona Militis*, Ch. 3; Dionysius, *Ecclesiastical Hierarchy*, throughout

[519] Cf. Ambrose, *On the Mysteries*; Augustine and others throughout; Cf. also Isidore, *De Ecclesiasticis Officiis*

many ages together keep untouched, are not vain, but profitable, pleasing to God, and much available to our salvation."[520]

True it is that the sectaries laugh at the ceremonies used in the sacraments; but themselves are indeed more to be laughed at, or rather bewailed, in that, trusting unto their blind judgment and mortal hatred (two pernicious counselors) they do wage battle against the most clear and evident truth. Surely of the ceremonies of baptism, even the most ancient divines do witness unto us: St. Denis,[521] St. Clement,[522] Tertullian,[523] Origen,[524] St. Cyprian,[525] St. Basil,[526] Saint Chrysostom,[527] St. Cyril.[528] Let the wicked scoff and blaspheme never so much, those fathers certainly with one consent do commend abrenunciation, exorcisms, holy water, holy chrism, and the sign of the cross. Almost twelve hundred years agone, wrote Saint Basil in this manner: "We do consecrate the water of baptism, and the oil of unction, and him also that receiveth baptism."[529]

But to give particular admonition of the ceremonies that are annexed unto all the sacraments, as it would be very long, so is it also very difficult, and to this our purpose not needful.

Yea, Origen doth plainly confess that in such ecclesiastical observances, there are many things which of necessity all must do, but the reason of them, why they are so done, is not yet sufficiently known.[530]

---

[520] John Damascene, *Sermon in de Defunctis*
[521] Cf. Dionysius, *Ecclesiastical Hierarchy*, Ch. 2
[522] Cf. Clement, *Epistle 3*
[523] Cf. Tertullian, *De Corona Militis*, Ch. 3
[524] Cf. Origen, *Homily 12 on Numbers*
[525] Cf. Cyprian, *Epistle 70*
[526] Cf. Basil, *De Spiritu Sancto*, Ch. 27
[527] Cf. Chrysostom, *Homily on Adam and Eve*
[528] Cf. Cyril of Jerusalem, *Catechetical Lectures 1, 2, 3, 4*
[529] Basil, *De Spiritu Sancto*, Ch. 27; Cf. Rabanus Maurus, *De Institutione Clericorum*, Bk. 1, Ch. 27-28; Isidore, *De Ecclesiasticis Officiis*, Bk. 2, Ch. 20; Ambrose, *On the Sacraments*, Bk. 1-3; *On the Mysteries*; Augustine, *On Marriage and Concupiscence*, Bk. 1, Ch. 22; Bk. 2, Ch. 33, 50; *A Sermon to Catechumens on the Creed*, Ch. 1
[530] Cf. Origen, *Homily 5 on Numbers*; Dionysius, *Ecclesiastical Hierarchy*, Ch. 1, 7; Augustine, *On Christian Doctrine*, Ch. 9

Of the Sacrament of Baptism

89. **What is baptism, and is it necessary to all?**

This is the first and most necessary sacrament of the new law, consisting in the outward washing of the body, and the due pronunciation of the words, according unto the institution of Christ.

A necessary sacrament, I say, not only for those that are of years of discretion,[531] but for infants also; and withal, effectual for them to life everlasting.[532] All are born the sons of wrath, and therefore even infants also have need to be purged from sin,[533] neither can they be cleansed and regenerated into the children of God without this sacrament.[534] For generally hath the lawmaker proclaimed that, "Unless a man be born again of water and the spirit, he cannot enter into the kingdom of God."[535] And in another place: "It is not the will of your Father which is in heaven, that one perish of those little ones."[536] But infants also not baptized should perish,[537] as of old in the synagogue of the Jews, children uncircumcised.[538]

Now forasmuch as there is but one baptism of Christ's faithful people,[539] which once received, it is very wicked to iterate,[540] whatsoever the long-since condemned Anabaptist do pretend,[541] we must say with the Constantinopolitan Council: "I confess one baptism, for the remission of

[531] Cf. Council of Trent, Session 6, Ch. 4; Session 7, "On Baptism," Can. 5; Augustine, *Tractate 13 on John*; Ambrose, *On the Mysteries*, Ch. 4; Clement, *Epistle 4 ad Julium*

[532] Cf. Fourth Lateran Council, Const. 1; Council of Milevi, Can. 2; Dionysius, *Ecclesiastical Hierarchy*, Ch. 7; Cyprian, Bk. 3, Epistle 8; Chrysostom, *Homily on Adam and Eve*

[533] Cf. Eph 2:3; Council of Trent, Session 5

[534] Cf. Augustine, *Epistle 28*; *On the Soul and Its Origin*, Bk. 3, Ch. 12; *On Merit and the Forgiveness of Sins, and the Baptism of Infants*, Bk. 1, Ch. 33

[535] Jn 3:5; Cf. Augustine, *On Merit and the Forgiveness of Sins, and the Baptism of Infants*, Bk. 3, Ch. 8, 21

[536] Mt 18:14; Cf. Bernard, *Sermon 66 on Canticle of Canticles*; *Epistle 140, ad Hil. de fons.*

[537] Cf. Augustine, *On Marriage and Concupiscence*, Bk. 1, Ch. 20; Bk. 2, Ch. 17; *Sermon 14, De Verbis Apostoli*

[538] Cf. Gn 17:14

[539] Cf. Eph 4:5; Basil, *De Spiritu Sancto*, Ch. 15

[540] Cf. Heb 6:4; *Apostolic Constitutions*, Bk. 6, Ch. 15; John Damascene, *An Exposition of the Orthodox Faith*, Bk. 4, Ch. 9

[541] Cf. First Council of Carthage, Can. 1; Council of Vienne; Council of Trent, Session 7, "On the Sacraments in General," Can. 9; "On Baptism," Can. 13; Augustine, *Tractate 11 on John*; Bede, *On John*, Ch. 3

sins";[542] and with St. Augustine: "To rebaptize a heretical man is certainly a sin; but to rebaptize a Catholic, a horrible wickedness,"[543] which for that cause is also prohibited by the emperor's laws.[544]

90. What things are principally to be noted about this sacrament?
The element that washeth, and the signification thereof, the word, the minister, and the effect of baptism. The element is simple water, the matter very necessary hereunto, which is naturally wont to wash away the filths of the body.[545] To which very aptly doth answer this signification: that by baptism the soul is cleansed from sin, and the man made just, as we mean to show hereafter.[546]

The word, wherein consisteth the form of the sacrament,[547] by Christ his appointment, is this: "I baptize thee in the name of the Father, and of the Son, and of the Holy Ghost."[548]

And although it be properly the office of priests to baptize, yet where this is very urgent necessity, others also may baptize, yea though they be wicked persons and heretics, so that they go not from the manner of the Church and her usual words.[549]

91. What profit and effect doth baptism yield?
That doubtless which by the teaching of Christ, and testimony of the apostles Sts. Peter and Paul, we learn, to wit: that by baptism both sins are

[542] Nicene-Constantinopolitan Creed
[543] Augustine, *Epistle 103*; *De Unico Baptismo contra Petilianum*, Ch. 13; Leo the Great, *Epistle 79 ad Nic.*; *Epistle 37 ad Leo. Rau.*
[544] Cf. C., Bk. 1, Ne Sanctum Bapt. Iteret. Cf. also Acts 2:38; Mk 16:16; Jn 3:22; 4:1; Ti 3:5; Mt 28:19; Eph 5:26; 1 Pt 3:21
[545] Cf. Jn 3:5; Eph 5:26; Acts 8:36; 10:47; Council of Trent, "On Baptism," Can. 2; Council of Florence; Chrysostom, *Homily 24 on John*
[546] Cf. Ti 3:5; Acts 2:38; 1 Cor 6:11
[547] Cf. Fourth Lateran Council; Council of Florence; Augustine, *On Baptism, against the Donatists*, Bk. 6, Ch. 25; Didymus, *De Spiritu Sancto*, Bk. 2
[548] Cf. Mt 28:19; Ambrose, *On the Mysteries*, Ch. 4
[549] Cf. Augustine, *Contra Epistolam Parmeniani*, Bk. 2, Ch. 13; *De Unico Baptismo contra Petilianum*, Ch. 9; *On Baptism, against the Donatists*, Bk. 3, Ch. 5; Bk. 7, Ch. 53; Hilary, *On Psalm 67*; Fourth Lateran Council, Const. 1; Council of Florence; Council of Trent, Session 7, "On Baptism," Can. 4

remitted and the Spirit is given, whereby both the old man is extinguished, and a new creature is made in Christ. For baptism rightly received doth not only yield this, that all sins be fully pardoned and taken away from the wicked man, but also that he, being once baptized, is perfectly renewed, and made truly innocent, just, holy, and worthy in Christ of the heavenly glory.[550] So that St. Paul hath justly said to all those that are baptized: "You are washed, you are sanctified, you are justified in the name of our Lord Jesus Christ, and in the Spirit of God."[551] And in another place he testifieth that baptism is the laver of regeneration, and of renovation of the Holy Ghost;[552] the laver also of water in the word of life.[553] And again he writeth: "As many of you as are baptized in Christ, have put on Christ."[554]

Very fitly and briefly doth St. Bernard comprise the principal effects of this sacrament: "We are washed in baptism," saith he, "because the handwriting of our damnation is canceled; and this grace is bestowed upon us, that now concupiscence cannot hurt us, yet so, that we keep ourselves from consent."[555]

Which concupiscence remaining in the regenerate is not of itself a sin, but an inclination unto sin (*fomes peccati*) as the divines do call it, left us, *ad agonem*, to strive withal, that the baptized by this occasion may more watchfully seek God's grace, and more fervently practice virtue, and more

[550] Cf. Mk 16:16; Acts 2:38; 22:16; 1 Pt 3:21; Ez 30:25; 1 Cor 6:11; Rom 6:3; Basil, *Homily 13, In Exhort. ad Bapt.*; *De Spiritu Sancto*, Ch. 15; Augustine, *Against Two Letters of the Pelagians*, Bk. 1, Ch. 13; Bk. 3, Ch. 3; *Enchiridion*, Ch. 64; Bede, *On John*, Ch. 3; John Damascene, *An Exposition of the Orthodox Faith*, Bk. 4, Ch. 10; Gregory the Great, Bk. 9, Epistle 39; Jerome, *Epistle 69 to Oceanus*; Gregory Nazianzen, *Oration 40, On Holy Baptism*; *In San. Lauracrum*; Clement of Alexandria, *Paedagogus*, Bk. 1, Ch. 6; Chrysostom, *ad Neoph. et ad Baptizand.*

[551] 1 Cor 6:11; Cf. Ambrose, *On the Sacraments*, Bk. 1, Ch. 4; Council of Florence; Council of Trent, Session 5, Can. 5

[552] Cf. Ti 3:5; Augustine, *Epistle 23*; *Quaestiones in Numeros*, q. 33; *Confessions*, Bk. 4, Ch. 4; Lactantius, *The Divine Institutes*, Bk. 3, Ch. 26; Cyprian, Bk. 2, Epistle 2

[553] Cf. Eph 5:26

[554] Gal 3:27; Cf. Rom 6:3

[555] Bernard, *De Coena Domini*; Cf. Cyprian, *De Bapt. Christ. et Ablut. Perdum*; Origen, *On Romans*, Ch. 6; Augustine, *Contra Julianum Haeresis Pelagianae Defensorem*, Bk. 1, Ch. 3, n. 7

valiantly striving, get themselves a greater crown.[556] Therefore, as St. Paul teacheth: "There is no damnation to them that are in Christ Jesus: that walk not according to the flesh,"[557] but according to the spirit; and that, according to the doctrine and example of Saint Paul, putting off the old man,[558] are renewed from day to day according to the inward man,[559] which is indeed the very property of the baptized.[560]

92. What doth the benefit received of so great a sacrament require at our hands?

First it requireth of us a special and continual gratitude of mind, that we may praise, love, and extol him: "Who, according to his mercy, hath saved us by the laver of regeneration, and renovation of the Holy Ghost, whom he hath poured upon us abundantly by Jesus Christ our Savior, that being justified by his grace, we may be heirs according to hope of life everlasting."[561]

Then so is the mystery of this sacrament to be remembered, that every man do oftentimes admonish himself of that notable promise and Christian profession,[562] which by his godfathers he made in the holy laver.[563] Therefore, let every Christian consider that, of the child of wrath and slave of Satan, he there was made the son of God, and a member and coheir of Christ,[564] and a lively temple of the Holy Ghost.[565]

---

[556] Cf. Jas 1:14; Rom 6:12; 7:7; Council of Trent, Session 5, Can. 5; Augustine, *On Marriage and Concupiscence*, Bk. 1, Ch. 23, 25; *Against Two Letters of the Pelagians*, Bk. 1, Ch. 13; *Retractions*, Bk. 2, Ch. 15; *On the Trinity*, Bk. 13, Ch. 16; *On Merit and the Forgiveness of Sins, and the Baptism of Infants*, Bk. 1, Ch. 39; Bk. 2, Ch. 33, 34

[557] Rom 8:1

[558] Cf. Col 3:9; Eph 4:22

[559] Cf. 2 Cor 4:16

[560] Cf. Rom 6:4

[561] Ti 3:5-7

[562] Cf. Origen, *Homily 12 on Numbers*

[563] Cf. Dionysius, *Ecclesiastical Hierarchy*, Ch. 7; Augustine, *On Marriage and Concupiscence*, Bk. 1, Ch. 20; *On Merit and the Forgiveness of Sins, and the Baptism of Infants*, Bk. 1, Ch. 19; *On Baptism, against the Donatists*, Bk. 4, Ch. 24

[564] Cf. Rom 8:1, 14; Gal 4:5

[565] Cf. 1 Cor 6:19

"Thou enteredst into the sanctuary of regeneration," saith St. Ambrose, "call to mind what thou wert demanded, recognize what answer thou didst make. Thou hast renounced the devil and his works, the world with her luxuriousness and pleasures."[566] "Be mindful of thy speech, and never let the process of thy obligation depart out of thy remembrance."[567] And it is an excellent speech of St. Paul, exhorting all those that are baptized: "Are you ignorant that all we which are baptized in Christ Jesus, in his death we are baptized? For we are buried together with him by baptism into death; that as Christ is risen from the dead by the glory of the Father, so we also may walk in the newness of life."[568]

Of the Sacrament of Confirmation

93. **Which is the other sacrament next unto baptism?**
Confirmation: which is a sacrament of the new law, "as sacred and holy," saith St. Augustine, "as baptism itself,"[569] which is ministered unto the baptized, with the imposition of the hands of a bishop, and the anointing with holy chrism.[570]

94. **What warrant have we to use this sacrament?**
It hath the testimony of divine scripture, according to the uniform sentence and interpretation of the fathers and the Church.[571] For hereunto belongeth that which St. Luke the evangelist writeth of the apostles, that they laid their hands upon the baptized, using this visible sign, ordained

[566] Ambrose, On the Mysteries, Ch. 2; Chrysostom, Homily 21, to the People of Antioch; Augustine, A Sermon to Catechumens on the Creed, Ch. 1
[567] Ambrose, On the Sacraments, Bk. 1, Ch. 2; Cyril of Jerusalem, Catechetical Lecture 1
[568] Rom 6:3-4; Cf. Gal 3:37; Augustine, De Fide et Operibus, Ch. 26
[569] Augustine, Answer to Petilian the Donatist, Bk. 2, Ch. 104
[570] Cf. Council of Elvira, Ch. 38; Council of Orleans, Can. 3; Council of Laodicea, Can. 48; Council of Meaux, Can. 6; Council of Florence; Council of Constance, Session 15; Council of Trent, Session 7; Bernard, Life of Malachy of Armagh; Peter Damian, Sermon 1, Dedicat. Eccles.; Isidore, De Ecclesiasticis Officiis, Bk. 2, Ch. 25-26; Rabanus Maurus, De Institutione Clericorum, Bk. 1, Ch. 30
[571] Cf. Cyprian, Bk. 1, Epistle 12; Augustine, On Baptism, against the Donatists, Bk. 5, Ch. 19-20; Tractate 6 on John

by God himself; because a new and more plentiful grace of the Holy Ghost was given to those which were newborn in Christ.[572] And therefore, when the apostles laid hands upon them, they received, as Saint Luke recordeth of those baptized, the Holy Ghost, to wit, with a certain increase and abundance of spiritual grace.[573]

But at this time, whereas the bishops do bear the room and possess the place of the apostles, God doth not defraud his Church of this so wholesome a grace, but, by the same bishops in this sacrament, worketh effectually,[574] so that, as testifieth St. Cyprian, "the verity is joined with the sign, and the Spirit is present in the sacrament."[575]

And hereunto doth appertain that canon of the Church, of old set down: "All the faithful ought to receive the Holy Ghost after baptism by the imposition of hands from a bishop, that they may be found perfect Christians; because when the Holy Ghost is infused, the faithful heart is dilated to prudence and constancy."[576]

95. **What things are necessary for the perfection of this sacrament?**
Three things are specially required thereunto: the proper matter of the sacrament, the due form of words, and a convenient minister.

The matter is compound of oil and baulme,[577] which being consecrated by a bishop, hath now of old obtained the name of holy chrism, and in this sacrament is, after a solemn manner, laid upon the forehead.[578]

The prescript form of words is this: "I do sign thee with the sign of the cross, and confirm thee with the chrism of salvation, in the name of the Father, and of the Son, and of the Holy Ghost."[579]

---

[572] Cf. Acts 8:17; 19:5; Cyprian, *Epistle ad Iubaianum*
[573] Cf. Ibid.
[574] Cf. Jerome, *Dialogue against the Luciferians*, Ch. 4
[575] Cyprian, *Sermon, De Unctione Chrismatis*
[576] Urban I, *Epistle to All Christians*, in the year 227
[577] Cf. Council of Braga, Ch. 4; Cyprian, *Sermon, De Unctione Chrismatis*; Gregory the Great, *On Canticle of Canticles*, Ch. 1; Fabian, *Epistle 3*, Ch. 1; Council of Florence
[578] Cf. Cyprian, *Sermon, De Unctione Chrismatis*; Bk. 1, Epistle 12; Basil, *De Spiritu Sanctu*, Ch. 27; Fabian, *Epistle 2*, in the year 241
[579] Cf. Council of Florence; 2 Cor 1:21; Eph 1:13

The minister of this sacrament is a bishop only; that the example, form, and tradition of the apostles may be kept.[580] Of which thing we have received a decree set down of old in this manner: "The sacrament of imposition of hands is to be had in great reverence, which cannot be done by any other, but by the high priests: neither is it read or known to have been done by any other in the apostles' time, but by the apostles themselves."[581]

96. And why are the baptized anointed with holy chrism?

Because that by the instinct of the Holy Ghost, the apostles have so delivered unto us, as St. Clement[582] and St. Denis,[583] the disciples of St. Peter and St. Paul do prove, and they delivered that doubtless, concerning the hallowing of chrism, which they have received of our Lord himself: as is thereof a grave witness, Fabianus,[584] who was both a martyr of Christ and high bishop of the Church.

Also, there is extant of this matter, such a precept of a most holy synod: "The baptized after baptism must receive the most holy chrism, and be made partakers of the kingdom of heaven."[585] Saint Cyprian allegeth this reason: that a Christian having once received chrism, to wit, unction or anointing, may be the anointed of God, and have in him the grace of Christ, and continually maintain holiness.[586]

And this visible ointment, wherewith the Church doth anoint the baptized, as St. Augustine teacheth,[587] doth signify the gift of invisible grace, wherewith the Holy Ghost doth with his internal unction replenish and

[580] Cf. Acts 8:14; Clement, *Epistle 4*; Urban; Melchiades; John Damascene, *Epistle 4*; Leo the Great, *Epistle 88 ad Episcopos Germaniae et Galliae*; Council of Worms; Council of Florence; Council of Trent

[581] Pope Eusebius, *Epistle ad Episcopos Tusciae et Campaniae*; Cf. Innocent I, *Epistle 1 ad Decent.*, Ch. 3; Acts 8:14; 19:6

[582] Cf. Clement, *Episte 4 ad Julium et Juliam*

[583] Cf. Dionysius, *Ecclesiastical Hierarchy*, Ch. 4, 2

[584] Cf. Fabian, *Epistle ad Orientales Episcopos*

[585] Council of Laodicea, Can. 48; Cf. Cornelius, *Epistle ad Fabium Antioch.* apud Eusebius, *Ecclesiastical History*, Bk. 6, Ch. 35; Theodoret, *Haereticarum Fabularum Compendium*, on Novatian

[586] Cf. Cyprian, Bk. 1, Epistle 12; *Sermon, De Unctione Chrismatis*; Cyril, *On Leviticus*, Bk. 9; Cyril of Jerusalem, *Catechetical Lecture 3*

[587] Cf. Augustine, *On the Trinity*, Bk. 15, Ch. 26; Pacian, *De Baptis.*; *Epistle 1, to Sympronian*

confirm Christ principally, who took his name of chrism, and then in like sort, all Christians.[588] Whereupon Tertullian, very fitly, alluding as it were to the nature of oil, hath written of this sacrament in this manner: "The flesh is anointed, that the soul may be consecrated; the flesh is signed, that the soul may be sensed; the flesh, by imposition of hands, is overshadowed, that the soul, by the Spirit, may be illuminated."[589] By which it is evident that they which reject holy chrism do greatly betray their own ignorance and folly, as manifestly denying the most ancient ordinance of the apostles, and rashly condemning the continual custom and tradition of the Church.[590]

97. What is the use and commodity of this sacrament?

In baptism, we are regenerate unto life; after baptism in this sacrament, "we are strengthened unto combat. In baptism, we are washed; by this after baptism, we are strengthened,"[591] that the Holy Ghost may be always present with the regenerate, as a keeper, and a comforter, and tutor. This is the doctrine of that holy high bishop and martyr Melchiades. And hereunto agreeth that which St. Clement testifieth he received of the apostles themselves: "When any man hath been regenerate by water, let him be afterward confirmed by a bishop with the sevenfold grace of the Holy Ghost: because otherwise he can never be a perfect Christian."[592] This sacrament therefore profiteth in marvelous manner,[593] that they which are by regeneration entered in the mysteries of faith, as infants

---

[588] Cf. Prosper, *Sententia*, n. 342; Augustine, *Tractate 33 on John*; *Sermon 47, De Verbis Domini*; Rabanus Maurus, *De Institutione Clericorum*, Bk. 1, Ch. 30; Isidore, *De Ecclesiasticis Officiis*, Bk. 2, Ch. 25

[589] Tertullian, *On the Resurrection of the Flesh*, Ch. 8

[590] Cf. Tertullian, *On Baptism*; Theodoret, *On Canticle of Canticles*, Ch. 1; Dionysius, Clement, Tertullian, Fabian, Cornelius, Cyprian, Cyril, Basil, Pacian, Amphilochius, Optatus of Milevis; Council of Rome under Silvester, Can. 5; Second Council of Carthage, Can. 3; Third Council of Carthage, 36; Fourth Council of Carthage, 36; First Council of Toledo, Ch. 20; First Council of Vaison, Can. 3; Council of Trent, Session 7, "On Confirmation," Can. 2; Cf. also Basil, *De Spiritu Sancto*, Ch. 27

[591] Melchiades, *Epistle to the Bishops of Spain*; Cf. Council of Florence; Peter of Cluny, Bk. 6, Epistle 1; Jn 3:5

[592] Clement, *Epistle 4 ad Julium*; Cf. Ambrose, *On the Sacraments*, Bk. 3, Ch. 2; *On the Mysteries*, Ch. 7

[593] Cf. Dionysius, *Ecclesiastical Hierarchy*, Ch. 2

newborn, and as yet weak and feeble, may wax greater in growth and be strengthened in Christ.[594]

These, as it were, novices in Christian warfare, the bishop admonisheth in anointing, that against so many enemies and daily dangers, they must be confirmed, *Spiritu principali*, with a principal Spirit.[595] He signeth with the cross their forehead, which is the seat of shamefastness, that they may constantly, and without fear, confess the name of our Lord. He giveth them also a blow on the cheek, that they may always remember how they must, with invincible patience, perform and finish their Christian warfare.[596]

Of the Sacrament of the Eucharist

98. What doth the name of the Eucharist signify?

This one name doth betoken that high and most Blessed Sacrament, than the which the Church hath nothing more honorable, more wonderful, more effectual or wholesome.[597]

And it is doubtless very worthily called the Eucharist, that is, "good grace," or "thanksgiving,"[598] because it containeth the principal and greatest gift of God, yea and the very fountain and author himself of all grace; and it admonisheth us of those special good things, for the receipt whereof we do owe thanksgiving, praise, and most sovereign glory to the supreme majesty of Almighty God.[599] For we could not have wished a greater benefit than that Christ Jesus our Lord, born of the Virgin Mary, crucified, and assumed into glory, should so give himself wholly unto us, that even

[594] Cf. 1 Pt 2:2
[595] Cf. Ps 50:14
[596] Cf. Augustine, *On Psalm 141*; Lk 9:26; Mt 10:33; 1 Pt 2:20; Lk 23:15; Mt 5:39; Acts 4:13, 31; 5:29, 41
[597] Cf. Dionysius, *Ecclesiastical Hierarchy*, Ch. 2-3; Council of Trent, Session 13, "Decree Concerning the Most Holy Sacrament of the Eucharist," Ch. 2-3
[598] Cf. Ambrose, *On the Sacraments*, Bk. 5, Ch. 3; Cyprian, *On the Lapsed*; Origen, *Contra Celsum*, Bk. 8
[599] Cf. Chrysostom, *Homily 60 ad Popul.*; *Homily 83 on Matthew*; *Homily 4 on John*; *Homily 5 on John*; *Homily 61, to the People of Antioch*

now at this present we truly receive his body and blood,[600] and are wholly incorporated unto him by this divine sacrament.[601]

99. **What things are specially contained in this sacrament?**
Three things are comprehended in the Holy Eucharist:[602] the visible forms, the truth of the body and blood of our Lord, and the effect of spiritual grace.[603]

For that which appeareth unto our eyes are visible forms, to wit, of bread and wine.[604] But that which under those forms, our faith and not our sense and reason doth apprehend, that is, the true body and blood of Christ our Savior.[605] And that which by participation of this sacrament we get is a certain singular grace of the Holy Ghost, to wit: the wholesome fruit and effect of the Eucharist,[606] as we will show hereafter.

100. **Which are the chief points necessary to be known touching this sacrament?**
There are five that do principally require the handling: the first, concerning the truth of the Eucharist; the second, touching the transubstantiation of bread and wine; the third, of the worship and adoration of the same; the fourth, of the oblation and sacrifice thereof; the last, of the receiving of the same under one or both kind. For of these in special, it is very profitable in these our days to have perfect knowledge and understanding.

101. **What therefore is to be believed, touching the verity of the Eucharist?**
This surely: that against all Capharnaites,[607] we do with the whole Church assuredly believe that, under the forms of bread and wine, the very true

---

[600] Cf. Chrysostom, *On the Priesthood*, Bk. 3; *Homily 2, to the People of Antioch; Homily 3 on Ephesians*

[601] Cf. Cyril, *On John*, Bk. 4, Ch. 16-17; Bk. 10, Ch. 13; Bk. 11, Ch. 26-27; Hilary, *On the Trinity*, Bk. 8; Irenaeus, *Against Heresies*, Bk. 5, Ch. 2; Cyril of Jerusalem, *Catechetical Lecture 4*; Chrysostom, *Homily 45 on John; Homily 61, to the People of Antioch*

[602] Cf. Cyril of Jerusalem, *Catechetical Lecture 4*

[603] Cf. Mt 26:26; Mk 14:22; Lk 22:19; 1 Cor 11:24

[604] Cf. Theophilus, *On Mark*, Ch. 14; *On Matthew*, Ch. 26; *On John*, Ch. 6; Cyril, *Epistle ad Calos.*; Ambrose, *On the Sacraments*, Bk. 4, Ch. 4; Bk. 6, Ch. 1

[605] Cf. John Damascene, *An Exposition of the Orthodox Faith*, Bk. 4, Ch. 14

[606] Cf. Augustine, *Tractate 26 on John*; others to be cited later

[607] Cf. Jn 6; Cyril, *On John*, Ch. 6; Augustine, *Tractate 27 on John*; Cyprian, *De Coena Domini*; Peter of Cluny, Bk. 1, Epistle 2

flesh of Jesus Christ and his true blood is given to in the Eucharist; by the ministry certes of the priest, but by the power and omnipotency of our Lord Jesus Christ,[608] with whom any word is not impossible.[609] "He spake, and they were made; he commanded, and they were created."[610] And he said in that supper which was prepared the day before his passion, when he had taken the bread first, and then the chalice into his hands,[611] and when his meaning was to assure every man both of the institution of this sacrament and also of the truth thereof, he, I say, most plainly and expressly said: "This is my body which is given for you."[612] He said: "This is my blood that shall be shed for many."[613] Concerning which institution he said also before: "My flesh is meat indeed, and my blood is drink indeed."[614] He said: "I am the living bread that came down from heaven."[615] "If any man eat of this bread he shall life forever; and the bread which I will give is my flesh, for the life of the world."[616] Neither are other testimonies of the evangelists and the apostle St. Paul obscure or hard to be known,[617] which do evidently avouch this faith unto us, that no man may doubt, but that Christ, according both to his divine

[608] Cf. Council of Ephesus; Second Council of Nicea, Act 6; Fourth Lateran Council, Const. 1; Council of Constance, Session 8; Council of Florence; Council of Trent, Session 13, Can. 1, 3; Ignatius of Antioch, *Epistle to the Smyrnaeans*; Theodoret, *Dialogue 3*; Tertullian, *On the Resurrection of the Flesh*, Ch. 8; *On Idolatry*, Ch. 7; Cyprian, *On the Lapsed*; Hesychius, *On Leviticus*, Ch. 22; Optatus of Milevis, *Against the Donatists*, Bk. 6; Leo the Great, *Sermon 7, De Pas.*; *Epistle 23*; Theodoret, *Dialogue 2*

[609] Cf. Lk 1:36; Mk 10:27

[610] Ps 148:5; Cf. John Damascene, *An Exposition of the Orthodox Faith*, Bk. 4, Ch. 14; *In Hist. Barlaam et Josaphat*, Ch. 19; *Sacra Parallela*, Bk. 3, Ch. 45; Ambrose, *On the Sacraments*, Bk. 4, Ch. 4-5; Cyril, *On John*, Bk. 4, Ch. 13; Peter of Cluny, Bk. 1, Epistle 2

[611] Cf. Lk 20; Mk 14; Mt 26; 1 Cor 11; Justin Martyr, *Second Apology*; Irenaeus, *Against Heresies*, Bk. 4, Ch. 32, 34; Juvencus, *Evang. Hist.*, Bk. 4; Tertullian, *Against Marcion*, Bk. 5, Ch. 1

[612] Lk 22:19

[613] Mk 14:24; Mt 26:28

[614] Jn 6:56; Cf. Hilary, *On the Trinity*, Bk. 8; Cyril, *On John*, Bk. 4, Ch. 16; Origen, *Homily 8 on Numbers*; Emisen., *Homily 5 De Pasc.*; Leo the Great, *Sermon 6, De Jejun. Sept. Mens. Cabil. 2*, Ch. 46

[615] Jn 6:51; Cf. Cyril, *On John*, Bk. 4, Ch. 15

[616] Jn 6:52; Cf. Cyril, *On John*, Bk. 4, Ch. 12; Theophilus, *On John*, Ch. 6; *On Mark*, Ch. 14; Peter of Cluny, Bk. 1, Epistle 2

[617] Cf. 1 Cor 10:16; 11:13

and human nature, is wholly in the Eucharist,[618] and doth remain with us even to the end of the world.[619]

Therefore, we have and do receive in the churches the very same flesh of Christ[620] that was seen in times past, in Palestine present with men. But the same here in this place is neither apparent unto the senses, nor subject to transmutation and corruption: as being invisible, impassible, immortal, shining with most excellent and divine glory, which at this time we cannot any otherwise behold than with the eyes of faith, but the saints in heaven do clearly see, with wonderful delight and pleasure.[621] And not-withstanding this, there be yet certain sacramentaries (O horrible and often condemned impiety) who, whilst they cannot reach with their senses, this mystery more to be adored than searched, they dare even to deny the same, marvelously depraving the words of the gospel, although most plain and evident. Which indeed is nothing else, but even, as it were, to take the sun out of the world, and to spoil God's spouse the Church of the most precious treasure of her true lover, and to bereave the faithful of the bread of life, that there may be nothing at all whereby their poor banished souls may be fed and sustained in the desert of this world.[622]

102. **And what is to be thought touching transubstantiation?**

Two things are here principally to be considered, and plainly professed: this one is that the priest, who consecrateth the Eucharist, must be ordered;[623] the other is that there is so much force and efficacy in those mys-

[618] Cf. Epiphanius, Ancoratus; Cyril of Jerusalem, *Catechetical Lecture 4*; Chrysostom, *Homily 83 on Matthew*; Leo the Great, *Sermon 6, De Jejun. Septimi. Mensis.*
[619] Cf. Mt 28:20; Council of Vienne, in Clem. tit. de Relig. et Vener. Sanct.
[620] Cf. Augustine, *On Psalm 98*; *On Psalm 33*; Prosper, *De Promiss. et Praedictionibus*, Pt. 2, Ch. 25
[621] Cf. Chrysostom, *Homily 2 on 2 Timothy*; *Homily 24 on 1 Corinthians*; John Damascene, *Sacra Parallela*, Bk. 2, Ch. 50; *Letter of the Presbyters and Deacons of Achaea*, on the history of St. Andrew
[622] Cf. Second Council of Nicea, Act 6, tom. 3; Council of Rome; Council of Vercelli under Leo IX; Council of Tours under Victor II; Council of Rome under Nicholas II; Council of Rome under Gregory VII; Council of Constance, Session 8, on article 3 of John Wycliffe; Council of Trent, Session 13, Can. 1
[623] Cf. Fourth Lateran Council, Const. 1; Chrysostom, *On the Priesthood*, Bk. 3; Jerome, *Epistle 14 to Heliodorus*, Ch. 7; *Epistle 146 to Evagrius*

tical and consecratory words, whereby such a priest doth, in Christ's room, consecrate the bread and wine upon the altar:[624] that the bread is suddenly changed into the body, and the wine into the blood of our Lord.[625]

A very wonderful transmutation indeed, and to be measured only by faith, which is brought to pass by the omnipotent power of Christ working by those very words; and it is not without cause called by the holy Catholic Church transubstantiation, because the substance of bread and wine is most certainly converted into the body and blood of Christ.[626] "For if the speech of Elijah were of such force to cause fire to come from heaven, shall not the speech of Christ (for this collection hath St. Ambrose made) be of force to change the substance of the elements? Of the works of the whole world thou hast read: 'He spake, and they were made; he commanded, and they were created.'[627] The speech therefore of Christ, which was able to make of nothing that which was not before, is it not able to change those things which are already, into that which they were not? For it is no less to give new natures to things, than to change natures."[628] And there is nothing more evident than the speech of Christ, saying, "this is my body, this is my blood,"[629] insomuch as there is no place at all left of suspicion, that after consecration there is bread and wine remaining in the Eucharist.[630]

[624] Cf. Justin Martyr, *Second Apology*; Irenaeus, *Against Heresies*, Bk. 5, Ch. 2; Ambrose, *On the Sacraments*, Bk. 4, Ch. 4; *On the Mysteries*, Ch. 9; Augustine, *Sermon 28*, *De Verbis Domini*; Cyprian, *De Coena Domini*; Chrysostom, *Homily 2 on 2 Timothy*; *On the Treason of the Jews*; Cf. also Bassarionem, on the same subject; Gregory of Nyssa, *Catechetical Oration*, Ch. 37; *Oration, De Bapt.*; Prosper, *De Consid.*, dist. 2, Ch. "Nos autem"

[625] Cf. Eusebius of Emesa, *Homily 5 De Pasc.*; Cyprian, *De Coena Domini*; Cyril of Jerusalem, *Catechetical Lectures 1, 3, 4*; Ambrose, *On the Sacraments*, Bk. 5, Ch. 4; Bk. 4, Ch. 4-5; *De Fide*, Bk. 4, Ch. 5; Chrysostom, *Homily 83 on Matthew*; *De Encaen.*; John Damascene, *Exposition of the Orthodox Faith*, Bk. 4, Ch. 14; Peter of Cluny, Bk. 1, Epistle 2

[626] Cf. Fourth Lateran Council, Const. 1; Council of Trent, Session 13, "Decree Concerning the Most Holy Sacrament of the Eucharist," Ch. 4; Session 13, Can. 2; Council of Rome under Gregory VII; Council of Constance, Session 8, articles 1-2; Council of Florence, et Lanfranc

[627] Ps 148:5

[628] Ambrose, *On the Mysteries*, Ch. 9; Cf. Ambrose, *On the Sacraments*, Bk. 4, Ch. 4

[629] Mt 26:26, 28; Mk 14:22, 24

[630] Cf. Theophylactus, *On Matthew*, Ch. 26; *On John*, Ch. 6; Gregory of Nyssa, *Catechetical Oration*, Ch. 37; Guitmund, Bk. 3

103. **Ought we to reverence and adore this sacrament?**

Yea undoubtedly; for so doth the office of religion require at our hands, that we creatures do give unto our Creator, and servants unto our Lord and Redeemer most mighty and sovereign, whom we believe to be present in the Eucharist, the honor and worship due unto him.[631]

For of him the scripture itself pronounceth: "Let all the angels of God adore him."[632] And again: "All the kings of the earth shall adore him, all nations shall serve him."[633] Then the divine prophet in another place, when he doth contemplate this sacrament and the greatness thereof, thinketh it not enough to say, "The poor shall eat and shall be satisfied, and shall praise our Lord."[634] But he addeth this also: "All the families of nations shall adore in his sight."[635] And again: "All those which are fat of the earth, have eaten and adored."[636]

The sages and some other like are commended by the evangelists, because they exhibited divine honor unto Christ being yet in mortal flesh, falling down before him and adoring him.[637] But now have we the same Christ in the Eucharist: not mortal but immortal, wonderful in glory and marvelous in might and power.[638] And this faith do we justly give testimony of, with a religious worship both of body and mind, when with reverence and submission we do exhibit the office of Christian humility and dutiful gratitude, before that dreadful and always most venerable majesty of Almighty God.[639]

---

[631] Cf. Augustine, On Psalm 98; Ambrose, De Spiritu Sancto, Bk. 3, Ch. 12; Mt 4:10; Apoc 14:7; 19:10; 22:9; Council of Trent, Session 13, "Decree Concerning the Most Holy Sacrament of the Eucharist," Ch. 5; Session 13, Can. 6; Peter of Cluny, Bk. 1, Epistle 2

[632] Heb 1:6; Ps 96:7

[633] Ps 71:11

[634] Ps 21:27; Cf. Euthymius, On Psalm 21; Eusebius, In Catena; Augustine, On Psalm 21; Epistle 120 ad Honor., Ch. 24, 27

[635] Ps 21:28

[636] Ps 21:30

[637] Cf. Mt 2:11; Chrysostom, Homily 24 on 1 Corinthians; Homily 8 on Matthew; Jn 9:38; Mt 14:33; 9:18; 28:17; Lk 24:52

[638] Cf. Rom 6:9; Ps 94:3

[639] Cf. Chrysostom, Homily 61 ad Pop.; Homily 3 on Ephesians; On the Priesthood, Bk. 6; Homily 1 on Isaias; Homily 3 contra Anom.; Homily 4 contra Anom.; Nilus of Sinai, Epistle ad Anast.; Ambrose, Oration 1 Prep. Ad Misam.; Gregory Nazianzen, Oration 11 in Gorgon.; Gregory the Great, Dialogues, Bk. 4, Ch. 58; Origen, Homily 5 in divers.

104. What then must our belief be concerning the Sacrifice of the Altar?

This undoubtedly: that the Eucharist is not instituted only to that end, that Christians may receive the same as a wholesome food; whereupon it is called "meat," "drink," "lively bread," and "the bread of life,"[640] but also to the intent that it may be offered as a sovereign and most proper sacrifice of the new testament, insomuch as it hath now of old obtained the name of a "host," a "sacrifice," an "oblation," and "holocaust."[641]

And it is offered for a continual memory and thanksgiving for the passion of our Lord,[642] and that it may be available unto the faithful, both to do away the evils and obtain the good things both of this life and the life to come;[643] and that it may not only profit the living, but the dead also, to forgiveness of sins, as most grave fathers do out of divine scripture and tradition apostolical avouch.[644]

This is that singular great and incomparable sacrifice, which Christ at his last supper, ordaining under the form of bread and wine, gave charge to his apostles, as to the first and chief priests of the new testament, and to their successors,[645] to offer, saying, "Do this, for a commemoration of me."[646]

---

[640] Cf. Jn 6:48, 51, 55; 1 Cor 10:16; 11:26; Prv 9:5

[641] Cf. Dionysius, *Ecclesiastical Hierarchy*, Ch. 3; *Epistle* 8; Ignatius of Antioch, *Epistle to the Smyrnaeans*; Justin Martyr, *Dialogue with Trypho*; Basil, *Sermon 2, De Baptismo*, Ch. 2; Tertullian, *On Prayer*, Ch. 14; Augustine, *Epistle 23*; *Contra Faustum*, Bk. 20, Ch. 21; Fulgentius, *Ad Monimum*, Bk. 2, Ch. 2, 5; Theodoret, *Ecclesiastical History*, Ch. 20; Alcimus Avitus, *De Spiritualis Historiae Gestis*, Bk. 5, Ch. 10; John Damascene, *In Hist. Barlaam et Josaphat*, Ch. 12, 19; Peter of Cluny, Bk. 1, Epistle 2

[642] Cf. Chrysostom, *Homily 17 on Hebrews*

[643] Cf. Liturgies of Sts. James, Basil, and John Chrysostom; Augustine, *City of God*, Bk. 22, Ch. 8; Chrysostom, *Homily 77 on Isaias*; *Homily 18 on Acts of the Apostles*; Gregory the Great, *Dialogues*, Bk. 4, Ch. 57; Bede, *Ecclesiastical History of the English Church*, Bk. 4, Ch. 22

[644] Cf. Clement, *Epistle 3*; Irenaeus, *Against Heresies*, Bk. 4, Ch. 32; Chrysostom, *Homily 3 on Philippians*; *Homily 69 ad Popul.*; John Damascene, *Oration de Defunct.*

[645] Cf. Irenaeus, *Against Heresies*, Bk. 4, Ch. 32; Eusebius, *Demonstratio Evangelica*, Bk. 1, Ch. 10; Cyprian, *Epistle 63*; Augustine, *City of God*, Bk. 10, Ch. 20; *Contra Faustum*, Bk. 20, Ch. 21; *On Psalm 33*, conc. 2

[646] Lk 22:19; Cf. Chrysostom, *Homily 83 on Matthew*; *Homily 24 on 1 Corinthians*; Martial of Limoges, *Epistle ad Burdegalenses*, Ch. 3; Dionysius, *Ecclesiastical Hierarchy*, Ch. 3; *Apostolic Constitutions*, Bk. 5, Ch. 19; Peter of Cluny, Bk. 1, Epistle 2

This is that oblation, which was figured by divers similitudes of sacrifices in the time both of the law of nature and the law of Moses,[647] as being a sacrifice containing in it all those good things as then signified by them, as the consummation and perfection of them all.[648] This is that perpetual sacrifice, which shall not be abolished but about the end of the world, as Daniel testifieth.[649]

To this belongeth the priesthood according to the order of Melchizedech, which also David affirmed that it should be and continue in Christ.[650]

This is that clean and pure oblation, which neither any unworthiness or malice of the offerers can pollute; which, alone succeeding very many sacrifices of the Jews' law, is offered and sacrificed among the Gentiles in every place,[651] that is to say, all the world over, to celebrate the name of our God and Redeemer, as we read in Malachi.[652]

This is the oblation of the Mass, the sacrifice, the liturgy, unto which do give invincible testimony,[653] the canons and traditions of the apostles,[654] the holy councils,[655] the general consent and continual custom of the whole Church, Greek and Latin, East and West.[656]

Which Sacrifice of the Mass, if we weigh the whole matter uprightly, is in truth a certain holy and lively representation, and also an unbloody

[647] Cf. Gn 4:4; 8:21; 14:18; Ex 12:6
[648] Cf. Augustine, City of God, Bk. 10, Ch. 20; Contra Faustum, Bk. 6, Ch. 5
[649] Cf. Dn 12:11; 9:27; Hippolytus, On the End of the World; Chrysostom, Homily 49, operis imperf.
[650] Cf. Ps 104; Heb 7:1, 11; Gn 14:18; Cyprian, Epistle 63; Eusebius, Demonstratio Evangelica, Bk. 5, Ch. 3; Jerome, Epistle 46 to Marcella, Ch. 2; Epistle 73 to Evagrius; Augustine, On Psalm 33, conc. 2; Epiphanius, Adversus Haeresus, n. 55.; John Damascene, Exposition of the Orthodox Faith, Bk. 4, Ch. 14
[651] Cf. Nm 28:3; 29:1; Augustine, City of God, Bk.17, Ch. 20; Peter of Cluny, Bk. 1, Epistle 2
[652] Cf. Mal 1:11; Cf. Martial of Limoges, Epistle ad Burdegalenses, Ch. 3; Justin Martyr, Dialogue with Trypho; Irenaeus, Against Heresies, Bk. 4, Ch. 32-34; Chrysostom, On Psalm 95; Augustine, City of God, Bk. 19, Ch. 23; Bk. 18, Ch. 35
[653] Cf. Acts 13:2
[654] Cf. Apostolic Canons, Can. 3, 9; Apostolic Constitutions, Bk. 6, Ch. 23
[655] Cf. First Council of Nicea, Can. 14; Council of Laodicea, Can. 19, 58; Council of Ephesus, Epistle to Nestorius; Council of Trent, Session 22, Ch. 1
[656] Cf. Liturgies of Sts. James, Basil, John Chrysostom, Ambrose, Gregory, etc.

and effectual oblation of our Lord's passion, and of that bloody sacrifice which was offered for us upon the cross.[657]

Whereby first it cometh to pass that a lively memory, faith, and gratitude from us toward our Redeemer is daily stirred up and confirmed, according to that: "Do this for a commemoration of me."[658] Of which words, the Church hath been such a diligent interpreter, that she hath in such sort ordained all external furniture belonging unto this unbloody sacrifice, holy vestments, vessels, ceremonies, and all manner of actions: that the standers-by may have nothing else to behold, but that holy commemoration, and the majesty of so great a sacrifice may be the more set forth, and the minds of the faithful, by means of these exterior signs and helps, more easily lifted up, and, as it were, led with the hand to the meditation of heavenly things, which do lie hidden in this sacrifice.[659]

Also hereby, it cometh to pass that the fruit of the oblation of Christ made upon the cross, and of our redemption, may be applied unto us and to all the faithful, as well alive as dead.[660]

---

[657] Cf. The very name of the Mass is read in these places: Alexander I, Epistle 1; Telesphorus; Felix I, Epistle 2; Hyginus et Soter apud Gratianum; Evaristus apud Ivonem; Fabian in Cod. Decretor., Bk. 16; Felix IV, *Epistle 1*; *Rule of St. Benedict*, Ch. 17; Damasus in Alexander I, Sixtus I, Telesphorus, and Felix I; Damasus, *Epistle 4*; Second Council of Carthage, Ch. 3; Council of Agde, Ch. 21, 47; Ambrose, Bk. 5, Epistle 33; Augustine, *Sermon 91, De Temp.*; *Sermon 237, De Temp.*, Ch. 8; *Sermon 251, De Temp.*; Council of Milevi, Ch. 12; Fourth Council of Carthage, Ch. 84; Leo the Great, *Epistle 81 to Dioscorus*; *Epistle 88 to the Bishops of Gall and Germany*; Victor. Utic., Bk. 2; John Cassian, *De Ordine Psal.*, Bk. 3; Gregory the Great, Bk. 1, Epistle 12; Bk. 4, Epistle 10; Council of Rome under Sylvester; Council of Lerida, Ch. 4; Council of Valencia, Ch. 1; First Council of Orleans, Can. 18

[658] Lk 22:19; 1 Cor 11:24

[659] Cf. On the ceremonies of the Mass see: Dionysius, *Ecclesiastical Hierarchy*, Ch. 3; Isidore, Alcuin, Remigius, Rabanus Maurus, Amalarius, Rupert, Innocent III, Council of Trent, Session 22, "Doctrine on the Sacrifice of the Mass," Ch. 5; Can. 7; Chrysostom, *Homily 3 on Ephesians*; *Homily 14 on Ephesians*; Prudentius, *Peristephanon*, Hymn 2; Optatus of Milevis, *Against the Donatists*, Bk. 6; Jerome, ad Theoph. ante libros eius Pascha.; Cyril of Jerusalem, *Catechetical Lecture 5*; Clement, *Epistle 2 ad Frat. Dom.*; Bede, *Ecclesiastical History of the English Church*, Bk. 1, Ch. 29

[660] Cf. Cyprian, *Epistle 66*; Chrysostom, *Homily 41 on 1 Corinthians*; *Homily 21 on Acts of the Apostles*; John Damascene, *Oration de Defunct.*; Augustine, *On the Care of the Dead*, Ch. 1; *Sermon 32, De Verbis Apostoli*, Ch. 1, 2; *Confessions*, Bk. 9, Ch. 11-13; Epiphanius, *Adversus Haeresus*, n. 75

For which cause St. Cyprian giveth testimony, that this sacrament is both a medicine and a holocaust to heal infirmities and to purge iniquities;[661] and Martial, the disciple of the apostle St. Peter, writeth thus: "That which the Jews upon envy did sacrifice, thinking thereby to blot out his name upon the earth: that same do we for our salvation offer upon a sanctified altar, knowing well that, by this only remedy, life is given unto us and death put to flight."[662] We omit other fathers, witnesses of the same faith and doctrine, that we may keep that brevity that we purposed in the beginning.

By all which things it is apparently evident that Christ, two sundry ways, is called and is indeed for us a sacrifice, to wit: after a bloody and an unbloody manner.[663] For he offered himself a bloody sacrifice for us upon the cross,[664] that unto the type of the paschal lamb, which was offered among the Jews, he, the true Lamb without spot, the very truth unto the figure, might answer.[665] But at the last supper, as also upon the altar, his pleasure was that the same should be offered, after a manner and ceremony unbloody,[666] even as St. Cyril calleth it;[667] to the intent that the oblation of Melchizedek, who offered bread and wine, might be made perfect; and he remain true priest according to the order of Melchizedek, and his priesthood continue forever, without any other to succeed in his room.[668]

---

[661] Cf. Cyprian, *De Coena Domini*; Cf. also Liturgies of Sts. James, Basil, and John Chrysostom

[662] Martial of Limoges, *Epistle ad Burdegalenses*, Ch. 3; Cf. Jerome, *On Titus*, Ch. 1; Ambrose, *On the Duties of the Clergy*, Bk. 1, Ch. 48; *On Psalm 38*; Alex., *Epistles 1 and 2*; Gregory of Nazianzen, *Oration 3*; Augustine, *Sermon 4, De Innoc.*; Third Council of Braga, Can. 1; Gregory the Great, *Homily 37 on the Gospels*; Council of Trent, Session 22, "Doctrine on the Sacrifice of the Mass," Ch. 2

[663] Cf. Council of Ephesus, Epistle to Nestorius; Second Council of Nicea, Act 6, tom. 3; Augustine, *Contra Faustum*, Bk. 20, Ch. 21

[664] Cf. Eph 5:2; Heb 10:14

[665] Cf. Ex 12:3; Mk 14:12

[666] Cf. Eusebius, *Demonstratio Evangelica*, Bk. 1, Ch. 10; Gregory of Nazianzen, *Oration 4*; *In Carm. Ad Episc. et ad Constantinop.*; Gregory of Nyssa, *Oration 1 in Resur. Christi*.

[667] Cf. Cyril, *Epistle 10 to Nestorius*; et interp. Anat. 11.

[668] Cf. Gn 14:18; Heb 7:1; Ps 109:4; Jerome, *On Matthew*, Ch. 26; Oecumenius, *On Hebrews*, Ch. 5; Sedulius, *Carmen Paschale*, Bk. 3; Claudius Marius, *On Genesis*, Bk. 3

There, once and at one only place of Judea, he offered this sacrifice, whereof St. Paul writing unto the Hebrews doth discourse;[669] but here he is sacrificed more often, and in every place,[670] to wit, all over the Church, as it is confirmed by the prophet Malachi.[671] There he was offered unto death, and here for a perpetual and lively remembrance of his death, and a wholesome participation thereof, which floweth from thence, as it were, from the head unto the members, to the intent that the fruit and effect of that sacrifice offered upon the cross might be daily exhibited and applied unto us, by this Sacrifice of the Mass.[672]

105. **Is the Eucharist to be received under one kind only, as of bread, or under both kinds, of bread and wine?**

Forasmuch as belongeth to priests, or those that sacrifice, it is manifest that they must receive the sacrament under both kinds; whereas otherwise, they cannot orderly either consecrate or offer the Eucharist. The reason whereof depending of the nature of the sacrifice itself, there is no need to allege in this place.

But concerning the rest of the faithful which do not themselves sacrifice, we must thus much confess that they are not bound by any divine commandment to receive the Blessed Sacrament under both kinds, but that it is sufficient for their salvation to communicate under one kind. For if we look into the state of the primitive Church, we shall find that it was ministered unto the faithful sometimes under one and sometimes under both kinds.[673] And if we go unto the holy scripture, it doth in such manner speak of this sacrament that it useth to make mention sometimes of the bread and the cup, sometimes of the bread only.[674] For where we read,

---

[669] Cf. Heb 9:25; 10:14

[670] Cf. Chrysostom, *Homily 17 on Hebrews*; Augustine, *Epistle 23*; Theophylactus, *On Hebrews*, Ch. 5, 7, and 10; Oecumenius, *On Hebrews*; Photius, *On Hebrews*

[671] Cf. Mal 1:11

[672] Cf. Peter of Cluny, Bk. 1, Epistle 2

[673] Cf. Tertullian, *Ad Uxorem*, Bk. 2, Ch. 5; Cyprian, *On the Lapsed*; Origen, *Homily 13 on Exodus*; Basil, *Epistle ad Caesariam*; Jerome, *Apology* for his books *Against Jovinian*, Ch. 6; Peter of Cluny, *De Miraculis*, Bk. 1, Ch. 1

[674] Cf. 1 Cor 10:16; 11:26; Acts 2:42

"Unless you eat the flesh of the Son of man, and drink his blood, you shall not have life in you,"[675] we read also, "If any man eat of this bread he shall live forever."[676] And he which said, "He that eateth my flesh, and drinketh my blood, hath life everlasting,"[677] hath also said, "The bread which I will give is my flesh, for the life of the world."[678] And again, the same that affirmed, "He that eateth my flesh, and drinketh my blood, abideth in me and I in him,"[679] affirmed this also: "He that eateth this bread, shall live forever."[680] To omit what St. Luke allegeth, touching the breaking of bread only.[681] Neither do we want the example of Christ himself, who first at the last supper ordained this sacrament under both kinds, and delivered it unto his apostles;[682] but afterward being at Emmaus with his two disciples, he gave them the Eucharist under one kind only, and immediately after withdrew himself, as the fathers do interpret this place of the gospel.[683]

We must not therefore condemn either those who, contenting themselves with one kind only, do abstain from the use of the cup, and are ready to have abstained many ages since; or those that of old, when so the Church did allow, had in public use both kinds.[684]

But use and experience, the master of matters, hath taught by little and little that for the more profit of the people, and less danger, and for many respects it is very conveniently done, that the chalice being left,

[675] Jn 6:54; Council of Trent, Session 21, Can. 1
[676] Jn 6:52
[677] Jn 6:55
[678] Jn 6:52
[679] Jn 6:57
[680] Jn 6:59
[681] Cf. Lk 24:30, 35; Acts 2:42; 20:7; 27:35; Augustine, *Epistle 36 to Casulanus*; Chrysostom, *Homily 17 Operis Imperf.*; Isich., *On Leviticus*, Ch. 9
[682] Cf. Mt 26:26; Mk 14:22; Lk 22:19; 1 Cor 11:24
[683] Cf. Lk 24:30; Theoph., *On Luke*, Ch. 24; Bede, *On Luke*, Ch. 24; Chrysostom, *Opus Imperfectum in Matthaeum*, Homily 17; Augustine, *The Harmony of the Gospels*, Bk. 3, Ch. 25
[684] Cf. Eusebius, *Ecclesiastical History*, Bk. 6, Ch. 36; Augustine, *Homily 26 ex 50*; *Sermon 252, De Temp.*; Ambrose, *On the Death of Satyrus*; Paulinus of Nola, *Life of St. Ambrose*; Amphilochius, *Life of Basil*; Bede, *Ecclesiastical History of the Church of England*, Bk. 4, Ch. 14, 24; Theodoret, *Historia Philothea*, 26 quae est Simeonis; Evagrius, *Ecclesiastical History*, Bk. 4, Ch. 3; Gregory of Tours, *Glory of the Martyrs*, Bk. 1, Ch. 86; Gulielmus, *Life of St. Bernard*, Bk. 1, Ch. 11

the Communion under one kind only be retained. And thus hath the Church long since decreed to be done, not swerving at all herein from the ordinance and commandment of her spouse (for she is the pillar and ground of truth,[685] and a faithful dispenser of the mysteries of God,[686]) but employing that power which she hath received of her spouse in dispensing the mysteries to edification, and the common profit of the faithful, as the state and condition of times and men, which enforceth alteration even in sacred things, doth seem to require.[687]

For the very words of the gospel do give us to understand that Christ, at his last supper, dealt with those unto whom he gave commission not only to receive, but also to consecrate and offer the Eucharist,[688] yea and to direct and govern the whole Church. To the judgment, wisdom, and authority of those he left, to appoint laws unto posterity and according to the diversity of times orderly to dispose, as well in most other things appertaining unto Christian weal, as in the manner and order of communicating the Eucharist unto the faithful.[689]

This same even out of Saint Paul[690] doth St. Augustine prove, and it may easily be convinced by many decrees of the apostles.[691]

Neither have we reason to think that the laity have any wrong, if in this, as also in most other things, they be not made equal unto priests.[692] For it is most certain that Christ is not divided into two parts, according unto the two distinct signs of this sacrament, but that as well under one as under both kinds, yea under a little particle of a consecrated host, Christ is wholly given and wholly received in flesh, in soul, in blood, and in Godhead. And where Christ is received whole and perfect, there cannot be wanting the full fruit and effectual grace of so great a sacrament.[693] And therefore, the

---

[685] Cf. 1 Tm 3:15
[686] Cf. 1 Cor 4:1
[687] Cf. 2 Cor 10:8; 13:10; Council of Trent, Session 21, "Decree on the Communion of Both Species, and the Communion of Infants," Ch. 2
[688] Cf. Mt 26:20; Mk 14:17; Lk 22:14; Justin Martyr, *Second Apology*
[689] Cf. Acts 20:28; 1 Pt 5:2; Lk 10:16; Eph 4:11, 14
[690] Cf. 1 Cor 11:34
[691] Cf. Augustine, *Epistle 54 to Januarius*, Ch. 6
[692] Cf. Mt 18:18; Jn 20:23; 1 Tm 3:2, 8, 13; 4:14; Ti 1:5
[693] Cf. Basil, *Epistle ad Caesariam*; Cyril, *Epistle ad Calos.*; *On John*, Bk. 4, Ch. 14;

laity are here defrauded of no commodity at all, whether thou regardest the thing itself contained in the sacrament, to wit, Christ, God and man, or dost require the fruit and grace which is given unto those that receive the Blessed Sacrament for the health of their souls, but they receive as much under one kind, as they should under both, if it were allowable.[694]

Of which matter, certes, there is no more any place left either to doubt or to dispute:[695] since that the Holy Ghost, who, according to the promise of Christ, doth teach and govern the Church, hath set down unto us a most certain and plain sentence,[696] and, again and again, confirmed the same with the inviolable authority of a most holy synod.[697] Whereupon it may evidently be concluded that this custom of receiving under one kind is not contrary unto the commandment of God; is ratified by the lawful authority of the Church; is approved by long continuance of time and general consent of the faithful; is commended with most sure reason and profit; and finally, is to be assuredly accounted for a law, which by none, but by the Church herself, may be changed.

And yet neither the adversaries themselves, though here they bark and keep astir, are able to show when such custom of communicating began. So that it is a wonder to see some yet, for all this, who, being carried away with a show of private devotion, do otherwise persuade themselves, and do conspire herein with the new rebels and contemnors of the Church,[698] against the reverend authority of the whole Church. These men truly ought to fear, lest, whilst they stand so much upon the outward signs of the sacrament and give themselves wholly to contentiousness, they lose the internal benefits of the sacrament, yea and Christ himself altogether; so that it were far better for them to abstain from any use of the sacrament at

Council of Florence; Eusebius of Emesa, *Homily 3 De Pasc.*; Council of Trent, Session 13, "Decree Concerning the Most Holy Sacrament of the Eucharist," Can. 3; de cons. dist. 2. c .*qui manducat. etc. singuli.*

[694] Cf. Jn 6:42, 52; 1 Cor 10:16
[695] Cf. Augustine, *Epistle 54 to Januarius*, Ch. 5
[696] Cf. Lk 12:31; Jn 14:16; 16:12; Is 59:21
[697] Cf. Council of Constance, Session 13; Council of Basel, Session 30; Council of Trent, Session 21
[698] Cf. 1 Tm 3:15; Mt 18:17

all.[699] For so much as neither faith nor sacraments are profitable to any, but to those only who persist in the unity of the Church.[700] So that hereupon Saint Augustine hath said: "All the sacraments of Christ are received not to salvation but to judgment, without the chair of unity."[701] And again: "What doth either sound faith, or happily, the sound sacrament of faith profit a man, whereby the deadly wound of schism, the sound health of charity is destroyed?"[702] And truly there is no doubt, but that they do grievously sin against Christ himself, who presume to abuse this most holy badge of unity, to make it as a badge of schismatical division.[703]

106. **What profit cometh by the Eucharist being received as it ought to be?**
Very much doubtless, and exceeding great. For, "This is the holy banquet wherein Christ is received, the memory of his passion is solemnized,[704] the mind is replenished with grace, and a pledge of future glory is given us,"[705] as the Church, moved by the feeling and experience of these fruits, doth notably sing.

This is the bread that descended from heaven, and giveth life to the world, and upholdeth and strengtheneth our minds in spiritual life.[706]

This is that holy Synaxis or Communion, which signifieth and causeth also the faithful to be linked together amongst themselves, as members of one and the same body, and to be associated unto the merits of all saints and devout persons;[707] moreover, (which is a more blessed and happy thing) it uniteth them fast unto Christ their head,[708] that they may abide in him, and he in them, and so by that means they may obtain life everlasting.[709]

[699] Cf. Augustine, *Contra Cresconium*, Bk. 1, Ch. 33
[700] Cf. Augustine, *Epistola ad Catholicos contra Donatistas*, Ch. 4
[701] Augustine, *Answer to Petilian the Donatist*, Bk. 3, Ch. 40
[702] Augustine, *On Baptism, against the Donatists*, Bk. 1, Ch. 8
[703] Cf. Augustine, *City of God*, Bk. 21, Ch. 25; Council of Trent, Session 13, Ch. 2, 8
[704] Basil, *Sermon 1, De Baptismo*, Ch. 3
[705] Ambrose, *On Psalm 118*, Sermon 15, verse 4; Council of Trent, Session 13, "Decree Concerning the Most Holy Sacrament of the Eucharist," Ch. 2
[706] Cf. Jn 6:33, 36, 49, 52, 59; Theophylactus, *On John*, Ch. 6; Cyril, *On John*, Ch. 6
[707] Cf. 1 Cor 10:17; Council of Florence
[708] Cf. Chrysostom, *Homily 45 on John*; *Homily 61 ad Pop.*; Hilary, *On the Trinity*, Bk. 8; Leo the Great, *Sermon 14 De Pas.*; Cyril, *On John*, Bk. 1, Ch. 26; Bk. 20, Ch. 13; Bk. 4, Ch. 17; Gregory of Nyssa, *Catechetical Oration*, Ch. 37
[709] Cf. Jn 6:57

This is that voyage provision of our peregrination,[710] which is the manna given unto the fathers; it bringeth comfort, delight, virtue, and grace most effectual, without all comparison, unto those that are wandering in the desert and warfare of this life, and traveling from hence unto the heavenly Jerusalem.[711]

And two effects principally (as most excellently teacheth St. Bernard) doth this sacrament work in us: "For in the least sins it diminisheth our feeling, and in the greater sins it cutteth off consent. If any of you do not feel neither so often, nor such vehement motions of anger, envy, lechery, or such other like, let him give thanks to the body and blood of our Lord, because the virtue of the sacrament worketh in him; and let him be glad that a most festered sore doth now draw near to perfect soundness."[712] And the same again in another place: "This body of Christ is a medicine unto the sick, and a way to the wayfaring pilgrims, which strengtheneth the weak, delighteth the strong, and cureth languishing faintness. By this a man is made more meek to take correction; more patient to abide labor; more fervent in love; in taking heed, more circumspect; more prompt in obedience; more devout in thanksgiving."[713]

No marvel therefore that great Ignatius hath written, willing us to "come often and speedily unto the Eucharist, and (as he calleth it) to the glory of God. For when this is continually done, the powers of Satan are expelled, who bendeth all his endeavors into fiery darts to sin."[714] This

[710] Cf. First Council of Nicea, Can. 12; Second Council of Orleans, Can. 12; Third Council of Orleans, Can. 24; Chrysostom, *On the Priesthood*, Bk. 6; Paulinus, *Life of Ambrose*; Eusebius, *Ecclesiastical History*, Bk. 6, Ch. 36; Nicephorus, *Church History*, Bk. 8, Ch. 31; Bk. 13, Ch. 37; Cedre. in Maur. et Phoca. imp.; Gregory the Great, *Homily 40 on the Gospels*

[711] Cf. Ex 16:13; Dt 8:16; Ws 16:20; Jn 6:49; Alcimus Avitus, *De Spiritualis Historiae Gestis*, Bk. 5, Ch. 20

[712] Bernard, *Sermon De Coena Domini*; Cf. Cyril, *On John*, Bk. 4, Ch. 17; Bk. 3, Ch. 37; John Cassian, *Conferences of the Desert Fathers*, Col. 22, Ch. 26

[713] Citatur a B. Thoma., opusc. 59, Ch. 5; Cf. Chrysostom, *Homily 24 on 1 Corinthians*; *Homily 51 on Matthew*; Peter of Cluny, Bk. 1, Epistle 2

[714] Ignatius of Antioch, *Epistle to the Ephesians*, Ch. 13

bread is a medicine causing immortality, a preservative, never to die, but to live in God through Jesus Christ.[715]

107. **What things are required for the worthy receiving of the Eucharist, and reaping the fruits and commodities thereof?**

The answer is easy of the apostle himself: "Let a man prove himself: and so let him eat of that bread."[716] As also, St. Augustine hath said: "In the body of Christ our life doth consist: let him therefore change his life, who meaneth to receive life."[717]

And this proving of a man's self and change of life consisteth specially in four things, to wit: there must be faith, penance, attention of mind, and a decent composition of the Christian man.

Faith requireth thus much: that thou dost not doubt any wit at all of those things that we have said, and other the like appertaining unto this mystery.[718] And that, thou shalt accomplish, in case thou rest wholly and simply upon the faith and sentence of the Church, as doubtless it is necessary.[719]

Penance, whereof (we will speak hereafter more at large), requireth a detestation of sin, and a plain and sincere confession unto a priest, and absolution obtained for the same.[720]

Then must the mind of necessity be present,[721] seriously converting itself, by meditations and devout prayers unto this so great a sacrament.[722]

---

[715] Cf. Basil, *Epistle ad Caesariam*; Ambrose, *On the Sacraments*, Bk. 5, Ch. 4; Chrysostom, *Homily 61, to the People of Antioch*; Cyprian, *Sermon 6, On the Lord's Prayer*; Jerome, *Epistle 71, to Lucinius*; Cyril, *On John*, Bk. 3, Ch. 37; John Cassian, *Conferences of the Desert Fathers*, Col. 23, Ch. 21

[716] 1 Cor 11:28; Cf. Theoph., *On 1 Corinthians*, Ch. 11; Anselm, *On 1 Corinthians*, Ch. 11; Gregory the Great, *On 1 Kings*, Bk. 2, Ch. 1; Gregory of Nyssa, *De Perf. Christ. forma*.

[717] Augustine, *Sermon 1, De Temp.*

[718] Cf. Basil, *The Shorter Rules*, q. 172

[719] Cf. 1 Tm 3:15

[720] Cf. Basil, *Sermon 1, De Baptismo*, Ch. 3; *Sermon 2*, Ch. 3; Cyprian, *On the Lapsed*; Council of Trent, Session 13, "Decree Concerning the Most Holy Sacrament of the Eucharist," Ch. 7; Hesychius, *On Leviticus*, Ch. 26; Chrysostom, *Homily 30 on Genesis*; *Homily 10 on Matthew*; Peter of Cluny, *De Miraculis*, Bk. 1, Ch. 2-3, 5

[721] Cf. Chrysostom, *Homily 83 on Matthew*; *Homily 3 on Ephesians*; *Homily 60, to the People of Antioch*; *Homily 6, to the People of Antioch*

[722] Cf. Ambrose, *in Orat. ante Missam*

Last of all the decent demeanor and composition I spake of doth require that no man come unto this Holy Communion, but chaste,[723] fasting,
modest, humble,[724] with submission, and without all indecency.[725] But they
that receive the Holy Eucharist unworthily do not receive life, but judgment unto themselves, and are guilty of the body and blood of our Lord,
as witnesseth the apostle; and shall be grievously condemned with Judas
and the Jews, the bloody enemies of Christ our Savior.[726]

Of the Sacrament of Penance

108. **What is the sacrament of penance?**

It is that in which is given the absolution of a priest from sins, which a
man hath truly detested and rightly confessed.

Which power of absolving, to the intent that we might have certain
in the Church, this divine promise was made unto priests:[727] "Receive ye
the Holy Ghost: whose sins you shall forgive, they are forgiven them: and
whose you shall retain, they are retained."[728] Then in another place: "Amen
I say to you," saith our Lord, "whatsoever you shall bind upon earth, shall
be bound also in heaven: and whatsoever you shall loose upon earth, shall
be loosed also in heaven."[729]

By which it plainly appeareth that the effect of this sacrament is excellent and full of comfort, as being the means whereby are remitted

[723] Cf. Augustine, *Sermon 3, De Temp.*; *Sermon 252, De Temp.*; John Cassian, *Conferences of the Desert Fathers*, Col. 22, Ch. 5; *Institutes of the Coenobia*, Bk. 6, Ch. 8

[724] Cf. Augustine, *Epistle 54 to Januarius*, Ch. 6

[725] Cf. Origen, *Homily 5*, in divers.; John Cassian, *Conferences of the Desert Fathers*,
Col. 22, Ch. 7

[726] Cf. 1 Cor 11:27; Chrysostom, *Homily 45 on John*; *Homily 61, to the People of Antioch*;
Basil, *Sermon 2, De Baptismo*, Ch. 3; Theodoret, *On 1 Corinthians*, Ch. 11; John Cassian,
Conferences of the Desert Fathers, Col. 22, Ch. 5; Peter of Cluny, *De Miraculis*, Bk. 1, Ch. 25

[727] Cf. Council of Trent, Session 14, "Doctrine on the Sacrament of Penance," Ch.
6; Can. 10; Ambrose, *On Repentance*, Bk. 10, Ch. 2, 7; Bk. 2, Ch. 2

[728] Jn 20:22-23; Cyril, *On John*, Bk. 12, Ch. 56; Gregory the Great, *Homily 26 on the
Gospels*; Chrysostom, *Homily 85 on John*

[729] Mt 18:18; Cf. Cyprian, *Epistle 54 to Cornelius*; Hilary, *On Matthew*, Can. 16; Pacian, *Epistle 1, to Sympronian*; Jerome, *Epistle 14 to Heliodorus*, Ch. 7; Augustine, *City of God*,
Bk. 20, Ch. 9; Chrysostom, *Homily 5, De Ver. Esaiae Vidi Dominum*

all manner of sins, though never so foul and abominable; and they absolved without any difference, that have guilty consciences in the sight of Almighty God; and this by the ministry of a priest, through the divine ordinance of Christ. And therefore, the power and authority of priests is now far more excellent, and more to be accounted of, than of old it was,[730] as being those persons unto whom it is granted—I do not say, "to allow," as already purged, but—altogether to purge, not the leprosy of the body, but the filths of the soul, as witnesseth Saint Chrysostom.[731] And St. Augustine: "What other thing doth the Church," saith he, "unto whom it is said, 'What things you shall loose shall be loosed,' but that which our Lord said to his disciples, 'Loose him and let him go'?"[732]

109. **Wherefore is this sacrament of penance needful?**

That a man having fallen after baptism and become the enemy of God, obtaining by means of this sacrament remission of sins, may be reconciled unto God, and of a dead man be made alive, and of wicked become just. For which cause, the fathers do not unadvisedly call penance the second table after shipwreck,[733] to wit, by the which, every man may be transported out of the whirlpool of mortal sin as out of a shipwreck, into the grace and favor of Almighty God, though loaden and pestered with many, and those very heinous, sins.[734]

---

[730] Cf. Lv 4:22, 27; 5:4, 15; 6:2; 13:2, 17, 37; 14:2, 18; Mt 8:4; Lk 17:14

[731] Cf. Chrysostom, *On the Priesthood*, Bk. 3, n. 6

[732] Augustine, *Sermon 8, De Verbis Domini*, Ch. 1-2; *Sermon 44, De Verbis Domini*; *Tractate 49 on John*; *Homily 27 ex 50*; *On Psalm 101*, conc. 2; Jn 11:44; Cf. Council of Trent, Session 14, "Doctrine on the Sacrament of Penance," Ch. 1; Can. 1; Session 6, "Decree on Justification," Ch. 14; Can. 29; Council of Florence, Session 15; Gregory of Nyssa, *Life of Moses*; Bernard, *Life of Malachy of Armagh*

[733] Cf. Pacian, *Epistle 1, to Sympronian*; Jerome, *On Isaiah*, Ch. 3; *Epistle 130 to Demetrias*, Ch. 6; Ambrose, *De Lapsu Virginis Consecratae*, Ch. 8; Council of Trent, Session 6, "Decree on Justification," Ch. 14; Session 14, Can. 2; Tertullian, *De Paenitentia*, Ch. 7; Ez 18:30; 33:11

[734] Cf. Ambrose, *On Repentance*, Bk. 1-2; Augustine, *De Conjugiis Adulterinis*, Bk. 1, Ch. 28; Bk. 2, Ch. 16; Fourth Lateran Council, Const. 1; Council of Trent, Session 14, "Doctrine on the Sacrament of Penance," Ch. 2; Council of Florence; Jerome, *Against the Pelagians*, Bk. 2

110. **When is this sacrament taken as it ought to be, and worketh effectually?**
When he that sueth for remission of his sins doth use three parts or acts:
contrition, confession, and satisfaction, which do comprehend the full
conversion of a man unto God, the duty of a penitent, and his perfect
renewing. Of which St. Chrysostom speaketh in this manner: "Perfect
penance doth constrain the sinner to suffer all things willingly: contrition
in his heart, confession in his mouth, and in his actions, nothing but humility."[735] This to be wholesome penance St. Chrysostom affirmeth, that
by those very means that we offend God (which certes we do by heart,
word, and deed) by the same we may be reconciled unto God: in heart by
contrition, in mouth by confession, in deed by satisfaction.[736]

To contrition appertaineth that place: "A troubled spirit is a sacrifice
to God: a contrite and humble heart, O God, thou wilt not despise."[737]

Confession, St. Luke doth notify in these words: "Many of them that
believed, came confessing and declaring their deeds."[738] And the apostle
St. James teacheth: "Confess your sins one to another."[739]

And to satisfaction do belong those worthy fruits of penance, which St.
John Baptist requireth, and amongst them alms is accounted.[740] Of these,
Daniel the prophet saith thus: "Redeem thy sins with alms, and thy iniquities with mercy toward the poor."[741] "A great offense hath need of great satisfaction,"[742] saith St. Ambrose. And hereunto also is referred that which
St. Paul saith of mourning for those Corinthians, because they had not as
yet done penance for the uncleanness, and fornication, and incontinency
which they had committed.[743]

[735] Chrysostom, *Sermon De Paenit.*
[736] Cf. Kgs 16:5; Ps 50:19, 5; 6:7; 37:7, 18; 101:4, 10; 2 Kgs 12:13; 24:10; 3 Kgs 21:25;
Jon 3:7ff
[737] Ps 50:19
[738] Acts 19:18; Cf. Nm 5:6ff
[739] Jas 5:16; Bede, *On James*, Ch. 5
[740] Cf. Mt 3:2; Lk 3:8; Acts 26:20
[741] Dn 4:24
[742] Ambrose, *De Lapsu Virginis Consecratae*, Ch. 8, n. 37
[743] Cf. 2 Cor 12:21; Cf. also Council of Florence; Council of Trent, Session 14,
"Doctrine on the Sacrament of Penance," Ch. 3; Can. 4

111. **What is contrition?**

It is a grief of mind, and a detestation conceived for sin, because Almighty God is therewith displeased, joined with a full purpose of amendment of life.

This contrition is procured:[744] if a man do diligently behold the foulness, enormity, and multitude of his sins; if he carefully think upon that sovereign goodness offended, of the grace of God, and other gifts lost; if he do deeply weigh and stand in awe of the inevitable necessity of the uncertain hour of death, the horrible severity of the judgment to come, and the everlasting pains prepared for sinners.[745]

Hereunto appertaineth that of Hezekiah: "I will recount unto thee all my years in the bitterness of my soul."[746] And that of David: "I stood in awe of thy judgments."[747] And that which he also, in lamenting manner, doth pray: "I am afflicted and too much humbled: I did roar with the sighs of my heart."[748] And a little after: "I will declare my iniquity, and I will think for my sin."[749]

Also, it is an express speech of God himself unto a sinner: "Thou hast left thy first charity, be mindful therefore from whence thou art fallen and do penance."[750] And Christ in the gospel: "Fear him," saith he, "who after he hath killed, hath power to cast into hell. Yea, I say unto you, fear him."[751] Now finally, this grief of contrition doth prepare us to remission of sins, in case it be joined with a confidence of God's mercy,[752] and a desire of performing those things which do belong to the sacrament of penance.[753]

---

[744] Cf. Chrysostom, *On Psalm 50*; *De Compunct.*, Bk. 1-2; Augustine, *De Paenit. Medic.*, Ch. 9; Ambrose, *De Lapsu Virginis Consecratae*, Ch. 8; Council of Trent, Session 14, Can. 5

[745] Cf. Heb 9:27; Soph 1:15; Mt 25:41; Mk 9:43

[746] Is 38:15

[747] Ps 118:120

[748] Ps 37:9

[749] Ps 37:19

[750] Apoc 2:4-5; Cf. 2 Cor 12:21; 7:9

[751] Lk 12:5; Cf. Mt 10:28

[752] Cf. Ambrose, *On Repentance*, Bk. 1, Ch. 1

[753] Cf. Augustine, *De Paenit. Medic.*, Ch. 11; *Enchiridion*, Ch. 65; Ambrose, *On Psalm 37*; *De Lapsu Virginis Consecratae*, Ch. 8; Cf. also Council of Trent, Session 14, "Doctrine on the Sacrament of Penance," Ch. 4; Council of Florence; Augustine, *Sermon 3 in Nat.*

112. Is confession necessary?

Yea verily: but not only as some do falsely suppose that interior confession which is to be done in the presence of God every day,[754] according to the example of holy David, who saith, "I have said I will confess against myself my injustice unto our Lord,"[755] but also this exterior confession which is done unto a priest, of all the sins which do come into a man's mind, after diligent search and examination of his conscience.[756]

So is it written of men of the primitive Church: "Many of them that believed came confessing and declaring their deeds."[757] Which manner of confessing to be very necessary, not only the holy laws of the Church[758] and the reverent writings of the fathers do confirm,[759] but also the divine words of Christ do conclude and declare, when he saith, "Whose sins you shall forgive, they are forgiven them. And whose you shall retain, they are retained."[760] But to remit and retain sins (whereas this is an office of a judge) no priest can have authority, except he first examine and know very perfectly the sinner's cause whereof he hath to judge. Neither can this knowledge be had, before that the party which committeth himself to be judged and absolved by the priest, as his judge[761] and physician, doth so discover and lay open his wounds in such distinct and several manner by

Do.; *De Paenit. Medic.*, Ch. 2; *Homily 50 ex 50*, Ch. 15; Fulgentius, *De Remissio Pecat.*, Bk. 1, Ch. 12

[754] Cf. Chrysostom, *Homily 42 on Matthew*

[755] Ps 31:5

[756] Cf. Origen, *Homily 1 on Psalm 37*; *Homily 2 on Leviticus*; Chrysostom, *On the Priesthood*, Bk. 3; Gregory of Nyssa, *Oration in eos qui in alios acerbius judicant*; Peter of Cluny, *De Miraculis*, Bk. 1, Ch. 3-6; Bk. 2, Ch. 32

[757] Acts 19:18

[758] Cf. Fourth Lateran Council, Const. 21; Council of Florence; Council of Trent, Session 14, "Doctrine on the Sacrament of Penance," Ch. 5

[759] Cf. Clement, *Epistle 1 ad Frat. Do.*; Dionysius, *Epistle 8 ad Demoph.*; Tertullian, *De Paenitentia*, Ch. 8-10, 12; Origen, *Homily 1 on Psalm 37*; *Homily 2 on Leviticus*; Cyprian, *On the Lapsed*; Pacian, *Paraenesi ad Paenit.*; Jerome, *On Ecclesiastes*, Ch. 10; Chrysostom, *Homily 30 on Genesis*; *Homily 16 on Matthew*

[760] Jn 20:23

[761] Cf. Augustine, *City of God*, Bk. 20, Ch. 9; Gregory the Great, *Homily 26 on the Gospels*; Chrysostom, *On the Priesthood*, Bk. 3; *Homily 5, De Verb. Esa.*; Jerome, *Epistle 14 to Heliodorus*, Ch. 7

voluntary confession, that the priest may plainly perceive where the sins are to be loosened, and where they are to be bound.[762]

113. What do the fathers write of confession?

They certes do with one consent not only commend and approve unto us the benefit of confession, and the perpetual practice of it in the Church, but the bond also and necessity thereof.

And to allege amongst very many a few, and those most approved witnesses. First, St. Basil the Great saith thus: "It is judged necessary that sins be confessed unto those to whom is committed the dispensation of the mysteries of God: for so the very penitents of ancient times are found to have confessed their sins unto holy men."[763]

Then, St. Cyprian: "I beseech you my brethren," saith he, "everyone to confess his sin, whilst yet he that sinneth remaineth in this world; whilst his confession may be admitted; whilst every man's satisfaction and remission given by the priests is acceptable unto our Lord."[764]

Hereunto accordeth the sentence of St. Augustine, who teacheth in this manner: "Do ye penance, such as is done in the Church, that the Church may pray for you. Let no man say within himself, 'I do it in secret, I do it before God alone: God who pardoneth me knoweth that I do in heart.' Was it therefore said in vain, 'Whatsoever you shall loose in earth shall be loosed in heaven'?[765] Were the keys given to the Church of God in vain? Do we frustrate the gospel of God? Do we frustrate the words of Christ? Do we promise you that which he denieth? Do we deceive you?"[766] And in another place: "There are," saith he, "that do think it sufficient for their salvation if they confess their sins to God alone, unto whom nothing is hidden, and every man's conscience lieth open. For they will not, or they

[762] Cf. Fourth Lateran Council, Const. 11; Council of Worms, Ch. 25; Origen, *Homily 1 on Psalm 37*; *Homily 2 on Psalm 37*

[763] Basil, *The Shorter Rules*, q. 288; Cf. Basil, *The Shorter Rules*, q. 229; *Epistle 3* can. ad Amphil. can. 73

[764] Cyprian, *On the Lapsed*, n. 29; Cf. Cyprian, *Epistle 10*; *Epistle 55*; *Homily 39 ex 50*, Ch. 3; *Homily 41*; *Homily 50*, Ch. 4-5

[765] Mt 18:18; Cf. Jn 20:23

[766] Augustine, *Sermon 392 ad Conjugatos*, n. 3

are ashamed, or they disdain to show themselves unto priests, whom yet our Lord hath by Moses ordained to discern between leper and leper.[767] But I will not have thee deceived with this opinion, and be ashamed thereby to confess them unto the vicegerent of our Lord, either languishing with the shamefastness, or stiff-necked with indignation. For of reason in like manner must we admit him for our judge, which our Lord doth not disdain to be his vicar."[768] And it is no less evident that Leo the Great hath left in writing: "The manifold mercies of God doth succor the falls of men, that not only by the grace of baptism, but also by the medicine of penance, the hope of life everlasting might be repaired: that they which had violated the benefit of regeneration, condemning themselves in their own judgment, might come to remission of sin; the succors of God's goodness being so ordained, that pardon cannot be had at God's hands, but by the supplication of priests. For the mediator of God and men, Christ Jesus,[769] hath given this power to prelates of the Church, that they might both admit unto penance those which confess, and receive them being purged with wholesome satisfaction, to the communion of the sacraments, by the gate of reconciliation."[770]

114. What ought we to think of satisfaction?

Truly thus much: that there is one kind of satisfaction proper unto Christ our Redeemer; and another common to all faithful penitents; that was once accomplished in the body of Christ crucified, when that immaculate Lamb took away the sins of the world;[771] that they which by nature were the sons of wrath, might be reconciled unto God; but this, which belongeth unto penitents, is done every day in the Church by the members of Christ, when being sorry for our sins, we do after confession perform those things which the priest, when he gave absolution, enjoined, or when of our own

---

[767] Cf. Lv 13:2; 14:2; Lk 17:14; Mt 8:4

[768] Augustine, *De Visit. Infirm.*, Bk. 2, Ch. 4

[769] Cf. 1 Tm 2:5

[770] Leo the Great, *Epistle 91 ad Theod.*; Cf. Leo the Great, *Epistle 80 ad Episc. Campaniae*

[771] Cf. Heb 9:22; Eph 5:2, 26; 4:32; 1 Jn 2:2; Jn 1:29

accord we do bring forth the worthy fruits of penance, whereby we may in some part at the least recompence the faults and offenses of our life past.[772]

This is a certain satisfaction both of revengement and of purgation; and it is so far from obscuring the benefit and satisfaction of Christ our Redeemer, that it doth more commend and set forth the same.[773] For that satisfaction of his going before, and especially cooperating with us, we do, according unto the scripture, use judgment and justice, taking revengement upon ourselves for our sins, and cleansing the relics of sin that remain in us; procuring and deserving for ourselves the more plentiful grace of God; finally, professing by these means that we do willingly embrace the cross of Christ,[774] deny ourselves, mortify our flesh, and being stricken with a hatred of old Adam in us, do endeavor to perfection, whilst we do with fervent zeal and courage strive against the motions of a depraved mind.[775] After this sort did holy David, the Ninevites, and others give themselves to satisfaction, whom it is manifest to have done penance in sackcloth, ashes, sighing, mourning, fasting, and other afflictions; and they are read to have been grateful and approved unto God therefore.[776] And this part of penance the scripture confirming and commending unto us crieth out: "Turn ye to me with all your heart, in fasting, in weeping, and lamentation."[777] And in another place: "Convert and do penance for all your iniquities: and iniquity shall not be unto you in destruction."[778] And St. Paul teacheth

---

[772] Cf. Eph 2:3; 2 Cor 5:18; Cyprian, *Epistle 59*; *Epistle 10*; Tertullian, *De Paenitentia*, Ch. 5, 7-9; Council of Trent, Session 14, "Doctrine on the Sacrament of Penance," Ch. 8-9

[773] Cf. Ex 32:3; Nm 12:9; 14:19, 27; 20:10, 24; Ps 98:6, 8; 2 Kgs 12:7, 13; Augustine, *On Merit and the Forgiveness of Sins, and the Baptism of Infants*, Bk. 2, Ch. 34; *Contra Faustum*, Bk. 2, Ch. 67; Gregory the Great, *Moralia in Job*, Bk. 9, Ch. 27; 2 Kgs 24; Prv 11:31; Eccles 5:2; Augustine, *Tractate 124 on John*

[774] Cf. Chrysostom, *Homily 80 ad Pop.*; Is 56:1; Ez 18:21, 27; Jer 2:3; 2 Cor 7:9; Ps 50:1, 6; Chrysostom, *On Isaiah*, Ch. 56; *On Matthew*, Ch. 3

[775] Cf. Lk 9:23; Mt 16:24; Rom 6:2, 6; Eph 4:22; Col 3:5

[776] Cf. 2 Kgs 12:13; 1 Par 21:16; Ps 34:13; 98:11; Jon 3:5; 3 Kgs 21:27; 1 Mc 2:14; 3:47; 2 Mc 3:20; Mt 11:21; Lk 6:13; Jdt 4:8, 16; 7:4; 8:5; 9:1; Jl 2:12; Dn 9:3; Jb 42:6; Jer 6:26; 4:8; 25:34; 48:37; 49:3; Ez 7:18; Lam 2:10

[777] Jl 2:12

[778] Ez 18:30

also that the sadness which is according to God doth work penance.[779] And he giveth a general admonition that: "If we did judge ourselves, we should not be judged of our Lord."[780]

And for that cause we shall not need to discourse of the name of satisfaction, which certes in the fathers is very familiar, seeing that the thing itself is expressly set down in holy scripture.[781]

115. **Let us see some sentences of the fathers touching satisfaction.**

Saint Cyprian, that most holy martyr, teacheth in this manner: "Look how much Almighty God is prone to pardon by the piety of a Father, so much is he to be feared by the majesty of a judge. Let a deep wound have diligent and long physic. Let not the penance be less than the fault: we must pray more earnestly; pass over the day in lamenting; the nights in watching and weeping; spend the whole time in mournful tears; lie upon the ground in ashes; and wallow in sackcloth and filth."[782] And again the same: "God is to be beseeched and to be pacified with our satisfaction; our sins must be pondered; our actions and secret intentions surveyed; and the deserts of our conscience weighed."[783] And a little after: "The way of penance which the priests showeth us, let us embrace: let us use the vital remedies which he taketh out of heavenly scriptures, and laying open the burden of our conscience before him, let us demand the wholesome medicine for those secret wounds which we have confessed. And let us not cease to do penance, and call upon the mercy of our Lord; lest that which seemeth but little in the quality of the sin be augmented by the negligence of satisfaction."[784]

And Saint Augustine hath said very plainly: "That it is not sufficient for a man to amend his manners and to leave his misdeeds; unless by the sorrow of penance, by the sighings of humility, and by the sacrifice of a

---

[779] Cf. 2 Cor 7:9

[780] 1 Cor 11:31

[781] Cf. Gregory the Great, *On 1 Kings*, Ch. 9; Basil, *The Shorter Rules*, q. 12

[782] Cyprian, *On the Lapsed*, n. 35; Cf. Cyprian, *Epistle 55 to Cornelius*; *Epistle 10 ad Clerum*

[783] Cyprian, *On the Lapsed*, n. 21; Cf. Cyprian, *De Eleemosynis*

[784] Cyprian, *On the Lapsed*, n. 28

contrite heart, together with the cooperation of alms, satisfaction be made to God for those things also that have been committed."[785]

Then in St. Jerome we find it thus written: "The body is to be afflicted which hath spent much time in delicacy; long laughter must be recompensed with continual weeping; the soft linen and precious silks must be changed into the sharpness of haircloth."[786]

To this end also is this speech of St. Ambrose: "He that doth penance ought not only to wash away his sin with tears; but also to cover his faults with more reformed actions, that sin may not be imputed unto him."[787] And again in another place: "For a great wound, a deep and long medicine is necessary. Great wickedness must of necessity have great satisfaction."[788]

Finally, so saith St. Gregory: "It is to be seriously thought and considered: that he which knoweth himself to have committed things unlawful must endeavor to abstain from some things that are lawful; that thereby he may make satisfaction unto his Creator."[789]

116. Is there any place for satisfaction after death?

For the explication of this point, we must consider the diverse estates of them that die. For some of them do keep the grace of God and innocency of life, even to their end. Unto whom appertaineth that saying of Manasses, that, "Unto just persons and those which have not sinned, as Abraham, Isaac, and Jacob, penance was not ordained."[790] Others have sinned indeed, and fallen from the grace of God which once they received, but they have purged in this life the filth of their sins with the worthy works of penance:

---

[785] Augustine, Homily 50, Ch. 5; Cf. Augustine, Enchiridion, Ch. 70-71, 65

[786] Jerome, Epistle 108, "Epitaph for Paula," n. 15; Cf. Chrysostom, Homily 10 on Matthew

[787] Ambrose, On Repentance, Bk. 2, Ch. 5; Bk. 1, Ch. 16

[788] Ambrose, De Lapsu Virginis Consecratae, Ch. 8; On Repentance, Ch. 2

[789] Gregory the Great, Homily 34 on the Gospels; Cf. Eusebius of Emesa, Ad Mon., Homily 5 and 10; Theodoret, In epit. divinor. decret. cap. De paenit.; Haereticarum Fabularum Compendium, de Audianis

[790] Prayer of Manasses

David,[791] Hezekiah,[792] St. Peter,[793] and St. Mary Magdalen.[794] Both these kinds have no need of satisfaction after death, but are altogether free from all bond thereof.

But far more in number are those of a middle sort, and yet not very evil, as St. Augustine showeth, who have not performed perfect penance for the sins in their lifetime,[795] and therefore are to be saved by fire; that, whatsoever was wanting of convenient satisfaction in this life may be paid unto God's justice in another.[796] "For there shall not enter any polluted thing into that city."[797]

Therefore, that we may answer to the question proposed: such kind of persons departed must abide some satisfaction, yea and that most painful, after their death. Which yet nevertheless God of his great mercy is wont to release by the devout intercession of those that are alive, that so they which are departed, being helped in the Church by the suffrages of their brethren and members, may be lightened of their sins and of the terrible pains due unto the same.[798] And hereunto belongeth that which the authority of holy scripture delivereth: "It is a holy and wholesome cogitation to pray for the dead, that they may be loosened from their sins."[799] Whereupon Judas the Maccabee was commended, for that being moved with a singular

---

[791] Cf. 2 Kgs 12:13; Ps 6:7

[792] Cf. Is 38:3

[793] Cf. Mt 26:57ff

[794] Cf. Lk 7:37

[795] Cf. Augustine, *Enchiridion*, Ch. 10; Bede, *On Proverbs*, Ch. 11

[796] Cf. 1 Cor 3:15. So doth St. Augustine expound this place: *On Psalm 37*; *City of God*, Bk. 21, Ch. 26; *De Fide et Operibus*, Ch. 16; *On Psalm 80*. So doth also Origen, *Homily 12 on Jeremias*; *Homily 13 on Jeremias*; *Homily 25 on Numbers*; *Homily 6 on Exodus*; Ambrose, *On 1 Corinthians*, Ch. 3; *On Psalm 118*, Sermon 20; Jerome, *On Amos*, Ch. 4; *On Isaias*, end of the last book; *Against Jovinianus*, Bk. 2, Ch. 13; Cf. also Gregory the Great, *Dialogues*, Bk. 4, Ch. 39; Bede, *On Luke*, Ch. 3

[797] Apoc 21:27; Cf. Ps 14:1; 23:3

[798] Cf. Augustine, *On Psalm 37*; *City of God*, Bk. 21, Ch. 26; *De Fide et Operibus*, Ch. 16; *On Psalm 80*; *City of God*, Bk. 21, Ch. 24; *Homily 16 ex 50*; *Sermon 41 de Sanctis.*; Gregory the Great, *Dialogues*, Bk. 4, Ch. 39; Bernard, *De Obitu Humberti*; John Damascene, *Oration De Defunct.*; Council of Florence; Council of Trent, Session 6, Can. 30; Session 25, Pt. 1

[799] 2 Mc 12:46; Cf. 1 Kgs 21:12; Bede, *On 1 Kings*, Ch. 21; 2 Kgs 1:12; 3:31; Tb 4:18; Ecclus 7:37; 17:18; 38:14; Jer 16:6; 2 Tm 1:17; 1 Jn 5:16

religious zeal, he did with great care and sumptuousness procure that not only prayers, but also sacrifice should be offered for the sins of the souls departed.[800]

In this doctrine do agree the reverend councils and fathers, which have delivered the true doctrine of the Church.[801] Of whom to allege one instead of many, and him a witness most worthy of credit, St. Augustine writeth thus: "In the books of the Machabees, we read sacrifice to have been offered for the dead. But although it were nowhere extant in the old scriptures, yet is the authority of the universal Church not small, whose practice in this behalf is most evident: where, in the prayers of the priests, which are made unto our Lord at his altar, the commendation also of those that are departed hath a peculiar place."[802] And again: "It is to be thought," saith he, "that there shall be no purgatory pains after that last and terrible judgment."[803] And what can be more plainly spoken than those words? "It is not to be doubted but that by the prayers of the holy Church, and by the most wholesome sacrifice, and by alms which are bestowed for their souls, those which are departed be helped, that our Lord may deal more mercifully with them than their sins have deserved. For this hath been delivered by the fathers, and the universal Church observeth: that for those which are departed in the communion of the body and blood of Christ, when their memory is made at the sacrifice in the due place, prayers also are poured out unto God; and it is expressly mentioned that the sacrifice

[800] Cf. 2 Mc 12:43-46
[801] Cf. Fourth Council of Carthage, Can. 79, 95; Eleventh Council of Toledo, Can. 12; Council of Tribur, Can. 31; First Council of Braga, Can. 34; Council of Florence; Council of Trent, Session 25; Session 22, "Doctrine on the Sacrifice of the Mass," Ch. 2; Can. 3
[802] Augustine, *On the Care of the Dead*, Ch. 1
[803] Augustine, *City of God*, Bk. 21, Ch. 16; Cf. Mt 12:32. Which place is expounded of remission of sins in the other world by prayers of the Church by St. Augustine, *City of God*, Bk. 21, Ch. 24; *Contra Julianum*, Bk. 6, Ch. 5; Gregory the Great, *Diaglogues*, Bk. 4, Ch. 39; Bede, *On Mark*, Ch. 3; Bernard, *Homily 66 on Canticle of Canticles*; Peter of Cluny, *Contra Petrobrusianos Hereticos*; Rabanus Maurus, *De Institutione Clericorum*, Bk. 2, Ch. 44; Cf. also Mt 5:26. Which place also is expounded of purgatory by Tertullian, *On the Soul*, Ch. 17; Cyprian, Bk. 4, Epistle 2; Origen, *Oration 35 on Luke*; *Epistle on Romans*; Eusebius of Emesa, *Homily 5 De Epiph.*; Ambrose, *On Luke*, Ch. 12; Jerome, *On Matthew*, Ch. 5; Bernard, *De Obitu Humberti*; Mal 3:3; Phil 2:10; Apoc 5:3-12

is offered for them. And when, for the helping of them, works of mercy are exercised, who may doubt but that they are available unto them, for whom prayers are not in vain offered? It is not at all to be doubted but these things do profit the dead, yet such only who lived so before death, that these things might be profitable to them after death."[804] Thus writeth St. Augustine above 1200 years agone; to omit many also more ancient than himself: St. Cyprian,[805] Origen,[806] St. Denis,[807] St. Clement,[808] who with one consent do all accord in this doctrine. Wherefore, St. Chrysostom doth in plain terms exhort, "both that we ourselves to our power do help them that are departed, and put others in mind also to pray and give alms for them. For it was not unadvisedly decreed by the apostles that in the dreadful mysteries, commemoration should be made of those that are departed. For they knew well that they should gain much, and reap no small commodity thereby."[809] Thus writeth St. Chrysostom.

Finally, this is that which to this day the holy Church, a faithful interpreter of the scriptures, hath taught against the Aerians,[810] that there is a certain purgatory, or emendatory fire,[811] as St. Augustine calleth it, in which the faithful souls departed in Christ must suffer and satisfy for the punishment of those sins for which wholly satisfaction was not made in this life by penance;[812] except, as Saint Augustine speaketh, they be relieved by the devotion of their friends that are alive.[813]

[804] Augustine, *Sermon 32, De Verbis Apostoli*, Ch. 1-2; Cf. Isidore, *De Ecclesiasticis Officiis*, Bk. 1, Ch. 18; Rabanus Maurus, *De Institutione Clericorum*, Bk. 2, Ch. 44

[805] Cf. Cyprian, *Epistle 52*; *Epistle 66*

[806] Cf. Origen, *Oration 35 on Luke*; *Epistle on Romans*

[807] Cf. Dionysius, *Ecclesiastical Hierarchy*, Ch. 7

[808] Cf. Clement, *Epistle 1*; *Apostolic Constitutions*, Bk. 6, Ch. 29

[809] Chrysostom, *Homily 3 on Philippians*; Cf. Chrysostom, *Homily 41 on 1 Corinthians*; *Homily 69 ad Pop.*; John Damascene, *Oration De Defunct.* Athanasius and Gregory of Nyssa apud John Damascene

[810] Cf. Epiphanius, *Adversus Haeresus*, n. 75; Augustine, *De Haeresibus*, n. 53; John Damascene, *De Haeresibus*

[811] Cf. Council of Trent, Session 24; Session 6; Council of Florence,

[812] Cf. Augustine, *On Psalm 37*; *De Genesi Contra Manichaeos*, Bk. 2, Ch. 20; Gregory the Great, *Expositio in Psalmos Poenitentiales*, third psalm; *Dialogues*, Bk. 4, Ch. 39; Bernard, *Sermon 66 on Canticle of Canticles*

[813] Cf. Augustine, *Enchiridion*, Ch. 29, n. 110; *On the Care of the Dead*, Ch. 1, 4, 18

117. What is the commendation and dignity of penance?

Penance is the beginning of the preaching of the gospel; the joy of angels in heaven; the strait way upon earth, and that narrow gate by which the faithful do travel toward life and lay violent hands upon the kingdom of heaven. She erecteth them that be fallen; cureth the wounded; strengtheneth the weak; quickeneth the dead; restoreth those that are lost; and finally, all things that sin doth impair, penance doth renew and refresh in us. By her we give a testimony of a hatred of our life past, of the contempt of ourselves, and of all submission.[814] She being our guide: we mourning, find comfort; being wounded, we are cured; being humble, we are exalted.[815] This is she whereby we overcome the devils and the pestilence of vice; we drive away deserved punishments; we pacify God's wrath; we purchase grace; and get glory everlasting.[816] Hereupon are those speeches of Christ in the gospel: "Do penance, for the kingdom of heaven is at hand."[817] "I came not to call the just, but sinners to penance."[818] "Unless you have penance, you shall likewise perish."[819] But he finally doth true penance, to conclude all these things with the words of St. Cyprian, "who, obeying the precepts of God and the priests, with his obedience and works of justice, doth win our Lord."[820]

Of the Sacrament of Extreme Unction

118. What ought to be our belief touching the sacrament of extreme unction?

That certes which the Catholic Church doth constantly teach, to wit: that this is a sacred sign, ordained in consecrated oil, that hereby heavenly

---

[814] Cf. Augustine, *De Vera et Falsa Poenit.*, Ch. 1; Basil, *De Ver. Paenit.*; Chrysostom, *Homily and Sermon, De Paenit.*

[815] Cf. Mt 5:5

[816] Cf. Jer 18:8; Ez 18:21; 33:11; Jon 3; Mt 3:6; 2 Cor 7:10; Acts 11:18

[817] Mt 4:17

[818] Lk 5:32

[819] Lk 13:5

[820] Cyprian, *Epistle 14*; Cf. Mt 3:2; 4:17; Mk 1:4; Lk 5:7, 10; Mt 7:13; 11:12

virtue may by God's ordinance be applied unto sick persons, for the health not only of the souls, but of their bodies also.[821]

Unto which sacrament Saint James the apostle giveth most clear and evident testimony, forasmuch as he hath written these very words: "Is any man sick among you? Let him bring in the priests of the church, and let them pray over him, anointing him with oil in the name of our Lord. And the prayer of faith shall save the sick; and our Lord shall lift him up; and if he be in sins, they shall be remitted him."[822]

119. What doth the apostle teach by these words?

He showeth first of all that the element, or matter of this sacrament, is oil consecrated, as noteth well St. Bede, by the benediction of a bishop.[823] And it signifieth cheerfulness of mind and an internal strengthening which, through the grace of God, the sick man feeleth by the virtue of this sacrament.[824]

Then doth the same apostle set down the proper minister of this sacrament, to wit, a priest, who with prayer is decently to exercise this holy unction.[825] Neither was it without some signification of the minister of this sacrament written of the apostles, that: "They anointed with oil many sick, and healed them."[826]

[821] Cf. Council of Nicea ex Arab. Latinum factum, Can. 69; Council of Constance, Session 15; Council of Florence; Council of Trent, Session 14; Innocent I, *Epistle ad Decentium*, Ch. 8; Peter Damian, *Sermon 1, Dedicat. Eccles.*; Bernard, *Life of Malachy of Armagh*; Council of Worms, Can. 72; Council of Chalons, Ch. 48; Council of Meaux, apud Burchardus, Bk. 4, Can. 75; Council of Meaux, apud Ivonem, Pt. 1, Ch. 269; Second Council of Aix-la-Chapelle, Can. 8; Council of Mainz, under Rabano.; Alcuin, *De Offic.*, Ch. 12; Hugh of St. Victor, *De Sacramentis*, Pt. 15, Bk. 2, Ch. 2-3; Origen, *Homily 2 on Leviticus*; Chrysostom, *On the Priesthood*, Bk. 3; Augustine, *In Speculo*; *Sermon 215, De Temp.*
[822] Jas 5:14-15; Cf. Bede, *On James*
[823] Cf. Bede, *On Mark*, Ch. 16; *On Luke*, Ch. 8; *On James*, Ch. 5; Innocent I, *Epistle ad Decentium*, Ch. 8; Council of Meaux, apud Burchardus, Bk. 4, Can. 75; Council of Meaux, apud Ivonem, Pt. 1, Ch. 269
[824] Cf. Theophylactus, *On Mark*, Ch. 6
[825] Cf. Chrysostom, *On the Priesthood*, Bk. 3; Origen, *Homily 2 on Leviticus*
[826] Mk 6:13; Cf. Theophylactus, *On Mark*, Ch. 6; Bede, *On Mark*, Ch. 6

Furthermore, the parties that receive this sacrament are by Saint James called sick persons, because, as the manner and custom of the Church is, this holy unction is only celebrated in grievous and dangerous sicknesses.[827]

120. **What is the profit and effect of this sacrament?**

First, it availeth to remission of such sins as the sick person hath not already purged by the remedies of penance: that he may before all things be eased of the burden, and cured of the malady of his sins.[828]

Then profiteth it also, either to drive away or to assuage the infirmity of the body, so far forth as it is expedient for the sick person to be delivered of the same.[829]

Last of all, it is of force to minister comfort and confidence, of which certes there is special need in that last agony and departure; at what time the dying man must have very sore conflicts, both with most bitter pains, and also with most horrible fiends. Wherefore, although bodily health be not always hereby restored unto the sick person, who often chanceth to die after this unction received, yet a peculiar grace is given in this sacrament: to bear the force and troublesomeness of the disease more constantly, and to take death itself more easily.[830] And this is it, that by his apostles God hath promised: "The prayer of faith shall save the sick; and our Lord shall lift him up; and if he be in sins, they shall be remitted him."[831]

To the signifying certes of which effects, even the nature and native force of oil doth fully agree, Theophilacte showeth.[832] Wherefore it behooveth us exactly to observe that which St. Augustine doth most wholesomely admonish: "So often as any infirmity chanceth, let him that is sick receive the body and blood of Christ, and after that let him anoint his

---

[827] Cf. Peter of Cluny, *De Miraculis*, Bk. 1, Ch. 20; Bk. 2, Ch. 32

[828] Cf. Bernard, *Life of Malachy of Armagh*; Council of Trent, Session 14; Peter of Cluny, Bk. 6, Epistle 1

[829] Cf. Bernard, *Life of Malachy of Armagh*

[830] Cf. Cyril of Alexandria, *Oration, De Exitu Animae*; Gregory the Great, *Moralia in Job*, Bk. 2, Ch. 17-18; *Homily 39 on the Gospels*; John Climacus, grad. 6; Eusebius of Emesa, *Homily 1 ad Monat.*; Sulpicius Severus, *De Transitu S. Martini*

[831] Jas 5:15

[832] Cf. Theophylactus, *On Mark*, Ch. 6

body; that, that which is written may be accomplished in him: 'Is any man sick? Let him bring in the priests and let them pray over him, anointing him with oil in the name of our Lord. And the prayer of faith shall save the sick. And our Lord shall lift him up. And if he be in sins, they shall be remitted him.'"[833]

Of the Sacrament of Orders

121. **What is the sacrament of holy orders?**

It is that whereby a singular grace and spiritual power is given to some, that they may by open profession bear office in the Church.

This is the sacrament by which, as by a door, do necessarily enter the lawful dispensers of the mysteries and of the word of God, the ministers of Christ and his Church: as bishops, priests, deacons, finally, all those whosoever they be that do exercise functions in the Church orderly and with authority.[834]

For no man, as the scripture testifieth, taketh, or ought to take, "the honor to himself," to wit, of exercising the functions of the Church, "but he that is called of God as Aaron":[835] that is, unless he be consecrated by the sacrament of visible ordination;[836] and be by a bishop lawfully ordered, and sent to the work of some certain ministry, which in his degree he may exercise in the Church according to the laws of divine and apostolical tradition.[837]

---

[833] Augustine, *Sermon 215, De Temp.*; Jas 5:14-15; Cf. Augustine, *De Rect. Cathol. Convers.*; *De Visit. Infirm.*, Bk. 2, Ch. 4; *In Speculo*

[834] Cf. 1 Cor 4:1, Mal 2:7; 1 Tm 3:1; 5:17; Eph 4:11; 1 Cor 14:2, 19; 12:28

[835] Heb 5:4; Cf. Acts 1:24

[836] Cf. Cyprian, *Epistle 52*; Tertullian, *Prescription against Heretics*, Ch. 41; Fourth Lateran Council, Ch. 3; Innocent III, ad Metens. cap. cum. ex injuncto. Tit. de haer.

[837] Cf. Mt 10:1; Lk 9:1; Mk 16:15; Jn 20:21; 17:18; Acts 13:2; Ti 1:5; Cf. also Augustine, *Contra Epistolam Parmeniani*, Bk. 2, Ch. 13; *Of the Good of Marriage*, Ch. 24; *On Baptism, against the Donatists*, Bk. 1, Ch. 1; Leo the Great, *Epistle 81 ad Diosc.*; Gregory the Great, *On 1 Kings*, Ch. 10, 16; Gregory of Nyssa, *Oration, De Sanct. Bapt.*; Council of Florence; Council of Trent, Session 23; Ambrose, *On 1 Corinthians*, Ch. 12; Theoph., *On Luke*, Ch. 19; Peter of Cluny, Bk. 6, Epistle 1

122. **Are not all Christians priests alike?**

They may surely be so called in this sense: that, as priests are wont to exercise certain external sacrifices and sacred functions, so, as many as are regenerated in Christ,[838] may and ought daily to offer and diligently to exercise certain spiritual sacrifices, to wit: prayer, praises, thanksgivings, mortifying of the flesh, and others of like sort. So that for this cause they are said in holy scripture to be spiritual priests before God, and to offer up spiritual sacrifices.[839]

But if we take this name of priesthood properly: all indifferently are not priests, but those only unto whom the authority of the Church hath committed to be proper ministers of sacraments, and hath granted power and right to consecrate, offer, and distribute the Holy Eucharist, and both to remit and to retain the sins of men.[840] And of the priests and prelates of the new law, thus writeth Saint Paul: "The priests that rule well, let them be esteemed worthy of double honor, especially they that labor in the word and doctrine."[841] And this doubtless cannot appertain to women, whom the same apostle forbiddeth to teach in the Church, and biddeth to be silent;[842] neither can it concern the laity at all, whose part it is, after the manner of sheep,[843] to be fed, and not to feed; to be governed, not to prefer, but to submit and humble themselves unto their prelates, and to hear, observe, and do whatsoever they, sitting in the chair, shall say, whether they be good or evil, according as we read it commanded by the word of God.[844]

Wherefore, as in the Church triumphant there are angels different in order and power, who, with decent disposition, do faithfully execute and fulfill the

[838] Cf. Apoc 1:6; 5:10; 1 Pt 2:9

[839] Cf. 1 Pt 2:5; Rom 12:1; Ps 49:23; 50:19; Phil 4:18; Heb 13:15-16; Basil, *Sermon 2, De Baptismo*, Ch. 8; Augustine, *City of God*, Bk. 20, Ch. 10; Leo the Great, *Sermon 3, In Annivers. Pontificatus*; Ambrose, *On the Sacraments*, Bk. 4, Ch. 1

[840] Cf. Ignatius of Antioch, *Epistle to Hero*; Chrysostom, *On the Priesthood*, Bk. 3, 6; *Homily 60 ad Pop.*; Jerome, *Epistle 14 to Heliodorus*, Ch. 7; *Dialogue against the Luciferians*, Ch. 8; *Epistle 146 to Evagrius*; Victor., *De Persecutione Wandalica*, Bk. 2; Cyprian, *Epistle 54*

[841] 1 Tm 5:17

[842] Cf. 1 Tm 2:11; 1 Cor 4:34; Tertullian, *Prescription against Heretics*, Ch. 41; Epiphanius, *Adversus Haeresus*, n. 42, 40

[843] Cf. Leo the Great, *Epistle 2 ad Maxi.*

[844] Cf. Jn 10; 21:15; 1 Pt 5:2; 2:13; Heb 13:17; Rom 13:1; Mt 23:2; Lk 10:16; 1 Jn 4:6

offices imposed upon them;[845] so also the Church militant, which is the house of God and, as it were, a certain camp set in battle array, hath her peculiar ministers distinct from other Christians and disposed in godly order amongst themselves, for the prosecuting of the public and common functions of the Church upon earth, to wit, that for the benefit of the Christian people, they may even, by public profession and with due comeliness and majesty,[846] bestow their labors in those things which belong unto God and the health of souls.[847]

123. **In what place doth the scripture give testimony unto this sacrament?**
There truly where it teacheth of the apostles that, in choosing, appointing, and ordering of the ministers of the Church, they used imposition of hands.[848] For by this as by a certain and effectual token of present grace, which is exhibited and received in the giving of holy orders, is this sacrament which we speak of commended unto us.[849]

And therefore, St. Paul writing to Timothy, whom he had created bishop and admonishing him of the grace that he had received in this sacrament, doth speak in this manner: "Neglect not the grace that is in thee, which is given thee by prophecy, with imposition of the hands of priesthood."[850] And again, writing to the same bishop: "I admonish thee, that thou resuscitate the grace of God which is in thee, by the imposition of my hands."[851]

And, because it is very much material what kind of men be placed in every of the Church's functions, and do receive ecclesiastical power by means of this sacrament,[852] therefore, it is said to every bishop: "Impose hands on no man lightly, neither do thou communicate with other men's sins."[853]

---

[845] Cf. Col 1:6; Dn 7:10; Dionysius, *De Caelest. Hier.*, Ch. 10

[846] Cf. 1 Tm 1:15; Cant 6:9; Anacletus, *Epistle 1*; *Epistle 2*; *Epistle 3*; Isidore, *De Ecclesiasticis Officiis*, Bk. 2, Ch. 5ff

[847] Cf. Heb 5:1; 8:3; 13:17; 2 Cor 5:20

[848] Cf. Acts 6:6; 13:3; 14:22; 1 Tm 4:1, 14; 5:22; 2 Tm 1:6

[849] Cf. Ambrose, *De Dignitate Sacerdotali*, Ch. 5; Nicephorus, *Church History*, Bk. 12, Ch. 14

[850] 1 Tm 4:14; Cf. Theoph., *On 1 Timothy*, Ch. 4; Haymo, *On 1 Timothy*, Ch. 4

[851] 2 Tm 1:6; Cf. Theoph., *On 2 Timothy*, Ch. 1

[852] Cf. Leo the Great, *Epistle 87 ad Episc. Maur.*; Council of Rome under Sylvester, Ch. 11; Council of Trent, Session 23, "Decree on Reformation," Ch. 7, 12

[853] 1 Tm 5:22

124. How many degrees doth this sacrament contain in it?

It containeth, in general, lesser and greater orders: the lesser are four in number, to wit, of ostiaries, lectors, exorcists, and acolytes; and the greater are three, to wit, of subdeacons, deacons, and priests.[854] And of priests some are greater, some lesser known to be ordained by Christ.[855]

For the greater sort of priests are the apostles and bishops, their successors, excelling doubtless with a great power and reverend prerogative of dignity.[856] For it is their office (as the scripture testifieth) to take heed to themselves and to the whole flock, which they do receive of the Holy Ghost, to be cured and fed; to rule the Church; to reform the things that are wanting; and to ordain priests by cities.[857]

And the lesser sort of priests do attend in the ministry of the Church under bishops, as those seventy-two disciples did under the apostles;[858] do offer gifts and sacrifices for sins;[859] and are next unto the same bishops, as it were, workmen in our Lord's harvest.[860]

But the clerks of the four lesser orders have this proper office: to attend upon priests and bishops in many businesses and affairs; to dispose the people that do resort to holy things; and that they themselves, by little and little, as it were, by certain degrees, may be well informed and prepared to undertake greater offices in the Church.[861]

---

[854] Cf. Fourth Council of Carthage, Can. 6ff; Council of Laodicea, Can. 24; Council of Trent, Session 23; Ignatius of Antioch, *Epistle to the Antiochians*; Dionysius, *Ecclesiastical Hierarchy*, Ch. 3; Eusebius, *Ecclesiastical History*, Bk. 6, Ch. 35, ex epist. Corn.

[855] Cf. Lk 9:1; 10:1; Bede, *On Luke*, Ch. 9-10; Clement, *Epistle 1*; Anacletus, *Epistle 2*; *Epistle 3*

[856] Cf. Jerome, *Epistle 41 to Marcella*; Cyprian, *Epistle 69*; *Epistle 65*; Ignatius of Antioch, *Epistle to the Philadelphians*; Augustine, *On Psalm 44*

[857] Cf. Acts 20:28; 1 Pt 5:1; Heb 13:17; Ti 1:5; Acts 14:22

[858] Cf. Lk 10:1; Leo the Great, *Epistle 88 ad Episc. Gall.*; Innocent III, *De Myst. Altar.*, Bk. 1, Ch. 6

[859] Cf. Heb 5:1; 8:3

[860] Cf. Mt 9:37; Lk 10:2

[861] Cf. Fourth Council of Carthage, Can. 6ff; Isidore, *De Ecclesiasticis Officiis*, Bk. 2, Ch. 11ff; *Etymologiae*, Bk. 7, Ch. 12; Rabanus Maurus, *De Institutione Clericorum*, Bk. 1, Ch. 9ff; First Council of Aix-la-Chapelle under Ludovico Pio, Ch. 2ff; Council of Rome under Sylvester, Can. 3, 6, 9

But the other three greater orders do afford greater power, both in other things and in the holy mysteries of the Eucharist. Therefore, the subdeacon and deacon may be present at the said mysteries as ministers, and be next unto the priests themselves.[862] And although as touching the sacrament of orders and the authority of offering sacrifice, there be no difference between bishops and priests, yet are they more excellent and high than priests; if we consider the power and authority of governing the Church, of feeding souls, of confirming the baptized, and of ordering clerks.[863]

But it is not our intent at this present exactly to declare what functions and laws are prescribed to every particular order. Most certain it is that all orders are to be had in great estimation, and diligently to be kept and maintained. For most firm testimony is given unto the same by the holy discipline of the apostles' tradition and the Church's observance, which hath continued even unto this day.[864]

125. In what sort do the ancient fathers write of this sacrament?

Of this doth Saint Augustine, a doctor without doubt very Catholic, manifestly declare both his own and the Church's mind in these words: "In that, that our Lord is read to have breathed upon his disciples a few days after his resurrection, and to have said, 'Receive ye the Holy Ghost,'[865] ecclesiastical power is understood to have been given. For, because all things in the tradition of our Lord are done by the Holy Ghost, therefore, when a certain rule and form of this discipline is delivered unto them, it is said to them: 'Receive ye the Holy Ghost.' And because it appertaineth truly to ecclesiastical jurisdiction, he presently addeth, saying: 'Whose sins you retain shall be retained, and whose you remit, shall be remitted.'[866] Therefore, this inspiration, or breathing, is

---

[862] Cf. Fourth Council of Carthage, Can. 3ff; Isidore, *De Ecclesiasticis Officiis*, Bk. 2, Ch. 7; Rabanus Maurus, *De Institutione Clericorum*, Bk. 1, Ch. 6ff; Council of Aix-la-Chapelle, Ch. 6; Arator, *De Actibus Apostolorum*, Bk. 1, Ch. 13

[863] Cf. Damasus, *Epistle 4*; Isidore, *De Ecclesiasticis Officiis*, Bk. 2, Ch. 7; Jerome, *Dialogue against the Luciferians*, Ch. 4; Leo, *Epistle 88*; Second Council of Seville, Ch. 7; Epiphanius, *Adversus Haeresus*, n. 75, Aerianorum

[864] Cf. Ambrose, *On Ephesians*, Ch. 4

[865] Jn 20:22

[866] Jn 20:23

a certain grace which is infused by tradition onto those that receive orders, whereby they may be accounted more commendable. Whereupon the apostle saith to Timothy: 'Neglect not the grace which is in thee, which was given thee...by the imposition of hands of a priest.'[867] Therefore, once it ought to be done, that forever after this tradition might be thought not to be void of the gift of the Holy Ghost."[868] Hitherto St. Augustine.

There are extant also the *Canons of the Apostles*, in which it is thus decreed: "Let a bishop be created by two or three bishops; a priest by one bishop; so a deacon and others of the clergy."[869] Then a little after: "If any bishop, or priest, or deacon, or subdeacon, or lector, or chanter do not fast the holy Lent, or the Wednesday, or the Parasceve (which we now call Friday), let him be put out of orders; unless happily some infirmity of body do hinder him."[870]

And Caius, a famous pope and martyr, above 1300 years since, reckoneth up these degrees and orders, one after another, when he saith: "If any man shall deserve to be a bishop: first, let him be an ostiary, then a lector, afterward an exorcist. Then let him be consecrate an acolyte; after which, a subdeacon, deacon, and afterward priest. Finally, if he be worthy, let him be made bishop."[871]

Therefore, Saint Cyprian doth praise Cornelius the bishop, and writeth that he was commended and honorably spoken of by all good persons, as well of the clergy as of the people: "Because he came not suddenly to the bishopric, but having gone through all ecclesiastical offices, and often purchased favor at our Lord's hand, by divine services and administrations, he ascended to the high dignity of priesthood, by all the steps of religion. Then afterward, he never required the bishopric itself, nor desired it, nor violently usurped it; but being quiet, modest, chaste, humble, shamefast, and finally, even constrained, did undertake the same."[872]

---

[867] 1 Tm 4:14

[868] Augustine, *Quaestiones Vet. et Nov. Test.*, q. 93; Cf. *Contra Epistolam Parmeniani*, Bk. 2, Ch. 13

[869] *Canons of the Apostles*, Can. 1, 2

[870] *Canons of the Apostles*, Can. 68; Cf. canone in signes, dist. 59ff

[871] Caius, *Epistle ad Foelicem*; Cf. Damasus, *Pontificali de codem Caio*

[872] Cyprian, *Epistle 52*; Cf. Sozomen, *Epistle 1 to Hesychius*

Those orders therefore which the ancient and apostolical Church hath approved, as appeareth by the writings of Saint Denis,[873] Anaclete,[874] and Saint Jonatius;[875] and which also every age since hath embraced, those certes, the Church at this day cannot but conserve and defend.

126. What order in the Church is of greatest account?

The order of priests, or priesthood: of the wonderful and ever most reverend dignity, whereof St. Chrysostom and Saint Ambrose have set forth whole books. Of which also great Ignatius saith: "Priesthood is the sum of all honors which are amongst men; which if any man shall dishonor, he dishonoreth God and our Lord Jesus Christ, the first begotten of all creatures, and the only chief priest of God by nature."[876] Thus saith he. Yea it is evidently warranted by a divine oracle that, "the lips of the priest do keep knowledge, and they shall require that law at his mouth: because he is the angel of our Lord of hosts."[877] And again: "He that shall be proud, not willing to obey the authority of the priest who at that time doth minister to thy Lord God: let that man die by the decree of the judge, and thou shalt take away evil out of Israel, and all the people hearing will be afraid, that none from henceforward may swell with pride."[878] Hereupon also, the apostle willeth: "Against a priest, receive not accusation, but under two or three witnesses."[879] And this truly is written to Timothy, the bishop of the Ephesians, as that also which we cited before: "The priests that rule well, let them be esteemed worthy of double honor: especially they that labor in the word and doctrine."[880]

---

[873] Cf. Dionysius, *Ecclesiastical Hierarchy*, Ch. 5; *Epistle ad Demoph.*

[874] Cf. Anacletus, *Epistle 2*

[875] Cf. Jonatius, *Epistle ad Antiochensis*

[876] Ignatius of Antioch, *Epistle to the Smyraeans*; Cf. Chrysostom, *On the Priesthood*, Bk. 3; *Homily 4, De Verb. Esa. Vidi Dominum*; *Homily 5, De Verb. Esa. Vidi Dominum*

[877] Mal 2:7; Cf. Agg 2:12; Gregory the Great, *Pastoral Rule*, Bk. 2, Ch. 4

[878] Dt 17:12-13; Cf. Cyprian, *Epistle 55*; *Epistle 65*; Gregory the Great, Bk. 12, Epistle 31 ad Felicem

[879] 1 Tm 5:19; Cf. Fabian, *Epistle 2*

[880] 1 Tm 5:17

127. And what conception ought we to have of evil priests?

This is the ordinance of God, which cannot be abolished, that not only good but also evil priests be honored in the Church. For he will be acknowledged, received, heard, and observed in his ministers;[881] whereas he hath said: "Upon the chair of Moses have sitten the scribes and Pharisees. All things therefore whatsoever they shall say to you, observe ye, and do ye; but according to their works do you not, for they say and do not."[882] But amongst those that be evil, there is a choice to be made: that we may understand that, forasmuch as concerneth the office and authority of teaching, we do owe faith and obedience unto those only who, being lawfully ordained and sent by bishops, do profess the sound doctrine of the Church. But of others we must carefully beware, as of enemies and pestiferous persons.

Touching which matter the most ancient Irenaeus, most wisely admonisheth and teacheth in this manner: "We are bound to hear those that are priests in the Church, which both have succession from the apostles and have received the grace and Spirit of truth with this succession of bishop-like authority; but as for others, which depart from this principal succession: in what place soever they be gathered together, we must have them in suspicion, either as heretics and men of evil doctrine, or as sowers of schism and proud persons."[883] And a little after, "We must," saith he, "eschew all such, and cleave unto those who do keep (as we have said before) the apostolical doctrine, and do together with the order of priesthood, exhibit sound speech and conversation without offense, to the confirmation and correction of others."[884] Thus writeth that Irenaeus, whose master was Polycarp, the disciple of St. John the evangelist. And not unlike to this teacheth Tertullian, who doth exprobrate the heretics in this manner,

---

[881] Cf. Ecclus 7:31; Mt 10:40; Lk 10:16; Jn 22; Chrysostom, *Homily 2 on 2 Timothy*; *Homily 65 on Genesis*; Origen, *Homily 7 on Ezechiel*; Bernard, *Sermon 66 on Canticle of Canticles*; Augustine, *Epistle 137*; Eusebius apud John Damascene, *Sacra Parallela*, Bk. 3, Ch. 45

[882] Mt 23:2-3; Cf. Augustine, *Sermon 49, De Verbis Domini*, Ch. 5ff; Chrysostom, *Homily 85 on John*

[883] Irenaeus, *Against Heresies*, Bk. 4, Ch. 43; Cf. Irenaeus, *Against Heresies*, Bk. 3, Ch. 2-3

[884] Irenaeus, *Against Heresies*, Bk. 4, Ch. 44

saying: "Their ordinations are rash, light, and inconstant; sometimes they place Neophites, sometimes those that are tied to the world, sometimes even our apostates, that they may bind them with glory, whereas they cannot with truth. There is never more easy preferment than in the camps of rebels: where the very being is deserving. Therefore, one is a bishop today and another tomorrow; today he is a deacon, who tomorrow is a lector; today he is a priest, who tomorrow is a layman; for even unto laymen do they enjoin priestly offices."[885] Thus far Tertulian, very lively painting out unto us the perverse customs, not of his own time only, but of this our age also; and showing the preposterous endeavors of sectaries, in the disturbing of holy things and ordering of ministers.[886]

128. What is the virtue and effect of this sacrament?

The virtue certes is singular, and the effects are manifold. For they, which rightly receive these seven orders which we speak of, do also receive a spiritual grace and power, that they may wholesomely execute of such things as do appertain to the proper functions of their orders, and are appointed fit ministers between God and his people.[887] Whereupon St. Ambrose saith: "A man that is placed in the order of an ecclesiastical office hath grace, whatsoever he be; not truly of himself, but of his order, by the operation of the Holy Ghost."[888]

Furthermore, the said parties that receive orders have thereby a certain and evident testimony, whereby they may commend and approve both themselves and their ministries also unto others.[889]

And so it cometh to pass that they, being, as it were, marked with those orders, and being separated unto the ministry of the Church, are well known and esteemed according to their degree, and very worthily honored. But woe be to them whom not the example of Aaron, that was called by

---

[885] Tertullian, *Prescription against Heretics*, Ch. 41
[886] Cf. Epiphanius, *Adversus Haeresus*, n. 24, 49
[887] Cf. Council of Florence; Council of Trent; Augustine, *Contra Epistolam Parmeniani*, Bk. 2, Ch. 13; Gregory the Great, *On 1 Kings*, Ch. 10
[888] Ambrose, *On 1 Corinthians*, Ch. 12
[889] Cf. Acts 6:6, 8, 10; 13:2; 14:20; 15:2, 41; 1 Tm 4:14; Ti 1:5; Cyprian, *Epistle 76*

God, doth induce; but seditious humors and swelling of the mind, like unto Uzziah the king, doth carry headlong to the occupying and usurping,[890] by whatsoever means the offices of priestly dignity, upon whom this speech of God doth fitly fall: "I did not send prophets, and they did run. I did not speak to them, and they did prophesy."[891] And these, the scripture warneth us not to account as ministers of the Church, but to eschew as thieves, robbers, foxes, dogs, and wolves because they do not enter in by the door,[892] but either of their own rashness, or for the favor only of some civil magistrate, or the popular multitude,[893] they assume unto themselves ecclesiastical offices, seizing upon those holy functions,[894] without any lawful calling and ordering: "But how shall they preach unless they be sent?"[895] as St. Paul, being one himself that was separated unto the work, doth say.[896]

Doubtless, order being once broken, and priesthood taken away, the hierarchy and princely disposition of the Church, consisting as well of priests and other ministers, as also of bishops rightly ordered, would come to decay.[897] Neither should the Church be that which it is called, a camp set in battle array;[898] nor the true and lawful ministers of the Church should be discerned; the office and authority of teaching would become contemptible; the dispensation of the sacraments would be unfaithfully and preposterously performed, yea and altogether frustrate; finally, the functions of the Church would be perturbed; and (as the proof itself too much doth show) new and false doctrines would increase and swarm by the means of these new and false ministers of Christ his spouse: whereby the Church would often be shaken with sore and deadly commotions, as we in our days feel by experience. And for that cause the apostle Saint Paul hath not only set

[890] Cf. Nm 16:31; Heb 5:4; 1 Par 13:10; 2 Kgs 6:6; 2 Par 26:16

[891] Jer 23:21; 14:14; 27:15; 29:9

[892] Cf. Jn 10:1ff; Cant 2:15; Acts 20:29; Mt 7:15

[893] Cf. Council of Trent, Session 23, "Doctrine Touching the Sacrament of Order," Ch. 4

[894] Cf. Council of Laodicea

[895] Rom 10:15

[896] Cf. Acts 13:2

[897] Cf. Leo the Great, *Epistle 87 ad Episc. Afr.*; Gregory the Great, Bk. 4, Epistle 52; Dionysius, *Ecclesiastical Hierarchy*, Ch. 5

[898] Cf. Cant 6:9

down diverse degrees of ministers in the Church,[899] but hath also showed how wholesome and necessary they be, insomuch that he affirmeth that they were given by God unto the Church, (as it hath been said before): "To the consummation of saints, unto the work of the ministry, unto the edifying of the body of Christ...That now we be not children wavering and carried about with every wind of doctrine, in the wickedness of men, in craftiness to the circumvention of error."[900]

And certes, this is a most evident and sure note of the Church: in that we see that perpetual, and never as yet, at any time interrupted succession of bishops, and of lawful orders in the same, which God hath placed therein for the perfect government of this his kingdom. And therefore, this institution of ministers, as a most firm knitting together of the Church and a most precious bond to preserve unity, is the more carefully to be retained, and even in the evil ministers of the Church (as we said before) because of God's ordinance is ever to be honored.[901] Which St. Augustine, well understanding, saith: "Into that order of bishops, which is derived from Peter himself, even to Anastasius, who now sitteth in the same chair; if any traitor had in those days crept in, it had been nothing prejudicial unto the Church, and unto innocent Christians: for whom our Lord was so careful and provident, that he saith of evil prelates, 'Whatsoever they say, do ye; but according to their works, do ye not.'"[902] Thus far St Augustine.

---

[899] Cf. 1 Cor 12:28

[900] Eph 4:12, 14

[901] Cf. Irenaeus, *Against Heresies*, Bk. 3, Ch. 3; Bk. 4, Ch. 43; Optatus of Milevis, *Against the Donatists*, Bk. 2; Augustine, *Epistle 165*; *Epistle 42*; *Against the Fundamental Epistle of Manichaeus*, Ch. 4; *Psalmus contra Partem Donati*; Tertullian, *Prescription against Heretics*, Ch. 36

[902] Augustine, *Epistle 165*; Mt 23:3; Cf. Augustine, *Answer to Petilian the Donatist*, Bk. 2, Ch. 51

Of the Sacrament of Matrimony

129. **What is matrimony?**

Matrimony is a lawful conjunction of a man and a woman instituted by God, that they may lead together an undivided society of life.[903] I say, "lawful," that there may be mutual consent of both parts,[904] and that there be not found between them the degrees, as they call them, of consanguinity and affinity, and other things of the like sort, either prohibiting, or disanulling matrimony.[905] Of which matrimonial conjunction, if thou wouldst know the first author, it is God himself, most excellent and mighty, who joined the first couple and parents of mankind in paradise itself, and honored them with his benediction.[906] But if thou regard the end why it was instituted, it is no other but: the propagation of mankind to the glory of God;[907] and a familiar and faithful living together of man and wife;[908] and finally, the avoiding of fornication, in this imbecility of a corrupted nature.[909]

130. **How is matrimony a sacrament?**

In that the most strait conjunction which is between man and wife is a holy and convenient sign ordained by God, whereby is signified the most holy and firm conjunction of Christ the bridegroom and the Church his spouse.[910] This very sign profiteth unto Christian couples to receive the

[903] Cf. Augustine, *De Fide et Operibus*, Ch. 7; *On Marriage and Concupiscence*, Bk. 1, Ch. 10, 21; *Of the Good of Marriage*, Ch. 24; Ambrose, *On Ephesians*, Ch. 5; Peter Damian, *Sermon 1, Ded. Lucius 3*. in 5. decret. tit. 7. c. 9; Council of Constance, Session 15, Art. 8; Council of Trent, Session 24, Can. 1

[904] Cf. Gn 24:57; Tb 7:15; Ambrose, *De Institutione Virginis*, Ch. 6

[905] Cf. Calixtus I, *Epistle 2*; Fourth Lateran Council, Const. 50; Council of Trent, Session 24, Can. 3-4; "Decree on the Reformation of Marriage," Ch. 2ff

[906] Cf. Gn 2:23; Mt 19:6; 1 Cor 7:10; Eph 5:21

[907] Cf. Gn 2:23; Fulgentius, *Epistle 1*, Ch. 3; Isidore, *De Ecclesiasticis Officiis*, Bk. 2, Ch. 19

[908] Cf. Chrysostom, *Homily 20 on the Ephesians*, in morali exhort.; *Homily 5 on 1 Thessalonians*

[909] Cf. 1 Cor 7:9-10; Augustine, *De Genesi ad Litteram*, Bk. 9, Ch. 7; Chrysostom, *On Psalm 43*; *Homily 3, De Verb. Esa. Vidi Dominum*

[910] Cf. Ambrose, *On Ephesians*, Ch. 5; Augustine, *De Genesi ad Litteram*, Bk. 9, Ch. 7; Isidore, *De Ecclesiasticis Officiis*, Bk. 2, Ch. 19; Council of Florence; Council of Trent, Session 24, "Doctrine on the Sacrament of Marriage"

grace of God, when they do rightly enterprise matrimony.[911] Which grace maketh perfect natural love, and confirmeth an indissoluble unity between them, and sanctifieth them,[912] that they may not only be and abide two in one flesh according to their vocation, but ever preserve mutual fidelity, peace, love, and singular concord.[913] And so that is accomplished in them, which the apostle teacheth: "Marriage honorable in all, and the bed undefiled."[914]

Wherefore the same apostle St. Paul, where he handleth the mystery of such conjunction, saith plainly: "This is a great sacrament: but I speak in Christ and in the church."[915] So also St. Augustine: "Not only," saith he, "fruitfulness, the profit whereof consisteth in issue; not only chastity, whose band is fidelity; but also a certain sacrament of marriage is commended unto faithful couples. Whereupon the apostle saith, 'Husbands love your wives as Christ also loved the church.'"[916] And again, the same holy father: "In marriage, of more value is the holiness of the sacrament, than the fruitfulness of the womb."[917]

131. **Can matrimony ever be dissolved?**

That matrimony cannot be dissolved, but that the bond thereof is perpetual, those words of the first man Adam do declare: "A man shall leave his father and mother and shall cleave to his wife, and they two shall be in one flesh."[918] Which thing Christ also confirmed, when he repeated the words of Adam, even as the words of God himself, adding this also: "That which God hath joined together, let not man separate."[919] And in another

[911] Cf. Tb 3:16; 6:16; 8:9; Evaristus, *Epistle 1*; Council of Trent, Session 24, "Decree on the Reformation of Marriage," Ch. 1
[912] Cf. Chrysostom, *Homily 20 on Ephesians*; Ambrose, *On Abraham*, Bk. 1, Ch. 7
[913] Cf. Gn 2:24
[914] Heb 13:4; Cf. Fulgentius, *Epistle 2*, Ch. 5
[915] Eph 5:32; Ambrose, *On Ephesians*, Ch. 5; Leo the Great, *Epistle 92 ad Rust.*
[916] Augustine, *On Marriage and Concupiscence*, Bk. 1, Ch. 10, 21; Eph 5:25
[917] Augustine, *Of the Good of Marriage*, Ch. 18
[918] Gn 2:24
[919] Mt 19:5; Mk 10:7-8; Cf. Origen, *Tractate 7 on Matthew*

place he teacheth: "Everyone that dismisseth his wife and marrieth another committeth adultery; and he that marrieth her that is dismissed from her husband, committeth adultery."[920] Moreover, St. Paul, setting forth this law of God, and inviolable ordinance touching the perpetual firmness of the knot of wedlock, saith: "To them that be joined in matrimony, not I give commandment, but our Lord: that the wife depart not from her husband; and if she depart, to remain unmarried, or to be reconciled to her husband. And let not the husband put away his wife."[921] And afterward, he addeth: "A woman is bound to the law, so long time as her husband liveth."[922]

Therefore, even although there be no hope at all of any issue, and never so many discommodities of life and hard chances do fall out, yet matrimony once contracted standeth in force, and is so firm and sure, especially if it be consummate, that so long as life lasteth, it can never be dissolved. And for that cause, one party cannot wholly be divorced from the other,[923] unless happily it be, (before any carnal copulation had between them) for to take in hand some rule of religious life.[924] But where certain causes do occur, for which sometimes married folks may be separated, the band is not therefore broken, but the community of the bed and cohabitation, which was before, is hindered.[925] The cause whereof, we say, doth consist in Christ himself who hath joined and linked unto himself with a special, perpetual, and most inseparable union the Church, his only spouse and ever most dear unto him.[926] And not only this same conjunction, which is between man and wife, hath such firmness of a matrimonial bond, but it doth also utterly exclude all polygamy (that is, to wit:) that divers women

[920] Lk 16:18; Mk 10:11-12; Cf. Rom 7:2; *Apostolic Canons*, Can. 48; Ambrose, *On Luke*, Ch. 16
[921] 1 Cor 7:10-11; Augustine, *De Conjugiis Adulterinis*, Bk. 2, Ch. 5, 9; *Homily 49 ex 50*, Ch. 2; Council of Milevi, Can. 17
[922] 1 Cor 7:39; Rom 7:2
[923] Cf. Augustine, *Of the Good of Marriage*, Ch. 7, 15, 18, 24; Jerome, *Epistle 77, to Oceanus on the Death of Fabiola*, Ch. 1; Isidore, *De Ecclesiasticis Officiis*, Bk. 2, Ch. 19
[924] Cf. Decret. Bk. 3. tit. 32. Ch. 2, 14; Council of Trent, Session 24, Can. 6
[925] Cf. Council of Florence; Council of Trent, Session 24, Can. 7, 8; Augustine, *De Conjugiis Adulterinis*, Bk. 1, Ch. 11
[926] Cf. Eph 5:22, 32; Cant 5:1-2, 9

do not marry to one man, or one woman be espoused to divers husbands.[927] Wherefore Christ, to the intent that he might both more firmly establish and reduce matrimony to that more pure and primitive estate, which it had at the beginning, very significantly hath said: "They two shall be in one flesh."[928] And again: "Now are they not two but one flesh."[929]

132. Is matrimony permitted to everyone?

No surely, for the holy apostles have delivered, as Epiphanius saith, that it is a sin to turn unto marriage, after virginity once decreed and established by vow.[930] And St. Jerome affirmeth it to be such and so great a sin, that he saith, that virgins that marry after consecration, they are not so much adulteresses, as incestuous persons.[931] And St. Augustine saith: "A virgin, which if she had married had not sinned; being once a nun, if she marry, shall be reputed an adulteress from Christ. For she hath looked back from the place, unto which she came before."[932]

Therefore, that which the apostle saith: "It is better to marry than to be burnt,"[933] as St. Ambrose doth learnedly declare, "appertaineth to her that is not yet promised; to her that hath not as yet received the veil. But she that hath espoused herself to God, and hath received the holy veil, she is now married; she is now joined to an immortal husband. And if now she will marry, according to the common law of wedlock, she committeth adultery, she becometh the handmaid of death."[934] Thus writeth St. Ambrose.

---

[927] Cf. Isidore, *De Ecclesiasticis Officiis*, Bk. 3, Ch. 19; Council of Trent, Session 24, Can. 2

[928] Gn 2:24; Mt 19:5

[929] Mk 10:8

[930] Cf. Epiphanius, *Adversus Haeresus*, n. 61 contra Apostolicos

[931] Cf. Jerome, *Against Jovinianus*, Bk. 2, Ch. 7; Basil, *De Virginitate*; *De Lapsu Virginis Consecratae*

[932] Augustine, *On Psalm 83*, n. 4; Cf. Augustine, *On Psalm 75*; *Of the Good of Widowhood*, Ch. 8-9, 11; Oecumenius, *On 1 Corinthians*, Ch. 7; Cyprian, *Epistle 62*; Chrysostom, *De Virginitate*, Ch. 39; Fulgentius, *Epistle 1*, Ch. 6-7

[933] 1 Cor 7:9

[934] Ambrose, *De Lapsu Virginis Consecratae*, Ch. 5, n. 21; Cf. Jerome, *Against Jovinianus*, Bk. 1, Ch. 7; Augustine, *De Conjugiis Adulterinis*, Bk. 8, Ch. 15; *Of the Good of Widowhood*, Ch. 8; Oecumenius, *On 1 Corinthians*, Ch. 7; Isidore, *De Ecclesiasticis Officiis*, Bk. 2, Ch. 17; Leo the Great, *Epistle 92 ad Rust.*, Ch. 14

Wherefore that was a very worthy decree of Jovinian the emperor, and put into the Codex by the emperor Justinian:[935] "If any man dare presume, I will not say to ravish, but even to assail by enticements, holy virgins for to marry them: let him be punished with death."[936]

Now the same reason in every respect, and the same judgment standeth in force concerning monks,[937] and those that have received holy orders.[938] For they have damnation, if, letting loose the bridle to licentiousness, they frustrate or (as the apostle speaketh) "make void their first faith"[939] given to God and to the Church. Who have voluntarily barred themselves of wedlock, either expressly by vow, binding themselves to the observance of a sole and single life; or by taking of holy orders, at the least virtually and in effect approving and protesting the same.[940]

Let them therefore give ear unto the word of God: "If thou hast vowed anything to God, delay not to perform."[941] And, "Whatsoever thou hast vowed, do thou perform."[942] Then in another place: "Vow ye, and pay your vows to your Lord God."[943] Yea and Christ himself teacheth: "No man putting his hand to the plough and looking back is apt for the kingdom of God."[944]

---

[935] Cf. Sozomen, *Church History*, Bk. 6, Ch. 3; Nicephorus, *Church History*, Bk. 10, Ch. 39

[936] L. Si quis. C. de Sanct. Episc. et Cler. Second Council of Tours, Can. 21

[937] Cf. Basil, q. 14 diff. expl.; *Sermon 1, De Instit.*; *Constitutiones Monasticarum*, Ch. 22; *Epistle ad Monachum Lapsum*; Chrysostom, *Epistle 6 to Theodore after His Fall*; Leo the Great, *Epistle 92 ad Rust.*, Ch. 3, 14-15; Augustine, *On Psalm 75*; *Sermon 1, De Commun. Vita Cler.*, Ch. 4; Council of Chalcedon, Ch. 16

[938] Cf. Epiphanius, *Adversus Haeresus*, n. 59; in compend. doctr.; Jerome, *Against Jovinianus*, Bk. 1, Ch. 19; *Against Vigilantius*, Ch. 1; Augustine, *De Conjugiis Adulterinis*, Bk. 2, Ch. 20; Fulgentius, *Letter to Peter on the Faith*, Ch. 3; Gregory the Great, Bk. 3, Epistle 34; Leo the Great, *Epistle 92 ad Rust.*, Ch. 3; *Epistle 84*, Ch. 4; Bernard, *Sermon 65 on Canticle of Canticles*; Council of Trent, Session 24, Can. 9

[939] 1 Tm 5:12; Cf. Fourth Council of Carthage, Can. 104; Augustine, *Of the Good of Widowhood*, Ch. 8-9; Isidore, *De Ecclesiasticis Officiis*, Bk. 2, Ch. 18

[940] Cf. 6. Decret. Bk. 3. tit. 15.

[941] Eccles 5:3

[942] Ibid.; Cf. Dt 23:21

[943] Ps 75:12

[944] Lk 9:62; Cf. Bernard, *Epistle 2 ad Fulconen.*; Anselm, *Epistle 4*

133. Doth the Church therefore compel any to live single?

She truly being a most kind and careful mother constraineth not: as binding no man by law to live single, but of those that have of their own accord received that law (as hath been said), she requireth that they do not break religion, nor violate and cut off that covenant which they have religiously made with Christ and his Church.[945]

Therefore, are they justly urged to stand to their promises, and to keep that evangelical counsel which they have once firmly embraced; whereof St. Paul saith: "And he that joineth his virgin in matrimony, doth well (to wit, so long as she is not bound with the vow of single life[946]), and he that joineth not, doth better."[947] And again: "It is good for a man not to touch a woman."[948] For which cause, the evangelical eunuchs,[949] or as Tertullian calleth them, *voluntarii spadones*,[950] that have cut themselves for the kingdom of heaven:[951] that they may be "holy in body and spirit,"[952] in flesh, and yet without flesh, warfaring unto God, are both commended by Christ and have always been highly commended in the Church. And in this matter is a double error that we have to take heed of. The one is of those men which with Jovinian do so extol matrimony that they either match,[953] or prefer this estate before single life or virginity;[954] whereas St. Paul certes, and all the fathers do evidently affirm the contrary.[955] Another is of those which cavil that continency and single-life can hardly be performed by

[945] Cf. Bede, *De Tabern.*, Bk. 2, Ch. 9; *On Luke*, Ch. 1; Jerome, *On Titus*, Ch. 1; *Apology* for his books *Against Jovinian*, Ch. 3, 8; Origen, *Homily 23 on Numbers*; Ambrose, *Epistle 82*; *On the Duties of the Clergy*, Bk. 1, Ch. 50; Eusebius, *Demonstratio Evangelica*, Bk. 1, Ch. 9; *Canones dist.* 28, 82

[946] Cf. Theoph., *On 1 Corinthians*, Ch. 7; Jerome, *Against Jovinianus*, Bk. 1, Ch. 7; Gregory the Great, *On 1 Kings*, Ch. 15; Epiphanius, *Adversus Haeresus*, n. 61

[947] 1 Cor 7:38

[948] 1 Cor 7:1

[949] Cf. Mt 19:12

[950] Tertullian, *Ad Uxorem*, Bk. 1, Ch. 6

[951] Cf. Is 56:3; Jerome, *On Isaiah*, Ch. 56; Basil, *De Virginitate*; Augustine, *Of Holy Virginity*, Ch. 24-25

[952] 1 Cor 7:34

[953] Cf. Jerome, *Against Jovinianus*, Bk. 1, Ch. 2; Augustine, *De Haeresibus*, n. 82

[954] Cf. Council of Trent, Session 24, Can. 10

[955] Cf. 1 Cor 7:38

Christian men, and therefore they contend that no man ought easily to undertake it, or religiously to promise it. For these men understand not the plenty and abundance of the grace of the gospel, which is such and so great, given by Christ so many ages, and daily given to those that believe, ask, seek, and knock, that these men find the yoke of our Lord sweet and the way of continency no less pleasant than wholesome.[956] In the number of whom St. Paul was, who plainly affirmeth: "God is faithful, who will not suffer you to be tempted above that which you are able, but will make also with temptation issue."[957] Wherefore St. Augustine explicating in a certain place this sentence: "Vow, and pay your vows unto our Lord God,"[958] writeth thus: "Be ye not slothful to vow, for you shall not by your own strength fulfill the same. You shall fail, if you presume of yourselves. But if you presume of him to whom you do vow, spare not to vow: you shall perform it with security."[959] And again, in another place: "A happy necessity which forceth a man to that which is better."[960]

134. **What is the summary doctrine of the premises?**

Those things that have been hitherto spoken according to our purposed brevity are only to this end: that the simpler sort must have the Catholic verity, touching the seven sacraments of the Church. Which are found, certes, to be of two sorts.

For some, as the first five, do advance the particular welfare of every faithful man. And the rest (to wit, the two latter) do serve for the multiplying of God's people and propagation of the Church. Both which effects they do work by God's holy ordinance for our behoof most necessary.[961]

---

[956] Cf. Augustine, *Confessions*, Bk. 6; Bk. 8, Ch. 11; see commentary on Matthew 19, of the following: Origen, Jerome, and Chrysostom

[957] 1 Cor 10:13

[958] Ps 75:12

[959] Augustine, *On Psalm 75*

[960] Augustine, *Epistle 45*

[961] Cf. Council of Florence

For baptism doth regenerate to the spiritual life, which is in Christ.[962] Confirmation doth add force and strength unto the regenerate.[963] The Eucharist is meat, drink, and voyage provision unto the wayfaring man.[964] Penance, being a present remedy against all the maladies of the mind, doth erect a man when he is fallen, and cure him when he is wounded.[965] Then succeedeth extreme unction, which, in the last conflict with death, doth fence and comfort the passenger.[966] Then holy orders yieldeth ministers unto the Church, which may have authority in holy things, and may rightly govern, dispense, conserve, and apply all those things which we spoke of before.[967] Finally, matrimony increaseth the Christian people, and provideth for man's incontinency.[968]

Where also this difference is to be observed: that baptism, confirmation, and orders, being once given, can never be iterated.[969] Also, baptism must of necessity be taken of all;[970] the Eucharist, of those that have the use of reason;[971] penance, of those that are fallen.[972] But it is at thy discretion to use any of the rest, so that thou have none in contempt, or dost neglect them against justice and equity when the time requireth.

There are therefore the preservatives and divine remedies, which that Samaritan, full of all mercy, hath ordained and committed to the prelates of the Church to be dispensed, for the well curing undoubtedly of the sick, that is to say, of all sinners in the Church, even until that they obtain, if they will, their true and perfect health. Which remedies rightly to understand, wholesomely to receive, and faithfully to apply unto others, is not

[962] Cf. Jn 3:5
[963] Cf. Acts 8:17
[964] Cf. Jn 6:52, 56
[965] Cf. Jn 20:23; Ez 18:30-31
[966] Cf. Jas 5:15
[967] Cf. Ti 1:5; 1 Cor 4:1
[968] Cf. Eph 5:32; 1 Cor 7:2
[969] Cf. Council of Florence; Council of Trent, Session 7, "On the Sacraments in General," Can. 9; Augustine, *Contra Epistolam Parmeniani*, Bk. 2, Ch. 13
[970] Cf. Jn 3:5
[971] Cf. Council of Trent, Session 21, "Decree on Communion under Both Species, and the Communion of Infants," Ch. 4
[972] Cf. Apoc 2:5

a point certes of human cunning but of Christian wisdom.[973] Of which whereas we have now spoken enough, according unto the scope of our present purpose, it now remaineth that, by the help of Christ, we pass over to the other part of this work, which containeth Christian justice.

"Wisdom inspireth life into her children, and entertaineth those that seek her, and she will go before in the way of justice, and he that loveth her, loveth life."[974]

Of Christian Justice, Sin, and Virtue

135. **What things do belong to Christian justice?**

All such things may be reduced unto two points, which are comprehended in these words: "Decline thou from evil, and do good."[975] As also Isaiah teacheth: "Cease ye to do perversely, and learn to do well."[976] This is that which St. Paul admonisheth, that the old man with his acts must be put off, and the new man must be put on, in justice and holiness of truth. The first consisteth in knowing and eschewing sins, for they are unto mortal men the greatest evils that can be. And the latter standeth in the desire and pursuit of things that be good.[977]

But to the intent that we may perform both these offices appertaining to justice, God's grace hath been by Jesus Christ purchased and promised unto us, and is ever most necessary.[978] By means of which, both preventing us and cooperating with us,[979] that effect is wrought in us which St. John

---

[973] Cf. Lk 10:33; 1 Cor 4:1, Jn 20:23
[974] Ecclus 4:12-13
[975] Ps 36:27; Cf. Ps 33:15; 1 Pt 3:10, 14; Tb 4:23
[976] Is 1:16; Ecclus 3:32; Rom 12:10
[977] Cf. Col 3:8; Eph 4:16-20
[978] Cf. Bernard, *Sermon 1, De Pentec.*
[979] Cf. Augustine, *On Grace and Free Will*, Ch. 9, 15-16; *Enchiridion*, Ch. 32; Jerome, *Against Jovinianus*, Bk. 2, Ch. 2; Council of Trent, Session 6, Can. 2

affirmeth: "He that doth justice is just, even as he also is just."[980] Moreover, he addeth: "He that committeth sin is of the devil."[981]

Of Sin in General

136. What is sin?

"Sin," as witnesseth St. Augustine, "is a will to retain or obtain that which justice prohibiteth, and from which it is in man's power to abstain."[982] And in another place he teacheth that "sin is whatsoever is spoken, done, or desired, contrary to the law of God."[983] And Saint Ambrose: "What is sin," saith he, "but the transgression of God's law, and the disobeying of the heavenly precepts?"[984]

137. How many kind of sins be there?

Three: original, mortal, and venial.[985] The first we call original, which, being transfused by Adam the first father of mankind, and contracted by us in our very conception, is taken away by baptism in Christ.[986]

Whereof, St. Paul speaketh in this manner: "By one man sin entered into this world, and by sin death; and so unto all men death did pass, in which all sinned."[987] And again, speaking unto the baptized, to the intent that he might show that the force of Christian baptism did extend to the purging of this sin also, he plainly testifieths: "You are washed, you are

---

[980] 1 Jn 3:7

[981] 1 Jn 3:8; Cf. Augustine, *Sermon 19, De Temp.*; Chrysostom, *On Psalm 4*; *Homily 16 on Ephesians*; Prosper, *Sententia ex Augustine*, n. 98

[982] Augustine, *Of Two Souls*, Ch. 11; Cf. Augustine, *Retractions*, Bk. 1, Ch. 15, 13; *De Genesi ad Litteram Imperfectus*, Ch. 1

[983] Augustine, *Contra Faustum*, Bk. 22, Ch. 27; Cf. Augustine, *Against Two Letters of the Pelagians*, Bk. 1, Ch. 13

[984] Ambrose, *De Paradiso*, Ch. 8; Cf. Augustine, *Harmony of the Gospels*, Bk. 2, Ch. 4; Bede, *On 1 John*, Ch. 3

[985] Cf. Augustine, *Enchiridion*, Ch. 64

[986] Cf. Council of Trent, Session 5; Ps 50:7

[987] Rom 5:12

sanctified, you are justified in the name of our Lord Jesus Christ, and in the spirit of our God."[988]

But mortal sin is that actual sin (as they call it) which taketh away spiritual life, and bringeth the death of the soul of him that sinneth: which death separateth a man from God and his kingdom, and maketh him worthy of everlasting punishment.[989] Whereupon it is written: "The stipend of sin, death."[990] Injustice is the procurement of death, "and the ungodly have invited her, with hands and words."[991]

Finally, a venial sin is certes actual, but it is such a sin as doth not make a man the enemy of God, and whereof, pardon is easily obtained by the faithful at God's hand. Of this hath St. John said: "If we shall say that we have no sin, we seduce ourselves, and the truth is not in us."[992] And St. James confesseth plainly: "In many things we offend all."[993] And if we believe the wise man: "The just man falleth seven times a day, and riseth again."[994]

Now it is manifest that one sin is more grievous than another;[995] and it is agreeable both to human and divine justice also, that a greater punishment is due to the greater sin.[996] And for that cause hath Christ put this difference between the fault and the punishment of one that sinneth wittingly, and of another that sinneth unwittingly: "That servant," saith he, "that knew the will of his Lord, and prepared not himself, and did not according to his will, shall be beaten with many stripes. But he that knew not, and did things worthy of stripes, shall be beaten with few."[997] And in another place, speaking of the sin of anger and the degrees thereof, he hath given this sentence: "Whosoever is angry with his brother shall be in danger of judgment; and whosoever shall say to his brother, 'Raca,' shall be in danger of a council; and whosoever shall say, 'Thou fool,' shall be

[988] 1 Cor 6:11
[989] Cf. 1 Cor 6:9; Gal 5:19; Apoc 21:8
[990] Rom 6:23
[991] Ws 1:16
[992] 1 Jn 1:8; Cf. Augustine, *Against Two Letters of the Pelagians*, Bk. 3, Ch. 3
[993] Jas 3:2
[994] Prv 24:16; Cf. Eccles 7:21
[995] Cf. Jn 19:12
[996] Cf. Augustine, *City of God*, Bk. 21, Ch. 6; *Sermon 18, De Verbis Apostoli*, Ch. 4
[997] Lk 12:47-48

guilty of the hell of the fire."[998] Where, as St. Gregory saith: "According to the degrees of the fault, increaseth the order of the sentence";[999] whilst anger without voice is bound to judgment, wherein the case is discussed; anger in voice is designed to a council, where the sentence is determined; anger in voice and word is adjudged to hell fire, where finally the sentence is executed.

138. **Why is sin to be eschewed?**

First, because God hath commanded none to do wickedly, and hath given no man space to sin, but hateth all those that work iniquity.[1000]

As the scripture expressly testifieth, neither is anything more odious and hateful to God, who otherwise loveth all things that are, and prosecuteth nothing with hatred and punishment, but only sin,[1001] which truly neither in heaven, nor in earth, he suffereth to escape unpunished.[1002]

Moreover, sin (that we may see how execrable and abominable a thing it is) was the cause[1003] that Christ our Lord, who otherwise committed no sin himself, did undertake the cross, and suffer a most bitter death.[1004] For, "He was wounded for our iniquities, he was worn out for our wickedness: our Lord laid upon him the iniquity of us all."[1005] "He is the propitiation for our sins: and not for ours only, but also for the whole world's."[1006]

And therefore, certes, he hath washed us from our sins in his blood,[1007] that as many as ever are buried with him by baptism into death,[1008] they, being dead to sin, may live to justice,[1009] and always walk by his grace in

---

[998] Mt 5:22

[999] Gregory the Great, *Moralia in Job*, Bk. 21, Ch. 5; Cf. Augustine, *On the Sermon on the Mount*, Bk. 1, Ch. 9

[1000] Cf. Ps 5:7; Ecclus 12:3; Ws 14:9; Prv 15:8-9; Ex 23:7

[1001] Cf. Ws 11:25

[1002] Cf. Ps 14:11-12; 2 Pt 2:4-7; Lv 26:14-15; Dt 18:15-16

[1003] Cf. Bernard, *Sermon, De Nativitate Domini*

[1004] Cf. 1 Pt 2:21

[1005] Is 53:5

[1006] 1 Jn 2:2

[1007] Cf. Apoc 1:5

[1008] Cf. Rom 6:2

[1009] Cf. 1 Pt 2:13

newness of life.[1010] But they that after grace received in the baptism of Christ will voluntarily sin again: they sin against Christ, they persecute Christ, they crucify Christ again, and shall be punished by Christ the just judge, no less than the wicked heathens. For so St. Paul teacheth: "If we sin willingly, after the knowledge of the truth received, now there is not left a host for sins, but a certain terrible expectation of judgment."[1011] Of which persons the apostle St. Peter hath also said: "It was better for them not to know the way of justice, than after the knowledge, to turn back from that holy commandment which was delivered unto them."[1012] "Wherefore he that standeth, let him look that he does not fall,"[1013] for in falling, the latter things are become worse than the former, "they which commit sin and iniquity are enemies to their own soul";[1014] if we believe the angel Raphael. "For a man by malice killeth his own soul."[1015] "The soul which shall sin, she shall die."[1016] And nothing certes is more unhappy than that death, by which a man is forever separated from the company of all the saints, from the joy of the angels, and all heavenly inhabitants, and finally from that so sovereign and eternal good, in the knowledge and fruition whereof, consisteth certes the whole welfare and perfect blessedness of a man.[1017]

Besides all this, such is the nature and malignity of sin, that it doth not only draw men, even those that be just, from God, and from the grace and glory of God, but doth moreover enthrall them to most extreme and ever-lasting evils, both of body and soul;[1018] and not only in this life but also in the life to come, it maketh them most unhappy: insomuch as being brought into the power of the devils, they are delivered up to most grievous torments and all manner of evil forevermore.[1019] Wherefore, those examples

[1010] Cf. Rom 6:4
[1011] Heb 10:26-27
[1012] 2 Pt 2:21
[1013] 1 Cor 10:12; Cf. Lk 11:26; Mt 12:45
[1014] Tb 12:10
[1015] Ws 16:14
[1016] Ez 18:4; Cf. Jas 1:15; Ps 33:22; Rom 6:23
[1017] Cf. Mt 7:23; 25:11; Lk 13:27; Ps 6:9; Chrysostom, *Homily 24 on Matthew*; *Homily 48, to the People of Antioch*; *Epistle 5 to Theodore after His Fall*
[1018] Cf. Ez 18:24, 33, 12
[1019] Cf. Jdt 5:18; Ex 32:33; Nm 14:28; Ecclus 21:4; Ps 10:6; Lk 16:22-23

are to be noted, which everywhere in holy writ are mentioned, concerning the reprehension and punishment of sinners: as of Cain,[1020] Pharaoh,[1021] Nebuchadnezzar,[1022] the Sodomites,[1023] Egyptians,[1024] Israelites,[1025] and others, whose wickedness the just God hath persecuted in most marvelous and horrible manner. Those sentences also are to be observed, which teach that the mischievous pestilence of sin is to be eschewed and detested. As: "He that committeth sin is the servant of sin."[1026] "Hateful unto God is the wicked man and his wickedness."[1027] "Sin maketh people miserable."[1028] "Fly from sin as from the face of an adder."[1029] "Thou art a God that willeth not iniquity, neither shall the malicious dwell near unto thee, neither shall the unjust abide in thy sight."[1030] "He that shall sin in one thing, shall lose many good things."[1031] "All the days of thy life have thou God in mind, and take heed that thou do not at any time consent unto sin, and overpass the precepts of our God."[1032] These things do tend to this end: that a man may know God, a most just revenger of sin; and knowing him, may fear him; and fearing him, may have regard to his own salvation; and by regarding, may escape the horrible pains of sinners. For: "Many are the scourges of a sinner."[1033]

[1020] Cf. Gn 4:11-12
[1021] Cf. Ex 14:27
[1022] Cf. Dn 4:22
[1023] Cf. Gn 19:24; Ez 16:46
[1024] Cf. Ex 7:8-10, 12, 14
[1025] Cf. Dt 23:22; Nm 16:26
[1026] Jn 8:34
[1027] Ws 14:9
[1028] Prv 14:34
[1029] Ecclus 21:2
[1030] Ps 5:5-6
[1031] Eccles 9:18
[1032] Tb 4:6; Cf. Chrysostom, *Homily 8, to the People of Antioch; Homily 17 on Genesis; Homily 51 on John; Homily 37 on John; Homily 28 on Romans; Homily 41 on Acts of the Apostles; Homily on Jonah the Prophet*; Basil, *Homily on Psalm 33*; Augustine, *Expositio Quarumdam Propositionum ex Epistola ad Romanos*, n. 42
[1033] Ps 31:10; Cf. Ecclus 13:21

139. What way leadeth unto sin?

By three degrees especially we do fall into sin: by suggestion, delectation, and consent.[1034]

By suggestion certes of the enemy, whilst an evil cogitation or temptation, either by the world, the flesh, or the devil, is thrust into us; and by our own delectation, when that pleaseth too much the mind which an evil temptation suggesteth; and finally, with our own consent also, when as the will being allured, consenteth deliberately to the sin itself: by which consent, the sin is now consummate, so that it doth not only make a man unclean and unjust, and slay him spiritually, but also maketh him guilty of hell before God, although it be not always accomplished in act.[1035] And therefore, not in vain is it said that "in suggestion is the seed; in delectation, the nutriment; in consent, the perfection of sin."[1036]

And if we do exactly consider which are wont to be the degrees of sin, we shall find that first, of suggestion, there ariseth cogitation; of cogitation, affection; of affection, delight; of delight, consent; of consent, work; of work, custom; of custom, despair; of despair, defending of sin; of defending, boasting; of boasting, damnation.[1037] This is that long and horrible chain of sins: these be the ropes and fetters, wherewith a man being bound, Satan doth miserably cast him down headlong here into all manner of mischief, and at the last, into the bottomless pit of hell. And therefore is it very requisite to discern and observe very diligently these degrees and branches of sins, that we be not thereby deceived and endangered.[1038]

140. How are sins easily avoided?

First certes, if we do foresee the evils and dangers which do follow after sin; then, if we do presently stop and mightily resist their evil entrances and

---

[1034] Cf. Augustine, *On the Sermon on the Mount*, Bk. 1, Ch. 12; *On the Trinity*, Bk. 12, Ch. 12; Gregory the Great, *Homily 16 on the Gospels*; *Moralia in Job*, Bk. 4, Ch. 27

[1035] Cf. Jas 1:14; Bede, *On James*, Ch. 1; Tb 4:6; Rom 6:12; Mt 5:23

[1036] Gregory the Great, *Ad interrogationem II Augustini Cantuar.*

[1037] Cf. Gregory the Great, *Moralia in Job*, Bk. 4, Ch. 27; Isidore, *De Summo Bono*, Bk. 2, Ch. 23

[1038] Cf. Prv 5:22; Ps 118:61; 2 Kgs 11:6; Cf. Augustine, *Confessions*, Bk. 8, Ch. 5; Gregory the Great, *Moralia in Job*, Bk. 2, Ch. 12

suggestions by which we are easily solicited to sin;[1039] last of all, if we do endeavor to practice the virtues contrary to these sins: Christ in all these things assisting us.[1040]

Wherefore the Ecclesiasticus giveth warning: "Do thou not go after thy concupiscences, and from thy own will, see thou turn away: if thou dost grant unto thy soul her concupiscences, she will cause thee to be a joy to thy enemies."[1041] And hereupon it is also pronounced by a divine oracle: "Shalt thou not if thou do well, receive well? But if evil, thy sin shall presently be in the gates. But under thee shall be the appetite thereof, and thou shalt have dominion over it."[1042]

And here that spiritual armor taketh place, wherewith St. Paul will have the soldiers of Christ to be guarded against sin and all the deceits of the devil, that they may strive against sin, resist in the evil day, and extinguish all the darts of the most wicked one.[1043]

Of the Seven Capital Sins

141. **Which are the sins that are specially to be noted?**
Truly, those that are called capital, because they are, as it were, the fountains or heads of all the rest, and out of which, as out of a corrupted root, very pestilent fruits do spring, and, as it were, by a long race, all kind of vices, turpitudes, scandals, harms, corruptions, and mischiefs of mankind do descend, and break out with great violence.

142. **How many such capital sins are there?**
Seven; which are numbered in this manner: pride, covetousness, lechery, envy, gluttony, anger, sloth. But as these are ever to be detested and eschewed, so the seven virtues opposite unto these vices are to be followed

---

[1039] Cf. Ps 136:9; Jas 4:7; 1 Pt 5:8; Bernard, *Sermon 5, De Quadrag.*; *Sermon 29, Ex Parvis*; *Sermon 49 on Canticle of Canticles*
[1040] Cf. Rom 12; Eph 4; Phil 4:5, 8
[1041] Ecclus 18:30-31
[1042] Gn 4:7
[1043] Cf. Eph 6:11; Heb 12:3

with very great diligence and affection, if we seek the life of our soul. To pride is contrary humility;[1044] to covetousness, liberality;[1045] to lechery, chastity;[1046] charity oppugneth envy;[1047] abstinence is opposite to gluttony;[1048] patience to anger;[1049] finally, devotion, or godly diligence and diligent piety expelleth sloth.[1050]

143. What is pride, and what daughters doth she beget?

Pride is an inordinate appetite of excellency, whether it lurk in the mind, or appear in outward show.[1051]

She certes is the mother, prince, and queen of all vices,[1052] which principally begetteth this unhappy offspring: disobedience, boasting, hypocrisy, contention, pertinacity, discord, curiosity.[1053]

And to the intent that we might avoid this most pestiferous sin, holy Tobit giveth warning in this manner: "Do thou never permit pride to bear rule in thy thought or in thy word: for in it all perdition took the beginning."[1054] For this cause is that apostolical doctrine: "God resisteth the proud and giveth grace to the humble."[1055] Yea and if we believe Ecclesiasticus: "Pride is hateful before God, and men. God hath dried up the roots of proud nations and hath planted the humble out of those nations. Why therefore art thou proud, thou dust and ashes?"[1056]

[1044] Cf. Col 3:12

[1045] Cf. 2 Cor 9:5

[1046] Cf. Acts 24:25

[1047] Cf. 1 Cor 13:4

[1048] Cf. Ecclus 31:19, 31

[1049] Cf. Heb 10:36

[1050] Cf. 1 Cor 15:58; Cf. also Gregory the Great, *Moralia in Job*, Bk. 3, Ch. 31; John Cassian, *Conferences of the Desert Fathers*, Col. 5; Bk. 5ff

[1051] Cf. Chrysostom, *Homily 43, to the People of Antioch*; Bernard, *De Gradibus Humilitatis et Superbiae*; Gregory the Great, *Moralia in Job*, Bk. 34, Ch. 17ff; Bk. 23, Ch. 7; Prosper, *Epistle ad Demet.*; Isidore, *De Summo Bono*, Bk. 2, Ch. 38; Fulgentius, *Epistle 3*, Ch. 16-17

[1052] Cf. Gregory the Great, *Moralia in Job*, Bk. 31, Ch. 31; Prosper, *De Vita Contemplativa*, Bk. 3, Ch. 2; Augustine, *Epistle 56*; Bernard, *Sermon 3, Ex Parvis*; *Sermon 4, De Adv.*

[1053] Cf. Dt 17:12; Ws 5:8; Mt 23:11, 14, 27; Prv 13:10; Gn 49:7; Prv 6:16; 1 Tm 5:13

[1054] Tb 4:14; Cf. Ecclus 10:15; Chrysostom, *Homily 8 on John*

[1055] Jas 4:6; 1 Pt 5:5

[1056] Ecclus 10:7, 18, 9

144. What is covetousness, and of what manner of daughters is she the mother?
Covetousness is an inordinate appetite of having. For he is rightly deemed
covetous, not only that taketh by violence, but also that desireth another
man's or covetously keepeth his own.[1057]

The daughters of this bad mother are treason, fraud, fallacy, perjury,
disquietness, violence, unmercifulness or inhumanity, and hardness of
heart.[1058] The apostle condemneth this vice, so as he hath called it the service of idols;[1059] and besides, writeth thus: "They that will be made rich fall
into temptation and the snare of the devil, and many desires unprofitable
and hurtful, which drown men into destruction and perdition. For the root
of all evils is covetousness."[1060] And in another place, we find it written:
"Nothing is more wicked than a covetous man."[1061] Also, "Nothing is more
unjust than to love money. For this man setteth his very soul to sale."[1062]
And Christ himself testifieth: "You cannot serve God and mammon."[1063]
And again: "Be not careful for tomorrow."[1064] Which Saint Paul also more
expressly delivering, giveth this admonition: "Let your manners be without
avarice: contented with things present. For he said, 'I will not leave thee,
neither will I forsake thee': so that we do confidently say: 'Our Lord is my
helper.'"[1065] "Having food and wherewith to be covered, with these we are
content."[1066]

[1057] Cf. Basil, in ditescentes et avaros Homily 6 and 7; Prosper, De Vita Contemplativa,
Bk. 2, Ch. 15-16; Isidore, De Summo Bono, Bk. 2, Ch. 41; Augustine, De Libero Arbitrio,
Bk. 3, Ch. 17; Sermon 196, De Temp.; Ambrose, De Nabuthe Jezraelita; De Cain et Abel,
Bk. 1, Ch. 5

[1058] Cf. Gregory the Great, Moralia in Job, Bk. 31, Ch. 31; 2 Tm 3:4; 1 Cor 6:8; Ecclus
11:31, 33; Zac 8:17; Mt 6:24; Prv 22:22; 21:13

[1059] Cf. Col 3:5; Eph 5:5

[1060] 1 Tm 6:9-10; Cf. Is 5:8; Mk 10:24; Apoc 2:6, 9; Jas 5:1; Ecclus 31:5, 8, 11; Bar
3:16; Ps 48:17

[1061] Ecclus 10:9

[1062] Ecclus 10:10

[1063] Mt 6:24; Cf. Chrysostom, Homily 7 on John

[1064] Mt 6:34

[1065] Heb 13:5; Cf. Lk 12:15

[1066] 1 Tm 6:8

145. What is lechery, and what manner of offspring doth it engender?

Lechery is an inordinate appetite of unclean and libidinous pleasure.[1067] And it bringeth forth blindness of mind, inconsideration, inconstancy, headlongness, love of himself, hatred of God, too much desire of this life, a horror of death and future judgment, and desperation of eternal felicity.[1068]

Against this sin, which maketh the wise mad, and causeth men to become in manner beasts,[1069] thus writeth St. Paul: "Fly fornication. Every sin whatsoever a man doth is without the body; but he that doth fornicate sinneth against his own body."[1070] And in another place thus: "Fornication and all uncleaness, or avarice, let it not so much as be named among you, as becometh saints; or filthiness, or foolish talk, or scurrility, being to no purpose: but rather giving of thanks."[1071] And it is a wonderful thing that Christians are not marvelously ashamed, who do pollute themselves with filthy lust in the sight of God and his angels,[1072] whereas they have consecrated in baptism their bodies and members, as pure temples to the Holy Ghost, and to Christ our Lord.[1073] Hereupon again saith St. Paul: "Know you not that your members are the temple of the Holy Ghost, which is in you, whom you have of God, and you are not your own?"[1074] Then again: "Know you not that your bodies are the members of Christ? Taking therefore the members of Christ, shall I make them the members of a harlot?"[1075] And finally, he concludeth in this sort: "For you are bought with a great

---

[1067] Cf. Prosper, *De Vita Contemplativa*, Bk. 3, Ch. 6; Isidore, *De Summo Bono*, Bk. 2, Ch. 39

[1068] Cf. Gregory the Great, *Moralia in Job*, Bk. 31, Ch. 31; Os 4:11; 2 Kgs 11:14; Dn 13:56; Prv 13:3; Ws 4:12; Ps 51:6; 2 Tm 3:4; Ps 20:9; Jas 4:4; Eph 4:19

[1069] Cf. 3 Kgs 11:1; Ecclus 19:2; Jerome, *On Osee*, Ch. 4; Ambrose, *De Cain et Abel*, Bk. 1, Ch. 15; *De Noe et Arca*, Ch. 9

[1070] 1 Cor 6:18; Cf. Chrysostom, *On 1 Corinthians*, Ch. 6; Augustine, *Sermon 9, De Decem Chordis*, Ch. 10; *Sermon 16, De Verbis Domini*, Ch. 10

[1071] Eph 5:3-4; Cf. Jerome, *On Ephesians*, Ch. 5. See also the sixth precept of the decalogue.

[1072] Cf. Ambrose, *On Luke*, Ch. 4; Gregory the Great, *Moralia in Job*, Bk. 6, Ch. 31

[1073] Cf. 1 Cor 3:16; 2 Cor 6:16

[1074] 1 Cor 6:19

[1075] 1 Cor 6:15

price. Glorify and bear God in your body."[1076] "For fornicators and adulterers God will judge."[1077]

146. What is envy, and what daughters doth she bring forth?

Envy is a sadness for the good of another, and a hatred of another man's felicity:[1078] in respect of superiors, because he is not made equal unto them; and in respect of inferiors, lest they should be made equal unto him; and in respect of equals, because they are equal unto him, as Saint Augustine saith.[1079] And she hath to her daughters: hatred, whispering, detraction, exulting in other men's adversities, and affliction in their prosperity.[1080]

Cain is read to have envied Abel, his own brother;[1081] and Saul to have envied David the designed king, his son-in-law.[1082] This abominable vice, besides that it is void of all charity and humanity, it also maketh men most like unto devils.[1083] For, "by the envy of the devil death entered into the world; and they do imitate him which are of his part."[1084] Well, therefore, doth the apostle give warning: "Let us not be made desirous of vain glory, provoking one another, envying one another."[1085]

[1076] 1 Cor 6:20

[1077] Heb 13:4; Cf. 1 Cor 6:9; Eph 5:5; Gal 5:20; Apoc 21:8

[1078] *De hoc peccato scribit Cyprian, Sermon, de zelo et livore*; Basil, *Homily 11, De Invid.*; *Homily 21, in aliquot. scripture locos*; Chrysostom, *Homily 44, to the People of Antioch*; *Homily 45, to the People of Antioch*; Prosper, *De Vita Contemplativa*, Bk. 3, Ch. 5, 9; Isidore, *De Summo Bono*, Bk. 3; Ch. 25

[1079] Cf. Augustine, *De Genesi ad Litteram*, Bk. 11, Ch. 14; Prosper, *Sententia ex Augustine*, n. 292

[1080] Cf. Gregory the Great, *Moralia in Job*, Bk. 31, Ch. 31; 1 Jn 3:12; Rom 1:29; Prv 17:5; 24:17, 21; 28:22; Eccles 4:4

[1081] Cf. Gn 4:5; Jude 1:11

[1082] Cf. 1 Kgs 18:8

[1083] Cf. Gregory of Nyssa, *Life of Moses*; Jerome, *On Galatians*, Ch. 5; Gregory the Great, *Pastoral Rule*, Bk. 3, Ch. 10, Admonition 11; Augustine, *Sermon 83, De Temp.*; Bernard, *Sermon 24 on Canticle of Canticles*; *Sermon 49 on Canticle of Canticles*; *Sermon, De Triplici Custodia*

[1084] Ws 2:24-25; Cf. Chrysostom, *Homily 41 on Matthew*; Gregory the Great, *Moralia in Job*, Bk. 5, Ch. 33-34; Bk. 29, Ch. 1; Augustine, *Of Holy Virginity*, Ch. 31

[1085] Gal 5:26

147. What is gluttony, and which are her daughters?

Gluttony is an inordinate appetite of meat and drink;[1086] her daughters are foolish mirth,[1087] much talk, scurrility,[1088] uncleanness, dullness of sense and understanding. And what is more foul and unseemly than that a man should be inferior to beasts, which are content with a certain natural moderation, whilst he maketh himself a slave to his belly, to surfeiting and drunkenness, consuming his goods, hurting his health, bringing on diseases, and finally, shortening and cutting off his own life?[1089] For it is a very true saying: "By means of surfeiting, many have died; but he that is abstinent shall increase life."[1090] Again: "In much meat there shall be infirmity."[1091] Therefore, Christ commandeth: "Look well to yourselves, lest perhaps your hearts be overcharged with surfeiting and drunkenness."[1092] And Saint Paul dissuading us from drunkenness saith: "Be not drunk with wine wherein is riotousness."[1093] "Drunkards shall not possess the kingdom of God."[1094] And hence is it also, that the prophet giveth such a heavy threat unto drunkards: "Woe to you that are mighty to drink wine, and strong men to mingle drunkenness."[1095]

[1086] Cf. Gregory the Great, *Moralia in Job*, Bk. 30, Ch. 27; Bernard, *De Pas.*, Ch. 34
[1087] Cf. Gregory the Great, *Moralia in Job*, Bk. 31, Ch. 31
[1088] Cf. Ex 32:6; Jb 21:12; Prv 10:19; Eph 5:4; Gregory the Great, *Pastoral Rule*, Bk. 3, Ch. 19, Admonition 20; Chrysostom, *Homily 57, to the People of Antioch*
[1089] Cf. Is 28:7; Eccles 10:16; Chrysostom, *Homily 44 on John*; *Homily 58 on Matthew*; Jerome, *Against Jovinianus*, Bk. 2, Ch. 6ff; *On Ezechiel*, Ch. 44; *On Galatians*, Ch. 5; Cf. also on this vice in: Basil, *Homily, Inebriet. et Luxum.*; Augustine, *Sermon 231, De Temp.*; *Sermon 232, De Temp.*; Chrysostom, *Sermon, Cont. Luxum et Crapulam*; *Homily 1, to the People of Antioch*; Isidore, *De Summo Bono*, Bk. 2, Ch. 42-43; Ambrose, *De Helia et Jejunio*, Ch. 12ff
[1090] Ecclus 37:34; Cf. Ecclus 31:19; Ps 77:29; Nm 11:33; Dt 32:15; Prv 21:17
[1091] Ecclus 37:33
[1092] Lk 21:34; Cf. Burchardus, Bk. 34 de decret.; Ivon., Pt. 13, Ch. 68ff
[1093] Eph 5:18; Cf. Prv 20:1; Jerome, *On Titus*, Ch. 1; *Epistle 69, to Oceanus*, Ch. 4; Ambrose, *On Repentance*, Bk. 1, Ch. 14
[1094] 1 Cor 6:10; Cf. Gal 5:11; Os 4:11; Prv 31:4; Ecclus 19:2
[1095] Is 5:22; Cf. Is 5:11; 22:12; Prv 23:20, 29; Am 6:4; Lk 6:24

148. **What is anger, and what offspring hath she?**

Anger is an inordinate desire of punishing him by whom a man supposeth that he have been harmed. There doth spring from her these detestable daughters: brawling, swelling of the mind, contumelies, clamor, disdainfulness, and blasphemy.[1096]

This is a pernicious poison of the mind, overthrowing all vigor of judgment and wisdom, and impairing the health of the mind, yea and oftentimes also of the body.[1097] For which cause hath Ecclesiastes given warning: "Be not thou swift to be angry, for anger resteth in the bosom of a fool."[1098] And the doctor of the Gentiles hath given charge: "Let all bitterness, and anger, and indignation, clamor and blasphemy, be taken away from you with all malice. And be gentle to one another, merciful, pardoning one to another, as also God in Christ hath pardoned you."[1099] But against angry, contentious, and contumelious persons, that dreadful sentence of Christ is already pronounced: "Whosoever is angry with his brother shall be in danger of judgment; and whosoever shall say to his brother, 'Raca,' shall be in danger of a council. And whosoever shall say, 'Thou fool,' shall be guilty of hell fire."[1100]

149. **What is sloth, and which be her branches?**

Sloth is a languishing of a mind that is slack and negligent to do well. And specially it is a sadness about some spiritual matter. She bringeth forth these daughters: malice, rancor, pusillanimity, desperation, dullness

[1096] Cf. Gregory the Great, *Moralia in Job*, Bk. 31, Ch. 31; Prv 29:22; Jb 15:2, 13; Ecclus 19:28; Eph 4:31

[1097] Cf. Basil, *Homily 10, De Ira.*; Chrysostom, *Homily 20, to the People of Antioch, et seq.*; *Homily 6 on Acts of the Apostles*; *Homily 3 on Matthew*; *Homily 18 on Matthew*; Gregory the Great, *Moralia in Job*, Bk. 5, Ch. 30ff

[1098] Eccles 7:10; Cf. Ecclus 8:19; 28:1; 30:26; Prv 12:16; 15:1, 18; 18:6, 14; 22:24; 26:21; 27:3; Jb 5:2; Ps 4:5; 30:10

[1099] Eph 4:31-32; Cf. Col 38:12; Bernard, *Sermon 13, in Psalm. Qui habitat*; Ambrose, *On the Duties of the Clergy*, Bk. 1, Ch. 21; Augustine, *On Psalm 4*; *De Vera Religione*, Ch. 45; *Epistle 87*; *Epistle 149*; Gregory the Great, Bk. 8, Epistle 51 ad Leont.; *Pastoral Rule*, Bk. 3, Ch. 16, Admonition 17

[1100] Mt 5:22; Cf. Gregory the Great, *Moralia in Job*, Bk. 21, Ch. 5; Augustine, *On the Sermon on the Mount*, Bk. 1, Ch. 19; *Enchiridion*, Ch. 79

about the necessary commandments, and a wandering of the mind about things unlawful.[1101]

Of this sin are those men guilty that are idle, lither,[1102] and as the scripture calleth them, lukewarm, and finally, everyone that doth pass over this time of grace and day of salvation in vain affairs and endeavors.[1103] And the end of this sin is that which Christ teacheth in the gospel: "Every tree which yieldeth not good fruit shall be cut down, and shall be cast into the fire."[1104] And in another place: "The unprofitable servant cast ye out into the utter darkness."[1105] Neither hath he omitted to tell us what in the mean season he would have us to do, that we may eschew sloth,[1106] saying: "Take heed, watch and pray, for you know not when the time is."[1107] "Strive to enter by the narrow gate, because many, I say to you, shall seek to enter, and shall not be able."[1108] These things we have briefly touched to the intent that they which are not already taught the ways of justice may not only know and discern the chief diseases and detestable plagues of mankind which we have showed, but also endeavor according to the prescript of God's law, to abandon from themselves and others, and utterly to expel the same. "Happy is that man which hath not walked in the counsel of the wicked, and hath not stood in the way of sinners, and hath not sit in the chair of pestilence,"[1109] as the kingly psalmist singeth, notifying unto us the first part of justice and happiness, in the front of his first canticle.

[1101] Cf. Gregory the Great, *Moralia in Job*, Bk. 31, Ch. 31; Ecclus 33:29; Prv 15:13
[1102] Cf. Mt 20:3, 6; 22:5
[1103] Cf. Apoc 3:15; Prv 6:3; 10:4, 26; 13:4; 18:8-9; 19:15, 24; 20:4; 21:25; 22:13; 24:30; 25:20; 26:13; 28:19; Ecclus 5:8; 7:16; 14:2; 22:1; Ps 72:5; Jer 48:10, 70; Rom 13:11; 2 Cor 7:10; Gal 3:5; Apoc 2:4
[1104] Mt 3:10; Cf. Mt 7:18; 21:19; Lk 13:7; Jn 15:2
[1105] Mt 25:30; Cf. Mt 25:26
[1106] Cf. Ecclus 6:23; Eccles 9:10; 2 Thes 3:7; Gal 6:9-10; Heb 12:12; Rom 12:11; Phil 4:4
[1107] Mk 13:33; Cf. Mk 13:35; Mt 24:42; 25:13; Jn 9:4; Eph 5:14, 16; Apoc 3:2-3
[1108] Lk 13:24; Cf. Mt 7:13; 11:12
[1109] Ps 1:1; Cf. Bernard, *Sermon 35, Ex Parvis*; Cf. also Bernard, *Sermon 3, De Ascensione*; *Sermon 6, De Ascensione*; Gregory the Great, *Pastoral Rule*, Bk. 3, Ch. 15, Admonition 16

Of Alien Sins

150. **What sins are called alien sins?**

Those which, although they be wrought and accomplished by the hands and deeds of other men, yet they are worthily imputed unto us, and do make our conscience guilty of damnation in the sight of God. And therefore, of this may that be understood which the scripture commandeth: "Do thou not communicate with other men's sins."[1110] And that which the kingly prophet prayeth: "From my secret sins cleanse me O Lord, and from alien sins spare thy servant."[1111] Hereunto doth St. Basil the Great[1112] refer that which Saint Paul wrote to the Ephesians: "Communicate not with the unfruitful works of darkness, but rather reprove them."[1113] Then that also of the same apostle: "Withdraw yourselves from every brother walking inordinately, and not according to the tradition which they have received of us."[1114]

151. **How many in number are these alien sins?**

Nine; as they are for the most part committed nine manner of ways, to wit: by counsel; by commanding; by consent; by provocation; by praise or flattery; by silence; by winking or indulgence; by participation in the fault; and by wicked defending or maintaining the same.

152. **When is an alien sin committed by counsel?**

At such time certes as we are the authors and instruments of evil counsel, which others do or may follow. Let Caiphas be an example, who by his counsel incensed and provoked the senate of the Jews to work the death of Christ.[1115] But commended on the contrary part is Joseph of Arimathea, and is called a good and just man, because he had not consented to the

---

[1110] 1 Tm 5:22; Cf. Basil, *De Vera Virg.*
[1111] Ps 18:13; Cf. Euthymius, *On Psalm 18*; Augustine, *De Libero Arbitrio*, Bk. 3, Ch. 10
[1112] Cf. Basil, *Sermon 2, De Baptismo*, Ch. 9; Augustine, *Sermon 18, De Verbis Domini*, Ch. 18
[1113] Eph 5:11
[1114] 2 Thes 3:6
[1115] Cf. Jn 11:49ff

counsel and acts of them,[1116] to wit, of the high priests and Pharisees, wickedly conspiring to put Christ to death.[1117] Of the same sort of men was that Demetrius who, with other artificers for the tendering of his own lucre and gain, filled in a manner the whole city of the Ephesians with a great tumult and sedition against St. Paul and his doctrine.[1118] Herein also did offend that infamous Herodias, King Herod's adulteress. For her dancing daughter, by her counsel and persuasion, did wickedly obtain the body's head of the glorious St. John Baptist, which she cruelly before had requested.[1119]

153. When is commanding an alien sin?

When by our decree, commission, or commandment, any wrong doth redound to our neighbor, or any evil whatsoever is committed. In this manner, David the king killed innocent Uriah, not certes with his own or with his servant's hands, but working it and charging it by letter that he should be slain in the battle.[1120] And Pilate the president was guilty of Christ's death, because for the favor of the Jews, although otherwise after a manner unwilling, he adjudged him and delivered him over by his authority to be crucified.[1121] So did Pharaoh and Herod bind themselves with a monstrous crime, when they made the tyrannical law of murdering the infants of the Hebrews.[1122] "But woe be unto them that make unjust laws."[1123]

154. When doth consent make us guilty of an alien sin?

When that which is wickedly done by others hath, as it were, our voice to go with it, or is, at the least, in secret sort by us approved.[1124] So sinned

[1116] Cf. Lk 23:50; Ps 1:1; Gn 49:5; Jb 21:16

[1117] Cf. Jn 11:53; Mt 26:3

[1118] Cf. Acts 19:24; 2 Kgs 10:3; 16:20; 17:1, 5; 3 Kgs 12:4; 21:25; 2 Par 22:3; 25:16, 20; 1 Esd 4:5; Est 5:10; Dn 6:5; 1 Mc 1:12; 2 Mc 1:11; 4:32; Acts 14:18

[1119] Cf. Mk 6:24; Mt 14:8; Cf. also Ecclus 27:28; 6:7; 8:20; 37:7, 9; Jb 5:13; 12:13, 16; 18:5, 7; Is 19:11, 13; Ps 7:16; 9:16; Prv 26:27; Eccles 10:8

[1120] Cf. 2 Kgs 11:15

[1121] Cf. Jn 19:16; Lk 23:25

[1122] Cf. Ex 1:16; Mt 2:16

[1123] Is 10:1; Cf. Mt 15:3; Mk 7:9; Cf. also 1 Kgs 22:17; Jdt 2:5; Est 3:12; Dn 3:5; 6:16; 1 Mc 1:43; 2 Mc 6:1; Mk 6:27; Acts 23:2

[1124] Cf. Irenaeus, *Against Heresies*, Bk. 4, Ch. 46

Saul, consenting to the death of the Protomartyr, Saint Steven.[1125] Also, herein offended above forty men of the Jews, who by vow bound and armed themselves to put St. Paul to death.[1126] Finally, herein offended the citizens of Jerusalem, giving their voices to their magistrates, that Christ might suffer death,[1127] so that St. Peter for that cause, upbraiding them, said: "The author of life you killed."[1128] Wherefore that sentence of St. Paul is to be noted: "Not only they which do evil things, but they also which consent unto the doers, are worthy of death."[1129]

And hereunto may be referred that which we read in St. Cyprian: "He is not free from wickedness that gave commandment to have it accomplished; nor he clear from crime who, not withstanding, he never committed the same, yet giveth his consent that it shall be otherwise given out, and publicly registered."[1130]

155. When do we contract an alien sin by provocation?

When we do wittingly provoke another to anger, revenge, blasphemy, cruelty, or other such like vices, whether it be done by word or deed, or any other means howsoever. As when Job's wife, wantonly scorning her most patient husband, did also persuade him, so much as lay in her, to blaspheme God.[1131] And Tobit's wife, as troublesome as the other, often molesting and exasperating her husband with her reproachful speeches, brought the matter to this pass: that the afflicted man was constrained to bewail his domestical injury with sighs, and tears, and prayers unto Almighty God.[1132] But Ecclesiasticus admonisheth the contrary, saying: "Keep thyself from contention, and thou shalt diminish sins. For an angry man doth kindle contention, and a man a sinner will molest his friends;

[1125] Cf. Acts 7:60
[1126] Cf. Acts 23:12
[1127] Cf. Mt 27:20; Mk 15:11
[1128] Acts 3:15; Cf. Acts 2:23
[1129] Rom 1:32
[1130] Cyprian, *Epistle 31, quae est Cleri. Romani ad Cyprianum*; Cf. Lv 20:4; Nm 16:24, 26; Jdt 8:9; Est 14:15; Lk 11:47
[1131] Cf. Jb 2:9
[1132] Cf. Tb 2:15; 3:7

and in the midst of them that are in peace, soweth enmity."[1133] And so hath Solomon said: "An evil man always seeketh chidings, but the cruel angel shall be sent against him."[1134]

156. When are we spotted with an alien sin by praise or flattery?

When we commend any man in misdeeds of lewd behavior, or as though the thing were very well done, we give a spur to him that runneth amiss, that he may hold on his wicked course. "But woe be unto them that sew cushions under every elbow; and do make pillows under the heads of persons of every age to take souls,"[1135] as the prophet saith. And into this vice do preachers sometime fall, and magistrates naughtily flattering the common people, whilst they do openly favor and approve their licentiousness.[1136] And therefore, rightly saith Isaiah: "O my people, they that call thee happy, these are they that deceive thee, and bring to naught the way of thy steps."[1137] For which cause St. Paul commandeth us to shun those doctors that, by sweet speeches and benedictions, do seduce the hearts of innocents.[1138] "For because the sinner is praised in the desires of his soul, and the wicked man is accounted happy: the sinner will provoke our Lord,"[1139] as the kingly prophet testifieth.

157. When doth an alien sin fall upon us through our silence?

When our unseasonable silence bringeth detriment to our subject, or to any other person. For example sake: if by office it belong unto us to teach, admonish, or correct our brother, or the whole people, and we omit the same without just cause, when we may do good. For which cause our Lord

[1133] Ecclus 28:10-11; Cf. Prv 15:18; 18:6; 22:10; 26:17; 29:22; 30:33
[1134] Prv 17:11; Cf. Prv 3:30; Is 33:1; Cf. also 1 Kgs 1:6; Ps 105:16; 2 Mc 14:27; Gal 5:15, 26; Eph 6:4; Col 3:21
[1135] Ez 13:18
[1136] Cf. Jer 14:13; 23:13, 17; 27:9; 28:15; 29:8; Lam 2:14; Mi 3:5; 3 Kgs 22:6
[1137] Is 3:12; Cf. Is 9:15; 30:10
[1138] Cf. Rom 16:18; 2 Pt 1:12, 14; Jerome, *Against the Pelagians*, Bk. 1, Ch. 9; *Against Jovianus*, Bk. 2, Ch. 19
[1139] Ps 10:3-4; Cf. Ps 54:22; Prv 1:10; 16:29; 17:15; 29:5; Eccles 7:6; Jer 9:3, 8; Cf. also Prv 24:24, 28; 27:2, 5-6; 28:23; Ps 140:5; Is 5:20; Chrysostom, *Homily 2, De David et Saule.*; Cyprian, *On the Lapsed*; Basil, *Homily on Psalm 61*; Augustine, *On Psalm 134*

by Isaiah testifieth to everyone that preacheth: "Cry, do not cease, as a trumpet exalt thy voice, and show unto my people their wickedness, and to the house of Jacob their sins."[1140] Hear moreover the danger they stand in, who are not without cause called "dumb dogs, not able to bark":[1141] "If when I say to a wicked man, (saith our Lord) 'Thou shalt die the death,' if thou do not warn him, and speak to him, that he may forsake his wicked way, and live: the wicked man himself shall die in his iniquity, but I will require his blood at thy hand."[1142] So necessary a thing it is to be observed, which Saint Paul not without great protestation doth require: "Preach the word, urge in season, out of season, reprove, beseech, rebuke in all patience and doctrine."[1143] And again, in another place: "Them that sin, reprove before all: that the rest also may have fear."[1144]

158. When are we by winking or indulgence entangled with alien sins?

So often as that thing which by our power or authority may and ought to be amended and punished, we, notwithstanding, suffer to go unpunished, and to wax worse and worse.

Herein do magistrates offend, when they bear the sword in vain, and are not as they are called, God's ministers and revengers unto wrath to those that behave themselves wickedly or seditiously.[1145] This was the sin of King Saul, when, contrary to the commandment of God, he spared his enemies the Amalekites.[1146] The same sin was also incurred by King Ahab, when he received into favor Benhadab the king of Syria; for which cause he did not escape the severe sentence of the prophet giving this

[1140] Is 58:1; Cf. Jer 23:22; 26:2; 50:1; Jo 1:2; 1 Cor 9:16

[1141] Is 56:10

[1142] Ez 3:18; Cf. Ez 33:7; Jerome, On Ezechiel, Ch. 33; Gregory the Great, Homily 11 on Ezechiel; Acts 20:18; Is 6:5; Est 4:13ff

[1143] 2 Tm 4:2; Cf. Ti 1:9, 13; 2:15; Chrysostom, Homily 6 on Philippians

[1144] 1 Tm 5:20; Cf. Lv 19:17; Augustine, Sermon 15, De Verbis Domini, Ch. 7; Sermon 16, Ch. 4, 7-8; Cf. also Bernard, De Nativitate Ioannis Baptistae; Gregory the Great, Pastoral Rule, Bk. 2, Ch. 4; Augustine, Epistle 109; Homily 7 ex 50; Prosper, De Vita Contemplativa, Bk. 1, Ch. 20; Isidore, De Summo Bono, Bk. 3, Ch. 44-46

[1145] Cf. Rom 13:4; Ws 6:3; Ps 2:10; Augustine, Retractions, Bk. 2, Ch. 5; Epistle 48; Epistle 50; Epistle 204; Tractate 11 on John; Bernard, Sermon 66 on Canticle of Canticles

[1146] Cf. 1 Kgs 15:9; Jdt 20:13; Nm 25:4

threat: "This saith our Lord: 'Because thou hast dismissed out of thy hand a man worthy of death, thy life shall be for his life, and thy people for his people.'"[1147] Hereunto may be referred that which the apostle willeth the Corinthians: "Take away the evil from among yourselves. Know you not that a little leaven corrupteth the whole paste? Purge the old leaven."[1148]

Secondly, herein do fathers and mothers, masters and mistresses offend, whilst they, with a certain dissembling and favorable indulgence, do mar those in bringing them up that are committed to their charge, and by their negligence and sloth do suffer them to fall into great hazard and danger.[1149] So we read the sons of Eli to have been depraved through the default only of their father's indulgence, who, for that cause, was grievously punished for his too much lenity.[1150]

Hereunto may also be added that sin which is commonly called the omission of brotherly correction, admonition, or reprehension.[1151] Forasmuch as Christ hath warned us to correct our brother, once, and twice, and the third time that we may win him when he sinneth.[1152] Although some do distinguish between this manner of omission and the former sufferance which we spake of, making them two different kinds of alien sins.[1153]

159. How do we contract an alien sin by participation?

Then especially, when we are partners in gain with thieves and extortioners; also, when we do wittingly together with others challenge or retain goods unjustly gotten, or which any way do belong to other men;

[1147] 3 Kgs 20:42

[1148] 1 Cor 5:13, 6, 7; Cf. Ex 22:18; Dt 13:1, 6, 12; 17:12; 18:20; 3 Kgs 18:19, 40; Jerome, *On Galatians*, Ch. 5; Gregory the Great, Bk. 32, Epistle 31

[1149] Cf. Augustine, *On Psalm 50*; Gregory the Great, *Dialogues*, Bk. 4, Ch. 18; Chrysostom, *Homily 9 on 1 Timothy*; Eph 6:4; Heb 12:7; Prv 13:18, 24; 22:15, 6; 23:13; 29:15, 17, 21; Ecclus 7:25; 22:3-5; 30:1

[1150] Cf. 1 Kgs 3:11; 4:17; 3 Kgs 1:6

[1151] Cf. Prv 9:7; 15:5, 10, 12; 24:14-15; 25:12; 27:5-6; 28:23; 29:1; Ecclus 7:6; 10:28; 11:7; 19:13, 17; 20:1, 4; Ps 140:5; Col 1:28; 1 Thes 5:14; 2 Thes 3:15; 1 Tm 5:20; 2 Tm 2:25; 4:2; Ti 1:9-10; 2:15

[1152] Cf. Mt 18:15

[1153] Cf. Ambrose, *Sermon 8 on Psalm 118*; Origen, *Homily 9 on Jeremias*; Jerome, *Epistle 109 to Riparius*; Augustine, *On Psalm 50*; *Sermon 15, De Verbis Domini*; Chrysostom, *Oration 1, Against the Jews*

and then, moreover, when we are enriched with the spoil of others. And hereunto seemeth to belong that which the psalmist saith, to run with the very thieves themselves, and to have portion with the adulterers.[1154] This did Isaiah object unto the people of the Jews: "Thy princes be unfaithful, companions of thieves, all do love gifts and follow rewards."[1155] And yet more grievously do they sin who do manifestly make a gain unto themselves of another man's filthiness, as bawds do; or such as dare give lodging and harbor unto thieves, or notorious, dishonest, and factious persons, where they may have cover for themselves or for their things.[1156]

160. When do we, by defending, commit an alien sin?

When we either protect malefactors, or defend and publish another man's doctrine, though it be perverse and wicked. When also by our care and endeavor, we labor to further and maintain that which is appointed against equity and justice. Against such persons there thundereth out this divine oracle: "Woe unto you that call evil good; and good, evil: making darkness, light; and light, darkness; making bitter, sweet; and sweet, bitter."[1157] And again: "Thou shalt not follow the multitude to do evil; neither shalt thou in judgment yield to the sentence of many, so to decline from the truth."[1158]

And this shall suffice touching alien sins, as they call them, which now certes in these days do reach very far, and are over licentiously committed every day, especially by magistrates. And there is commonly so little heed taken of them, that most men do think them not to be sins at all, nor make any account of them; although oftentimes with the filth of these sins, they defile and make guilty of perpetual torments, both their own and other men's consciences. And all these kinds mentioned before may be reduced to three kinds and in few words comprehended, as showeth

---

[1154] Cf. Ps 49:18; Augustine, *On Psalm 129*

[1155] Is 1:23

[1156] Cf. Dt 23:18; Cf. also Tb 2:21; Prv 1:14; 29:24; Nm 16:26; Ecclus 5:1; 2 Par 20:36; Gregory of Tours, *Glory of the Confessors*, Ch. 36, 71; *Glory of the Martyrs*, Bk. 1, Ch. 38, 72; Bk. 2, Ch. 13-17, 20; Theodoret, *Ecclesiastical History*, Bk. 3, Ch. 11-12; Victor., *De Persecutione Wandalica*, Bk. 1; Jo 7:24; Dn 5:23; 2 Mc 3:24; 5:15; 9:5; 1 Mc 6:12

[1157] Is 5:20; Cf. Is 10:1

[1158] Ex 23:2

St. Basil. For that we fall into the participation of another man's error or sin, it cometh to pass, either by deed and act; or by will only, and a certain purpose of the mind; or by some careless negligence, if at any time others be defrauded of the duty that we owe in admonishing them, and seeking their amendment.[1159]

But the worst kind of sinning of all others, without comparison, is when a man sinneth against the Holy Ghost.

Of Sins against the Holy Ghost

161. **What is a sin against the Holy Ghost?**

It is maliciously and contemptuously to reject the grace and liberality of God being offered, which grace, certes, is peculiarly attributed to the Holy Ghost, as to the fountain of all goodness. And this is to sin without any remedy or redress: insomuch that according to the speech of Christ, for such and so great a sin, no forgiveness is obtained either in this world, or in the world to come.[1160] For after this manner, Almighty God dealeth with us, that he giveth neither grace upon earth, nor glory in heaven to any other, but unto those only which having once known sin, do detest it; and setting before their eyes that which is good, do make choice of a righteous course of life. But from these sins is far banished both detestation of sin and the choice also of that good which were to be followed; and that, moreover, is clean rejected whereby the Holy Ghost doth use of his singular grace to withdraw a man from sin. And for this reason, they, which are fettered with such kind of sins, do either never get the grace of God, or seldom and very hardly. For these sins are not committed of human imbecility and frailty, which were to sin against the Father and the might and power of the Father, as we see in St. Peter the apostle who denied Christ;[1161] nor yet of ignorance, which were to sin against the Son and the wisdom of the Son, as was Saul his case, when he persecuted the Church;[1162] but that

---

[1159] Cf. Basil, *Sermon 2, De Baptismo*, Ch. 9
[1160] Cf. Mt 12:31; Mk 3:28; Lk 12:10
[1161] Cf. Mt 26:74; Gregory the Great, *Moralia in Job*, Bk. 25, Ch. 16
[1162] Cf. 1 Tm 1:13; Acts 9:1

which is far worse without comparison, these sins are committed of malice and obstinacy of mind, as we see, for example, in those most perverse and obstinate Pharisees.[1163]

162. **How many sins are there against the Holy Ghost?**

There are of that kind accounted six, and their names commonly used are these: presumption of the mercy of God, or of the impunity of sin; desperation; oppugning of the known truth; envying of brotherly charity; obstinacy; and impatience. But more plainly and significantly they may be thus numbered.

1. Confidently to abuse the mercy of God.
2. Utterly to despair of the grace of God, or of his own salvation.
3. Rebelliously to oppugn the truth of religion against his own conscience.
4. Vehemently to be moved with a fettled envy, because of the increase of salvation and virtue in his brother.
5. With an obstinate mind, to persist wittingly in a fault.
6. Without purpose of amendment, never to make an end of a lewd and perverse kind of life.

163. **What manner of presumption maketh a sin against the Holy Ghost?**

That which maketh a man to trust only in the mercy of God, and to be hardened and emboldened to sin, all manner of respect, of God's justice and fear being laid aside. And thus certes do very many sin at this day, who flattering themselves with a holy faith in Christ,[1164] do like beasts wallow and rot in the midst of the filth of sins;[1165] and not to themselves only, but to others also dare promise security: if only they have confidence in the merits of Christ, and in the grace of God apprehended by faith;[1166] although in the meantime the fruits of penance be nothing

---

[1163] Cf. *Summa Theologiae*, II-II, q. 14

[1164] Cf. Augustine, *De Fide et Operibus*, Ch. 14, 22; *Enchiridion*, Ch. 67; *De Haeresibus*, n. 54; Jerome, *On Osee*, Ch. 4

[1165] Cf. Jl 1:17

[1166] Cf. 2 Pt 2:18; Eccles 8:14; Council of Trent, Session 6, "Decree on Justification," Ch. 9; Can. 12-14; Jerome, *On Daniel*, Ch. 4

regarded.[1167] But to all these doth the doctor of the Gentiles cry out: "Dost thou contemn," saith he, "the riches of the goodness of God, and patience, and longanimity, not knowing that the benignity of God bringeth thee to penance?"[1168] And for that cause, he in another place is so far off from willing men to vaunt of only faith,[1169] that he biddeth even the faithful themselves, every one, to work their salvation with fear and trembling; commending unto them a faith not dead and idle,[1170] as Saint James calleth it,[1171] but lively and effectual, which worketh duly by charity.[1172] Against this abominable sin thus exclaimeth the Ecclesiasticus: "Of the remission of sin be thou not without fear, neither do though add sin upon sin. And do not say: 'The mercy of our Lord is great; he will have compassion upon the multitude of my sins.' For mercy and anger do soon approach from him, and his anger doth look upon sinners."[1173] Rightly therefore saith the prophet: "I will sing mercy and judgment unto thee, O Lord."[1174] Then in another place: "The honor of the king loveth judgment."[1175]

164. How doth a man sin against the Holy Ghost by desperation?

When the contrary vice unto presumption, whereof we spake before, doth to possess the mind of a man, that he casteth off all hope, either of obtaining pardon before God, or of attaining unto life everlasting.

After this sort sinned Cain, by despair, as himself testifieth by his speech, when he saith: "Greater is my iniquity than that I may deserve

[1167] Cf. Lk 3:8-9; 13:3; Mt 3:8, 10; Acts 26:20; Ecclus 2:22
[1168] Rom 2:4; Cf. Eccles 8:11; Ecclus 15:21; Augustine, *Tractate 33 on John*; *Homily 50 ex 50*, Ch. 4; Isidore, *De Summo Bono*, Bk. 2, Ch. 13
[1169] Cf. 1 Cor 13:1
[1170] Cf. Phil 2:12; Ps 2:11; Prv 28:14; Rom 11:20; 1 Cor 4:4; 10:12
[1171] Cf. Jas 2:14ff
[1172] Cf. Gal 5:6
[1173] Ecclus 5:5-7; Cf. Eccles 9:1; Augustine, *De Perfectione Justitiae Hominis*, Ch. 15; *On Rebuke and Grace*, Ch. 13; *Homily 41 ex 50*; *Sermon 3, De Innoc.*; Gregory the Great, *Moralia in Job*, Bk. 16, Ch. 3
[1174] Ps 100:1; Bernard, *Sermon 52, Ex Parvis*; *Sermon 6 on Canticle of Canticles*; Augustine, *Sermon 351, De Utilitate Agendae Paenitentiae*, Ch. 5
[1175] Ps 98:4; Cf. Gregory the Great, *On 1 Kings*, Ch. 3; *Moralia in Job*, Bk. 33, Ch. 15; Bk. 6, Epistle 22; Fulgentius, *Letter to Peter on the Faith*, Ch. 3; Bernard, *Sermon 38, Ex Parvis*

pardon."[1176] Thus sinned also Judas that traitor unto Christ, at what time, he, being moved with despair of salvation, like an unhappy wretch, hanged himself.[1177] But doubtless, there is no penance too late,[1178] as is manifest by the example of that thief which, upon the cross, even in those last moments of his life, obtained great grace and heavenly glory at the hands of Christ.[1179]

165. When doth he that oppugneth the truth sin against the Holy Ghost?
When that truth which concerneth the estate of faith and religion, not of ignorance but of malice, is purposely impugned, that thereby the sincerity of Catholic verity may be blemished.[1180] Of this sin were the Pharisees guilty, whose chiefest care we see to have been, as maliciously as falsely, to blaspheme Christ, to persecute the doctrine of the gospel,[1181] and to suppress the testimony of the apostles, and that even against their own consciences.[1182] Not unlike unto these are they that are said by the prophet "to sit in the chair of pestilence,"[1183] and are called by St. Peter "lying masters that do bring in sects of perdition,"[1184] finally, by St. Paul, "heretics,"[1185] "men corrupted in mind, reprobate concerning the faith,"[1186] "attending to

---

[1176] Gn 4:14; Cf. Bernard, *Sermon 11 on Canticle of Canticles*

[1177] Cf. Mt 27:3; Acts 1:18; Eph 4:19; 2 Kgs 2:20

[1178] Cf. Ez 18:21, 27; 33:11; 1 Jn 1:7, 9; 2:1; Jer 3:1; Is 1:18; Ps 144:8; Ecclus 17:21, 28

[1179] Cf. Lk 23:40; Augustine, *Retractions*, Bk. 1, Ch. 19; *On Rebuke and Grace*, Ch. 15; *Sermon 18, De Temp.*, Ch. 16; Leo the Great, *Epistle 91 ad Theo.*; Council of Trent, Session 14, "Doctrine on the Sacrament of Penance," Ch. 7; Cf. also Augustine, *Sermon 58, De Temp.*; *On Psalm 50*; Gregory the Great, *Moralia in Job*, Bk. 8, Ch. 14; Isidore, *De Summo Bono*, Bk. 2, Ch. 14; Chrysostom, *Homily 2 on Psalm 50*; Bernard, *Sermon 5, De Nativitate Domini*

[1180] Cf. Leo the Great, *Epistle 10 ad Flav.*, Ch. 1; Augustine, *De Genesi ad Litteram*, Bk. 7, Ch. 9; *Tractate 18 on John*; *De Utilitate Credendi ad Honoratum*, Ch. 1; *City of God*, Bk. 18, Ch. 51; Bk. 21, Ch. 25

[1181] Cf. Mt 12:24; 15:2; 21:45; 22:15; Jn 7:48; 12:10, 19

[1182] Cf. Acts 4:16; 5:18

[1183] Ps 1:1

[1184] 2 Pt 2:1

[1185] Ti 3:10

[1186] 2 Tm 3:8

spirits of error,"[1187] "subverted and condemned by their own judgment."[1188] Among whom may be numbered that same seducer Elymas, whom St. Paul publicly reprehending, said with great vehemency: "O full of all guile and all deceit, son of the devil, enemy of all justice, thou ceasest not to subvert the right ways of our Lord."[1189]

To this kind also is referred blasphemy of the Spirit, which sin Christ doth greatly rebuke in the Jews, and maketh it worse than other sins.[1190] And would to God that this sin did not reign in these our days. For against the Holy Ghost do they also blaspheme (as writeth Damasus), who, against the holy canons of the fathers, indicted by the instinct of the Holy Ghost, "do anything willingly or malepertly, or presume to speak, or willfully give their consent to them that have a mind so to do. For it is manifest that such a presumption is one kind of the blasphemies against the Holy Ghost,"[1191] thus saith Damasus.

166. How is envy of brotherly grace a sin against the Holy Ghost?

When we are stricken with a great grief and sorrow, because of the splendor and increase of virtues and God's gifts in which our brother doth excel.

Which sin seemeth to be rather proper unto the devil than unto man: whereas the devil doth most wrathfully take the increase and continuance of the grace of God in man;[1192] and for that cause he is not only an accuser of our brethren,[1193] but also an implacable adversary of God and of all good men, who, as a roaring lion, goeth about seeking whom he may devour.[1194] There were among the Jews such sons of Satan, who did altogether envy unto the Gentiles, the lately springing grace of the gospel, as we read in the Acts of the Apostles.[1195]

[1187] 1 Tm 4:1

[1188] Ti 3:11

[1189] Acts 13:10

[1190] Cf. Mt 12:31

[1191] Damasus, *apud Gratianum*, 25 *quaeft. 1. violatores*

[1192] Cf. Ws 2:24

[1193] Cf. Apoc 12:10

[1194] Cf. 1 Pt 5:8

[1195] Cf. Acts 11:2; 13:45; Gn 4:5; Cf. also Augustine, *On the Sermon on the Mount*, Bk. 1, Ch. 22; *Retractions*, Bk. 1, Ch. 19

167. What kind of obstinacy is that which is a sin against the Holy Ghost?

That certes which beareth an obstinate mind against him that giveth him good admonition, so that he will not suffer him felt by any means to be withdrawn from his damnable course.

With this sin was King Pharaoh notably attainted, who although he were so often admonished by Moses, and sometimes afflicted with very sore scourges from God,[1196] yet notwithstanding in his tyrannical purpose, he obstinately persisted, and perished.[1197] Famous also was that incorrigible obstinacy of the Jews,[1198] whom St. Steven, painting out, as it were, in their colors, saith: "With a hard neck and with uncircumcised ears, you have always resisted the Holy Ghost."[1199] And not unlike unto them are those at this day that, being addicted unto new sects, may not abide so much as to hear or read any Catholic instructions, but, even like to the serpent called the asp, shutting their ears against the sweet melody of the sound doctrine of the Church,[1200] they seem to say: "Depart thou from us, and we will not have the knowledge of thy ways";[1201] which is nothing else than as St. Paul speaketh: "According to their hardness and impenitent heart, to heap to themselves wrath, in the day of wrath, and of the revelation of the just judgment of God."[1202] For as Solomon also teacheth: "To a man, that with a hard neck contemneth him that correcteth him, a sudden destruction shall come upon him, and health shall not follow him."[1203]

168. When is a sin of impenitency committed?

When a man without any end or measure of his sins, which truly he should wash away by wholesome penance, resolveth moreover that he never will do any penance at all. Of this kind of persons, who are such desperate and

[1196] Cf. Ex 7ff; Augustine, *Quaestiones in Exodum*, q. 18, 24; *Sermon 88, De Temp.*; Gregory the Great, *Moralia in Job*, Bk. 31, Ch. 11; Bk. 11, Ch. 5
[1197] Cf. Ex 14
[1198] Cf. Jer 5:3; 8:5; Is 48:4; Zac 7:11; Gn 49:7
[1199] Acts 7:51
[1200] Cf. Ps 57:5
[1201] Jb 21:14
[1202] Rom 2:5
[1203] Prv 29:1; Cf. Bernard, *Sermon 42 on Canticle of Canticles*; Cf. also Augustine, *Enchiridion*, Ch. 83; *On Psalm 58*, conc. 1; Gregory the Great, *Homily 11 on Ezechiel*; Bernard, *De Consideratione*, Bk. 1, Ch. 2; *Sermon, De Conversione ad Clericos*, Ch. 4

pitiful sinners and so will remain, both their life and their death is most abominable;[1204] forasmuch as, if not in words, yet in deed they seem to say: "We have entered into league with death, and with hell we have made a pact."[1205] And of these also may that saying be understood, which St. John avoucheth: "There is a sin to death, for that I say not that any man ask."[1206]

Thus much concerning the sins against the Holy Ghost, which are doubtless most grievous, and which Almighty God either never or very hardly doth pardon. For which cause, we ought often to guard ourselves, and to confirm others against the same, that we may observe that saying: "Contristate not, extinguish not the Spirit of God."[1207] "This day if you hear his voice, harden not your hearts."[1208] "Let none of you be obdurate with the fallacy of sin."[1209] "For a hard heart shall be in evil case at the last."[1210] Now, therefore, let us come to those sins which are also not a little heinous, and are wont to be called, "sins that cry unto heaven."

Of Sins That Cry unto Heaven

169. **What sins are those that are said to cry unto heaven?**
Those which, notably above others, are known to have a manifest and exceeding wickedness, and do singularly purchase to those which commit them God's indignation and vengeance. Of this sort there are four numbered in holy scripture, to wit: willful murder,[1211] sodomy,[1212] oppression of the poor,[1213] and defrauding the laboring man's hire.[1214]

[1204] Cf. Ps 33:22
[1205] Is 28:15; Cf. Is 3:8-9; Ps 51:3, 7; Prv 2:14
[1206] 1 Jn 5:16; Cf. Augustine, *On Rebuke and Grace*, Ch. 12; *Retractions*, Bk. 1, Ch. 19
[1207] Eph 4:30; 1 Thes 5:19
[1208] Ps 94:8
[1209] Heb 3:13
[1210] Ecclus 3:27; Cf. Ecclus 3:7; Cf. also Augustine, *Sermon 21, De Verbis Domini*, Ch. 12-13; *Epistle 50 to Boniface*; Gelasius I, *in tomo de anathematis vinculo.*
[1211] Cf. Gn 4:10
[1212] Cf. Gn 18:20
[1213] Cf. Ex 22:23
[1214] Cf. Dt 24:15; Jas 5:4; Cf. also Augustine, *Enchiridion*, Ch. 30; *Annotationes in Job*, Ch. 30; *Locutiones de Genesi*; *Quaestiones in Exodum*, q. 5; Gregory the Great, *Pastoral Rule*, Bk. 3, Ch. 31, Admonition 32; *Expositio in Psalmos Poenitentiales*, second psalm

170. How doth the scripture teach that willful murder is revenged?

In most grievous manner doubtless, as Almighty God showeth in these words, wherein he rebuketh Cain the first manslayer: "What hast thou done?" saith he, "the voice of the blood of thy brother crieth to me from the earth. Now therefore shalt thou be cursed upon earth."[1215] And in another place God's own voice doth testify: "Whosoever shalt shed man's blood, his blood shall be shed also, for to the image of God was man made."[1216] The kingly psalmist singeth: "Men of blood shall not live half their days."[1217] For this is a very heinous wickedness, and he doth a most horrible injury to his neighbor that bereaveth him of his life without lawful authority.[1218] For which cause, Christ himself saith also: "All that take the sword, shall perish with the sword."[1219]

171. And what is extant in holy scripture touching the sin of Sodom and the punishments thereof?

"The men of Sodom," saith the scripture, "were very naught, and sinners before God too too much."[1220] This horrible and abominable sin Saint Peter,[1221] and Saint Paul,[1222] do reprove; yea nature herself doth abhor; and the scripture also doth declare the greatness of so foul a wickedness, in these words: "The cry of the Sodomites and the Gomorians is multiplied, and their sin is aggravated too too much."[1223] For which cause the angels do speak thus unto the just man Lot, who did greatly abhor from the outrageous filthiness of the Sodomites:[1224] "We will destroy this place, because the cry of the them hath increased before our Lord, who hath sent us to

---

[1215] Gn 4:10-11; Cf. Ambrose, *De Cain et Abel*, Bk. 2, Ch. 9
[1216] Gn 9:6; Cf. Ex 21:12, 14; Lv 24:17; Nm 35:16, 20; Dt 19:11; 1 Jn 3:15
[1217] Ps 54:24
[1218] Cf. Augustine, *Contra Faustum*, Bk. 2, Ch. 70
[1219] Mt 26:52; Cf. Apoc 13:10; Cf. also Council of Ancrya, Can. 22; Council of Epaone, Can. 31; Council of Tribur, Can. 54ff
[1220] Gn 13:13
[1221] Cf. 2 Pt 2:6
[1222] Cf. Rom 1:24; 1 Tm 2:10; Eph 5:5; Jgs 19:22; 20:46
[1223] Gn 18:20
[1224] Cf. 2 Pt 2:6

destroy them."[1225] "Therefore, our Lord rained down upon Sodom and Gomorrah brimstone and fire, from out of heaven, and overthrew those cities, and all the country about."[1226] Neither doth the scripture leave untouched the causes which moved the Sodomites and may also move others to this so grievous a sin. For thus we read in Ezechiel: "Behold this was the iniquity of Sodom thy sister: pride, fullness of bread, and abundance, and the idleness of her and her daughters; and they did not stretch their hand to the needy and poor."[1227]

And of this vice, which can never be sufficiently detested, are they guilty who do not fear to break the law of God, yea and the law of nature written in Leviticus, which is this: *Cum masculo non commiscearis coitu foemineo, quia abominatio est. Cum omni pecore non coibis, nec maculaberis cum eo.*[1228] Which sin, if it be committed, we are admonished in the same place that the very earth is polluted with such horrible and abominable lusts, and that God's wrath is very much provoked against the people,[1229] and that the crime is to be punished with death.[1230] For which cause St. Paul doth not once only rebuke the liers with mankind; and he condemneth also unclean and effeminate persons,[1231] of which one was Onan son of Judah who could not escape the present revenge of God, for that he sinned against his own body, and, worse than any beast, would violate the honesty and order of nature.[1232]

172. **What doth the scripture propose touching the oppression of the poor?**

"Thou shalt not make sad the stranger," saith our Lord, "neither shalt thou afflict him: for you yourselves were strangers in the land of Egypt. Ye shall not hurt the widow and the fatherless. If you do hurt them, they will cry

[1225] Gn 19:13

[1226] Gn 19:24-25; Cf. Ws 10:6; Dt 29:23; Jude 1:7; Gn 13:10; Gregory the Great, *Moralia in Job*, Bk. 14, Ch. 10; Augustine, *City of God*, Bk. 16, Ch. 30; Tertullian, *Apology*, Ch. 40; *De Sodoma*, Ch. 4

[1227] Ez 16:49

[1228] Lv 18:22-23; Cf. Dt 27:21; Chrysostom, *Homily 4 on Romans*; Tertullian, *On Modesty*, Ch. 4; Augustine, *Confessions*, Bk. 3, Ch. 8; *Epistle 109*

[1229] Cf. Lv 20:13, 15; Ex 22:19; Jl 3:3

[1230] Cf. *L. cum vir nubit. C. ad legem Jul. de adult.*

[1231] Cf. 1 Cor 6:9; Rom 1:24; 1 Tm 1:10; Gal 5:10-11

[1232] Cf. Gn 38:9; Jerome, *On Ephesians*, Ch. 5

out unto me, and I will hear their cry; and my fury shall take indignation, and I will strike you with the sword, and your wives shall be widows and your children orphans."[1233]

For which cause the Egyptians were scourged with so many plagues, and with their most cruel king and tyrant Pharaoh,[1234] who spared not to kill the very infants of the Hebrews,[1235] were finally drowned[1236] because of their cruelty, more than barbarous, against the Israelites. "I have seen," saith our Lord, "the affliction of my people in Egypt, and I have heard their cry, because of the hardness of those that are overseers of the works; and knowing their grief, I came down to deliver them out of the hands of the Egyptians."[1237] For this cause doth our Lord threaten by Isaiah the prophet: "Woe they that make unjust laws, and writing, have written injustice, that they might oppress the poor in judgment, and do violence to the cause of the humble of my people; that widows might be their prey, and that they might spoil the fatherless."[1238] And in the same prophet there is extant this complaint of cruel and unjust magistrates: "Thy princes are infidels, companions of thieves: all do love bribes; they follow after rewards. They do not give judgment to the fatherless, and the cause of the widow doth not enter in unto them."[1239] Again: "Their collectors have spoiled my people."[1240] And there is no doubt, but that cities and provinces by reason of this abominable sin, which is committed by tyrannical magistrates, are oftentimes brought into extreme danger.

173. **What finally doth the scripture teach, concerning the withholding or diminishing of the laborer's wages?**

We read in the apostle St. James how vehemently he doth upbraid rich men with their cruel sparing, and egregious wickedness in defrauding poor

[1233] Ex 22:21-24; Cf. Dt 15:9; 24:10; Ecclus 35:16; Jer 21:12; 22:3; Mal 3:5; 2 Kgs 12:3
[1234] Cf. Ex 7ff
[1235] Cf. Ex 1:8
[1236] Cf. Ex 14:27
[1237] Ex 3:7-8
[1238] Is 10:1-2; Cf. Dt 27:19; Jb 24:1; Mt 23:14
[1239] Is 1:23; Cf. Jer 5:28; Zac 7:9; Ps 93:3; Am 5:11
[1240] Is 3:12; Cf. Is 3:14

laborers: "Behold, the hire of the workmen that have reaped your fields, which is defrauded by you, crieth; and their cry hath entered into the ears of the Lord of Sabaoth."[1241] And Ecclesiasticus writeth in this manner: "The bread of the needy is the life of the poor man: he that defraudeth him is a man of blood. He that taketh away the bread in sweat is he that killeth his neighbor. He that sheddeth blood and he that defraudeth the hired man are brethren."[1242]

Therefore, it is decreed by the law of God: "Thou shalt not deny the hire of thy poor and needy brother, or of the stranger that abideth with thee in the land and is within thy gates; but the very same day, thou shalt render to him the price of his labor before the sunset, because he is poor, and thereby he sustaineth his life; lest he cry against thee to our Lord, and it be reputed to thee for a sin."[1243]

174. **To what end is all this discourse of sins to be referred, and what is the use and commodity thereof?**

This discourse belongeth to the first part of Christian justice, which consisteth in knowing and fleeing of evils; and the use and commodity thereof is rightly to discern, and being discerned, utterly to eschew those things which are verily evils, contrary to God, pernicious unto men; and if in case any of them be committed, then diligently to endeavor to purge the same.

Hereby we learn also how a wise man differeth from a fool, and a just man from a wicked person: "For a wise man feareth and declineth from evil; but a fool leapeth over and is confident."[1244] "For a fool doth not receive the words of wisdom, except thou speak those things which his heart is set upon,"[1245] as witnesseth Solomon; who also writeth thus: "The paths of just persons, as a bright shining light, proceedeth and increaseth even unto a perfect day; the way of the wicked is dark and

---

[1241] Jas 5:4
[1242] Ecclus 34:25-27; Cf. Ecclus 7:22
[1243] Dt 24:14-15; Cf. Lv 19:13; Tb 4:15; Mal 3:5
[1244] Prv 14:16
[1245] Prv 18:2

obscure: they know not where they fall."[1246] Many certes are shamefully ignorant of those pernicious plagues of the mind, the sins that we have declared; others, although they know them never so well, yet do they not avoid and detest them.[1247] But worst of all are others who are obdurate with the custom of sin;[1248] of which kind, it is thus said: "A wicked man when he is come into the bottom of sins, contemneth, but shame and reproach doth follow him."[1249] And this kind of men doth contemn those things especially which Christian justice doth require, not only for the marking and discerning of vices, but also for the necessary avoiding and purging of the same.[1250]

Of the Purging of Sins

175. **And by what means are sins purged?**

Here, first of all, it is out of controversy that Christ is unto us a propitiator[1251] and that Lamb of God that taketh away the sins of the world, who only could deserve for us remission of sins, and make purgation of the same.[1252]

Then is it most certain that God doth purify men's hearts by faith, as St. Peter saith, because that without faith (which is the door and foundation of man's salvation) none can obtain, or hope for remission, or purging of their sins.[1253] And as touching faith, they are utterly destitute thereof, who, not consenting with the faith of the Church,[1254] do with a certain

[1246] Prv 4:18-19
[1247] Cf. Augustine, *On Grace and Free Will*, Ch. 4; *De Libero Arbitrio*, Bk. 3, Ch. 22; Bernard, *Epistle 77 ad Hugon.*; Chrysostom, *Homily 26 on Romans*
[1248] See before of obstinacy; Cf. Augustine, *Enchiridion*, Ch. 80
[1249] Prv 18:3
[1250] Cf. Council of Trent, Session 5, Can. 3; Session 6, "Decree on Justification," Ch. 2, 7
[1251] Cf. Rom 3:24; 1 Jn 2:1; 4:10; 1:7
[1252] Cf. Jn 1:36; Mt 1:21; 1 Cor 1:30; 1 Tm 2:5; Heb 1:3; 9:12; Acts 4:12
[1253] Cf. Acts 15:9; Heb 11:1, 6; Gal 2:16; 3:8; Rom 3:24; Lk 7:50; Eph 2:8; Council of Trent, Session 6, "Decree on Justification," Ch. 8
[1254] Cf. Augustine, *Tractate 67 on John*; Leo, *Sermon 4, De Nat. Dom.*

vain confidence promise unto themselves and others remission of sins, and grace of justification through Christ.[1255]

But they that, persevering in the faith and unity of the Church, do desire to be delivered from their sins have many ways proposed unto them in scripture for the taking away of their sins, amongst which the principal is the sacrament of penance.[1256] Which, being despised, it is to no purpose to use any other remedies for deadly sins.[1257] For this hath Christ the physician of souls ordained, not only as a present, but also as a necessary medicine, to be of force against any leper of sin whatsoever; and commending the same, he hath said to the priests: "Whose sins you shall remit, they are remitted them."[1258]

Secondly, sins are cleansed and purged by alms, because it is written: "Alms delivereth from all sin and from death; and will not suffer a soul to go into darkness."[1259] Therefore, the prophet giveth this admonition: "Redeem thy sins with alms, and thy iniquities with the mercies of the poor."[1260]

Thirdly, sins are remitted, when, although we have been never so much wronged, yet we do forgive our brother the offense; our Lord having said: "If you will forgive men their offenses, your heavenly Father will forgive you also your offenses."[1261]

Fourthly, the same effect is wrought when, by admonishing our brother that sinneth, we do win him and bring him to amendment, as it is written: "He which maketh a sinner to be converted from the error of his way, shall save his soul from death, and covereth a multitude of sins."[1262]

Fifthly, hereunto belongeth the abundance of sincere charity, which is very puissant and mighty to obtain and accomplish all good things; for

---

[1255] See before of presumption, p. 164-165.
[1256] Cf. Origen, *On Leviticus*, Bk. 2; Augustine, *Contra Cresconium*, Bk. 2, Ch. 12; Chrysostom, *Conc. 4.*, *De Lazar.*, at the end; *Homily 6 on John*
[1257] See before of the sacrament of penance, p. 106-119.
[1258] Jn 20:23
[1259] Tb 4:11; Cf. 12:8; Ecclus 3:15, 33; Prv 13:8; 15:27; 16:6; Lk 11:41
[1260] Dn 4:24; Cf. Is 1:17-18; Heb 13:16; See after, of alms.
[1261] Mt 6:14; Cf. Lk 6:37; Mk 11:25; Ecclus 28:2
[1262] Jas 5:20

PETER CANISIUS

which it is said of Mary Magdalen: "Many sins are forgiven her, because she loved much."[1263] "For charity covereth the multitude of sins."[1264]

Sixthly, hereunto is available the sacrifice of a contrite heart, which God never despiseth, and a humble knowledge of a man's self, and confession of his sins.[1265] For our Lord hath "respect upon the prayer of the humble, and doth not despise their petitions,"[1266] insomuch that hereupon holy David also testifieth of himself: "I have said: I will confess against myself my injustice unto our Lord, and thou hast remitted the impiety of my sin."[1267] And St. John generally, to all that do truly confess, promiseth this grace: "If we confess our sins," saith he, "he is faithful and just for to forgive us our sins, and to cleanse us from all iniquity."[1268] Therefore, the Ninevites, when they did earnestly persevere in works of humility and penance, appeased the present wrath of God, and turned away the imminent destruction of their city and country.[1269] And therefore, of them we read it thus written: "God saw their works, because they were turned from their evil ways; and God took compassion of the evil which he had spoken that he would do to them, and did it not."[1270]

Thus, finally, we learn by the testimony of holy scripture that, by these and other means and offices of true piety done by the grace of Christ, this effect is wrought: that the sins of faithful penitents in the Church (as we said before) are purged and taken away;[1271] in regard whereof the apostle warneth: "Having therefore these promises, my dearest, let us cleanse ourselves from all inquination of the flesh and spirit, perfecting sanctification in the fear of God."[1272] And with no less vehemency speaketh St. James: "Cleanse," saith he, "your hands you sinners; and purify your hearts you

[1263] Lk 7:47
[1264] 1 Pt 4:8; Prv 10:12
[1265] Cf. Ps 50:19; Lk 18:13; Mt 18:32; Ecclus 21:1
[1266] Ps 101:18
[1267] Ps 31:5
[1268] 1 Jn 1:9
[1269] Cf. Jon 23:5; Mt 12:41; Lk 11:32; 3 Kgs 21:29; Ws 11:24; Cyprian, *Epistle 40*; *Epistle 8*; *Epistle 26*
[1270] Jon 3:10; Cf. Nm 25:11; Ps 105; 30
[1271] Cf. Prv 10:2; Acts 8:22; 2 Cor 7:10
[1272] 2 Cor 7:1; Cf. 2 Tm 2:19, 21

double of mind. Be miserable, and mourn, and weep; let your laughter be turned into mourning, and joy into sorrow. Be humble in the sight of our Lord, and he will exalt you."[1273] For it is not sufficient for a man to amend his manners, and to leave his misdeeds. (That we may again use the words of St. Augustine:) "Unless by the sorrow of penance, by the sighings of humility, and by the sacrifice of a contrite heart, together with the cooperation of alms; satisfaction be made to God, for those things also that have been committed otherwise, who so shall know that any mortal sins do bear sway in him."[1274] As the same saint writeth: "Except he worthily amend himself and (if he have space) do penance alongside and give large alms, and refrain from the sins themselves, he cannot be purged with that transitory fire whereof the apostle hath spoken,[1275] but shall be tormented without any redress in the everlasting flame."[1276] For not deadly sins, but little sins are purged and cleansed after this life.

176. **And what conception ought we to have of little sins?**

This surely: that such lighter sins as the wandering of the mind, an idle word, immoderate laugther, and such like, which are called quotidian, or venial sins, and without the which this life is not passed over, "for in many things we offend all,"[1277] as we also noted before although they are not deadly, and do seem little in outward appearance, yet they are not to be contemned.[1278] For so much as they displease God, or (as St. Paul speaketh) they "contristate the Holy Ghost,"[1279] they darken and obscure the conscience, they diminish the fervor of charity, and they do hinder the procetending of virtues, and draw a man oftentimes to

---

[1273] Jas 4:8; Cf. Ez 18:27

[1274] Augustine, *Homily 50 ex 50*, Ch. 15; Cf. Augustine, *Enchiridion*, Ch. 70; Cyprian, *On the Lapsed*, at the end; and others, as before of satisfaction, p. 112-118.

[1275] Cf. 1 Cor 3:13; Augustine, *Homily 16 ex 50*; *Enchiridion*, Ch. 67; *De Fide et Operibus*, Ch. 16; *De Octo Dulcitii Quaestionibus*, q. 1

[1276] Augustine, *Sermon 41, De Sanctis*

[1277] Jas 3:2; Cf. 1 Jn 1:8; Eccles 7:21; Prv 24:16; Ps 31:6

[1278] Cf. Augustine, *Sermon 9, De Decem Chordis*, Ch. 11; *On Psalm 129*; *Sermon 244, De Temp.*; *Sermon 244, De Temp.*; *Tractate 12 on John*

[1279] Eph 4:30

greater vices and dangers.[1280] For which cause it is written: "He that despiseth little things, shall by little and little fall."[1281] "He that loveth danger, shall perish in it."[1282] "He that shall sin in one thing, shall lose many good things."[1283]

Therefore, these blots and filths of the soul, as much as may be, are to be eschewed, for as we read: "There shall not enter into the heavenly Jerusalem any polluted thing."[1284] And except they be washed away in this life, they do burden a man after his death, and cannot certes be cleansed without the bitter pains of purgatory fire;[1285] which fire, although it be not everlasting, yet, if we believe Saint Augustine, "it is more sharp and grievous than whatsoever a man can suffer in this life."[1286]

177. What then are the remedies to purge the lighter sort of sins?

For the washing away of such filths of the soul in this life, the primitive Church hath acknowledged and used these remedies: a humble accusation of a man's self; our Lord's Prayer; knocking of the breast; and other the like devout exercises, either toward God, or toward our neighbor; and afflictions of the body, voluntarily and devoutly undertaken.[1287] Which remedies, wise men certes so much the more willingly and seriously do embrace, by how much they do more perfectly know, and more diligently weigh and consider the severity of God's justice in revenging of sin.[1288] Which may be expressly showed even by that one dreadful

---

[1280] Cf. Chrysostom, *Homily 87 on Matthew*; *Homily 8 on 1 Corinthians*; *Sermon, De levium peccatorum periculis*; Bernard, *Sermon 1, De Conversione Pauli*; *Tractate, De praecepto et dispensat.*, Ch. 14
[1281] Ecclus 19:1
[1282] Ecclus 3:27
[1283] Eccles 9:18
[1284] Apoc 21:27; Cf. Ps 14:2; 23:4
[1285] Cf. See above of satisfaction, p. 112-118.
[1286] Augustine, *On Psalm 37*; *Sermon 41, De Sanctis*; Cf. Gregory the Great, *Expositio in Psalmos Poenitentiales*; Cf. also Augustine, *Enchiridion*, Ch. 78; *City of God*, Bk. 21, Ch. 27; Isidore, *De Summo Bono*, Bk. 2, Ch. 18
[1287] Cf. Augustine, *Epistle 108*; *Enchiridion*, Ch. 71-72; *Tractate 12 on John*; *Sermon 41, De Sanctis*; *City of God*, Bk. 21, Ch. 27; *Homily 50 ex 50*, Ch. 13; Fourth Council of Toledo, Can. 9
[1288] Cf. Jb 24:12; Prosper, *Sententia ex Augustine*, Ch. 210; Augustine, *On Psalm 58*

speech of Christ: "I say unto you that every idle word that men shall speak, they shall render an account for it in the day of judgment";[1289] also by that speech of St. Peter: "The just man shall scarce be saved."[1290] Insomuch that for this cause Job, a man otherwise just and innocent, hath said: "I did fear all my works knowing that thou didst not spare him that sinneth."[1291] And the apostle Saint Paul: "It is horrible to fall into the hands of the living God"[1292] "But if we did judge ourselves (as the same apostle warneth us) we should not be judged."[1293] Therefore, "Blessed is that man that is always fearful; but he that is of a hard heart shall fall into evil."[1294]

178. Is it sufficient to abstain from sin?

Christian justice, whereof we have hitherto treated, proposeth two parts, and as equally necessary commendeth them unto us in these words: "Decline from evil, and do good."[1295] As also St. Paul teacheth: "Hating evil and cleaving to good."[1296] Therefore, "It is not sufficient," as St. Augustine hath plainly said, "to abstain from evil; except that be done which is good, and it is a small matter to hurt no man, except thou dost endeavor to do good to many."[1297] Wherefore, having now finished after our manner the first part of justice, which prohibiteth evils, it followeth now that, by the help of Christ, we go forward to speak of the other part also, which consisteth in the pursuit of those things which are good.[1298]

[1289] Mt 12:36
[1290] 1 Pt 4:18
[1291] Jb 9:28
[1292] Heb 10:31
[1293] 1 Cor 11:31
[1294] Prv 28:14
[1295] Ps 36:27; Cf. Ps 33:15; Augustine, On Psalm 36
[1296] Rom 12:9; Cf. 1 Pt 3:10-11; Tb 4:13; Is 1:16; Eccles 3:32; Col 3:8; Eph 4:16-17, 20; Jas 4:17; Mt 3:10; 7:19
[1297] Prosper, Sententia ex Augustine, Ch. 86; Cf. Augustine, City of God, Bk. 19, Ch. 14
[1298] Cf. Bernard, Sermon 34, Ex Parvis; Chrysostom, On Psalm 4; Homily 16 on Ephesians; Augustine, Sermon 59, De Temp.

Of Three Sorts of Good Works

179. In what good things doth Christian justice consist?

This justice extendeth so far, that it containeth in itself all the good things which are honestly, justly, and devoutly done; and proposeth the same unto us, as to be both desired and followed.[1299] Wherefore, thus doth the apostle admonish the faithful: "Walk worthy of God, in all things pleasing, fructifying in all good work."[1300] "Providing good things not only before God, but also before all men."[1301] For this is the true use and proper fruit of our vocation, and of Christian justice purchased by Christ, as witnesseth St. Peter: "That being dead to sins we may live to justice";[1302] that is to say, as St. Paul expoundeth it: "That denying impiety and worldly desires, we live soberly and justly and godly in this world."[1303] To this effect is that of the gospel proposed unto us: "That without fear being delivered from the hands of our enemies, we may serve him in holiness and justice before him all our days."[1304] For therefore hath Christ redeemed us "from all iniquity, that he might cleanse to himself a people acceptable, a pursuer of good works."[1305] For, "we are the work of God himself, created in Christ Jesus in good works, which God hath prepared that we should walk in them."[1306]

Thus doth St. Paul constantly write and warn all men about the observance and continual practice of Christian justice. And for this cause also St. John doth wisely admonish and absolutely define: "Little children, let no man seduce you. He that doth justice is just, even as he also is just. He that committeth sin is of the devil."[1307] And St. James expressly teacheth: "By works a man is justified and not by faith only. For even as the body

---

[1299] Cf. Chrysostom, *On Psalm 4*; *On Psalm 14*; *Homily 23 on Genesis*
[1300] Col 1:10
[1301] Rom 12:17; Cf. 2 Cor 8:21; Mt 5:17; 1 Pt 2:12
[1302] 1 Pt 2:24
[1303] Ti 2:12; Cf. Bernard, *Sermon 2, De Resur.*
[1304] Lk 1:74-75
[1305] Ti 2:14
[1306] Eph 2:10
[1307] 1 Jn 3:7-8

without the spirit is dead, so also faith without works is dead."[1308] Then again the same apostle: "He that hath looked in the law of perfect liberty, and hath remained in it, not made a forgetful hearer, but a doer of the work; this man shall be blessed in his deed."[1309] And no other meaning than this had St. Paul when he said: "Not the hearers of the law are just with God, but the doers of the law shall be just."[1310]

180. What profit do the works of Christian justice procure?

Very singular certes, and manifold, both in this life and in the life to come. For hereunto belongeth that speech of St. Paul: "Piety is profitable to all things, having promise of the life that now is, and of the life to come."[1311] Then in another place we find it written: "Of good labors there is glorious fruit."[1312]

For first these works proceeding from a lively faith, that is, from a faith working by charity, are not only signs of Christian vocation, but do also confirm and make sure the same in us.[1313] And therefore St. Peter the apostle, who in every place exhorteth to good works, hath added this also: "Brethren, labor the more, that by good works you may make sure your vocation and election: for doing these things you shall not sin at any time."[1314]

Secondly, they do augment grace in the believers[1315] and do perfect sanctification, as witnesseth the apostle;[1316] insomuch that hereupon Saint James also affirmeth that faith which doth work with works is also consummate by the same works.[1317]

[1308] Jas 3:24, 26; Cf. Augustine, *In Praefat.*, *On Psalm 31*; *De Fide et Operibus*, Ch. 14; Chrysostom, *Homily 2 on Genesis*

[1309] Jas 1:25

[1310] Rom 2:13

[1311] 1 Tm 4:8; Cf. Prv 11:17-18; 2 Par 15:7; Mt 10:41; 19:21, 29; Gn 12:1; 15:1; Ecclus 12:2; 36:18; Jer 31:16

[1312] Ws 3:15; Cf. Ws 10:17; Mal 3:14; 1 Cor 15:58; Heb 6:10

[1313] Cf. Gal 5

[1314] 2 Pt 1:10; Cf. Cyprian, *Epistle 57 to Cornelius*, at the end

[1315] Cf. 2 Cor 9:10; Col 1:10; 1 Pt 2:2

[1316] Cf. 2 Cor 7:1; Rom 6:22; Apoc 22:11; Ecclus 18:22; Council of Trent, Session 6, "Decree on Justification," Ch. 10

[1317] Cf. Jas 2:22

Thirdly, they engender a confidence of a good conscience, and do the more encourage to pray, and to obtain anything at God's hand,[1318] for it is written: "Alms shall be a great confidence before the high God to all them that do the same."[1319] And again: "My dearest, if our heart do not reprehend us, we have confidence toward God. And whatsoever we shall ask, we shall receive of him: because we keep his commandments, and do those things which are pleasing before him."[1320] There is an example extant in Hezekiah the king, who having confidence in a good conscience, and being approved therein by God's own voice, said: "I beseech thee, O Lord, remember, I pray thee, how I have walked before thee in truth, and in a perfect heart; and have done that which is good in thy sight."[1321]

Finally, they do cause that, laboring in the vineyard of Christ, we may receive the day penny, (to wit,) the promised reward of life everlasting,[1322] and the crown of justice,[1323] which, keeping the commandments of God in the Church,[1324] we do in Christ deserve.[1325] Therefore our Lord saith: "Call the work folks and pay them their hire."[1326] Holy David saith: "Thy servant keepeth them," (to wit,) the commandments of God, "in keeping them much retribution."[1327] And again: "I have inclined my heart to keep thy justifications forevermore, because of retribution."[1328] St. Paul also saith: "I have fought a good fight, I have consummate my course, I have kept the faith. Concerning the rest, there is laid up for me a crown of justice, which our Lord will render to me in that day, a just judge; and not only to me,

[1318] Cf. Jn 3:20; 1 Jn 4:17; Jas 2:25; Gal 6:4
[1319] Tb 4:12
[1320] 1 Jn 3:21-22; Cf. Jn 15:7; Augustine, *In Praefat., On Psalm 31*
[1321] Is 38:3; Cf. 4 Kgs 20:3; Ps 7:9; 16:1; 17:21, 25; 25:1; 34:24; 131:1
[1322] Cf. Mt 20; Augustine, *Tractate 67 on John*; Gregory the Great, *Diaglogues*, Bk. 4, Ch. 35
[1323] Cf. 2 Tm 4:8; Jas 1:12
[1324] Cf. Mt 19:17
[1325] Cf. Jn 3:21; 15:2, 4; Ecclus 16:15; Heb 13:16; Ws 3:5-6; 2 Thes 1:5-6; Apoc 3:4-5; Council of Trent, Session 6, "Decree on Justification," Ch. 16; Cyprian, *On the Unity of the Church*; Augustine, *Epistle 105*; *Of the Morals of the Catholic Church*, Ch. 25
[1326] Mt 20:8; Cf. Ws 5:16
[1327] Ps 18:12; Cf. Heb 11:6; Lk 14:14; Col 3:24; Eph 6:8; 2 Cor 4:17; Augustine, *On Psalm 93*
[1328] Ps 118:112; Cf. Mt 19:12; Augustine, *On Psalm 120*

but to them also that love his coming."[1329] Finally, Christ himself saith: "If though wilt enter into life, keep the commandments."[1330] And again: "They that have done good things shall come forth into the resurrection of life; but they that have done evil, into resurrection of judgment."[1331] Then in another place: "He that doth the will of my Father which is in heaven, he shall enter into the kingdom of heaven."[1332]

By all which it is made very manifest how much it standeth every one of us upon: if we desire life everlasting, to ponder those speeches of Almighty God: "He that is just, let him be justified yet; and let the holy be sanctified yet. Behold, I come quickly and my reward is with me, to render to every man according to his works."[1333] "Therefore, doing good let us not fail, for in due time we shall reap, not failing."[1334]

181. **How many kinds of good works be there, wherein Christian justice is chiefly seen and exercised?**

There are three kinds as we find in holy scripture, to wit: prayer, fasting, and alms. For other good deeds for the most part, which do proceed of a lively faith, and do set forth, increase, and consummate Christian justice, are easily reduced to these three fountains.[1335] Hereupon was that notable speech of the angel Raphael: "Prayer is good, with fasting; and alms, more than to hoard up treasures of gold."[1336] And Saint Augustine saith plainly: "This is the justice of a man in this life: fasting, alms, and prayer."[1337]

[1329] 2 Tm 4:7-8; Cf. Augustine, *Homily 14 ex 50*, Ch. 2; *On Psalm 83*; *On Psalm 100*; *Tractate 3 on John*; Second Council of Orange, Ch. 38; Mt 5:12; 6:4, 6, 17; 10:41; Apoc 2:7, 10, 26; 3:11; 14:13

[1330] Mt 19:17

[1331] Jn 5:29; Cf. Mt 25:34; Augustine, *On Psalm 49*

[1332] Mt 7:21

[1333] Apoc 22:11-12; Cf. Ecclus 18:22; Ps 61:12; Mt 16:27; Rom 2:6; 1 Cor 3:8

[1334] Gal 6:9; Cf. Ecclus 51:58; Augustine, *On Psalm 111*; *De Octo Dulcitii Quaestionibus*, q. 4

[1335] Cf. Augustine, *De Perfectione Justitiae Hominis*, Ch. 8, n. 17

[1336] Tb 12:8

[1337] Augustine, *On Psalm 42*

Of this doth Christ severally entreat in St. Matthew's gospel,[1338] and addeth promises of the heavenly reward prepared for those who, within the Church without hypocrisy, do sincerely fast, pray, and give alms.[1339] Hence is that faithful promise so often repeated: "The Father which seeth in secret will repay thee."[1340] And these be the very things wherein Christ (to the intent that we may live well and happily) would have our justice to abound,[1341] and so to shine before men, that they may see our good works and glorify the Father.[1342] To the performance of these, we are created and destinated in Christ: as the which things God hath prepared that we may walk in them.[1343] For these things done in charity, the just shall be received into the everlasting kingdom; and for neglecting of the same, the unjust shall be cast headlong into hell fire.[1344]

And as it is pharisaical and full of vanity, with the contempt of others to justify himself,[1345] and to trust to his own works; so is it Christian-like and lawful that a man, with humility, diligently attend unto good works,[1346] and if at any time he will glory, to glory in our Lord,[1347] who worketh in us to will and to accomplish, as witnesseth the apostle.[1348]

Of Fasting

182. **What is fasting?**

This word hath not one simple signification. A great and general fast, St. Augustine calleth, "to abstain from vices and unlawful pleasures of the

[1338] Cf. Mt 6
[1339] Cf. Augustine, *Sermon 60, De Temp.*
[1340] Mt 6:4, 6, 18
[1341] Cf. Mt 5:20
[1342] Cf. Mt 5:16
[1343] Cf. Eph 2
[1344] Cf. Mt 25:34; Jn 5:29
[1345] Cf. Lk 18:11
[1346] Cf. Rom 10:3; Council of Trent, Session 6, "Decree on Justification," Ch. 16
[1347] Cf. 1 Cor 1:21; 2 Cor 10:17
[1348] Cf. Phil 2:13; Cf. also Peter Chrysologus, *Sermon 43*; Leo the Great, *On the Fast of the Tenth Month*, Sermons 1 and 4; Bernard, *Sententiae*, Sect. 11

world."[1349] Then is there a philosophical fast, as some name it, consisting in a spare diet and temperance of meat and drink, and moral sobriety, wherewith the very heathens, according to the rule of right reason, do live temperately.[1350] Thirdly, there is an ecclesiastical fast, to wit, when according to the certain custom and prescript of the Church, we forbear flesh diet upon some certain days, and are content with one only repast.[1351] Which kind of fast is after a godly and Christian manner undertaken to perform God's service more religiously: to tame the flesh, and make it subject to the spirit; to yield the worthy fruits of penance; to exercise obedience; and finally, to obtain any grace and favor at God's hands.[1352]

183. **But what answer is to be made unto those that do reprehend and contemn the law of the ecclesiastical fast?**

First, such persons are to be admonished that they do not falsely attribute unto Catholics that which the apostle doth detest, and the Church hath ever, in the Jews, Manichees, and Priscillianists condemned; for that, either according to the law of Moses or of superstition, they do abstain from certain meats.[1353] "For Catholics," as St. Augustine answereth Faustus the Manichee, "whereas they abstain from flesh, they do it for to tame their bodies, and to restrain the more their souls from such motions as be contrary to reason, not for that they think the flesh itself to be unclean; neither do they abstain from flesh only, but also from some certain fruits of the earth: either always, as a few; or at certain days and times, as in the Lent, for the most part

---

[1349] Augustine, *Tractate 17 on John*; Cf. Augustine, *Quaestionum Evangeliorum*, Bk. 2, Ch. 18

[1350] Cf. Jerome, *Against Jovinianus*, Bk. 2, Ch. 9

[1351] Cf. *Apostolic Constitutions*, Bk. 5, Ch. 12, 14, 17-19; Isidore, *De Ecclesiasticis Officiis*, Bk. 1, Ch. 36ff; Rabanus Maurus, *De Institutione Clericorum*, Bk. 2, Ch. 17ff; Ivon., Pt. 4, Ch. 25ff; Burchardus, Bk. 25

[1352] Cf. Cyprian, *De Jejun. et Tentationibus Christi*; Athanasius, *De Virginitate*; Chrysostom, *Homily 1 on Genesis*; *Homily 2 on Genesis*; *Sermon 1, De Jejun.*; *Sermon 2, De Jejun.*; Basil, *Oration 1, De Jejun.*; *Oration 2, De Jejun.*; Augustine, *De Utilitate Jejunii*, Ch. 2-3; Ambrose, *De Helia et Jejunio*, Bk. 1; *Epistle 82*; Leo the Great, *On the Fast of the Seventh and Tenth Month*, Sermon 1, Pentecostes et Quadragesimae

[1353] Cf. 1 Tm 4:1; Col 2:16; Dt 14:3; *Apostolic Canons*, Can. 50, 52; Council of Gangra, Can. 2; First Council of Toledo, in assert. fid.; First Council of Braga, Can. 14, 32

everyone."[1354] Thus writeth Saint Augustine. And before him, the same also Epiphanius teacheth, where he confuteth the Arian heresy, which will have the set fasts of the Church to be at every man's discretion, and no man to be bound thereunto.[1355] But in that the order of time is observed in public fasts, as also in prayers and holy days, that doth confirm, set forth, and advance the order and public concord in the Church.[1356] Besides: private fasts, few would impose upon themselves, as being hindered from such endeavors, with a natural love of the flesh and care of the belly.

Now that it is of great importance, and of assured merit, reverently to embrace and diligently to observe such kind of fasts: St. Jerome proveth it so plainly against Jovinian, that none can doubt thereof anymore.[1357] Unto which may be added those things which we have taught before concerning the observance of the precepts of the Church, and that, for the avoiding of scandal and retaining of public discipline:[1358] "Neither only for wrath, but also for conscience sake,"[1359] as the apostle hath said.

And it is manifest, as the writers in all ages do prove,[1360] that this is both the perpetual discipline, custom, tradition, and decree of the Church, and

[1354] Augustine, *Contra Faustum*, Bk. 30, Ch. 5; Cf. Augustine, *On the Morals of the Manichaeans*, Ch. 13-14; *Contra Adimantum Manichaei Discipulum*, Ch. 14; Theod., *Epitome Divinorum*, decret., Ch. "De Abstin."; Bernard, *Sermon 66 on Canticle of Canticles*; Isidore, *De Ecclesiasticis Officiis*, Bk. 1, Ch. 44; Gn 1:29; 2:16; 9:3; Lv 10:8; Nm 6:3; Jdt 13:7, 13; Jer 35:6, 18; Dn 1:8; 10:2; Mt 3:4; Mk 1:6; Lk 1:15; Acts 15:20, 29; Rom 14:20; 1 Cor 8:13; 1 Tm 5:23; Third Council of Constantinople, Can. 56; Gregory the Great, *Ad August.* teste Gratian distinct. 4; Ivon., Pt. 4, Ch. 29; Athanasius, *Life of St. Anthony*; Jerome, *Life of Paulus the First Hermit*; *Life of St. Hilarion*; Epiphanius, *in compend. Doct. Eccles. Cathol.*

[1355] Cf. Epiphanius, *Adversus Haeresus*, n. 75; Augustine, *De Haeresibus*, n. 53; John Damascene, *De Haeresibus*

[1356] Cf. Jerome, *On Galatians*, Ch. 4; Leo the Great, *On the Fast of the Seventh Month*, Sermons 3 and 4; *Sermon 4, De Quadrag.*; Basil, *Oration 2, De Jejun.*

[1357] Cf. Jerome, *Against Jovinianus*, Bk. 2, Ch. 5, 10-11; Augustine, *De Haeresibus*, n. 22; Ambrose, *Epistle 82*

[1358] Cf. Augustine, *Epistle 54 to Januarius*, Ch. 2

[1359] Rom 13:5

[1360] Cf. Augustine, *Epistle 36 to Casulanus*; Epiphanius, *in compend.*; Calixtus, *Epistle 1 ad Bened.*; Leo the Great, *Sermon 1, De Pentecostes*; *Sermon 2, De Pentecostes*; *On the Fast of the Seventh Month*, Sermons 1 and 2; *On the Fast of the Tenth Month*, Sermon 8; Rabanus Maurus, *De Institutione Clericorum*, Bk. 2, Ch. 24; Council of Mainz, Ch. 34; Council of Selingstad, Ch. 2; Bernard, *In Vigilia S. Andreae*

hath been ever from the beginning: that upon certain days, especially of the Lent, this fast of the Church should be observed.[1361] So do the *Canons of the Apostles*,[1362] and the most holy councils teach.[1363] The Council of Gangra certes pronounceth them accursed that do contemn the common fasts of the whole Church.[1364] And the Toletane Council willeth them to be excommunicate who, without inevitable necessity and evident weakness, do eat flesh in Lent.[1365] And the holy fathers' zeal is most singular in commending, urging, and requiring fasting,[1366] especially that of Lent, which they will have accounted as instituted by the apostles.[1367] From this spirit of the fathers are they far off that do disburden themselves and others of the law of fasts, taking upon themselves the patronage not of evangelical liberty, but of licentiousness of the flesh. These fellows will not have the flesh with the vices and concupiscences to be crucified,[1368] and therefore, they favor not those things that are of the Spirit,[1369] but do rather extinguish the Spirit, contrary to the doctrine of the apostle.[1370] They do also resist the holy Church our mother, yea and Christ also,[1371] speaking and governing in the Church his spouse:[1372] wherefore they purchase unto themselves

[1361] Cf. Ignatius, *Epistle to the Philadelphians*; Epiphanius, *in compend.*; Theophilus of Alexandria, *Paschali. Maxim.*, Bk. 3, in sermon, de Quadragesima; see also the sermons on Quadragesima of the following: Ambrose, Augustine, Leo the Great, and Bernard; Origen, *Homily 10 on Leviticus*; Isidore, *De Ecclesiasticis Officiis*, Bk. 1, Ch. 36; Augustine, *Epistle 119*, Ch. 15; *On Psalm 110*

[1362] Cf. *Canons of the Apostles*, Can. 68

[1363] Cf. Council of Laodicea, Can. 50; Second Council of Braga, Can. 9; Fourth Council of Carthage, Can. 63; Council of Tribur, Can. 35; Council of Agde, Ch. 12

[1364] Cf. Council of Gangra, Can. 19; Council of Mainz, Can. 35

[1365] Cf. Eighth Council of Toledo, Can. 9; Telesphorus, *Epistle ad Univers.*; Theophilus of Alexandria, *Pasch.*, Bk. 3; Augustine, *Sermon 64, De Temp.*; Nicephorus, *Church History*, Bk. 17, Ch. 32; Chrysostom, *Homily 6 ad Pop.*; *Homily 1 on Genesis*; *Homily 2 on Genesis*

[1366] Cf. Basil, *Homily 2, De Jejun.*; Augustine, *Sermon 62, De Temp.*; Ambrose, *Sermons 23, 25, 34, 36, 37*

[1367] Cf. Jerome, *Epistle 41 against Montanus to Marcella*

[1368] Cf. Gal 1:24

[1369] Cf. 1 Cor 2:14

[1370] Cf. 1 Thes 5:19; Maximus, *in Litaniis*

[1371] Cf. Augustine, *Epistle 80 to Casulanus*

[1372] Cf. Lk 10:16; Mt 18:17; 1 Cor 14:37; 1 Thes 2:13; Acts 15:28; Jer 35:6, 18; 2 Mc 6:19; 7:1

assured damnation, whereas they abrogate and reject the holy and whole-some ordinance of fasts, always commended unto us by the Church.[1373]

184. **What doth the holy scripture teach concerning fasting?**

It is the voice of Almighty God himself, which by the prophet Joel crieth out unto sinners: "Be ye converted unto me in your whole heart, in fast-ing, weeping, and mourning."[1374] And a little after, "Sound the trumpet in Sion," saith he, "sanctify a fast, call the company, assemble the people together";[1375] or as others[1376] do read: "Sanctify a fast, preach the curing. That hereby we may learn that fast is sanctified by other good works, and, being sanctified, is available to the curing of sinners," as St. Jerome doth interpret.[1377] For as the same holy father[1378] gathereth out of holy writ, by fasting, Daniel, a man of desires,[1379] knew things to come; and the Ninevites appeased the wrath of God;[1380] and Elijah and Moses, with forty days hunger, were filled with the familiarity of Almighty God;[1381] and our Lord himself fasted so many days in the wilderness, that he might leave unto us solemn days of fasting;[1382] and he taught that the fiercer sort of devils cannot be vanquished but by prayer and fasting;[1383] the apostle saith that he fasted often;[1384] and in the psalms, the penitent saith: "I did eat my bread as ashes, and did mingle my drink with tears."[1385] And, "When they

---

[1373] Cf. Rom 13:2; Lv 23:27; 1 Kgs 14:24; 3 Kgs 13:16; Council of Trent, Session 25; Augustine, *Tractate 73 on John*; Ambrose, *Sermon 25*; *Sermon 36*; Chrysostom, *Homily 12 on 1 Timothy*; Rabanus Maurus, *De Institutione Clericorum*, Bk. 2, Ch. 25

[1374] Jl 2:12; Cf. Jl 1:14

[1375] Jl 2:15-16; Cf. Gregory the Great, *Homily 16 on the Gospels*; Maximus, *Homily 1, De Jejun. Quadrag.*

[1376] Cf. Augustine, *Sermon 60, De Temp.*; *Sermon 62, De Temp.*; *Sermon 69, De Temp.*; *Sermon 230, De Temp.*; Bernard, *Sermon 40, De Quadrag.*; Jerome, *On Daniel*, Ch. 6

[1377] Jerome, *Against Jovinianus*, Bk. 2, Ch. 17

[1378] Cf. Ibid.; Augustine, *Sermon 65, De Temp.*; Chrysostom, *Homily on Jonah*

[1379] Cf. Dn 9:3, 23; 10:3, 11

[1380] Cf. Jon 3:10

[1381] Cf. 3 Kgs 19:8; Ex 24:18; 34:28; Dt 9:9, 18

[1382] Cf. Mt 4:2; Lk 4:2

[1383] Cf. Mt 17:21; Mk 9:29

[1384] Cf. 1 Cor 11:27

[1385] Ps 101:10

were troublesome unto me, I did wear haircloth, I did humble my soul in fasting."[1386] What is more manifest than that which Christ affirmeth should come to pass,[1387] that when he (the spouse most dear unto his disciples) should be taken away, then they, though full of the Holy Ghost, should fast?[1388] Therefore, St. Paul exhorteth all the faithful: "Let us exhibit ourselves as the ministers of God, in much patience, in watchings, in fastings, in chastity."[1389] "For they that be Christ's have crucified their flesh with the vices and concupiscences."[1390]

Of Prayer

185. **What is prayer?**

It is a devout effect of our mind toward God, whereby we do faithfully demand whatsoever things are wholesome for us and others; whereby we do praise and celebrate the grace and power of Almighty God;[1391] or by any manner of means, exhibit ourselves devout before that sovereign and eternal Majesty.[1392] So that hereunto belongeth not only beseeching, but also adoration,[1393] oblation or sacrifice,[1394] invocation,[1395] praise,[1396] and thanksgiving.[1397]

[1386] Ps 34:13

[1387] Cf. Lk 5:35; Mk 2:20; Mt 9:15; Jerome, *On Matthew*, Ch. 9

[1388] Cf. Acts 13:3; 14:22

[1389] 2 Cor 6:4-5; Cf. Lk 2:37; Mt 6:16; Tb 3:10; Jdt 4:8; 8:6; Est 4:3; 14:2; Jer 36:9; Bar 1:5; 1 Mc 3:47; 2 Mc 13:12

[1390] Gal 5:24; Cf. Jdt 20:26; 1 Kgs 7:6; 31:13; 2 Kgs 1:12; 3:35; 12:16, 22; 3 Kgs 21:27; 1 Par 10:12; 2 Par 20:3; 1 Esd 8:21; 2 Esd 1:4

[1391] Cf. John Damascene, *An Exposition of the Orthodox Faith*, Bk. 3, Ch. 24; Augustine, *On the Sermon on the Mount*, Bk. 2, Ch. 3; *Sermon 230, De Temp.*; Basil, in *Julittam Mart.*; Chrysostom, *Homily 30 on Genesis*; Gregory of Nyssa, *De Oration.*

[1392] Cf. Ex 35; 2 Par 29

[1393] Cf. Mt 4

[1394] Cf. Mal 1; Is 56; Jn 4

[1395] Cf. Rom 10

[1396] Cf. Ps 17, 145

[1397] Cf. Is 56; 1 Tm 2; Augustine, *Epistle 59 ad Paul.*

The manner and exact form of praying,[1398] Christ hath prescribed, as we have already declared.[1399]

And there is no work more commended in holy scripture; none more familiar with devout and holy persons; none, that of more persons, and more often, and with greater diligence, and more necessarily is to be exercised in this life, than is prayer.[1400] It is a true saying: "The prayer of him that humbleth himself, shall pierce the clouds."[1401] Also, "It behooveth always to pray,"[1402] to wit, with a zealous affect of heart, and without hypocrisy, or respect of the praise of men,[1403] that is to say, in spirit and truth.[1404] Notwithstanding they that do pray do often use an external gesture and disposition of the body, together with many ceremonies.[1405] And therein they do very well, as appeareth by the examples of holy scripture. For even Christ our Lord sometimes with eyes lifted up to heaven,[1406] sometimes with loud voice,[1407] sometimes prostrate upon the ground,[1408] prayed unto his Father. The prayer also of Daniel[1409] and the Ninevites[1410] is the more commended, because it was not taken in hand without fasting, sackcloth, and ashes.[1411] And it is not in vain written of the publican that he made his prayer in the Temple, with a humble countenance, his eyes cast downward, and knocking of his breast. Which things certes though they seem external, and may be done even by wicked persons for ostentation sake,

---

[1398] Cf. Augustine, *Tractate 73 on John*; Basil, *Constitutiones Monasticae*, Ch. 2; Bernard, *Sermon 4, De Quadrag.*; *Sermon 5, De Quadrag.*; *Sermon, De Quatuor Modis Orandi*

[1399] Cf. Mt 6; Lk 11; See before of our Lord's Prayer.

[1400] Cf. Ps 140; Tb 12; Acts 10; Ex 32; Ps 105; Jer 7, 27; Jerome, *On Jeremias*, Ch. 7; *Epistle 128 to Gaudentius*, Ch. 3

[1401] Ecclus 35:21; Cf. Ps 105, 36; Jdt 9

[1402] Lk 18:1; Cf. Ecclus 18; 1 Thes 5

[1403] Cf. Mt 6

[1404] Cf. Jn 4:23-24

[1405] Cf. Tertullian, *Apology*, Ch. 30; Augustine, *On the Care of the Dead*, Ch. 5; Jerome, *Dialogue against the Luciferians*, Ch. 6; *Life of Paulus the First Hermit*; *On Illustrious Men*, on James the Just

[1406] Cf. Jn 17:1; 11:41

[1407] Cf. Mt 27:46, 50; Lk 23:46

[1408] Cf. Mt 26:39; Mk 14:35; Lk 22:41

[1409] Cf. Dn 9

[1410] Cf. Jon 3

[1411] Cf. Jdt 4, 9; 1 Mc 3

yet do they deserve praise and commendation, in that they both exercise the body devoutly, and bring it into the obedience of the Creator; and stir up the mind, confirm and strengthen it, in the interior worship. These are moreover certain testimonies of faith, humility, and piety, in no case to be neglected; as being things that do procure much edification, not only to the beholders, but also to the whole Church.[1412]

186. Why is it that it behooveth us so diligently and daily to pray?

First, because of the great and infinite commodities that redound to them that pray as they should. Then also, for that prayer is a proper and necessary exercise of faith. Moreover, it is everywhere commanded in divine scripture,[1413] and it hath a promise not only often repeated, but also such a one as is excellent and full of all consolation and sweetness: "I say to you," saith the truth himself, Christ, "all things whatsoever you ask praying, believe that you shall receive, and they shall come unto you."[1414] And again: "I say to you, ask and it shall be given you; seek and you shall find; knock and it shall be opened to you: for every one that asketh, receiveth: and he that seeketh, findeth; and to him that knocketh, it shall be opened."[1415] And again: "If you, being naught, know how to give good gifts to your children, how much more will your Father which is in heaven give good things to them that ask him?"[1416] "With such kind of speeches," as well noteth Saint Chrysostom, "and with such hope hath the Lord of all things provoked us to pray. It is our part that, being obedient to Almighty God,

---

[1412] Cf. Lk 18; Ex 9, 17; Dt 9; Nm 20; Ps 87, 140; 2 Par 6, 29; 3 Kgs 8; Dn 6; 1 Esd 9; Mt 2; Ex 7, 9, 20, 21; Eph 3, 6; 1 Cor 11; John Damascene, *An Exposition of the Orthodox Faith*, Bk. 4, Ch. 13. Of set times of prayer, see: Augustine, *De Haeresibus*, n. 57; Bede, *On Luke*, Ch. 18; Anselm, *On 2 Thessalonians*, Ch. 5; *Apostolic Constitutions*, Bk. 8, Ch. 40; Tertullian, *Apology*, Ch. 2; Cyprian, *On the Lord's Prayer*; Athanasius, *De Virginitate*; Basil, *Sermon 1, De Instit. Monach.*; *The Longer Rules*, q. 37; Chrysostom, *Homily 59 ad Pop.*; Jerome, *On Daniel*, Ch. 6; *Epistle 22 to Eustochium*, Ch. 17; *Epistle 108*, "Epitaph for Paula," Ch. 1; Council of Aix-la-Chapelle, Ch. 116ff; Ps 118:5; 54; Dn 6; Acts 3, 10, 16.

[1413] Cf. Mt 26; Mk 13; Lk 11, 18, 21; Ecclus 18, 21; Rom 12; Phil 4; Col 4; 1 Pt 4; 1 Thes 5, 6; 1 Tm 5; Heb 4; Lk 1, 4, 5

[1414] Mk 11:24; Cf. Mt 21:18ff

[1415] Lk 11:9-10; Mt 7:7-8; Cf. Jn 14, 15, 10; 1 Jn 3:5; Ps 49:114; Prv 15; 2 Par 7; Ecclus 2, 3, 38; Lv 4-6

[1416] Mt 7:11; Lk 11:13

we pass over our whole life in the praise of God and in prayer, using more diligence and care about the service of God, than about our own life. For so it will come to pass that we shall always lead our life worthy of a man."[1417] Thus far Saint Chrysostom.

187. **By what examples may we gather what the force and commodity of prayer is?**
The apostle St. James, to the intent he might explicate the virtue of prayer with an example, wrote thus: "Elias was a man like unto us passible; and with prayer he prayed that it might not rain upon the earth, and it rained not for three years and six months. And he prayed again, and the heaven gave rain. And the earth yielded her fruit."[1418] St. Augustine[1419] proveth the same thing with many more examples: Moses,[1420] and Samuel praying,[1421] the Jews overcame their enemies, the Amalekites, and the Philistines. Jeremiah, praying, is comforted and strengthened in prison.[1422] Daniel, praying, triumpheth amongst the lions.[1423] The three children, praying, do dance in the furnace.[1424] The thief, praying upon the cross, doth find paradise.[1425] Susanna, by prayer, is defended amidst the elders that accused her falsely.[1426] St. Steven, praying, is received into heaven, and heard in the behalf of Saul, amongst them that stoned him.[1427]

[1417] Chrysostom, *De Orando Deum*, Bk. 1; Cf. Chrysostom, *De Orando Deum*, Bk. 2; *Homily 5, De Incomprehensib. Dei Natura*; *Homily 71, to the People of Antioch*; *Homily 79, to the People of Antioch*; Gregory the Great, *Homily 17 on the Gospels*; *Expositio in Psalmos Poenitentiales*, sixth psalm; Cf. also Isidore, *De Summo Bono*, Bk. 3, Ch. 7; Augustine, *Sermon 226, De Temp.*; *Sermon 230, De Temp.*; *Epistle 121*, Ch. 8ff; *Sermon 5, De Verbis Domini*, Ch. 4ff; Cyprian, *On the Lord's Prayer*; Ambrose, *Concerning Virginity*, Bk. 3; *Sermon 93, De Nazario et Celso*
[1418] Jas 5:17-18; Cf. 3 Kgs 17-18; Lk 4; Ecclus 48
[1419] Cf. Augustine, *Sermon 22 ad fratres in eremo*
[1420] Cf. Ex 17; Jdt 4
[1421] Cf. 1 Kgs 7
[1422] Cf. Jer 32
[1423] Cf. Dn 6
[1424] Cf. Dn 3
[1425] Cf. Lk 23
[1426] Cf. Dn 13
[1427] Cf. Acts 7; Jerome, *Against Vigilantius*, Ch. 3; Augustine, *Sermon 1, De Sanctis*; *Sermon 4, De Sanctis*

By which examples, not only is declared the profit of prayer, but also the love and diligence of praying is commended unto us.[1428] Wherefore the apostolical writings do thus exhort us: "Pray without intermission, in all things give thanks."[1429] And again: "Pray one for another that you may be saved, for the continual prayer of a just man availeth much."[1430] In like manner: "This is the confidence which we have toward God, that whatsoever we shall ask according to his will, he heareth us."[1431] Moreover: "He that knoweth his brother to sin a sin not to death, let him ask and life shall be given him."[1432]

Of Alms and the Works of Mercy

188. What is alms?

It is a gift or benefit whereby, upon an affection of compassion, we do succor another man's misery. Hereunto belongeth that which the angel Raphael testifieth in Tobias: "Prayer is good, with fasting and alms."[1433] That we may understand, as St. Cyprian admonisheth, "that our prayers and fastings are little available unless they be helped with alms."[1434] "Good is mercy," saith St. Ambrose, "which of herself maketh men perfect, because it doth imitate the Father, which is perfect. Nothing doth so commend a Christian soul as mercy."[1435] Thus saith he. "Be ye therefore merciful, as your Father also is merciful,"[1436] that "you may be the sons of your Father which is in heaven, who maketh his sun to rise upon the good and the evil, and raineth upon

---

[1428] Cf. Gn 25; Ex 8-10, 14, 32; Nm 11-12, 14, 16, 21; 1 Kgs 1, 12; 4 Kgs 19-20; 2 Par 20, 33; 1 Esd 8, Tb 3; Jdt 9, 13; Ps 17, 119; Jon 2; 1 Mc 3-4; Acts 12

[1429] 1 Thes 5:17-18

[1430] Jas 5:16

[1431] 1 Jn 5:14

[1432] 1 Jn 5:16

[1433] Tb 12:8

[1434] Cyprian, *De Opera et Eleemosynis*; Cf. Peter Chrysologus, *Sermon 43*; Leo the Great, *Sermon 3, De Jejun. Pentecost.*; Os 6; Mt 6, 12; Prv 21; Phil 4; Heb 13

[1435] Ambrose, *On the Duties of the Clergy*, Bk. 1, Ch. 11; Cf. Chrysostom, *Homily 36, to the People of Antioch*; Augustine, *Sermon 76, De Temp.*; *Homily 36 ex 50*; Leo the Great, *Sermon 5, De Quadrag.*; *Sermon 10, De Quadrag.*; Gregory of Nyssa, *De Beatitudinibus*

[1436] Lk 6:36; Cf. Ps 32, 118, 144

the just and unjust."[1437] Thus saith Christ our Savior, and our Samaritan, full of all grace and mercy,[1438] who went throughout doing good and healing all that were oppressed of the devil.[1439]

189. In what manner doth the scripture commend alms unto us?

With many certes, and plain precepts, promises, and examples.[1440] Yea, St. Cyprian teacheth that in the gospel there is nothing more often commanded than that we persevere in giving alms, that we be not busied in earthly possessions, but rather lay up treasures in heaven.[1441] Hence are those speeches of Christ: "But yet, that which remaineth give alms,"[1442] and, "Behold all things are clean unto you."[1443] "Sell the things that you possess and give alms, make to you purses that wear not, treasure that wasteth not in heaven."[1444] And in another place: "Make unto you friends of the mammon of iniquity: that when you fail, they may receive you into the eternal tabernacles."[1445] In brief: "Give, and there shall be given to you."[1446] And for that cause, Daniel the prophet counseleth the wicked king: "Redeem thy sins with alms and thy iniquitites with the mercies of the poor."[1447] Then in another place we read: "Water doth quench the burning fire, and alms resisteth sins."[1448] And not of a man certes, but of an angel was that speech: "Alms delivereth from death, and she it is that purgeth

[1437] Mt 5:45

[1438] Cf. Lk 10

[1439] Cf. Acts 10; Cf. also Chrysostom, *Homily 13 on 2 Corinthians*; Augustine, *Sermon 30, De Verbis Domini*, Ch. 3

[1440] Cf. Dt 15; 1 Esd 8; Tb 4; Ps 40; Prv 11, 14, 19, 22, 15, 28; Ecclus 4, 7, 12, 17, 29; Ez 18; Mt 25; Lk 14

[1441] Cf. Cyprian, *De Opera et Eleemosynis*; Augustine, *Sermon 50*, Ch. 8ff; *Sermon 227, De Temp.*; *Homily 18*; *Homily 19*; *Homily 29*, Ch. 1ff; *Homily 47 ex 50*; Gregory Nazianzen, *Oration 16, De Paup. Amore*; Chrysostom, *Homily 32 ad Pop. et sequent.*

[1442] Lk 11:41; Cf. Jerome, *Epistle 120 to Hedibia*, q. 1

[1443] Lk 11:41; Cf. Augustine, *Enchiridion*, Ch. 75-77; *Sermon 30, De Verbis Domini*

[1444] Lk 12:33; Cf. Mt 6:19-20; Mk 10; 1 Tm 6

[1445] Lk 16:9; Cf. Augustine, *Sermon 25*, Ch. 3; *Sermon 35, De Verbis Domini*, Ch. 1ff

[1446] Lk 6:38; Cf. 2 Cor 8-9; 1 Tm 4; Rom 12; Jas 1

[1447] Dn 4:24; Cf. Prv 13; Ambrose, *Sermon 30*; *Sermon 31, De Helia et Jejun.*, Ch. 20; Leo the Great, *Sermon, De Collectis.*; Chrysostom, *Homily 25 on Acts of the Apostles*

[1448] Ecclus 3:33; Cf. Ambrose, *Sermon 15*; Chrysostom, *Homily 34 on Genesis*; *De Promiss. et Praedictionibus*, Pt. 2, Ch. 7

sins, and maketh a man to find mercy and life everlasting."[1449] Yea, and
Christ himself pronounceth: "Whosoever shall give drink to one of these
little ones a cup of cold water, only in the name of a disciple: Amen I say
to you, he shall not lose his reward."[1450] "Blessed therefore are the merciful,
for they shall obtain mercy."[1451] And contrariwise, as St. James affirmeth:
"Judgment without mercy to him that hath not done mercy."[1452]

190. **With what examples is the effect and profit of alms declared?**
In the holy scripture, Abraham and Lot, through hospitality, are said both
to have pleased God,[1453] and to have entertained angels.[1454] The alms of
Tobias[1455] and the centurion[1456] were so available that they ascended into
remembrance, in the sight of God, and had the holy angels not only for witnesses, but also for commenders. Zacchaeus moved by the words of Christ
(and of a prince of publicans, being made a mirror of mercy) giveth half
his goods to the poor, and is presently pronounced the son of Abraham
by Christ himself.[1457] Tabitha is praised by St. Luke as being full of good
works and alms, which she bestowed especially upon widows.[1458] So are
those devout matrons singularly commended in the gospel, which, with
Magdalen and Martha, did liberally minister of their goods to Christ our

---

[1449] Tb 12:9; Cf. Tb 4; Is 1; Prv 15, 16, 10; 1 Pt 4; Jas 5

[1450] Mt 10:42; Cf. Gregory the Great, *Homily 5 on the Gospels*; Ambrose, *Concerning Widows*; Leo the Great, *Sermon 4, De Quadrag.*; *Sermon 6, De Quadrag.*; *On the Fast of the Tenth Month, Sermon 6*

[1451] Mt 5:7

[1452] Jas 2:13; Cf. Prv 21

[1453] Cf. Gn 18-19

[1454] Cf. Heb 13

[1455] Cf. Tb 12

[1456] Cf. Acts 10. See notable examples of alms in these saints' lives: John the Almsgiver from Leontius, *Life of John the Almsgiver*; Martin from Sulpicius Severus, *Life of St.
Martin*; Paula from Jerome, *Epistle 108*, "Epitaph for Paula," Ch. 7; Paulinus from Gregory of Tours, *Glory of the Confessors*, Ch. 107 and Gregory the Great, *Dialogues*, Bk. 3,
Ch. 1; Tiberius from Gregory of Tours, *History of the Franks*, Bk. 5, Ch. 19; Benedict from
Gregory the Great, *Dialogues*, Bk. 2, Ch. 28-29; Martyrius from Gregory the Great, *Homily 39 on the Gospels*; Gregory from John the Deacon, *Life of St. Gregory*, Bk. 1, Ch. 10; Bk.
2, Ch. 22-23; Oswald from Bede, *Ecclesiastical History of the English Church*, Bk. 3, Ch. 6.

[1457] Cf. Lk 19

[1458] Cf. Acts 9; Johannes Moschus, *Pratum Spiriuale Sophronii*, Ch. 175, 185, 195, 201

Lord and to his poor disciples.[1459] And of Saint Laurence the Levite and martyr,[1460] it is most justly sung: "He dispersed, he gave to the poor: his righteousness remaineth forevermore."[1461]

191. What is mercy?

It is, as St. Augustine affirmeth, "a certain compassion in our heart of another man's misery, whereby we are compelled to yield succor, if it lie in our power."[1462] Which name of mercy is wont very often to be taken for alms. "And all manner of mercy," as witnesseth the divine scripture, "shall make a place unto every man according to the merit of his works."[1463] Very often and wonderfully doth Saint Chrysostom commend the same,[1464] and he doubteth not in a certain place to say: "Mercy is the fortress of salvation, the ornament of faith, the propitiation of sins: she it is that approveth the just persons, confirmeth the holy, and setteth forth the servants of God."[1465] Yea, and if we believe Saint Ambrose, "The whole sum of Christian discipline consisteth in mercy and piety."[1466]

192. Are the works of mercy of one kind only?

They are found to be of two sorts: forasmuch as some be corporal, some spiritual. Some are certes called corporal, because they are exercised for the relieving of the corporal misery of our neighbor; other spiritual, for that in them we do well provide and labor for the spiritual good of our neighbor.[1467] Of this diversity of mercy, the most bountiful Job giveth a most clear example, who witnesseth of himself: "From my infancy, hath

---

[1459] Cf. Lk 8, 10; Jn 12; 3 Kgs 17; 4 Kgs 4

[1460] Cf. Ambrose, *On the Duties of the Clergy*, Bk. 2, Ch. 8

[1461] Ps 111:9; Chrysostom, *Homily 55 on Genesis*

[1462] Augustine, *City of God*, Bk. 9, Ch. 5; Cf. Isidore, *De Summo Bono*, Bk. 3, Ch. 64; Gregory of Nyssa, *De Beatitudinibus*, Bk. 1

[1463] Ecclus 16:15

[1464] Cf. Chrysostom, *Homily 32 on Hebrews*; *Homily 9, De Paenit.*; *Homily 53 on Matthew*; *Homily 36, to the People of Antioch*

[1465] Chrysostom, *Homily, De Misericord. et Duabus Viduis*

[1466] Ambrose, *On 1 Timothy*, Ch. 4; Cf. Ambrose, *On Luke*, Ch. 3

[1467] Cf. Augustine, *Of the Morals of the Catholic Church*, Ch. 27-28; *Enchiridion*, Ch. 72; *Sermon 203, De Temp.*

mercy increased with me, and from my mother's womb she came forth with me."[1468] "I have been an eye to the blind, and a foot to the lame. I was the father of the poor, and the cause which I knew not, I did diligently search out. I did consume the grinding stones of the wicked man, and out of his teeth I did take the prey."[1469] Also: "The stranger stood not without doors, my door was open to the traveler."[1470]

193. **How many works of mercy be there both corporal and spiritual?**

There are seven accounted of each kind. And first certes the corporal works are these: to feed the hungry; to give drink to the thirsty; to clothe the naked; to redeem the captive; to visit the sick; to harbor pilgrims;[1471] to bury the dead.[1472]

And the spiritual works are these: to correct those that sin;[1473] to teach the ignorant;[1474] to give good counsel to them that are in doubt;[1475] to pray to God for the welfare of our neighbor;[1476] to comfort the sorrowful;[1477] to bear injuries patiently;[1478] to forgive offenses.[1479] Which offices of human piety are so plain and evident, especially unto Christians and to those which are not altogether barbarous, that they need not any long discourse.

194. **How are these declared in holy scripture?**

Very plainly certes, and in every place; as notably those words of Isaiah, or rather the precepts of God, do declare: "Break," saith he, "thy bread

---

[1468] Jb 31:18; Gregory the Great, *On Job*, Ch. 31

[1469] Jb 29:15-17

[1470] Jb 31:32

[1471] Cf. Mt 25

[1472] Cf. Tb 1-2, 12; 2 Kgs 2; Augustine, *City of God*, Bk. 1, Ch. 13; *On the Care of the Dead*, Ch. 3.

[1473] Cf. Mt 18; 1 Tm 5

[1474] Cf. Ecclus 18; 2 Tm 4; Is 52; Jer 15; Dn 12; Jas 5; Gal 6; Chrysostom, *Homily 3 on Genesis*; *Homily 10 on Genesis*; Clement of Alexandria, *The Stromata*, Bk. 1; Bernard, *Sermon 36 on Canticles of Canticles*; Gregory the Great, *Homily 17 on the Gospels*

[1475] Cf. Prv 27; Ecclus 5

[1476] Cf. Mt 5; Jas 5

[1477] Cf. Ecclus 7; 2 Cor 1

[1478] Cf. Ti 3; 1 Thes 5; Rom 15

[1479] Cf. Mt 5-6, 18; Mk 11; Ecclus 28

to the hungry; the needy and wandering bring into thy house; when thou shalt see a naked man, clothe him, and thy flesh do thou not despise."[1480] Of which offices, the great profit and commodity is after annexed in the same place: "Then thy justice shall go before thy face, and the glory of our Lord shall gather thee."[1481] And Saint John, who wholly laboreth in commending unto us brotherly charity and mercy, amongst other things teacheth: "He that shall have the substance of this world, and shall see his brother have need, and shall shut his bowels from him: how doth the charity of God abide in him?"[1482] And not content with this speech, he concludeth in most excellent manner: "My little children, let us not love in word and in tongue, but in deed and truth. In this we know that we are of the truth."[1483]

These are the works of the faithful, and of those that are truly just, which in the last judgment Christ will acknowledge and publicly approve: for the which he will allot the promised kingdom, and render a crown of justice unto the merciful, whom also himself calleth just.[1484]

Which works certes do afford so much the more of true praise and eternal reward, by how much the more sincerely, cheerfully, and liberally they are done by a Christian mind. Which then is performed, when there is as little respect as may be unto human vanity and desires, but they are wholly directed unto the glory of God, and the profit of our neighbor who is benefited.[1485] To this end are those speeches of holy scripture to be observed: "He that giveth, in simplicity;…he that showeth mercy, in cheerfulness."[1486] "Turn not away thy face from any poor man…According to thy ability be

[1480] Is 58:7

[1481] Is 58:8

[1482] 1 Jn 3:17; Cf. Jas 2; Basil, *Homily 7, In Divites Avaros*; Ambrose, *Sermon 81*; Gratia. Dist. 86; *On the Duties of the Clergy*, Bk. 3, Ch. 7; Gregory the Great, *Pastoral Rule*, Bk. 3, Ch. 21, Admonition 22; Gregory of Tours, *Glory of the Confessors*, Ch. 108

[1483] 1 Jn 3:18

[1484] Cf. Mt 15; Lk 14

[1485] Cf. Gregory the Great, *Pastoral Rule*, Bk. 3, Ch. 20, Admonition 21; Ambrose, *On the Duties of the Clergy*, Bk. 1, Ch. 30; Bk. 2, Ch. 21, 25; Chrysostom, *Homily, De Misericord. et Duabus Viduis*; *Homily 30 on 1 Corinthians*

[1486] Rom 12:8

thou merciful."[1487] "God loveth a cheerful giver."[1488] "In every gift, make
thy countenance cheerful."[1489] Pleasant is that man that taketh compassion
and profiteth.[1490] Christ certes in St. Luke describeth such a Samaritan,[1491]
as may be a notable example of exhibiting willingly the highest kind of
courtesy and perfect mercy even unto strangers and the undeserving:[1492]
But, "he that soweth sparingly, sparingly also shall reap,"[1493] as witnesseth
the apostle. And this shall suffice touching the corporal works of mercy.

195. But what doth the scripture testify of those that are spiritual?

"We," saith he, "that are stronger, must sustain the infirmities of the weak,
and not please ourselves. Let every one of you please his neighbor unto
God to edification. For Christ did not please himself."[1494] And again:
"Be ye gentle one to another, merciful, pardoning one another, as God
in Christ hath pardoned you."[1495] Again: "Be ye therefore followers of
God, as most dear children; and walk in love, as Christ also loved us."[1496]
Moreover: "Put ye on, therefore, as the elect of God, holy and beloved,
the bowels of mercy, benignity, humility, modesty, patience, supporting
one another. And pardoning one another, if any have a quarrel against
any man: as also our Lord hath pardoned us, so you also."[1497] And again:
"Admonish the unquiet, comfort the weak-minded, bear up the weak, be
patient to all."[1498]

[1487] Tb 4:7
[1488] 2 Cor 9:7
[1489] Ecclus 35:11
[1490] Cf. Ps 111
[1491] Cf. Lk 10
[1492] Cf. Gregory Nazianzen, *Oration 19, In Funere Patris*; Chrysostom, *Homily 21 on Romans*; *Homily 35, to the People of Antioch*; *Homily 37, to the People of Antioch*
[1493] 2 Cor 9:6
[1494] Rom 5:1-3
[1495] Eph 4:32
[1496] Eph 5:1-2
[1497] Col 3:11-13; Cf. Augustine, *Enchiridion*, Ch. 73-74; *Homily 6 ex 50*; *Homily 29 ex 50*, Ch. 1; *Homily 40 ex 50*, Ch. 3ff; *Sermon 203, De Temp.*; Gregory the Great, *Dialogues*, Bk. 4, Ch. 60
[1498] 1 Thes 5:14

These and many other things of like tenor doth Saint Paul everywhere inculcate; who, to the intent he might save all, was made all things to all men,[1499] so that hereupon himself testifieth: "Who is weak, and I am not weak? Who is scandalized, and I am not burnt?"[1500] And again: "I have great sadness, and continual sorrow in my heart. For I wished myself an anathema from Christ for my brethren."[1501] And in another place: "I most gladly will bestow, and will myself moreover be bestowed for your souls: although loving you more, I am loved less."[1502]

196. What is the sum of all the doctrine touching the performance of the works of mercy?

The apostle hath comprised the whole matter, as it were, in this one word: "Bear ye one another's burthens; and so you shall fulfill the law of Christ,"[1503] to wit, the law of charity, of which law again he saith: "If there be any other commandment, it is comprised in this word: Thou shalt love thy neighbor as thyself."[1504] And the apostle St. Peter: "Before all things," saith he, "having mutual charity continual among yourselves; because charity covereth the multitude of sins."[1505] Which precept or office of showing mercy and charity, as it is most agreeable to nature and reason, so doth it touch even all kinds of men without exception; insomuch that of this we read it written: "God hath given every man a charge of his neighbor."[1506] And he hath given charge in this manner, as Christ interpreteth: "All things whatsoever you will that men do to you, do you also to them: for this is the law and the prophets."[1507]

[1499] Cf. 1 Cor 9
[1500] 2 Cor 11:29
[1501] Rom 9:2-3
[1502] 2 Cor 12:15
[1503] Gal 6:2
[1504] Rom 13:9; Cf. Gal 5:14
[1505] 1 Pt 4:8
[1506] Ecclus 17:12
[1507] Mt 7:12; Cf. Lk 6:31

Of the Cardinal Virtues

197. **What meaneth the name and nature of cardinal virtues?**

Certain virtues be therefore called cardinal, because they be, as it were, fountains and hinges of all the rest; and as the door turneth upon the hinges, so the whole course of honest life consisteth of them,[1508] and the whole frame of good works doth seem after a sort to depend upon them.[1509] And they are accounted four in number: prudence, justice, temperance, and fortitude.[1510] Whereof it is thus written: "She teacheth sobriety, and prudence, and justice, and virtue: than which things there is nothing in this life more profitable unto men."[1511] Where, by *sobriety*, temperance; by *virtue*, fortitude is not obscurely signified.[1512] And all of them are so commended unto us, that we may assuredly understand that, by the eternal wisdom which is God, they are properly bestowed, and are received and exercised with very great fruit of man's salvation.[1513] Which virtues are called also officials, that is, appertaining to offices or duties, because that from them, as Saint Ambrose hath noted, do spring the diverse kinds of offices; and are derived all manner of duties appertaining to the ordinary life of man, according to every man's vocation.[1514]

198. **How are the cardinal virtues defined?**

Prudence is a virtue which, according to the rule of honesty, prescribeth what is to be desired and what is to be eschewed by a man. Justice is a virtue whereby we give every man his own. Temperance is a virtue moderating the pleasures of the flesh, which are felt in tasting and touching. Fortitude is a virtue whereby labors and dangers of death are constantly both undertaken and suffered out.

[1508] Cf. Ambrose, *On Luke*, Ch. 6; *On the Duties of the Clergy*, Bk. 1, Ch. 24; Prosper, *De Vita Contemplativa*, Bk. 3, Ch. 18

[1509] Cf. Gregory the Great, *Moralia in Job*, Bk. 2, Ch. 36

[1510] Cf. Ambrose, *Concerning Virginity*, Bk. 3; *On the Duties of the Clergy*, Bk. 2, Ch. 9

[1511] Ws 8:7

[1512] Cf. Augustine, *Retractions*, Bk. 1, Ch. 7

[1513] Cf. Prv 8; Ecclus 24

[1514] Cf. Ambrose, *On the Duties of the Clergy*, Bk. 1, Ch. 25

This is the noble chariot of virtues, whereby we are carried into heaven: these are the four rivers of paradise,[1515] as St. Augustine calleth them;[1516] of whom also this saying of worthy memory is extant: "That," saith he, "is the science and knowledge of human things, which knoweth the light of prudence, the decency of temperance, the strength of fortitude, the holiness of justice. For these are they which, fearing no fortune, we may behold to call truly our own."[1517]

199. How is prudence commended unto us in holy scripture?

Wisely doth Ecclesiasticus teach us in this manner: "My son, without advice do nothing, and after thy deed thou shalt not repent thee."[1518] And again: "A wise heart that hath understanding will keep itself from sin, and in the works of justice it shall have success."[1519] Also, the fountain of all wisdom and prudence,[1520] Christ, that true Solomon,[1521] teacheth thus: "Be ye wise as serpents, and simple as doves":[1522] to the intent that we may understand, that to perfect prudence, both are jointly required, to wit: both the simplicity of the dove, which maketh men meek and innocent; and the prudence of the serpent, which maketh men circumspect and provident; so that they neither deceive, nor be of others deceived. That shall be brought to pass if we conform ourselves to the doctrine of St. Paul: "See brethren," saith he, "how you walk warily: not as unwise, but as wise, redeeming the time because the days are evil. Therefore, become not unwise, but

[1515] Cf. Gn 2

[1516] Cf. Augustine, *De Genesi Contra Manichaeos*, Bk. 2, Ch. 10; Ambrose, *De Paradiso*, Ch. 3

[1517] Augustine, *Contra Academicos*, Bk. 1, Ch. 7; Cf. Augustine, *De Libero Arbitrio*, Bk. 1, Ch. 13; *Of the Morals of the Catholic Church*, Ch. 15; Ambrose, *On the Duties of the Clergy*; Prosper, *De Vita Contemplativa*, Bk. 3, Ch. 18ff; Bernard, *Sermon 35, Ex Parvis*; *Sermon 22 on Canticle of Canticles*

[1518] Ecclus 32:24; Cf. Ecclus 37; Prv 12-13

[1519] Ecclus 3:32; Cf. Ecclus 18, 33; Prv 14; Jb 28; Dt 4, 32; Cf. also Prv 3, 8; Ws 6-7

[1520] Cf. Ecclus 1:5

[1521] Cf. Mt 12; Lk 11

[1522] Mt 10:16; Cf. Theophil., *On Matthew*, Ch. 10; Jerome, *On Matthew*, Ch. 10; Augustine, *Quaestionum Septendecim in Evangelium Secundum Matthaeum*, q. 8; Gregory the Great, *Moralia in Job*, Bk. 1, Ch. 2; *Homily 30 on the Gospels*; Prosper, *De Vita Contemplativa*, Bk. 3, Ch. 29-30

understanding what is the will of God,"[1523] to wit, "good, acceptable, and perfect."[1524] And hereunto appertaineth that speech of Solomon: "He that goeth with wise men, shall be wise; a friend of fools shall become like unto them."[1525] And this also: "In the face of a wise man shineth wisdom."[1526] Finally, that which the same affirmeth: "The heart of a wise man shall possess knowledge, and the care of wise men seeketh doctrine."[1527]

200. **Of justice, what doth the holy scripture deliver unto us?**

"Justice advanceth the nation."[1528] "By justice the throne is established. Better is a little with justice, than many fruits with iniquity."[1529] And the office of this justice doth the apostle explicate unto us in these words: "Render to all men their due: to whom tribute, tribute; to whom custom, custom; to whom fear, fear; to whom honor, honor."[1530] Hereunto belongeth those parts of a just and happy man, thus set down in the psalm: "He that hath not done deceit in his tongue, nor hath caused evil to his neighbor, and hath not admitted a reproach against his neighbors;…he that sweareth to his neighbor, and doth not deceive; he that hath not given his money to usury,[1531] and hath not taken rewards against the innocent."[1532] By which we may easily see that the name of justice is here taken after a more strict manner than where we discoursed of Christian justice in general.

[1523] Eph 5:15-17; Cf. Col 4; 1 Pt 4; Prv 4; Eccles 2
[1524] Rom 12:2; Cf. 1 Thes 4
[1525] Prv 13:20; Cf. Ecclus 6
[1526] Prv 17:24; Cf. Eccles 8
[1527] Prv 18:15; Cf. Basil, *Constitutiones Monasticae*, Ch. 15; *Homily 12, In Principium Proverbiorum*; Bernard, *Sermon 49 on Canticle of Canticles*
[1528] Prv 14:34; Cf. Prv 15, 21; Ecclus 4
[1529] Prv 16:12, 8; Cf. Prv 25; Augustine, *City of God*, Bk. 4, Ch. 4; Bk. 19, Ch. 21; Gregory the Great, Bk. 7, Epistle 120 ad reges Franciae Theodoricum et Theobertum
[1530] Rom 13:7; Cf. Mt 22:17; Lk 2:3; 1 Tm 5; Bernard, *Sermon 3, De Adv.*; Augustine, *Sermon 19, De Verbis Domini*; *Contra Faustum*, Bk. 22, Ch. 74-74; Theoph., *On Romans*, Ch. 13
[1531] Cf. Ex 22; Lv 25; Dt 23; Ez 18, 22; Lk 6; Leo the Great, *On the Fast of the Tenth Month*, Sermon 6; Bernard, *Epistle 322 ad Spirenses*; Ambrose, *On Tobias*, Ch. 14-15; Jerome, *On Ezechiel*, Ch. 18; Third Lateran Council, under Alexander III, Pt. 1, Ch. 25
[1532] Ps 14:3-5; Cf. Mt 5; Chrysostom, *Homily 15 on Matthew*; Ambrose, *On the Duties of the Clergy*, Bk. 1, Ch. 28-29; *Sermon 16 on Psalm 118*; *De Paradiso*, Ch. 3; Augustine, *On Christian Doctrine*, Bk. 4, Ch. 18. See the seventh and eighth commandments.

201. How doth the scripture teach temperance?

For the eschewing of intemperance, this doth the scripture enjoin us: that we make not the provision of the flesh in concupiscences,[1533] nor that by gluttony our hearts be at any time overcharged with surfeiting and drunkenness.[1534] But it exhorteth to the exercise of temperance, where it willeth us to be sober and to watch,[1535] that is to say, by holy watchings and prayers, to be ready that we give not place to the devil.[1536] For which cause Ecclesiasticus also giveth this admonition: "Use, like a thrifty man, the things that are set before thee, that when thou eatest much thou be not had in contempt."[1537] Neither doth he forget to condemn drunkenness: "For much wine being drunk, maketh provoking, and anger, and many ruins."[1538] Yea, also as the same saith: "Wine and women make wise men to become apostates."[1539] Therefore, of drinking wine temperately, he addeth this also: "The exaltation of the soul and of the heart is wine moderately drunk; health to the soul and the body is sober drinking."[1540] And therefore, we read it written also in another place: "Blessed is the land whose princes do eat in due time, to refreshing, and not unto lechery."[1541] And, "He that is abstinent, shall increase life."[1542] But this virtue of temperance extendeth itself further than to the moderate taking of meat and drink.[1543] St. John Baptist (if ever any other) exhibited himself unto us a most perfect and absolute example of temperance, abstinence, yea, and of all manner of continency, when as he cut off from himself all manner of excess in diet and apparel, and

---

[1533] Cf. Rom 13; 1 Pt 2; Gal 5; 1 Cor 9
[1534] Cf. Lk 2. See before of gluttony and fasting.
[1535] Cf. 1 Pt 5; 1 Thes 5; 1 Tm 3; 2 Tm 4; Ti 1-2; Lv 10
[1536] Cf. Eph 4
[1537] Ecclus 31:19
[1538] Ecclus 31:38
[1539] Ecclus 19:2
[1540] Ecclus 31:36-37
[1541] Eccles 10:17
[1542] Ecclus 37:34
[1543] Cf. Prosper, *De Vita Contemplativa*, Bk. 3, Ch. 19; Ambrose, *De Jacob et Vita Beata*, Bk. 1, Ch. 2; Jerome, *On Ezechiel*, Ch. 44

contenting himself with a marvelous kind of frugality, passed over his life in the wilderness.[1544]

202. What admonisheth the scripture touching fortitude?

To the use and practice hereof, it exhorteth us sufficiently when it forbiddeth a perverse fear; and commendeth unto us confidence, cheerfulness, constancy, and magnanimity of a Christian mind:[1545] "The wicked man flieth when no man pursueth him," saith Solomon, "but the just man, as a confident lion, shall be without fear."[1546] And St. Peter giveth this admonition touching the enemies of faith and piety: "The fear of them, fear ye not, and be not troubled."[1547] "Who is he that can hurt you, if you be emulators of good? But if you suffer ought for justice, blessed are ye."[1548] And St. Paul, being himself an invincible soldier of Christ,[1549] doth often encourage others to true and Christian fortitude: "My beloved brethren," saith he, "be stable and unmoveable, abounding in the work of our Lord always, knowing that your labor is not in vain in our Lord."[1550] And again: "Brethren, be strengthened in our Lord and in the might of his power. Put you on the armor of God, that you may stand against the deceits of the devil," and, "resist in the evil day, and stand in all things perfect."[1551]

Of a man that hath fortitude, these are the proper speeches: "I have trusted in God, I will not fear what flesh can do unto me."[1552] "Our Lord is the protector of my life, of whom shall I tremble?... If whole armies stand

[1544] Cf. Mt 3, 11; Mk 1; Lk 1, 7; Bernard, *Sermon, De Nativitate Ioannis Baptistae*; Gregory the Great, *Homily 6 on the Gospels*

[1545] Cf. Mt 10, 8; Lk 12; Is 8, 35, 41, 43-44, 51; Jer 10; Ecclus 7, 34; Prv 3; Ps 3, 22, 26, 55, 117; Is 12; Heb 12

[1546] Prv 28:1; Cf. Jb 15, 6; Prv 29; Ecclus 22; Ps 13, 10, 12; Apoc 21; 2 Cor 1; Mt 11; Gal 3; Prv 15, 27; Ecclus 27

[1547] 1 Pt 3:14

[1548] 1 Pt 3:13-14; Cf. Mt 5; Lk 6

[1549] Cf. 1 Cor 4; 2 Cor 4, 6, 11-12; Acts 20-21; 2 Tm 4; Rom 8

[1550] 1 Cor 15:58; Cf. 1 Cor 16, 9; Rom 11; Gal 6; 2 Thes 3; Tb 2; Eccles 10; Ecclus 4-5, 11; 2 Par 15; Jas 5; Heb 10; Mt 10, 24; Bernard, *Epistle 129 ad Januenses*

[1551] Eph 6:10-11, 13; Cf. Is 40; Prv 14; 2 Par 16; Jas 4; 1 Pt 5; Prosper, *De Vita Contemplativa*, Bk. 3, Ch. 20; Ambrose, *On the Duties of the Clergy*, Bk. 1, Ch. 35ff

[1552] Ps 55:5

against me, my heart shall not be afraid."[1553] "If I shall walk in the midst of the shadow of death, I will not fear evils, because thou art with me."[1554] "Who shall separate us from the charity of Christ?"[1555] "I can do all things in him that strengtheneth me."[1556] This is that which the most courageous King David, as it were, sounding the alarm to all the sons of God, his fellow soldiers,[1557] doth say: "Do manfully and let your heart be comforted, all you that trust in our Lord."[1558] "In God we will do virtue, and he will bring to nothing those that trouble us."[1559] But that certes is a life worthy of a Christian man, wherein we do live wisely, justly, temperately, and with fortitude. Hence is it that golden mediocrity, that we do nothing too much nor too little.[1560] This is that which the scripture meaneth, when it saith: "Do thou not decline either on the right hand, or on the left."[1561]

Of the Gifts and Fruits of the Holy Ghost

203. How many gifts of the Holy Ghost be there?

They are found in Isaiah the prophet, and the fathers of the Church,[1562] to be seven: the Spirit of wisdom, of understanding, of counsel, of fortitude, of science, of piety, and finally, the Spirit of the fear of our Lord.

Which gifts certes, of spirits, are found to be after a more perfect manner in Christ Jesus our Lord than in any other.[1563] "For he is full of grace

[1553] Ps 27:1, 3
[1554] Ps 22:4
[1555] Rom 8:35
[1556] Phil 4:13
[1557] Cf. 1 Kgs 17; 2 Kgs 14, 16-17, 23; Ps 17
[1558] Ps 30:25
[1559] Ps 107:14; Cf. Heb 11; Dn 3; 1 Mc 2; 2 Mc 7; Acts 4; Apoc 2-3
[1560] Cf. Bernard, *De Consideratione*, Bk. 2, Ch. 10
[1561] Prv 4:27
[1562] Cf. Is 11; Jerome, *On Isaias*, Ch. 11; Ambrose, *De Spiritu Sancto*, Bk. 1, Ch. 20; Augustine, *Sermon 209, De Temp.*, Ch. 4; *Sermon 17, De Sanctis*, Ch. 2; *On the Sermon on the Mount*, Bk. 1, Ch. 3-4; *On Christian Doctrine*, Bk. 2, Ch. 7; Gregory the Great, *Homily 19 on Ezechiel*; *Moralia in Job*, Bk. 1, Ch. 28; Bk. 35, Ch. 7; Bernard, *Sermon, De Septem Donis Spiritus Sancti*
[1563] Cf. Origen, *Homily 3 on Isaias*; *Homily 6 on Numbers*

and truth."[1564] "In him doth inhabit all the fullness of the divinity corporally."[1565] "Of this fullness we all have received":[1566] who hath also given unto us of his Holy Spirit.[1567] "And if any man have not the Spirit of Christ, he is not his,"[1568] if we believe the apostle.

204. How many are the fruits of the Holy Ghost?

They are of the same apostle St. Paul, numbered twelve.[1569]

The first is charity, the most excellent kind of fruit, and the root also of all good things:[1570] "Without the which all other good things cannot profit,[1571] and which cannot herself be had without all other good things whereby a man is made good,"[1572] as saith St. Augustine.

Another fruit is joy; excelling in this: that a spiritual man doth serve God cheerfully and with alacrity.[1573]

The third is peace; which serveth to this end: that in the storms of this world, the tranquility of the mind be kept.[1574]

The fourth is patience; which consisteth in suffering adversity.[1575]

The fifth is longanimity; which doth declare the greatness of the mind in expecting good things to come.[1576]

The sixth is goodness; which hurteth no man and wisheth well to all.[1577]

The seventh is benignity; inviting to familiarities, sweet in speech, temperate in manners.[1578]

[1564] Jn 1:14
[1565] Col 2:9
[1566] Jn 1:16
[1567] Cf. 1 Jn 4
[1568] Rom 8:9
[1569] Cf. Gal 5; Jerome, *On Galatians*, Ch. 5; Theoph., *On Galatians*, Ch. 5; etc.
[1570] Cf. Col 3; 1 Jn 4; Augustine, *Tractate 87 on John*; Jerome, *On Galatians*, Ch. 5
[1571] Cf. 1 Cor 13; Augustine, *Tractate 5 on 1 John*
[1572] Augustine, *Tractate 87 on John*, n. 1
[1573] Cf. Phil 4
[1574] Cf. Lk 2; Phil 4; Ps 118
[1575] Cf. Lk 21; Jas 1
[1576] Cf. Hb 2; 2 Cor 6; Mt 10
[1577] Cf. Eph 5
[1578] Cf. Col 3

The eighth is mildness; which doth qualify and mitigate all the motions of anger.[1579]

The ninth is faith, or fidelity toward our neighbor; that we be faithful and observers of all covenants and promises.[1580]

The tenth is modesty; which excludeth all suspicion of haughtiness and arrogancy.[1581]

The eleventh is continency; whereby we do not only abstain from meat, but from all manner of wickedness.[1582]

The twelfth is chastity; which keepeth a chaste mind in a chaste body.[1583]

205. **How may we rightly use the doctrine concerning the gifts and fruits of the Holy Ghost?**

By this means surely: if with grateful minds we acknowledge from whence they come unto us, and feel the effectual virtue and use of them in ourselves; and show forth and preserve the same. They proceed, certes, from the fountain of all grace, that Father of lights, who in the same commendeth unto us his infinite goodness and charity;[1584] whilst through Christ, he doth so abundantly pour his Spirit upon us:[1585] "For the charity of God," as witnesseth the apostle, "is poured forth in our hearts, by the Holy Ghost which is given us,"[1586] to wit, according to this sevenfold grace, Christ so deserving in our behalf. "He that believeth," saith he, "as the scripture saith, out of his belly shall flow rivers of living water. And this he said of the Spirit that they should receive which believed in him,"[1587] as the evangelist himself expoundeth. "Otherwise, without Christ," as St. Jerome hath said, "neither can any man be wise, nor

---

[1579] Cf. Mt 5, 11; Prv 31
[1580] Cf. 1 Tm 3; Prv 12
[1581] Cf. Phil 4
[1582] Cf. Ecclus 37; Tb 1; 1 Thes 5
[1583] Cf. Ws 4; 1 Cor 7
[1584] Cf. Jas 1:17
[1585] Cf. Ti 3
[1586] Rom 5:5
[1587] Jn 7:38-39

intelligent, nor a counselor, nor courageous, nor learned, nor godly, nor full of the fear of God."[1588]

And the virtue and use of these spiritual goods do tend to this end: that the virtues theological and cardinal, which we have spoken of, may readily perform their force and proper operation in us. Also, they bring to pass that men do very willingly, and with sweetness, follow everywhere the Holy Ghost as guide, and, by him being moved and strengthened,[1589] do without fainting run forward in the way of the commandments of God, and are made truly spiritual,[1590] and the children of God: "Whosoever are led by the Spirit of God, they are the sons of God,"[1591] as witnesseth the apostle.

Of these gifts it were too long to discourse in particular, but from thence do proceed the most sweet fruits of the Holy Ghost, which do commend and set us forth as fruitful trees in the field of the Church,[1592] according to that saying: "Every good tree yieldeth good fruits; and the evil tree yieldeth evil fruits…Therefore, by their fruits you shall know them."[1593] Which fruits also do bring this commodity: that a Christian man be furnished and confirmed, as it were, with a certain spiritual armor, against the works of the flesh. For the rule of the apostle never faileth: "Walk in the Spirit, and the works of the flesh you shall not accomplish."[1594] And in another place it is written: "If by the Spirit, you mortify the deeds of the flesh, you shall live."[1595]

206. Which are the works of the flesh?

Those whereof the apostle thus discourseth: "The works of the flesh be manifest, which are: fornication, uncleanness, impudicity, lechery, serving of idols, witchcrafts, enmities, contentions, emulations, angers, brawls, dissentions, sects, envies, murders, inebrieties, comessations, and such like.

[1588] Jerome, *On Isaias*, Ch. 11
[1589] Cf. Ps 142, 50; Ws 1
[1590] Cf. Ps 118
[1591] Rom 8:14
[1592] Cf. Ps 51
[1593] Mt 7:17, 20; Cf. Jerome, *On Galatians*, Ch. 5
[1594] Gal 5:16
[1595] Rom 8:13

Which I foretell you, as I have foretold you, that they which do such things shall not obtain the kingdom of heaven."[1596] And afterward he addeth in the same place: "And they that be Christ's have crucified their flesh, with the vices and concupiscences."[1597] Then in another place: "They that are in flesh (to wit, they that walk according to the desires of the flesh) cannot please God."[1598] Therefore, the same apostle giveth this admonition: "Be not deceived. God is not mocked. For what things a man shall sow, those also shall he reap. For he that soweth in his flesh, of the flesh also shall reap corruption, but he that soweth in the Spirit, of the Spirit shall reap life everlasting."[1599]

Of the Eight Beatitudes

207. **Which are the beatitudes of the law of the gospel?**

Those certes which Saint Ambrose calleth our Lord's beatitudes and benedictions,[1600] which in St. Matthew's gospel are in this manner recounted eight in number.[1601]

1. Blessed are the poor in spirit, for theirs is the kingdom of heaven.[1602]
2. Blessed are the meek, for they shall possess the land.[1603]
3. Blessed are they that mourn, for they shall be comforted.[1604]
4. Blessed are they that hunger and thirst after justice, for they shall have their fill.[1605]
5. Blessed are the merciful, for they shall obtain mercy.[1606]

[1596] Gal 5:19-21; Cf. Augustine, *City of God*, Bk. 14, Ch. 2-3
[1597] Gal 5:24
[1598] Rom 8:8; Cf. Augustine, *Sermon 6, De Verbis Apostoli*, Ch. 9, 11
[1599] Gal 6:7-8
[1600] Cf. Ambrose, *On Luke*, Ch. 6
[1601] Cf. Mt 5. See commentary on Matthew 5, of the following: Hilary, Chrysostom, Jerome, Chromatius, Theophilus, Euthymius, Anselm, etc.
[1602] Cf. Lk 9; Is 66; Jas 2; Mt 18
[1603] Cf. Ps 36; Mt 11; Ps 26
[1604] Cf. Lk 6, 16; 1 Kgs 15; Jn 16; Is 61; Mt 26
[1605] Cf. Ws 1; Ps 15, 61; Is 65
[1606] Cf. Ps 40; Prv 11; Ecclus 29; Lk 6

6. Blessed are the clean of heart, for they shall see God.[1607]

7. Blessed are the peacemakers, for they shall be called the children of God.[1608]

8. Blessed are they that suffer persecution for justice, for theirs is the kingdom of heaven.[1609]

208. **Why is this doctrine of the beatitudes to be observed?**

Because it is the chiefest and greatest part of the law of the gospel, which Christ our lawmaker delivered upon the hill with his own most sacred mouth, that every man might consider what is contained and required in Christian justice besides faith;[1610] then also that they might understand how unto just persons a crown of justice, as Saint Paul calleth it,[1611] or a full and eternal reward[1612] doth not come without labor.[1613] For hereupon doth St. James also affirm: "Blessed is the man that suffereth temptation: for when he hath been proved, he shall receive the crown of life."[1614]

209. **And what is principally to be noted about the doctrine of the beatitudes?**

First of all, certes, ought to be observed that there be certain distinct degrees amongst them, as appeareth both by their number and order. Then, in every degree there are jointly proposed two things: whereof the one is the very act of virtue, or the merit and the beatitude (as they call it) of this life; the other is the reward of life everlasting, answerable to his proper and peculiar merit, which we may call the beatitude of our country. And as the first part offereth labor and difficulty to the believers, so the latter,

---

[1607] Cf. Ps 23, 50

[1608] Cf. Ps 36; Jn 14

[1609] Cf. Lk 6; 1 Pt 3; 2 Tm 3; Acts 14; Augustine, *On the Sermon on the Mount*, Bk. 1, Ch. 5; Cf. also Augustine, *On the Sermon on the Mount*, Bk. 1, Ch. 2ff; Chromatius, *In Declamatione de Octo Beatitudinibus*; Gregory of Nyssa, *De Beatitudinibus*; Leo the Great, *Homily, In Omnium Sanctorum*; Bernard, *Sermon 1, De Festo Omnium Sanctorum*; *Sermon 4, De Adventu Domini*

[1610] Cf. Is 53; Jas 4; Mt 5

[1611] Cf. 2 Tm 4

[1612] Cf. 2 Jn; Lk 6

[1613] Cf. 1 Cor 3; Mt 11; Lk 16

[1614] Jas 1:12; Cf. Ambrose, *On Luke*, Ch. 6

which in each degree is presently adjoined by the greatness of the proposed
reward, doth afford consolation, and easeth the labors, sweats, and agonies
which every man must sustain in Christian warfare. "For no man shall be
crowned unless he strive lawfully."[1615] "Everyone shall receive his own reward, according to his own labor."[1616] "What things a man shall sow, those
also shall he reap,"[1617] as constantly affirmeth the doctor of the Gentiles.
And therefore our Lord, before he comes to sit in dreadful judgment over
the world,[1618] stirreth us to the expectation of his coming with these words:
"Behold, I come quickly," saith he, "and my reward is with me, to render to
every man according to his works."[1619] "He that shall overcome, I will give
unto him to sit with me in my throne";[1620] which finally is the most high,
eternal, and absolute beatitude and happiness.

But most vain is the judgment of the world, touching beatitude and
happiness, by which in the mean season, many are deceived and brought
to destruction. For commonly and for the most part are accounted
happy: the rich and the mighty; those that excel in glory and authority;
those which abound with the goods of fortune; those which give themselves wholly to pleasure.[1621] But Christ layeth a double woe upon those
men.[1622] And boldly thus doth Isaiah cry out: "My people, they that call
thee happy, they deceive thee, and bring to naught the way of thy foot-
steps."[1623] "Blessed is the people to whom our Lord is God,"[1624] to wit:
that in living well and happily, he may always praise and magnify his
author and Creator.[1625]

[1615] 2 Tm 2:5
[1616] 1 Cor 3:8
[1617] Gal 6:8
[1618] Cf. Heb 10; Acts 17
[1619] Apoc 22:12
[1620] Apoc 3:21; Cf. Mt 19; Lk 22
[1621] Cf. Eccles 2, 5, 11; Ps 143; Ws 2
[1622] Cf. Lk 6; Is 5, 65; Am 6
[1623] Is 3:12
[1624] Ps 32:12; Cf. Ps 143; Augustine, *On Psalm 32*, conc. 2; *On Psalm 118*, conc. 1
[1625] Cf. Ambrose, *On Luke*, Ch. 6

Of the Evangelical Counsels

210. **Which are called the evangelical counsels?**

Those surely which, though they be not absolutely necessary for the getting of salvation, yet, to the intent that we may have a more ready and easy way to procure the same, they are proposed and counseled by our Savior Christ.[1626]

For which cause, the difference that the scripture hath set down between precepts and counsels is very diligently to be noted, that we may understand that the first are prescribed, as necessary to be observed;[1627] but the other are counseled and voluntarily undertaken, as furtherances of the perfect observation of the commandments.[1628] Hereupon the apostle, when he would give instruction about the leading of a single life, pronounceth this sentence: "As concerning virgins, a commandment of our Lord I have not; but counsel I give, as having obtained mercy of our Lord to be faithful."[1629] And to this end is that which St. Augustine hath plainly said: "A counsel is one thing, a commandment is another. Counsel is given to conserve virginity, to abstain from wine and flesh, to sell all that we have, and to give it to the poor; but there is commandment given to keep justice, to turn from evil, and to do good."[1630] And again: "He that shall willingly hear and fulfill a counsel shall have the greater glory; he that shall not fulfill a commandment, unless he be helped by penance, he cannot possibly avoid punishment."[1631] Unto St. Augustine consenteth St. Ambrose, when as he writeth thus: "That is not commanded which is above the law, but is rather persuaded by a counsel being given; and that which is the safer is showed unto us."[1632] Also: "Counsel inviteth them that are willing;

[1626] Cf. Augustine, *Sermon 65, De Temp.*; *Enchiridion*, Ch. 121; *De Conjugiis Adulterinis*, Bk. 1, Ch. 14; *Of Holy Virginity*, Ch. 14; *Quaestionum Evangeliorum*, Bk. 2, Ch. 19; Paulinus, *Epistle 4 ad Severum*

[1627] Cf. 1 Cor 7; Mt 19:16ff; Lk 10

[1628] Cf. 1 Cor 9; Mt 26; Mk 14; 3 Kgs 8; Gn 8; Nm 6

[1629] 1 Cor 7:25; Cf. Cyprian, *Sermon, De Nativitate Christi*

[1630] Augustine, *Sermon 61, De Temp.*

[1631] Ibid.

[1632] Ambrose, *Epistle 21 ad Eccles. Vercellens.*; Cf. Ambrose, *Concerning Widows*

the commandment bindeth even them that are unwilling."[1633] And of the same mind was St. Jerome, as these his words do declare: "Where counsel is given, there is the free choice of the offerer. Where a commandment is given, there is necessity of a servant."[1634] "But that deserveth a greater reward," saith he, "which is not constrained, and yet is offered."[1635]

211. How many evangelical counsels are there?

To recount them all in this place, it is not needful; but there are three principal, of embracing and professing poverty, chastity, and obedience; as the fathers have gathered out of holy scripture. Poverty appertaineth to those that once do forsake all worldly things, that after the example of St. Peter and the apostles, they may perfectly follow Christ.[1636] Chastity belongeth to those that have cut themselves for the kingdom of heaven.[1637] And as Tertulian hath said, do show themselves voluntarily eunuchs.[1638] And they do perform obedience, who, to the intent they may fully deny themselves, are not only utterly averted from all cupidities, but also from their own will,[1639] as the scripture admonisheth; whilst they do wholly submit themselves unto his will whom, in the stead of Christ, they have chosen to be their superior.[1640]

Such kind of counsels, Christ, the absolute example of evangelical perfection, hath not only taught in word, as we will presently show, but hath also confirmed the same unto us, by the example of his most holy life: who, when he was rich, for our sakes became poor,[1641] not having where

---

[1633] Ibid.

[1634] Jerome, *Against Jovinianus*, Bk. 1, Ch. 7

[1635] Jerome, *Epistle 22 to Eustochium*, Ch. 8

[1636] Cf. Mt 19; Acts 4; see commentary on Matthew 19, of the following: St. Marci, Cyprian, Anthony, Hilarion, Chrysostom, Paulini, Augustine, Gregory, Josaphat, Damascene, etc.

[1637] Cf. Mt 19; Eusebius, *Ecclesiastical History*, Bk. 2, Ch. 6; Nicephorus, *Ex Philone de Via Contemplativa*, Bk. 2, Ch. 16

[1638] Cf. Tertullian, *Ad Uxorem*, Bk. 1, Ch. 6

[1639] Cf. Mt 16; Lk 9

[1640] Cf. Ecclus 18; Gal 5; Basil, *The Shorter Rules*, q. 96

[1641] Cf. 2 Cor 8:9

to lay his head;[1642] who, born of a Virgin, persevereth a Virgin,[1643] and the spouse of all most holy virgins;[1644] who, finally, was so diligent in exhibiting obedience that, being subject to his mother a Virgin, yea, and that which is more, unto a carpenter,[1645] and being obedient even to the death of the cross,[1646] he witnesseth of himself: "I descended from heaven not to do mine own will, but the will of him that sent me."[1647]

212. In what place is evangelical poverty taught by Christ?

In St. Matthew's gospel, it is declared in that place which followeth the re-hearsal of the divine precepts; of which precepts it is said to everyone with-out exception: "If thou wilt enter into life, keep the commandments."[1648] And then after is the counsel proposed of undertaking voluntary poverty, with a particular form of words annexed, which might leave it to the free will of him which chooseth the same.[1649] For our Lord saith: "If thou wilt be perfect, go sell the things that thou hast and give to the poor, and thou shalt have treasure in heaven, and come follow me."[1650] Where our Lord doth not only give this counsel, but addeth also, as it were, a spur, and to the intent that men might be more willing to embrace this counsel, he proposeth the greatness of reward whereby he may allure and comfort them: promising that so it shall come to pass, that he, which by leaving all for Christ's sake is poor, shall have a treasure in heaven, shall receive a

---

[1642] Cf. Mt 8:20

[1643] Cf. Is 7:14

[1644] Cf. Jerome, *Epistle 22 to Eustochium*, Ch. 1, 6; Ambrose, *Concerning Virginity*, Bk. 1; *Sermon 90*

[1645] Cf. Lk 2; Mt 17

[1646] Cf. Phil 2; Mt 26; Rom 5

[1647] Jn 6:38

[1648] Mt 19:17

[1649] Cf. Jerome, *Epistle 14 to Heliodorus*, Ch. 6; *On Matthew*, Ch. 19; *Epistle 130 to Demetrias*, Ch. 7; *Epistle 120 to Hedibia*, q. 1; *Epistle 66 to Pammachius*, Ch. 3-4; Basil, *The Longer Rules*, q. 9; John Damascene, *In Hist. Barlaam et Josaphat*, Ch. 15; Chrysostom, *in illud Pauli, Salut. Prisc. et Aquilam*

[1650] Mt 19:21; Cf. Lk 18:22; Mk 10:21; Bede, *On Matthew*, Ch. 19; Theophylactus, *On Matthew*, Ch. 19

hundredfold, and possess life everlasting,[1651] which otherwise is very hard for rich men to come unto.[1652]

Such practicers and professors of poverty were the apostles,[1653] in whose name St. Peter said boldly unto Christ: "Behold, we have left all things, and have followed thee."[1654]

Of this number also were the Christians of the primitive Church who, as St. Luke testifieth,[1655] did sell their possessions and applied the money that came thereby to the common use: so that no man called anything his own, because nothing was private, but all things remained common amongst them.

But this poverty requireth that it be a voluntary and full resignation of riches, whereof, no property may be retained.[1656]

And here taketh place that famous sentence approved by the ancient fathers: "It is good by portions to give a man's substance to the poor, but it is better to give all at once with an intent to follow our Lord; and being free from care, to be poor with Christ."[1657]

[1651] Cf. Mt 19; see commentary on Matthew 19, of the following: Jerome, Euthymius, and Anselm; see also commentary on Mark and Luke, of Theophylactus and Bede; John Cassian, *Conferences of the Desert Fathers*, Col. 24, Ch. 26; Gregory the Great, *Homily 18 on Ezechiel*; Bernard, *In Declamat. de Deferendis Facult.*; Damian, *Sermon, De S. Bened.*

[1652] Cf. Mt 19

[1653] Cf. Lk 6; Ambrose, *On Luke*, Ch. 6; Leo the Great, *Sermon, De Omnibus Sanctis*; Chromatius, *On Matthew*, Ch. 5; Bernard, *Sermon 1, In Festo Omnium Sanctorum*; Tertullian, *Against Marcion*, Bk. 4, Ch. 14; Augustine, *City of God*, Bk 17, Ch. 4

[1654] Mt 19:27

[1655] Cf. Acts 4, 2; Jerome, *Epistle 130 to Demetrias*, Ch. 7; *On Illustrious Men*, on Mark; Augustine, *Epistle 89 ad Hilar.*; Possidius, *Life of Augustine*, Ch. 5; John Cassian, *Institutes of the Coenobia*, Bk. 7, Ch. 14, 17; *Conferences of the Desert Fathers*, Col. 3, Ch. 6

[1656] Cf. Acts 5; Jerome, *Epistle 130 to Demetrias*, Ch. 7; Basil, *Sermon 1, De Instit. Monach.*; *Constitutiones Monasticarum*, Ch. 19, 35; *The Shorter Rules*, q. 85; Augustine, Epistle 109; *Sermon 49, Ex Divers.*, Ch. 1ff; *Of the Morals of the Catholic Church*, Ch. 31; Jerome, *Epistle 22 to Eustochium*, Ch. 14; Gregory the Great, *Dialogues*, Bk. 4, Ch. 55; Bk. 10, Epistle 22

[1657] Gennadius of Massilia, *De Ecclesiasticis Dogmatibus*, Ch. 71; Cf. Ambrose, *On the Duties of the Clergy*, Bk. 1, Ch. 30; Jerome, *Against Vigilantius*, Ch. 5-6; Prosper, *De Vita Contemplativa*, Bk. 2, Ch. 9; Augustine, *Of the Good of Marriage*, Ch. 8

213. Where is the counsel of chastity commended?

Both in the gospels and in the apostles' writings. For Christ commendeth those kinds of eunuchs that have gelded themselves for the kingdom of heaven. And lest we should think that this is rather a commandment than a counsel, he addeth presently: "He that can take it, let him take it."[1658] "In which speech our Lord doth, as it were, exhort (as well doth St. Jerome interpret) and invite his soldiers to the reward of chastity, as if he said: 'He that can fight, let him fight: let him conquer and triumph.'"[1659] This can he do, unto whom it is given,[1660] "and it is given to all (as witnesseth the same holy father) that will ask, that will labor for to receive. 'For to everyone that asketh, it shall be given, and he that seeketh, shall find, and to him that knocketh, it shall be opened.'"[1661] Thus saith St. Jerome.[1662]

And to this chastity, holy scripture assigneth certes a reward; but to the chastity of virgins, it promiseth a particular and singular reward.[1663] For they that have not been defiled with women, but have remained virgins, do stand without spot before the throne of God, and do sing a new song before God and the Lamb, and do follow the Lamb whithersoever he shall go.[1664]

And the apostle hath said expressly: "It is good for a man not to touch a woman."[1665] And again, as concerning virgins: "A commandment of our Lord I have not, but counsel I give, as having obtained mercy of our Lord to be faithful. I think therefore that this is good for the present necessity,

[1658] Mt 19:12; Cf. Is 56; Basil, *De Virginitate*; Epiphanius, *Adversus Haeresus*, n. 58, contra Valesios; Augustine, *Of Holy Virginity*, Ch. 24-25

[1659] Jerome, *On Matthew*, Ch. 19; Cf. Jerome, *Against Jovinianus*, Bk. 1, Ch. 7; Cyprian, *On the Dress of Virgins*

[1660] Cf. Ws 8

[1661] Mt 7:8; Lk 11:10; Cf. Council of Trent, Session 24, Can. 9

[1662] Jerome, *On Matthew*, Ch. 19; Cf. Jerome, *Against Jovinianus*, Bk. 1, Ch. 7; Origen, *Tractate 7 on Matthew*; Augustine, *Confessions*, Bk. 6, Ch. 11; Chrysostom, *Homily 63 on Matthew*; Gregory Nazianzen, *Oration 31*

[1663] Cf. Ws 3, 4; Ecclus 26; Mt 13, 22; Mk 12; Lk 20

[1664] Cf. Apoc 14; Is 56; Ps 44; Cyril, *Catechetical Lectures 4, 12, 15*; Martial of Limoges, *Epistle ad Tolosan.*, Ch. 8-10; Cyprian, *On the Dress of Virgins*; Jerome, *On Philemon*; Augustine, *Of Holy Virginity*, Ch. 14, 27ff; Gregory the Great, *Pastoral Rule*, Bk. 3, Ch. 28, Admonition 29

[1665] 1 Cor 7:1

because it is good for a man so to do."[1666] And again, writing of the widow: "Let her marry (saith he) to whom she will: only in our Lord; but more blessed shall she be, if she so remain according to my counsel. And I think that I also have the spirit of God."[1667]

Unto the apostle very finely accordeth Saint Ambrose, when he writeth in these words: "Justly certes is the good wife commended, but more rightly is the devout virgin preferred, the apostle saying: 'He that joineth his virgin in matrimony, doth better':[1668] for the one thinketh of the things that be of the world; the one is bound with the bands of wedlock, the other is free from bands; the one is under the law, the other, under grace. Good is marriage, by means whereof there hath been found posterity of human succession; but better is virginity, whereby hath been achieved the inheritance of the heavenly kingdom, and the succession of heavenly merits hath been found. By a woman came care, by a Virgin was procured salvation."[1669] Hitherto St. Ambrose.

Now this chastity requireth that a man does, with deliberation and firm purpose, endeavor to live uncorrupted, and to lead a perpetual single life, void of all filth of the flesh, or venereous voluptuousness:[1670] that he may be holy both in body and spirit for Christ's sake.[1671] And in regard hereof, the apostle hath said: "He that hath determined in his heart, being settled,

[1666] 1 Cor 7:25-26; Cf. Jerome, *Against Jovinianus*, Bk. 1, Ch. 4ff; Ambrose, *On 1 Corinthians*; Theodoret, *On 1 Corinthians*; *Ep. Divin.* decret., Ch. "De Virgin."; Chrysostom, *De Virginitate*, Ch. 9ff

[1667] 1 Cor 7:39-40; Cf. Jdt 8, 15; Lk 2

[1668] 1 Cor 7:38; Cf. Ambrose, *Concerning Widows*; *Concerning Virginity*, Bk. 3; *In Exhort. ad Virgines*; *De Institutione Virginis*, Ch. 6, 15, 17; John Damascene, *An Exposition of the Orthodox Faith*, Bk. 4, Ch. 25; Athanasius, *De Virginitate*; Basil, *De Virginitate*; Gregory Nazianzen, *De Virginitate*; Augustine, *On Holy Virginity*; Fulgentius, *Epistle 3 ad Probam*, Ch. 9-10; Jerome, *Epistle 22 to Eustochium*, Ch. 8; *Against Jovinianus*, Bk. 1, Ch. 1; *Apology for his books Against Jovinian*, Ch. 1; Ignatius of Antioch, *Epistle to the Philadelphians*; Cyprian, *De Bono Pudicitiae*; Isidore, *De Summo Bono*, Bk. 2, Ch. 40

[1669] Ambrose, *Epistle 83 to Pope Siricius*; *Epistle 82 ad Vercellenses*

[1670] Cf. Basil, *In Praefat.*, *In Ascetica*; *Constitutiones Monasticarum*, Ch. 1; John Cassian, *Conferences of the Desert Fathers*, Col. 12, Ch. 4, 7

[1671] Cf. 1 Cor 7

not having necessity, but having power of his own will, and hath judged this in his heart, to keep his virgin, doth well."[1672]

214. How is the evangelical counsel concerning obedience proposed unto us?

Christ our Lord, first by the example of his most holy life, as we said before, then by his word, hath proposed and commended unto us the exact and perfect manner of this obedience. For he came not to do his own will, but the will of his Father;[1673] and of those unto whom we read that he was subject:[1674] he came to serve, and not to be served,[1675] insomuch that he humbled himself, being made obedient even to death, even the death of the cross.[1676]

Then by word also moving us to his imitation, he said: "If any man will come after me, let him deny himself, and take up his cross, and follow me."[1677] Which words may be certes very well understood as spoken generally to all; but yet after a more peculiar and perfect manner, they do belong unto those who, so far as frailty can reach, do so conform themselves unto Christ, that they will not in any one thing be governed by themselves; and do endeavor to live rather at another man's direction, than at their own, whilst they do follow of their own accord the will and commandment of another whom they have made their governor in Christ's room.[1678]

The superior of such persons, as teacheth St. Basil, doth bear the Person of Christ, and being made, as it were, an intercessor between God and men, doth sacrifice unto God the salvation of them that obey. And therefore, as sheep do obey their shepherd, going the same way that the shepherd leadeth them, so is it meet that such practicers of piety do obey their superiors: not curiously searching the things that are commanded, so that they

---

[1672] 1 Cor 7:37; Cf. Basil, *Homily on Psalm 44*
[1673] Cf. Jn 6:38
[1674] Cf. Lk 2:51; Bernard, *Sermon 3, De Circumcis. Domini*
[1675] Cf. Mt 20:28; Lk 22:27
[1676] Cf. Phil 2:8
[1677] Mt 16:24; Lk 9:23
[1678] Cf. Jerome, *Epistle 125 to Rusticus*, Ch. 6-7; Basil, *Sermon, De Abdicatione Rerum*; *Sermon, De Instit. Monach.*; *The Shorter Rules*, q. 96; *Constitutiones Monasticarum*, Ch. 23; Gregory the Great, *Moralia in Job*, Bk. 32, Ch. 21; Nicephorus, *Church History*, Bk. 11, Ch. 37

be free from sin; but with all alacrity and diligence, fulfilling those things that are prescribed.[1679] And of this superior, after St. Basil, St. Bernard also affirmeth: him whom we have in God's room, we ought to hear as God himself in those things which are not manifestly against God.[1680]

And such faithful and excellent followers of Christ, as have busily attended to the observation of the said counsels, the Church hath always had, as ancient histories do make mention; and amongst them, certain choice and approved companies of devout and religious men, who, above the custom and example of the common sort, forsaking at once all their goods and abandoning the pleasures of the flesh, have given themselves by profession to a holy obedience; only seeking and laboring that they might wholly conform themselves to the example of the obedient Christ, and to the perfection of the evangelical rule; leaving no place at all to their own proper will. Witnesses whereof very fit and substantial, we have St. Basil, St. Augustine, St. Jerome, St. Benedict, St. Gregory, Cassianus, St. Bernard, and other innumerable professors of evangelical perfection, and not only defenders, but most perfect observers of a monastical rule.[1681]

[1679] Cf. Basil, *Constitutiones Monasticarum*, Ch. 23; 1 Kgs 15; Eccles 4; Lk 10; Eph 6; Col 3

[1680] Cf. Bernard, *De Praecepto et Dispensatione*, Ch. 12-13, 23; *Epistle 2 ad Adam Monachum*

[1681] Cf. Philo, *De Vita Contemplativa*; et eodem Eusebius et Nicephorus; Josephus, *Antiquities of the Jews*, Bk. 18, Ch. 2; *The Jewish War*, Bk. 2, Ch. 7; Epiphanius, *Adversus Haeresus*, n. 29; Jerome, *Epistle 22 to Eustochium*, Ch. 15-16; *On Illustrious Men*, on Philo and Mark; Dionysius, *Ecclesiastical Hierarchy*, Ch. 6; Eusebius, *Demonstratio Evangelica*, Bk. 1, Ch. 8; Augustine, *On Psalm 132*; *Of the Morals of the Catholic Church*, Ch. 31, 33; *Confessions*, Bk. 8, Ch. 6; Ambrose, *Epistle 82*; John Cassian, *Conferences of the Desert Fathers*, Col. 18, Ch. 14ff; Gregory Nazianzen, *Oration 20*; Athanasius, *Life of St. Anthony*; Sulpicius Severus, *Life of St. Martin*; Isidore, *De Ecclesiasticis Officiis*, Bk. 2, Ch. 15; Sozomen, *Church History*, Bk. 1, Ch. 12; Gregory the Great, *Dialogues*, Bk. 2; Bk. 1, Epistle 33; Chrysostom, *Advers. Vitup. Monast. Vitae*; *Homily 5 ad Pop.*, cum sequent.; *Homily 4 on 1 Timothy*; Bernard, *Apol. Ad Guil. Abb.*; *Homily, De Bonis Margaritis*; Cf. also *De obedientia laude et perfectione*, see: Augustine, *City of God*, Bk. 14, Ch. 12; Jerome, *Epistle 130 to Demetrias*, Ch. 10; Gregory the Great, *Moralia in Job*, Bk. 35, Ch. 12; *On 1 Kings*, Bk. 2, Ch. 4; Bk. 4, Ch. 5; Bk. 6, Ch. 2; John Cassian, *Institutes of the Coenobia*, Bk. 4, Ch. 10; *Conferences of the Desert Fathers*, Col. 2, Ch. 11; Col. 4, Ch. 20; Bernard, *Sermon, De 3 Ordinibus Ecclesiae*; *Ad Milites Templi*, Ch. 13; *Sermon, De Virtute Obedient.*

215. In brief: What conception ought we to have of the evangelical counsels?
This surely: that they be provocations and certain helps very profitable, which do yield armor unto weak persons against the baits of the world and the flesh; which do further the endeavors of good men in the race of true piety; which does make the spirit more at liberty to perform the functions of religion and divine worship;[1682] and which moreover are much available, as we have declared, for the achieving of the reward of eternal life, and more ample glory in the kingdom of heaven.[1683]

But the whole sum of evangelical perfection standeth in this: that as much as thou mayest, thou endeavor to get charity,[1684] and that thou follow Christ.[1685] And him thou dost imitate, if, according to thy power, thou dost seek to conform thyself to Christ, who was both poor[1686] and a virgin,[1687] and subject to others,[1688] and obedient even to the death of the cross;[1689] if with the apostle St. Paul,[1690] neglecting those things that are behind, with unwearied labor thou dost travail toward those things that are before, and dost stretch out thyself every day to the prize of the supernal vocation, utterly forsaking in the mean season, as much as thou canst, thy own proper will, and submitting it to a man for God's sake,[1691] that thou mayest pursue the better gifts,[1692] and mayest both choose the best part,[1693] and with faithfulness conserve the same even to the end.[1694]

[1682] Cf. 1 Jn 2; Lk 14; Mt 19, 13; 1 Cor 7; Ecclus 31; Prv 29; Jgs 17, 21; Gal 5
[1683] Cf. Mt 9; Gregory the Great, *Moralia in Job*, Bk. 26, Ch. 25
[1684] Cf. 1 Cor 13; 1 Jn 2, 4; Col 3; Augustine, *Of the Morals of the Catholic Church*, Ch. 33
[1685] Cf. Lk 9
[1686] Cf. 2 Cor 8; Mt 8
[1687] Cf. 1 Pt 1
[1688] Cf. Lk 2
[1689] Cf. Phil 2
[1690] Cf. 1 Pt 2
[1691] Cf. Phil 3; Ps 83; Bernard, *Epistle 253 ad Garinum Abbatem*; *Epistle 341 ad Monachos Sanct. Bertini*; *Sermon 2, De Purific. B. Mariae*; Augustine, *Epistle 137 ad Hipponenses*
[1692] Cf. 1 Cor 12
[1693] Cf. Lk 10
[1694] Cf. Apoc 2

Of the Four Last Things of a Man

216. **Which are called "the four last things of a man"?**

These surely: death, judgment, hell, and the kingdom of heaven; called
certes "the last things," because that amongst all the things that can chance
unto a man, they challenge unto themselves the very last place.[1695] For
death, according to the common saying, is the last line of things. After
death followeth the judgment of God, as Saint Paul also hath declared in
these words: "It is appointed to men to die once, and after this, the judgment."[1696] To wit, both that particular which everyone hath at his death;[1697]
and that last and general judgment, which expecteth all men at the end of
the world, as we have already declared.[1698]

And some are judged (those that die in mortal sin) to be delivered to everlasting pains in hell;[1699] others, who departing this life, are adorned with
the marriage garment of charity, that they may enjoy the most happy life in
the kingdom of heaven.[1700] That is it which the evangelical verity affirmeth:
"They that have done good things, shall come forth into the resurrection
of life, but they that have done evil, into the resurrection of judgment."[1701]
"For the Son of man shall come in the glory of his Father, with his angels:
and then will he render to every man according to his works."[1702]

217. **What instruction doth the scripture give us of death?**

"As by one man sin entered into this world, and by sin death, so unto all
men death did pass,"[1703] as St. Paul affirmeth. Therefore, although nothing

[1695] Cf. Ecclus 7, 28, 38; Dt 32; Prv 19; Bernard, *Sermon, Primord. Mediis et Novissimis*
[1696] Heb 9:27
[1697] Cf. Augustine, *On the Soul and Its Origin*, Bk. 2, Ch. 4; *Tractate 49 on John*;
Chrysostom, *Homily 14 on Matthew*
[1698] See on the Creed, above.
[1699] Cf. Lk 16; Mt 25
[1700] Cf. Mt 22; Augustine, *Post Collationem contra Donatistas*, Ch. 20; Gregory the
Great, *Homily 38 on the Gospels*
[1701] Jn 5:29; Cf. Mt 25
[1702] Mt 16:27
[1703] Rom 5:12; Cf. Ws 1; Council of Milevi, Can. 1; Augustine, *De Praedest. et Gratia*,
Ch. 3

be more uncertain unto us than the hour of death,[1704] for "a man knoweth not his end,"[1705] yet nothing can be more sure than death itself. For which cause it is written: "All of us die, and as waters we fall into earth, which do not return again."[1706] And Ecclesiasticus confirming the same: "And a king (saith he) is today, and tomorrow he shall die; and when a man dieth, he shall inherit serpents, and beasts, and worms."[1707]

And because it concerneth us much in what manner and how well prepared we die, therefore, so often in the gospel is this repeated unto us: "Be watchful";[1708] also: "Be ye ready, for at what hour you think not, the Son of man will come."[1709] And we shall be watchful and ready to entertain death, if every man do for his own part earnestly and in all his life meditate that which is written: "Before death work justice, because there is not in hell to find meat."[1710] As also Christ himself hath said: "The night cometh when no man can work."[1711] "Walk whilst you have the light, that the darkness overtake you not."[1712]

But fitly doth the prophet put a difference between the death of the good and the evil. For of these he saith: "The death of sinners is very evil."[1713] To wit, of them, who like the obstinate Jews, do die in their sin

[1704] Cf. Gregory the Great, *Homily 13 on the Gospels*; Augustine, *On Psalm 144*; *Homily 27 ex 50*, Ch. 3, 2; *Soliloquiorum Animae*; Hugo of St. Victor, *De Anima*, Bk. 1, Ch. 3

[1705] Eccles 9:12; Cf. Jas 4; Ecclus 11, 14; Lk 12

[1706] 2 Kgs 14:14; Cf. Eccles 2; Ps 89, 101, 102; Jb 8, 14; 1 Pt 1; Augustine, *City of God*, Bk. 13, Ch. 10-11; *Sermon 21, De Verbis Domini*, Ch. 2-3; Innocent III, *De Contemptu Mundi*, Bk. 1, Ch. 24

[1707] Ecclus 10:12-13; Cf. Jb 17; Ps 48; Bar 3; Ecclus 41; Prosper, *Sententia ex Augustine*, last number

[1708] Mt 25:13; 26:41; Mk 13:33, 35-36; Cf. Augustine, *Epistle 80 to Hesychius*; *De Diversis Quaestionibus Octoginta Tribus*, q. 59

[1709] Lk 12:40; Cf. Apoc 3:2-3; 16:15; Cyprian, *Epistle 52 ad Anton.*; Augustine, *Sermon 3, De Innocentibus*; *Tractate 33 on John*; Gregory the Great, *Moralia in Job*, Bk. 16, Ch. 31

[1710] Ecclus 14:17; Cf. Eccles 9, 12; Gal 6; Augustine, *On Christian Doctrine*, Ch. 11-12; Fourth Lateran Council, Const. 21; Council of Trent, Session 14; Council of Nantes, Ch. 4; Gregory the Great, *Dialogues*, Bk. 4, Ch. 58; Possidius, *Life of Augustine*

[1711] Jn 9:4; Cf. Augustine, *Enchiridion*, Ch. 110; *Tractate 44 on John*

[1712] Jn 12:35; Cf. Lk 19

[1713] Ps 33:22; Cf. Prv 11; Ws 5; Ps 10; Augustine, *Sermon 47 ad fratres in eremo*; *Sermon 59 ad fratres in eremo*; Hugo of St. Victor, *De Anima*, Bk. 1, Ch. 2; Bk. 3, Ch. 23; Bk. 4, Ch. 13; Innocent III, *De Contemptu Mundi*, Bk. 2, Ch. 42

without penance, and for that cause do so perish, that they are to be tormented perpetually in hell with the rich glutton.[1714] But of the other he testifieth: "Precious in the sight of our Lord is the death of his saints."[1715] For to such this death of the body is nothing else but an end of this earthly peregrination, and a conclusion of the miseries of this mortal life: a quiet sleep and secure repose, the beginning of true life, and a wished passage to most happy immortality;[1716] with the desire whereof the apostle burning and being weary of this life: "I desire," saith he, "to be dissolved, and to be with Christ."[1717] "Blessed are those servants that when the Lord cometh he shall find watching."[1718] And, "Blessed are the dead which die in our Lord."[1719] And, "A just man, if he shall be prevented with death, he shall be in a refreshing."[1720]

218. In what sort doth holy scripture admonish us of judgment?

"It is horrible to fall into the hands of the living God,"[1721] and of Christ the judge, before whose tribunal we must all be manifested,[1722] and every man must render account for himself:[1723] "For all things that are done, God will bring into judgment, for every fault: whether it be good or evil."[1724] And therefore not only unto sinners, but also unto saints[1725] oftentimes the expectation of this judgment is terrible.[1726] This did holy David fear,

---

[1714] Cf. Lk 16; Gregory the Great, *Dialogues*, Bk. 4, Ch. 38; *Homily 12 on the Gospels*; Bede, *Ecclesiastical History of the English Church*, Bk. 5, Ch. 14-15

[1715] Ps 115:15

[1716] Cf. 2 Cor 5; Gregory the Great, *Dialogues*, Bk. 4, Ch. 11ff; Cyprian, *On Mortality*; Ambrose, *De Bono Mortis*, Ch. 2ff

[1717] Phil 1:23; Cf. Lk 2; Ps 41, 83, 141; Nm 23

[1718] Lk 12:37

[1719] Apoc 14:13

[1720] Ws 4:7

[1721] Heb 10:31; Cf. Bernard, *Sermon 8, in Psal. Qui habitat*

[1722] Cf. 2 Cor 5

[1723] Cf. Rom 14; Lk 16, 12, 19

[1724] Eccles 12:14; Cf. Eccles 11; 1 Cor 4; Rom 2; Ws 1; Ecclus 11; Mt 12, 16; Apoc 20, 21; Ps 61; 2 Tm 4; John Damascene, *Oration De Defunct.*; Cyril of Alexandria, *Oration, De Exitu Animae*; Leontius, *Life of John the Almsgiver*

[1725] Cf. 1 Pt 4; Soph 1; Ps 74; Bernard, *Sermon 55 on Canticle of Canticles*; Gregory the Great, *Moralia in Job*, Bk. 8, Ch. 13

[1726] Cf. Heb 10

so that he did earnestly pray: "Enter not into judgment with thy servant O Lord."[1727] This feared Job also, notwithstanding he was innocent, and his fear[1728] he expresseth in these words: "What shall I do when God shall arise to judgment? And when he shall ask, what shall I answer him?"[1729] "As swelling waves over me, I always feared Almighty God, and his weight I could not bear."[1730] "I did fear all my works, knowing that thou wouldst not spare him that offendeth."[1731]

And certes that judge is to be feared, whose power we cannot escape, whose wisdom is infallible, justice inflexible, judgment unrevocable.[1732] Of which it is thus written: "The zeal and furor of the man (to wit, of Christ the judge) shall not spare in the day of revenge, nor yield to any man's petition, nor will take for redemption never so many gifts";[1733] who also of himself and his judgment (lest any man should be ignorant) hath foretold this unto all men: "When I shall take time, I will judge justice."[1734] "I the Lord searching the heart, and proving the reins: who do give to every one according to his way, and according to the fruit of his inventions."[1735] "I come to gather together their works, and their cogitations, with all nations and tongues; and they shall come and see my glory."[1736]

But of the day of the last judgment,[1737] which is also called in scripture "the day of our Lord," "the day of anger," "the great and horrible day";[1738] the apostle Saint Peter teacheth in this manner: "The day of our Lord shall

[1727] Ps 142:2
[1728] Cf. Jb 1
[1729] Jb 31:14
[1730] Jb 31:23; Cf. Gregory the Great, *Moralia in Job*, Bk. 21, Ch. 15-16
[1731] Jb 9:28; Cf. Jb 24; Eccles 9; 1 Cor 4
[1732] Cf. Augustine, *Sermon 9, De Decem Chordis*, Ch. 1-2; Prosper, *De Vita Contemplativa*, Bk. 3, Ch. 12; Bernard, *Epistle 1*; Innocent III, *De Contemptu Mundi*, Bk. 3, Ch. 15
[1733] Prv 6:34-35
[1734] Ps 74:3; Cf. Bernard, *Sermon 55 on Canticle of Canticles*
[1735] Jer 17:10; Cf. Jer 11, 20, 32; Prv 16; Heb 4; 1 Par 28; Mal 3; Ps 7, 43
[1736] Is 66:18; Cf. Jude 1; Mt 10
[1737] Cf. Augustine, *City of God*, Bk. 20, Ch. 1-2, 30; Bk. 18, Ch. 53; *Epistle 78*; *Epistle 80 to Hesychius*; Hippolytus, *On the End of the World*; John Damascene, *An Exposition of the Orthodox Faith*, Bk. 4, Ch. 27
[1738] Cf. Soph 1; Jl 2, 3; Is 13, 24, 66; Jer 23; Mal 3, 4; Dn 7; Apoc 20, 6; Ps 96, 59; Mt 24, 25, 13, 3; Ws 5

come as a thief, in the which the heavens shall pass with great violence, but the elements shall be resolved with heat, and the earth and the works that are in it shall be burnt. Therefore, whereas all these things are to be dissolved, what manner of men ought you to be in holy conversations and godlinesses? Expecting and hastening unto the coming of the day of our Lord, by which the heavens burning shall be resolved, and the elements shall melt with heat of fire?"[1739]

And that we may find Christ then a gentle judge, and that day wherein "heaven and earth shall pass"[1740] joyful unto us: most excellent is this counsel of the wise man: "Before sickness apply the medicine, and before judgment examine thyself, and in the sight of God thou shalt find propitiation."[1741] "For if we did judge ourselves, we should not be judged."[1742] "To him that feareth our Lord, it shall be well at the last, and in the day of his death he shall be blessed."[1743]

219. And what of hell and the pains thereof?

As nothing is more miserable than death, as nothing also is more terrible than judgment, especially to the children of this world, persisting obstinately in sin, so can there nothing be imagined more intolerable and unfortunate than hell and the pain thereof. "For there (as witnesseth divine scripture) is weeping and gnashing of teeth."[1744] There "their worm dieth not, and the fire quencheth not."[1745] There "the land is dark, and covered with the mist of death." There "the shadow of death and no order, but perpetual horror

---

[1739] 2 Pt 3:10-12; Cf. Augustine, *City of God*, Bk. 20, Ch. 16, 18; Chrysostom, *Homily 46, to the People of Antioch*, et seq.; Ephrem, *Judicio Extremo*; *De Vera Poenitentia*; Augustine, *Sermon 67, De Temp.*; Isidore, *De Summo Bono*, Bk. 1, Ch. 30; Cyril of Jerusalem, *Catechetical Lecture 15*; Jerome, *Epistle 14 to Heliodorus*, Ch. 9; Gregory the Great, *Homily 1 on the Gospels*; *Homily 12 on the Gospels*; *Moralia in Job*, Bk. 26, Ch. 24-25; Augustine, *meditat. Anselmus de miseria hominis.*, Ch. 4; Bernard, *De Interiori Domo*, Ch. 38
[1740] Lk 21:33; Cf. 1 Cor 7:31; Apoc 21:4
[1741] Ecclus 18:20; Cf. 2 Pt 3; Lk 21; Ti 2; 1 Thes 5; Lk 17; Chrysostom, *Homily 5, De Poenit.*
[1742] 1 Cor 11:31
[1743] Ecclus 1:13; Cf. Gregory the Great, *Moralia in Job*, Bk. 31, Ch. 21; Augustine, *Sermon 120, De Temp.*
[1744] Mt 8:12; 13:42, 50; 22:13; 24:51; 25:30; Lk 13:28
[1745] Mk 9:43, 45, 47; Cf. Is 66:24; Ecclus 7:19; Jdt 16:21

inhabiteth."[1746] There "their part shall be in the pool burning with fire and brimstone, which is the second death."[1747] There "they shall be tormented day and night, forever and ever."[1748] There finally that shall be found true by experience which the just judge hath foretold in these words, to all those that are to be tormented in hell: "Behold, my servants shall eat, and you shall be hungry; behold, my servants shall drink, and you shall be thirsty; behold, my servants shall rejoice, and you shall be confounded; behold, my servants shall sing praises for the exultation of their heart, and you shall cry for the grief of heart, and because of the contrition of spirit, ye shall howl."[1749] Therefore, the kingly prophet calleth upon all kings and princes, and setteth before them the pains that are to come for the wicked, with this severe admonition: "And now kings understand ye, be ye instructed, ye that judge the earth.[1750] (For 'to the stronger, there remaineth a stronger torment, and a most hard judgment shall pass upon them that are in authority.'[1751]) Serve ye our Lord in fear, and exult unto him with trembling; apprehend ye discipline, lest that our Lord be angry, and you do perish from the just way. When his anger shall suddenly wax hot."[1752] Hereupon Christ himself also hath thus spoken to every man: "Fear him who after he hath killed, hath power to cast into hell. Yea I say to you, fear him."[1753] For as it is momentary which in this life delighteth, so is it everlasting which in hell tormenteth.[1754]

[1746] Jb 10:21, 22; Cf. Jude 1; Gregory the Great, *Moralia in Job*, Bk. 9, Ch. 45ff; John Cassian, *Confess. Theologica*, Pt. 3; Ephrem, *De Vera Poenitentia*, Ch. 7-8

[1747] Apoc 21:8; Cf. Apoc 14, 18-20; Ps 10, 20; Dt 32; Jb 24; Rom 2; Is 3; Prv 19; Ecclus 21

[1748] Apoc 20:10; Cf. Apoc 9; Jb 7, 20; Ps 48; Is 33; Mt 3, 25; 2 Thes 1; 2 Pt 2

[1749] Is 65:13-14; Cf. Lk 6, 16; Cyril of Alexandria, *Oration, De Exitu Animae*; Augustine, *Enchiridion*, Ch. 3ff; *Sermon 181, De Temp.*, Ch. 18; *De Triplici Habitaculo*, Ch. 2; Cyprian, *Ad Demetr.*; *Sermon, De Ascensione Christi*; Bernard, *Epistle 253*, meditat. Ch. 3; *Sermon 8, in Psal. Qui habitat*; Hugo of St. Victor, *De Anima*, Bk. 8, Ch. 13; Innocent III, *De Contemptu Mundi*, Bk. 3, Ch. 2ff; Council of Florence

[1750] Ps 2:10

[1751] Ws 6:9, 6; Cf. Is 5

[1752] Ps 2:11-13

[1753] Lk 12:5; Cf. Mt 10:28

[1754] Cf. Chrysostom, *De Providentia Dei*, Bk. 1; *Homily 5, to the People of Antioch*; *Homily 55, to the People of Antioch*; Augustine, *On Psalm 49*; Bernard, *Sermon, De Conversione ad Clericos*, Ch. 5; Cf. also Chrysostom, *Epistle 5 to Theodore after His Fall*; Cyril of Alexandria, *Oration, De Exitu Animae*; Prosper, *De Vita Contemplativa*, Bk. 3, Ch. 12; Gregory the Great, *Dialogues*, Bk. 4, Ch. 28-29, 42ff; Isidore, *De Summo Bono*, Bk. 1, Ch. 31-32

220. **What do we learn out of holy scripture of the kingdom of heaven?**

God hath prepared his kingdom for the elect, from the beginning of the world:[1755] a heavenly kingdom,[1756] an eternal kingdom,[1757] a most blessed kingdom,[1758] whereof Saint Paul plainly confesseth: "The passions of this time are not condign to the glory to come."[1759] "The eye hath not seen, nor ear hath heard, neither hath it ascended into the heart of man, what things God hath prepared for them that love him."[1760] "O holy city Jerusalem, new, descending from heaven, prepared of God, as a bride adorned for her husband."[1761] Whereof Saint John, very well acquainted with divine matters, heard these things from heaven and wrote them: "Behold the tabernacle of God with men, and he will dwell with them, and they shall be his people, and he God with them, shall be their God. And God shall wipe away all tears from their eyes, and death shall be no more, nor mourning, nor crying, neither shall there be sorrow anymore, which first things are gone."[1762] There is heard the voice of the great trumpet, and "as the voice of many waters, and as the voice of great thunders saying: 'Alleluia: because our Lord God omnipotent hath reigned, let us be glad, and rejoice, and give glory unto him: because the marriage of the Lamb is come.'"[1763]

"Blessed be they that are called to the supper of the marriage of the Lamb";[1764] but more blessed they that being called, do come to that supper, all impediments being taken away, and bring their wedding garment, that

[1755] Cf. Mt 25
[1756] Cf. 2 Tm 4
[1757] Cf. 2 Pt 1
[1758] Cf. Lk 14; Augustine, *Sermon 37, De Sanctis*; Cyprian, *On Mortality*
[1759] Rom 8:18; Cf. 2 Cor 4; Acts 14; 2 Tm 2, 4
[1760] 1 Cor 2:9; Cf. Is 64:4
[1761] Apoc 21:2; Cf. Apoc 22; Mt 13, 22; Ws 3, 5; Dn 12; 1 Cor 5; Phil 3; Jn 14
[1762] Apoc 21:3-4; Cf. Apoc 7; 1 Cor 13; 1 Jn 3; Is 25, 33, 49, 51, 60, 65-66; Ps 16, 26, 30, 35, 86, 114, 149; Chrysostom, *Epistle 5 to Theodore after His Fall*; Anselm, *Epistle 2*; *De Similitudinibus*, Ch. 47ff; Hugo of St. Victor, *De Anima*, Bk. 4, Ch. 15-16
[1763] Apoc 19:6-7; Cf. Ps 83; Augustine, *On Apocalypse*, Ch. 19; *City of God*, Bk. 10, Ch. 16; Bk. 22, Ch. 29-30; *De Libero Arbitrio*, Bk. 3, Ch. 25; *A Sermon to the Catechumens on the Creed*, n. 17; *On the Trinity*, Bk. 1, Ch. 13; *On the Catechizing of the Uninstructed*, Ch. 25; *Tractate 4 on 1 John*, meditat. Ch. 22, 25; *Soliloquiorum*, Ch. 21, 35, 36; *Manual.*, Ch. 6-7, 16-17
[1764] Apoc 19:9

they may sit down in the kingdom of God,[1765] with Abraham, Isaac, and Jacob.[1766] And we shall not need to ask, "O Lord who shall dwell in they tabernacle? or who shall rest in thy holy hill?" The answer is ready: "He that entereth without spot and worketh justice."[1767] Or if thou takest more delight in the speech of Christ: "He that doth the will of my Father which is in heaven, he shall enter into the kingdom of heaven."[1768] This is a holy city, and it also requireth holy citizens: "There shall not enter into it any polluted thing."[1769]

221. **What is the use and commodity of the whole doctrine concerning the four last things?**

First of all, to know and seriously to meditate these things, it is profitable to this end: that we may the more easily be withdrawn from the care, affection, and love of those things which are transitory, vain, and floating in this world. For, "Vanity of vanities saith Ecclesiastes: Vanity of vanities, and all is vanity."[1770] "I saw all things that are done under the sun, and behold, all is vanity and affliction of spirit."[1771]

Then they do not only, being well considered, avert a man from vain cogitations and earthly cares; but also do terrify him from all liberty, custom, and proneness to sin.[1772] Hence is that golden sentence: "In all thy works remember thy last things, and thou shalt never sin."[1773]

[1765] Cf. Lk 14; Gregory the Great, *Homily 36 on the Gospels*; *Homily 37 on the Gospels*; Prosper, *De Vita Contemplativa*, Bk. 1, Ch. 2ff; Bk. 3, Ch. 32; Bernard, *Sermon, De Triplici Genere Bonorum*, Ch. 4, meditat.

[1766] Cf. Mt 8; Lk 13, 12, 22; Gregory the Great, *Homily 13 on the Gospels*

[1767] Ps 14:1-2; Cf. Ps 23; Is 33; Rom 2; Mt 5; Bernard, *Sermon, De Conversione ad Clericos*, Ch. 25

[1768] Mt 7:21; Cf. Mt 19, 25; Apoc 2-3, 7; Bernard, *Sermon 2, De verb. Apost. non est regnum Dei esca et potus*

[1769] Apoc 21:27

[1770] Eccles 1:2; Cf. Jerome, *On Ecclesiastes*, Ch. 1; Gregory the Great, *On 1 Kings*, Bk. 5, Ch. 2

[1771] Eccles 1:14

[1772] Cf. Augustine, *De Genesi Contra Manichaeos*, Bk. 2, Ch. 28; *Sermon 120, De Temp.*; Gregory the Great, *Homily 39 on the Gospels*; Isidore, *De Summo Bono*, Bk. 3, last chapter

[1773] Ecclus 7:40; Cf. Bernard, *Sermon 1, In Festo Omnium Sanctorum*; *Sermon, De Primordiis Mediis et Novissimis Nostris*

Moreover, they do admonish a wise man that, in all affairs, he do nothing rashly, but that first he set before himself the last things, and having foreseen the end, do go on in the high roadway,[1774] that he may neither decline on the right hand, or on the left, from that which is right.[1775]

But specially the memory and contemplation of such things doth cause that the fear of God, which is the fountain of true wisdom, the guardian of all virtue, and a necessary schoolmaster in all the life of man, may confirm and set us forward in the zeal of justice and goodness.[1776] For, "the fear of God expelleth sin; and he that is without fear, cannot be justified."[1777] "They that fear our Lord, will inquire what things are well pleasing unto him…They will prepare their hearts, and in his sight they will sanctify their souls."[1778] Finally: "They that fear our Lord, will keep his commandments, and will have patience until he behold them, saying: 'If we do not penance, we shall fall into the hands of our Lord.'"[1779]

But the children of this world, who love vanity and seek after a lie,[1780] "who rejoice when they do evil, and triumph in things that be worst,"[1781] before whose eyes the fear of God is not: they do nothing less than think of these matters.[1782] "It is a people without counsel, and without wisdom: would to God they were wise, and did understand, and foresee the last things."[1783] With them we see it fall out daily by experience, that which holy Job saith: "They hold the tabor and the lute, and rejoice at the sound of the instrument. They pass over their days in pleasures, and in a moment they descend into hell."[1784] "So laughter shall be mingled with grief, and the end of joy is mourning."[1785]

[1774] Cf. Dt 32

[1775] Cf. Prv 4

[1776] Cf. Ecclus 1; Ps 110; Prv 1, 9; Jb 28; Eccles 7; Prv 14; Chrysostom, *Homily 15, to the People of Antioch*; *Homily 2 on 2 Thessalonians*; Augustine, *Tractate 90 on 1 John*; *On Psalm 127*

[1777] Ecclus 1:27-28

[1778] Ecclus 2:19-20; Cf. Augustine, *Sermon 13, De Verbis Apostoli*, Ch. 13, 18; *Of Holy Virginity*, Ch. 38; *Sermon 214, De Temp.*

[1779] Ecclus 2:21-22

[1780] Cf. Ps 4

[1781] Prv 2:14

[1782] Cf. Ps 13

[1783] Dt 32:28-29; Cf. Bernard, *Sermon 2, In Die Apost. Petri et Pauli*; *Epistle 292*

[1784] Jb 21:12-13

[1785] Prv 14:13; Cf. Chrysostom, *Epistle 5 to Theodore after His Fall*; John Damascene, *In Hist. Barlaam et Josaphat*, Ch. 5, 12-14

222. **What is the sum of those things that are contained in this book?**

The sum of the whole work is comprised in two things: in Christian wisdom and justice. To wisdom are these points referred, to wit: of faith and the Creed; of hope and our Lord's Prayer; of charity and the ten commandments. For faith, hope, and charity are those virtues wherein the divine scripture comprehendeth the true wisdom of man, as Saint Augustine hath noted.[1786] Then is there further annexed a discourse of the precepts of the Church, and of the sacraments. For as the foresaid virtues cannot stand without the sacraments and perfect observance of the precepts of the Church; so, being joined with them, they are effectually grafted in us; and being grafted, are confirmed, augmented, and brought to perfection. Therefore, in explicating those things which we reduce unto wisdom is the first part of the book concluded.

The latter, which treateth of justice, doth briefly demonstrate two parts thereof, belonging both to the fleeing of evil things and the pursuing of those which are good.[1787] For to abstain from evil (as witnesseth Saint Chrysostom) is not sufficient for us to salvation, except therewith all be annexed the following of good things and the action of virtue. Therefore, to either of these two parts we have applied some discourses, which do chiefly serve to the observing of the difference of good and evil.[1788] But the force and largeness of all justice, Tobit, a man no less wise than just, doth briefly comprehend: where he admonisheth his son, and consequently in him all the children of God in particular, with these words: "Fear not my son: we lead surely a poor life, but we shall have many good things if we fear God, and abstain from all sin, and do well."[1789] Thus, finally we learn the exact duty of a Christian man, which doth not only require faith, but a life also ordered according to the rule of Christian wisdom and justice. For a wise heart that hath understanding, as the scripture testifieth, will keep itself from sin, and will have success in the works of justice.[1790]

[1786] Cf. Augustine, *Retractions*, Bk. 2, Ch. 63; *Enchiridion*, Ch. 2-3
[1787] Cf. Ps 33, 36
[1788] Cf. Chrysostom, *On Psalm 4*; see as well Question 174 and following, above.
[1789] Tb 4:23
[1790] Cf. Ecclus 3

But to the intent that we may not pass the bands of our intended brevity, let this be the end and conclusion of this doctrine appertaining to the instruction of Christians, and those especially of the simpler sort. All which things we will close up with one word of Ecclesiastes, as with a notable seal of the whole life of man, making this conclusion: "Fear God, and keep his commandments. For this is all a man."[1791]

"Confirm this O God, which thou hast wrought in us."[1792]

[1791] Eccles 12:13
[1792] Ps 67:29

CAPITA DOCTRI-
NAE CHRISTIANAE

compendio tradita, vt sit veluti
paruus Catechismus Ca-
tholicorum.

CAPVT PRIMVM.

De Fide & Symbolo
Fidei.

Quis dicendus est Christianus atq̃
Catholicus?

QVI Baptismatis Sacramento ini-
tiatus, IESV Christi veri Dei at-
què hominis salutarem doctrinã
in eius Ecclesia profitetur, neque sectis Act. 12.
vel opinionibus vllis ab Ecclesia Catholica alienis adhæret.

Quibus dè rebus primùm docendi
sunt Christiani?

De Fide, Spe, Charitate, Sacramentis,
& officijs iustitiæ Christianæ.

Quid est Fides?

Donum Dei, ac lumen, quo illustratus
homo firmiter assentitur omnibus quæ
Deus reuelauit, & nobis per Ecclesiam
credenda proposuit: siue scripta illa sint,
siue non sint.

B 5   Quæ

Page of Institutiones Christianae Pietatis, *an early edition of the Small Catechism.*
Cologne: M. Cholinus, 1571. Bridwell Library Special Collections, SMU.

AN

INTRODUCTION

TO THE

CATHOLICK

FAITH

Containing

A brief explication of the Christian Doctrine.

Lord, what wilt thou have me to do?
Act. 9. 7.

By John Cousturier.

1633

To the Reader

Christian reader,

If thou didst behold the thoughts and affections couched in my heart, thou wouldst among the rest view my wishes of thy salvation: which because neither I can express, nor thou see, give me leave in a word to put thee in mind of that, thy greatest and only good. This life is but a moment, whereupon eternity dependeth: eternity of punishments in hell, or of joys in heaven; eternity of weal or woe of thy soul, that soul which Christ our Lord prized so much, that out of his infinite goodness he would ransom it with the expense of his life and sacred blood. This thou believest. What then will it profit thee, to gain the whole world, if thou let pass this moment and neglect that soul, which (if thou wilt) is to be companion of the angels in never-fading felicity? Thou knowest what answer faith maketh to thy conscience; and I hope thou desirest to do what thy conscience suggesteth to be meet, and consequently to know what a Christian ought to believe and do, that he may be saved. This little Introduction instructeth thee in both; for in it thou shalt find what the holy Church proposeth to be believed, as also how to return to God by penance, and have recourse unto him by prayer; which three things are in a special manner necessary for thy salvation, which, again and again, I wish may be thy only care. And that this care may be the greater, I beseech thee, for God's and thy own sake, seriously to weigh and frequently to consider, in the silence of thy recollected mind, these words of the great doctor of the Church, St. Austin,[1] which are here adjoined.

Three sayings of St. Austin most worthy to be noted; taken out of his first book of faith, *ad Petrum*.

1. Hold for most certain, and in no wise doubt, that not only all pagans, but also Jews, heretics, and schismatics, who die out of the Catholic Church, shall go to never-ending fire, prepared for the devil and his angels.

---

[1] Editor's note: This is the common moniker used among English Catholics for St. Augustine of Hippo.

2. Hold for most certain, and in no wise doubt, that no heretic or schismatic, baptized in the name of the Father, and of the Son, and of the Holy Ghost, if he be not united (by faith and charity) to the Catholic Church, though he give never so great alms, yea die for the name of Christ, can in any wise be saved. For neither baptism, nor ever so great almsdeeds, nor death undergone for the name of Christ can be profitable to salvation, as long as one remaineth in the wickedness of heresy or schism, which leadeth to damnation.

3. Hold for most certain, and in no wise doubt, that not all who are baptized according to the rites of the Catholic Church shall receive everlasting life, but only those who after baptism live righteously, that is, abstain from vices and desires of the flesh. For as faithless heretics shall not have the kingdom of heaven, so naughty Catholics shall never inherit the same.

These are the words of St. Austin, that great light of God's Church; I pray God they may be imprinted and even rivetted in thy heart, and therein work that effect, which (together with thy prayers), I desire. Farewell.

The Sum of the Christian Catholic Faith

The Apostles' Creed

1. I believe in God the Father Almighty, Creator of heaven and earth.
2. And in Jesus Christ his only Son our Lord.
3. Who was conceived by the Holy Ghost, born of the Virgin Mary.
4. Suffered under Pontius Pilate; was crucified, dead, and buried.
5. Descended into hell; the third day he rose again from death.
6. Ascended into heaven, sitteth at the right hand of God the Father Almighty.

7. From thence he shall come to judge the quick and the dead.
8. I believe in the Holy Ghost.
9. The holy Catholic Church, the communion of saints.
10. Remission of sins.
11. Resurrection of the flesh.
12. Life everlasting. Amen.

Our Lord's Prayer

Our Father which art in heaven, 1) hallowed be thy name. 2) Thy kingdom come, 3) thy will be done in earth, as it is in heaven. 4) Give us this day our daily bread, 5) and forgive us our trespasses, as we forgive them that trespass against us. 6) And lead us not into temptation, 7) but deliver us from evil. Amen.

The Angelical Salutation

Hail Mary, full of grace, our Lord is with thee; blessed art thou amongst women, and blessed is the fruit of thy womb, Jesus. Holy Mary, Mother of God, pray for us sinners, now and in the hour of our death. Amen.

The Ten Commandments

I am the Lord thy God;
1. Thou shalt have no other gods before me.
2. Thou shalt not take the name of God in vain.
3. Remember that thou sanctify the feasts.
4. Honor thy father and mother.
5. Thou shalt not murder.
6. Thou shalt not commit adultery.
7. Thou shalt not steal.
8. Thou shalt not bear false witness.
9. Thou shalt not desire thy neighbor's wife.
10. Thou shalt not covet thy neighbor's goods.

The Seven Sacraments

1. Baptism.
2. Confirmation.
3. Eucharist.
4. Penance.
5. Extreme unction.
6. Order.
7. Matrimony.

Three Theological Virtues

1. Faith.
2. Hope.
3. Charity.

Four Cardinal Virtues

1. Prudence.
2. Justice.
3. Fortitude.
4. Temperance.

Seven Gifts of the Holy Ghost

1. Wisdom.
2. Understanding.
3. Counsel.
4. Fortitude.
5. Knowledge.
6. Piety.
7. Fear of God.

Twelve Fruits of the Holy Ghost

1. Charity.
2. Joy.
3. Peace.
4. Patience.
5. Benignity.
6. Goodness.
7. Longanimity.
8. Mildness.
9. Faith.
10. Modesty.
11. Continency.
12. Chastity.

Two Precepts of Charity

1) Thou shalt love the Lord thy God, with thy whole heart, with thy whole soul, with all thy strength, and with all thy mind, 2) and thy neighbor as thyself.

The Commandments of the Church

1. To keep certain appointed days holy, with leaving work and hearing Mass.
2. To keep fast and abstinence certain days.
3. To pay tithes to the pastors of the Church.
4. To be confessed of their pastor, at least once a year.
5. To receive the Blessed Sacrament, and that at Easter, or thereabouts.

To which may be adjoined:
6. Not to marry at certain times, and in certain degrees, nor privily without witness.

The Works of Mercy Corporal

1. To feed the hungry.
2. To give drink to the thirsty.
3. To clothe the naked.
4. To visit and ransom the captives.
5. To harbor the harborless.
6. To visit the sick.
7. To bury the dead.

Works of Mercy Spiritual

1. To correct the sinner.
2. To instruct the ignorant.
3. To counsel the doubtful.
4. To comfort the sorrowful.
5. To bear patiently wrongs.
6. To forgive all injuries.
7. To pray for others, both quick and dead.

The Eight Beatitudes

1. Blessed are the poor in spirit, for theirs is the kingdom of heaven.
2. Blessed are the meek, for they shall possess the land.
3. Blessed are they that mourn, for they shall be comforted.
4. Blessed are they that hunger and thirst for righteousness, for they shall be filled.
5. Blessed are the merciful, for they shall find mercy.
6. Blessed are the clean in heart, for they shall see God.
7. Blessed are the peacemakers, for they shall be called the sons of God.
8. Blessed are they that suffer persecution for righteousness sake, for theirs is the kingdom of heaven.

The Five Senses of the Body

1. Sight.
2. Hearing.
3. Smelling.
4. Taste.
5. Touching.

The Office of Christian Justice

To decline from evil, or sin. To do good, or the office of justice.

Of Sin

Sin is double, original and actual; which actual again is either mortal or venial.

The Seven Capital or Deadly Sins

1. Pride.
2. Covetousness.
3. Lechery.
4. Anger.
5. Gluttony.
6. Envy.
7. Sloth.

To which these virtues are contrary:
1. Humility.
2. Liberality.
3. Chastity.
4. Patience.
5. Abstinence.
6. Charity.
7. Devotion.

The Six Sins against the Holy Ghost

1. Despair of salvation.
2. Presumption to be saved without merits.
3. To impugn the known truth.
4. Envy at another man's grace.
5. Obstinacy in sin.
6. Final impenitence.

Things Necessary for the Repentant Sinner

1. Contrition of heart.
2. Entire confession to a priest, capable and approved.
3. Satisfaction by work.

True contrition consisteth in hearty displeasure of sin past, for the love of God; and full resolution not to sin anymore.

Sins That Cry Vengeance in the Sight of God

1. Willful murder.
2. Carnal sin against nature.
3. Oppression of the poor.
4. To defraud workmen of their wages.

Nine Ways of Being Accessory to Another Man's Sin

1. By counsel.
2. By commandment.
3. By consent.
4. By provocation, or leading others.
5. By praise or flattery.
6. By concealing the faulty.
7. By partaking.

8. By holding our peace, and not speaking unto such as be under our charge.
9. By dissembling, or not finding fault, and letting when we may, or have charge.

Three Kinds of Good Works

1. Almsdeeds.
2. Prayer.
3. Fasting.

Three Evangelical Counsels

1. Voluntary poverty.
2. Perpetual chastity.
3. Entire obedience.

The Four Last Things to Be Remembered

1. Death.
2. Judgment.
3. Hell.
4. Heaven.

This summary of our Christian faith is to believe in general that there is but one only God, and yet that in him there are three Persons in one nature, that is, God the Father, God the Son, God the Holy Ghost; of which the second Person, to wit, God the Son, the time appointed by his eternal providence being come, took man's flesh upon him, remaining God and man together, and conversing with men about the space of three-and-thirty years, taught them the way to heaven; and withal did found and build his Church by the means as well of his own preaching, as of his apostles and their successors; and for the conservation and continuance thereof, besides that, he left a visible chieftain or head in his place, that is to say, a high priest or supreme bishop, who is our holy father the pope, whom he hath promised that his faith shall never fail; he ordained also his sacraments, which are in number seven, by means whereof, as by certain conduits, he doth communicate his gifts and graces to Christians, for to engender, nourish, strengthen, heal, augment, and conserve them in the spiritual life.

And concerning this point of the Church, every Christian ought firmly to believe and rest most assured of two things. First, that this same Church cannot err, or fail, and much less fall; both because it is always guided and directed by the Holy Ghost, who is infallible, as also for that her spouse Jesus Christ hath promised never to forsake her. Secondly, that those only, which remain in this Church, believing what she believeth, and living as she commands, can be saved, and no others; whence it follows that all heathens, idolaters, Jews, and heretics are in the way of perdition and death everlasting, as all those that during the deluge were out of the ark of Noah.

"Some things we learn, that we may only know them; and some other things we learn, that we may also do them."[2]

"He that will not hear the church, let him be to thee as the heathen and the publican."[3]

[2] Augustine, *On Psalm 118:6*
[3] Mt 18:17

A BRIEF EXPLICATION OF THE SUMMARY AFORE-GOING; OR, THE LITTLE CATHOLIC CATECHISM WRITTEN BY R.F.P. CANISIUS OF THE SOCIETY OF JESUS

Of Faith and the Apostles' Creed

1. **Who is to be called a Christian and a Catholic?**
He that being baptized doth profess the wholesome doctrine of Jesus Christ, God and man, in his Church, and doth not follow any sects or opinions contrary to the same.

2. **What are Christians chiefly to be instructed in?**
In faith, hope, charity, the sacraments, and the duties of Christian justice.

3. **What is faith?**
Faith is a gift of God, and a light, wherewith a man being illuminated believeth all things which God hath revealed, and by his Church propounded unto us to be believed, whether they be written, or not written.[4]

4. **Which is the sum of faith, or of things to be believed?**
The Apostles' Creed, divided into twelve articles.

5. **Which are those twelve articles?**
These: I believe in God the Father Almighty, etc., as before.

[4] Cf. Heb 11

6. **What is the meaning of the first article: "I believe in God the Father"?**
It declares the first Person in the Godhead, to wit, the heavenly and eternal Father, to whom nothing is impossible or hard to do; who of nothing hath created heaven and earth with all other things, both visible and invisible, and having created them, doth likewise conserve and govern them with wonderful goodness and wisdom.[5]

7. **What signifies the second article: "And in Jesus Christ his only Son"?**
It demonstrates the second Person in the Godhead, to wit, Jesus Christ, the natural and only Son of God, who was begotten of him from eternity and is consubstantial to the Father, and our Lord and Redeemer, who delivered and saved us when we were lost.[6]

8. **What signifies the third article: "Who was conceived by the Holy Ghost"?**
It lays open the mystery of our Lord's incarnation; because the same Son of God descending from heaven, took human nature upon him, but altogether after a singular and unspeakable manner: as being conceived without a father by the virtue of the Holy Ghost, and born of the immaculate Virgin Mary.[7]

9. **What signifies the fourth article: "Suffered under Pontius Pilate"?**
It doth treat of the mystery of man's redemption. For the same true Son of God, according to that our human nature thus taken upon him, did suffer the very extremity of most cruel punishments, for to redeem us and all sinners. Insomuch as though he was the "Lamb without spot,"[8] he was notwithstanding crucified under the president Pontius Pilate, died upon the cross, and afterward was buried.[9]

[5] Cf. Gn 1; Jn 5
[6] Cf. Mt 16; Lk 1
[7] Cf. Mt 1; Lk 1; Jn 1
[8] Ex 12:5; 1 Pt 1:19
[9] Cf. Mt 17; Jn 4

10. **What signifies the fifth article: "He descended into hell"?**

It comprehends the mystery of the resurrection of Christ;[10] who according to his soul, descended to deliver the fathers out of *limbus*;[11] and the third day after his death, re-assuming his body by his own power, returned to life again.

11. **What signifies the sixth article: "He ascended to heaven"?**

It shows the mystery of the glorious ascension of Christ, who, having accomplished the work of our redemption, departed from this world to his Father, and by his own power ascended triumphant into heaven, and there, in the eternal glory of his Father, is placed above all.[12]

12. **What signifies the seventh article: "From thence he shall come to judge the quick and the dead"?**

It doth set the day of judgment before our eyes, when Christ shall descend again from heaven, visible in his human nature, to give that dreadful judgment upon all, good and bad, and shall reward everyone according to his works.[13]

13. **What signifies the eighth article: "I believe in the Holy Ghost"?**

It doth express the third Person in the Trinity, to wit, the Holy Ghost, who, proceeding from the Father and the Son, is with them one, true, and eternal God, and so reigneth with the Father and the Son, and accordingly is adored and glorified together with them both.[14]

14. **What signifies the ninth article: "The holy Catholic Church"?**

It doth teach us four things to be believed concerning the Church. First, that the Church is one, that is: established in one Spirit of Christ Jesus, in one doctrine of faith and sacraments, in one head and

[10] Cf. Acts 2; Mt 18
[11] Cf. Eph 4; 1 Cor 5
[12] Cf. Acts 1; Mk 16
[13] Cf. Mt 25
[14] Cf. 1 Jn 5

governor of this universal Church, namely, the vicar of Christ and St. Peter's successor.[15]

Secondly, that this same Church is holy; because both it is made holy by Christ the head and spouse thereof, to whom it is joined by faith and sacraments, and also is continually governed and directed by the Holy Ghost.

Thirdly, that the same Church is catholic or universal; because, being spread through the whole world, it comprehends all faithful Christians that have been, are, and shall be at all times.[16]

Fourthly and lastly, that in this same Church there is a communion of saints, that is, not only of the faithful yet living here on earth, but also of those who, freed from the mortality of flesh, do either reign in heaven, or being to reign there hereafter, are as yet detained in purgatory to be cleansed of the remaining ordure of their sins; which saints, as members of one body, do mutually assist one another with their good works, merits, and prayers, and are partakers of the virtue of the most Holy Sacrifice of the Mass and sacraments of holy Church.[17]

15. **What signifies the tenth article: "Forgiveness of sins"?**
It offereth the present grace of God to all sinners, lest any do ever despair of obtaining pardon of his sins, so he persevere in the Catholic Church, and duly use the sacraments of the same.

16. **What signifies the eleventh article: "The resurrection of the flesh"?**
It doth affirm that all the dead are to be raised to life; and also doth confirm the last day of judgment. For we are all to appear before the judgment seat of Christ in our flesh, that everyone may receive his reward, good or evil, according as he hath behaved himself in his body, well or ill.[18]

---

[15] Cf. Eph 4, 5; 1 Cor 6; Jn 14, 16
[16] Cf. Mk 16; Dn 2
[17] Cf. Rom 12; Eph 4; Ps 12
[18] Cf. Jb 19; 1 Cor 13; Jn 5, 11; 1 Thes 4

17. **What signifies the twelfth and last article: "And life everlasting"?**

It showeth the happy immortality which is to be the reward of true faith and Christian virtue;[19] to the end we may certainly know that after this life there is remaining another far different and truly blessed, secure, and everlasting, which is promised to all that do believe in Christ and obey him.

18. **What is the sum of all these articles of belief?**

With heart and mouth, I do confess our Lord God, than whom nothing can be imagined more wise or good; and that he is both one in divine essence and nature, and threefold in Persons, to wit, Father, Son, and Holy Ghost, so as these three are one: one, true, eternal, immense, and incomprehensible God, of whom, by whom, and in whom are all things. The Father is the Maker of all things; the Son, the Redeemer of mankind; the Holy Ghost, the Sanctifier and governor of the Church or the faithful of Christ. To this most holy and undivided Trinity, therefore, do the three principal parts of the Creed answer: the first, which treats of our creation, answering to the Father; the second, which treats of our redemption, to the Son; and the third, which treats of our sanctification, to the Holy Ghost.

19. **What is the Church?**

It is a congregation of all those that do profess the faith and doctrine of Christ, which here on earth is governed under one head and chief pastor, next to Christ.[20]

20. **Which be those that are altogether separated from this Church?**

First the Jews and all infidels; secondly, heretics, to wit, those which, being baptized, do stubbornly maintain errors against the Catholic faith; thirdly, schismatics, who of their own accord do sever themselves from the peace and unity thereof; and lastly, those that lawfully by ecclesiastical power are excluded from the communion of saints, and the suffrages and divine services of the Church: whence they are also called excommunicated persons.

[19] Cf. Mt 25
[20] Cf. 1 Cor 12; 1 Pt 5; Jn 21; Mt 16

All which are both dismembered from the body of Christ, which is the Church, and consequently remain devoid of spiritual life and salvation; and unless they repent, become slaves to Satan, and guilty of never-ending death. And all such persons are carefully to be shunned by Catholics; but heretics especially and schismatics are to be eschewed and abhorred no less than contagious and deadly diseases.

21. **Which is finally the plain, short, and direct rule of faith whereby Catholics are discerned from heretics?**

It is this: to profess the faith of Christ, and full authority of the Church; and to hold that ratified and established which the pastors and doctors of the Catholic Church have concluded upon to be believed. If, moreover, any do not hear the Church, "let him be unto thee (saith Christ himself) as a heathen and a publican."[21] For he shall not have God to be his Father who will not have the Church to be his mother.[22]

Of Hope and Our Lord's Prayer

22. **What is hope?**

Hope is a virtue infused by God, whereby with assured confidence we expect the happiness of our salvation, and life everlasting.[23]

23. **Whence do we learn the manner how we ought to hope and pray aright?**

Out of our Lord's Prayer, which Christ himself, our blessed Lord and master, hath taught and prescribed by his own most sacred mouth.[24]

[21] Mt 18:17
[22] Cf. Cyprian, *On the Unity of the Church*, n. 6
[23] Cf. 1 Pt 1; Rom 5
[24] Cf. Mt 6; Lk 11

24. Rehearse our Lord's Prayer.
Our Father, etc., as before.

25. What meaneth the beginning of this prayer: "Our Father, which art in heaven"?
It is a little preface, as it were, which puts us in mind of that highest benefit, whereby God the Father through Christ hath adopted us for his children and heirs.[25] And besides, by this sweet and loving name of *Father*, we are stirred up both to love him again and to pray with greater confidence.

26. What doth the first petition express: "Hallowed be thy name"?
It doth express unto us the due and hearty wishes which the children of God have: in desiring that always and in all places, the knowledge, fear, honor, love, and worship of his eternal majesty and whatsoever in fine doth belong to the glory of our highest and most indulgent Father, may be advanced.

27. What do we ask in the second petition: "Thy kingdom come"?
We ask the glory of the kingdom of heaven, and everlasting happiness to be given us, that shortly we may come to reign with Christ forever.

28. What do we ask in the third petition: "Thy will be done"?
We ask and implore the help of God's grace, that sincerely, cheerfully, and constantly we may fulfill the will of God the Father, on earth, as the blessed do it in heaven.[26]

29. What do we ask in the fourth petition: "Give us this day our daily bread"?
We ask that all necessaries belonging to the nourishment and sustenance of our life, both corporal and spiritual, may be afforded us: as are food, clothing, God's word, and the sacraments of the Church.[27]

[25] Cf. Rom 1; Gal 4
[26] Cf. Rom 8
[27] Cf. Jn 6; Mt 4

30. What do we ask in the fifth petition: "And forgive us our trespasses"?

We crave pardon and forgiveness of our sins, being ready likewise to forgive others that trespass against us.[28]

31. What do we ask in the sixth petition: "And lead us not into temptation"?

We crave in this so great frailty of our life to be succored and upheld by heavenly strength, and to be defended against the world, the flesh, and the devil: that in no wise we yielding to temptation may give consent to sin.[29]

32. What do we ask in the seventh and last petition: "But deliver us from evil"?

We demand the goodness and assistance of God, that he may deliver and rescue us from misery, both of body and soul, whether it be in this life, as far as is convenient for our salvation, or in the life to come.[30] And we add *Amen*, or, "So be it," to show the desire and hope we have of obtaining what these seven petitions do contain.

33. What is the sum of the above-said petitions of this prayer?

The first four petitions do declare what we are to demand and hope for in this life; of which the chiefest is the honor and glory of His Divine Majesty; the next is our own happiness; then, the obedience we owe to God; and lastly, necessary sustenance for body and soul. These are the things that summarily are contained in the first four petitions.

34. What is the effect of the rest?

The three latter contain the evils which we are to pray that God will turn away from us, as are: sins, which do debar us from the kingdom of God; temptations, which, unless we be protected by the help of God, of their own force are enough to draw us to sin; and lastly, the calamities both of this life and the life to come, so as our Lord's Prayer doth teach us both how to demand good things and seek the avoidance of evil.

[28] Cf. Mt 6; Lk 6
[29] Cf. Eph 6
[30] Cf. 1 Tm 2

35. **How do you say the *Ave Maria?***
    Hail Mary, etc., as above.

36. **From whence came this manner of praying to the Mother of God?**
    First, from the example of the angel Gabriel and St. Elizabeth; then, from the custom and consent of holy Church.[31]

37. **But what fruit doth this salutation bring us?**
    It doth renew in us the wholesome remembrance of the sacred Virgin, and of our Lord's incarnation wrought by her means; and it doth further put us in mind to purchase the said Blessed Virgin's favor and her intercession with God for us.

38. **What do we learn out of this salutation?**
    We learn thereby to know the excellent endowments and high praises of the incomparable Virgin; as that she was replenished with most ample gifts of God and divine virtues; that she was a Virgin and a Mother; that she was Mother of the King of kings, Christ Jesus our Lord and God, and consequently to us, a Mother of life.

Of Charity and the Ten Commandments

39. **What is charity?**
    Charity is a virtue infused by God, whereby we love God for himself, and our neighbor for God.[32]

[31] Cf. Lk 1
[32] Cf. Lk 10; Mt 22

40. **How many are the precepts of charity?**

Two chiefly, which our Lord God hath set down in these words: "Thou shalt love thy Lord God with all thy heart, with all thy soul, and with all thy mind, and with all thy strength; this is the first and greatest commandment. And the second is like to this: Thou shalt love thy neighbor as thyself"; of these precepts or commandments "depends all the law and the prophets."[33]

41. **By what sign doth our charity or love to God manifest itself?**

If you keep his commandments: "For this is the love of God, that we keep his commandments; and his commandments are not heavy," as witnesseth St. John the apostle.[34] And Christ himself doth teach: "He that hath my commandments and keepeth them, is he that loveth me."[35]

42. **How doth our love to our neighbor show itself?**

That is sufficiently expressed by St. Paul in these words: "Charity is patient, it is benign: charity envieth not, it dealeth not perversely; is not puffed up; is not ambitious, seeks not her own, is not provoked to anger, it thinks not evil; rejoiceth not upon iniquity, but rejoiceth with the truth; suffereth all things, believeth all things, hopes all things, beareth all things."[36]

43. **Why therefore are the ten commandments given us?**

Though there be two precepts or commandments of charity, wherein the fullness of the law doth consist, yet are the ten commandments adjoined, to the end that all may the more clearly understand what doth appertain to the performance of our charity, both to God and our neighbor.

[33] Mt 22:37-40
[34] 1 Jn 5:3
[35] Jn 14:21
[36] 1 Cor 13:4-7

44. **Which are the ten commandments?**

I am thy Lord God. Thou shalt have no other gods before me, etc., as above.[37]

45. **What is the meaning of the first commandment: "Thou shalt have no other gods before me"?**

It forbids and condemns idolatry, or the worship of false gods, witchcraft, divining, and all superstitious observations, and finally, all ungodly worship; and on the contrary, it requires that we believe, serve, and invoke one most good and omnipotent God.[38]

46. **Is it not lawful then to worship and pray to saints?**

It is; not in that manner which we are commanded to worship and pray to God, as being our Creator, our Redeemer, and giver of all good things, but in a degree far inferior, to wit, as the beloved friends of God, and our intercessors and patrons with God.[39]

47. **Is the use of pictures of Christ and his saints contrary to this commandment?**

In no wise; because to that which is commanded in these words: "Thou shalt not make to thyself any graven image," the reason is presently added, "to adore it,"[40] that is, as the heathens do, who set up images of false gods, and impiously worship their idols. But we, after a pious manner delivered us by our forefathers, do in pictures worship Christ and his saints, whom the pictures do represent.[41]

[37] Cf. Ex 20
[38] Cf. Ex 23; Dt 18
[39] Cf. John Damascene, *An Exposition of the Orthodox Faith*, Bk. 4, Ch. 15; Col 4; 2 Thes 3
[40] Dt 20:4, 5
[41] Cf. Dn 4; Gregory the Great, Bk. 11, Epistle 13; Second Council of Nicea

48. **What forbids the second commandment: "Thou shalt not take the name of thy God in vain"?**

It forbids the abusing of the name of God, and the irreverence which is committed by forswearing and blaspheming people that, without some great cause of truth and reverence, do swear by God, his saints, or any creature.[42]

49. **What doth the third commandment enjoin us: "Remember thou keep holy the sabbath-day"?**

It commands the sabbath-day (or day determined by the Church) to be kept and celebrated by performing of good and holy actions; which is done by going to Church, hearing of Mass, and assisting otherwise at divine service. But to work and employ oneself in servile labors it utterly forbids.[43]

50. **What doth the fourth commandment enjoin us: "Honor thy father and mother"?**

It commands us to yield reverence, obedience, and help to those who, next to God, are the authors of our life; and to satisfy them by all manner of duties. Then it commands us to account our magistrates, as well temporal as spiritual or ecclesiastical, to be in the rank of our parents and superiors, and that willingly we obey them and respect their power and authority.[44]

51. **In what manner shall we reverence ecclesiastical power and authority?**

By yielding due respect and obedience to holy and general councils, to the received ordinances and decrees of the apostles and fathers, to approved customs of our ancestors, and finally, to the high pastors, bishops, and prelates of the Church. Whereas those do sin most grievously that slight and violate divine service, and ecclesiastical ordinances and ceremonies; also those that oppose themselves against such like councils and prelates, and infringe rights belonging to priests, or usurp churches, profaning sacred and hallowed things.

[42] Cf. Ecclus 23; Jer 4; Mt 5
[43] Cf. Dt 5; Jer 17
[44] Cf. Eph 6; Col 3; Rom 13; Heb 13

52. **What meaneth the fifth commandment: "Thou shalt not kill"?**

It forbids open violence, murder, and all manner of wrong that may be offered our neighbor in his body and life. And withal it prohibits anger, hatred, rancor, disdain, and all other affections any ways tending to the hurt of our neighbor.[45]

53. **What doth the sixth commandment forbid: "Thou shalt not commit adultery"?**

It forbids fornication, adultery, and all other unclean and unlawful acts in that kind, as also whatsoever else is contrary to purity, chastity, and modesty.[46] For even he that doth but behold a woman with bad desire, hath already committed the sin in his heart, saith our Savior Christ.[47]

54. **What is forbidden in the seventh commandment: "Thou shalt not steal"?**

By it is forbidden all unlawful taking and usurping of another man's goods; as done by stealing, robbing, usury, unjust gain, deceit, cozening, fraudulent bargains, and finally, by all kinds of exchanges and dealings whereby Christian charity is limited and our neighbor circumvented.[48]

55. **What is forbidden in the eighth commandment: "Thou shalt not bear false witness against thy neighbor"?**

By this commandment is forbidden false witness-bearing, lying, and all misusing of the tongue against our neighbor; as is done by tale-tellers, backbiters, ill-speakers, flatterers, liars, and forswearers.[49]

56. **What do the two last commandments forbid: "Thou shalt not covet thy neighbor's wife, nor his goods"?**

They forbid the coveting of another man's wife and goods; because whatsoever belongeth to another man is not only unlawful for us to possess

---

[45] Cf. Mt 5; Dt 5; Ex 20
[46] Cf. 1 Cor 6; Mt 5; Eph 5; Heb 13
[47] Cf. Mt 5:28
[48] Cf. 1 Cor 6; Eph 4; 1 Tm 4
[49] Cf. Eph 4; 1 Pt 2; Jas 4

unjustly and at our own pleasure, but we ought not so much as with our will to desire it, so that being content with what is our own, we may live without all envy, emulation, and covetousness.[50]

57. **What is the sum and end of the ten commandments?**
This: that God and our neighbor may sincerely be loved by us;[51] which was anciently signified by the distinguishing of these commandments into two tables, made by God himself. For in the first table were delivered three commandments, peculiarly belonging to the love of God; and in the second were contained the other seven, pertaining to the love of our neighbor.[52]

58. **In what manner do the commandments of the first table teach the love of God?**
In this: that they forbid and take away all vices most contrary to the true worship and honor of God, as are idolatry, apostasy, heresy, perjury, superstition; and command, on the other side, true and pure worship and service of God to be faithfully performed with heart, mouth, and deed; and where this is done, the only true God is served and adored with that true divine worship proper to him alone, called *latria*.

59. **How do the commandments of the second table declare our love to our neighbor?**
In this: that they orderly comprehend our duty toward our neighbor, to wit: that we do not only honor our elders and superiors, but also endeavor to do good to all in deed, word, and will, and to be hurtful to none, whether we regard the body of our neighbor, or the party joined to us in wedlock, or the goods of fortune.[53]

---

[50] Cf. Mt 5; Dt 5
[51] Cf. 1 Jn 5
[52] Cf. Ex 20
[53] Cf. Ti 2; 1 Cor 13

60. **What is the sum and effect of the commandments concerning the love of our neighbor?**

This: what thou wilt not have another to do to thee, that do thou not to another. "But all things whatsoever you will that men do to you, do you also to them. For this is the law and the prophets."[54]

61. **Are there any other besides the ten commandments?**

There are, and those not only profitably but also necessarily to be kept, especially the commandments of the Church, whom, as our most holy mother and the spouse of Christ, we her children are all bound to hearken to and obey.[55]

62. **How many are the commandments of the Church?**

There be chiefly five.

1. Keep holy days appointed by the holy Church.
2. Hear Holy Mass devoutly upon Sundays and holy days.
3. Observe the fasting days commanded, and abstinence from forbidden meats.
4. Confess thy sins (at least) once a year to thine own pastor or priest, or to another with license.
5. Receive the Blessed Sacrament at the least once a year, and that about Easter.

63. **What fruit doth the keeping of these commandments bring us?**

These and the like commandments and ordinances of the Church do first exercise our Christian faith, humility, and obedience; and then do nourish, maintain, and adorn divine service, and well-ordered discipline, and public tranquility; and do withal wonderfully avail that all things in the Church be performed with order and decency. And besides we do merit much toward our salvation if we keep the said commandments with due love and charity.[56]

---

[54] Mt 7:12
[55] Cf. Mt 1, 13; Council of Agde
[56] Cf. 1 Cor 13

Of the Sacraments

64. What is a sacrament?

It is a visible sign of an invisible grace, instituted by God for our sanctification.[57] For one thing it is, which we see in the sacrament, and another, which we receive therein: we see the outward sign, but we receive the inward, hidden, and spiritual grace, which is called the thing (or effect and fruit) of the sacrament.[58]

65. How many sacraments be there?

There be seven; which being instituted by our Savior Christ, delivered by his apostles, and still from time to time continuing in the Catholic Church, are come even to these our days. And they be these: baptism, confirmation, Eucharist, penance, extreme unction, order, and matrimony.[59]

66. Why are sacraments so much to be reverenced and had in so great account?

First, because they are instituted by God our Savior in the new law;[60] secondly, because they not only signify, but also, as certain holy vessels of the divine Spirit, contain the grace of God whereof we stand in need, and confer the same in great plenty to all that duly do receive them; and withal because they are most present and sovereign remedies against sin, and divine medicines of our Samaritan;[61] and lastly, for that the grace, which good Christians have already, is thereby conserved, increased, and amplified in them.

[57] Cf. Augustine, *On Christian Doctrine*, Bk. 3
[58] Cf. Ambrose, *On the Sacraments*, Bk. 1, Ch. 3, n. 10
[59] Cf. Fourth Lateran Council; Council of Constance, "Condemned Articles of John Hus," n. 8; Council of Florence, "Bull of Union with the Armenians"; Council of Trent, Session 7, "On the Sacraments in General," Can. 1
[60] Cf. Council of Florence, "Bull of Union with the Armenians"
[61] Cf. Lk 10

67. **Why are solemn and ecclesiastical ceremonies used in the administration of the sacraments?**

For many and weighty respects. First, to the end that those who behold the administration of the sacraments may be put in mind that no profane thing is here acted, but certain hidden and celestial things, full of divine mysteries, which indeed require a special reverence. Secondly, that in those who come to the sacraments, they may further and augment the interior devotion which God especially doth require; whereof ceremonies are as it were the signs, testimonies, and exercises. Thirdly, that those who administer the sacraments may perform their office with greater worthiness and profit; whilst in so doing, they faithfully observe the institutions of the ancient Church, and follow the steps of the holy fathers. For it is clear that most of these ceremonies, by a continual succession in the Church, are derived from the apostles' times even to these our days. Lastly, by these ceremonies there is maintained a well-ordered and religious discipline, and public tranquility preserved, which oftentimes is much disturbed by alteration and novelty of external rites and accustomed ceremonies.

68. **What is baptism?**

It is the first and most necessary sacrament of the new law, which is once ministered with water, wherein we are spiritually born anew, and receiving full remission of our sins, adopted the children of God, and enrolled to be the heirs of life everlasting.[62]

69. **What is confirmation?**

It is a sacrament, administered by a bishop to those that are baptized; wherein by holy chrism and sacred words, grace is bestowed upon them, and strength of spirit increased both to believe firmly, and constantly to confess the name of our Lord, when need so requires.[63]

---

[62] Cf. Jn 3
[63] Cf. Acts 8, 19; Council of Florence, "Bull of Union with the Armenians"

70. **How many things are necessary to be known concerning the doctrine of the Holy Eucharist or Blessed Sacrament?**

Five. The first is the truth thereof. The second is the change of bread and wine into the body and blood of Christ. The third, a due adoration thereof. The fourth, the oblation of it. And the fifth, the receiving of the same.[64]

71. **What is the truth of this sacrament of the Eucharist?**

This it is: that Christ, true God and man, is truly and entirely contained and present with us in this sacrament, after a priest rightly ordained hath consecrated the bread and wine with those mystical words prescribed and delivered by the same our Savior Christ.[65]

72. **What change is there made by virtue of those words wherewith the priest doth consecrate this holy sacrament?**

This: that by these words, through the power of Christ, the bread and wine are changed and transubstantiated into the body and blood of our Lord; so as the said bread and wine after consecration do altogether cease, and are not at all in the Eucharist.[66]

73. **What adoration is due to this sacrament?**

The very same truly which is due to Christ our Lord and eternal God whom we acknowledge to be there present; and therefore, we do humbly worship this sacrament with greatest devotion, both internal and external, and with such religious reverence, both of body and mind, as is requisite.[67]

74. **Why is this sacrament held to be an oblation?**

Because it is the sacrifice of the new law, that is, a pure and unbloody offering succeeding the bloody sacrifices of the Judaical law; which sacrifice is celebrated in Holy Mass for all the faithful Christians, living and dead. Whence it proceeds that the Eucharist is not only of devotion received by

---

[64] Cf. Mt 2; 1 Cor 11
[65] Cf. Mt 26; Mk 14; Lk 22; Jn 6
[66] Cf. Mt 26; Fourth Lateran Council, Const. 1
[67] Cf. Mt 4; Apoc 14; Ps 98

Christian people, but also is by priests daily offered in continual remembrance of the passion and death of our Blessed Savior, and also availeth for expiation of sins; and in that kind hath always been so celebrated in the Church.

75. **What is to be observed in the receiving this sacrament?**
That which faith and the authority of our holy mother the Church doth teach us, to wit, that it is sufficient for a lay person to receive Christ wholly under one kind, or sign of bread alone, and that by this receiving of the sacrament, it followeth that whosoever cometh and receiveth worthily doth thereby obtain abundant grace of God, and afterward life everlasting, which is the true and entire fruit of this sacrament; and this becomes the more effectual, the oftener this sacred and wholesome Communion is worthily frequented.[68]

76. **What is penance?**
Penance is a second table after shipwreck, and a sacrament necessary for all that have fallen into sin after baptism, in which sacrament remission of sins both is demanded by the penitent, and given by the priest.

77. **How many parts be there of penance?**
There are three. 1) Contrition, or grief of a soul detesting her sins, and aspiring to a better life.[69] 2) Confession, or an expression of one's sins made unto a priest.[70] 3) Satisfaction, or a revenge and punishment taken of one's self for his offenses, thereby to bring forth fruits worthy of true penance.[71]

78. **What is extreme unction?**
Extreme unction is a sacrament, whereby the sick in greatest troubles of their sickness are, with holy oil and sacred words of our Savior, eased,

[68] Cf. Council of Constance, Session 13; Council of Florence, "Bull of Union with the Armenians"; Lk 24; Acts 2
[69] Cf. Ps 50
[70] Cf. Jas 5
[71] Cf. Mt 3

comforted, and strengthened, the more happily to depart out of this world, and their bodies also, if so to God it seem expedient, are restored to health.[72]

79. **What is order?**

Order is a sacrament, by which power is given to priests and other ministers of the Church, duly and decently to undergo ecclesiastical functions.[73]

80. **What is matrimony?**

Matrimony is a sacrament, whereby man and woman lawfully contracting do enter into an inseparable fellowship and company of living together; and are endowed with divine grace, both with honesty and Christian care to beget and bring up children, as also to the end that the sin of filthy lust and incontinency may thereby be avoided.

81. **Is there any difference amongst the sacraments?**

There is truly; for baptism, confirmation, and order, being once ministered, are never more reiterated to the same party, as the rest are. Also, baptism of necessity must be received of all; the Eucharist, of such as are of years of discretion; and penance, of those that are fallen into sin after baptism. As for the rest, it is free for every man's choice to use them; so as yet none contemn or neglect them when time requires.

[72] Cf. Jas 5; Council of Florence, "Bull of Union with the Armenians"
[73] Cf. Mt 10; 1 Tm 3; Acts 13

Of the Duties of Christian Justice

82. How many are the duties of Christian justice?
These two: decline from evil, or sin; and do good, or the duty of righteousness.[74]

83. How can a man avoid sin and do good, or perform righteousness?
A Christian, though he be not able of himself, yet strengthened with the grace and Spirit of Christ, can and ought, as much as the condition of this life doth permit, to live justly and keep the commandments.

84. How manifold is sin?
Twofold: original and actual.[75]

85. What is original sin?
Original sin is that which we bring with us from our birth, and is forgiven us by baptism through Christ.[76]

86. What is actual sin?
Actual sin is that which we say, do, or covet against or besides the law of God or the Church.[77]

87. How manifold is actual sin?
It is twofold: mortal, so called because it bringeth present death to the soul, for "the soul that sinneth...shall die";[78] and venial, so called because it is easily pardoned, without which in this life even the just do not live.

[74] Cf. Is 1; 1 Jn 3
[75] Cf. 2 Cor 5; Lk 1; Rom 8
[76] Cf. Rom 6
[77] Cf. Augustine, *Contra Faustum*, Bk. 22, Ch. 27
[78] Ez 18:4, 20; Cf. Jas 1

88. **By what degrees do we fall into sin?**

By these three: suggestion of the enemy; delight of our own part; and consent, or a determinate will to sin.[79]

89. **Which are the highest degrees of sinners?**

These, to wit: when men do wittingly and willingly sin of mere malice; and when also they do glory in their sin, and oppose themselves against such as admonish them, and wholly do contemn their wholesome admonitions.[80]

90. **Why is sin to be eschewed?**

Because it offends our Lord God, and deprives the offender of the chiefest good and brings him the greatest harm; whilst it takes away from him the blessed fruition of God, and doth engulf him in the everlasting pains of hell.

91. **Which are those that are called capital sins?**

Those from which, as from certain heads and fountains, all other sins do proceed.

92. **How many are those capital sins?**

Seven: pride, covetousness, luxury, envy, gluttony, anger, and sloth.[81]

93. **By what means may these sins be shunned and overcome?**

If we do cooperate with the grace of Jesus Christ, seriously considering the danger and damage these sins bring unto us, withal exercising the seven virtues opposite unto them.

94. **Which be those virtues that are opposite to the capital sins?**

These seven: humility, liberality, chastity, benignity, temperance, patience, devotion or diligent serving of God.[82]

---

[79] Cf. Jas 1ff
[80] Cf. Ps 5; Rom 2, 6
[81] Cf. Gregory the Great, *Moralia in Job*, Bk. 3
[82] Cf. 2 Pt 1

95. **Which are the sins that are said to be committed against the Holy Ghost?**
Those that of their own malice do so exclude God's grace, that they can neither be forgiven in this world but very hardly, nor in the world to come.[83]

96. **How many are the sins against the Holy Ghost?**
Six: presumption of the mercy of God or impunity of sin, desperation, impugning of the known truth, envy at fraternal charity, obstinate stubbornness, and impenitence.

97. **Which are the sins that are said to call to heaven for revenge?**
Those that of themselves are most abominable, and openly do break all laws of human charity; whence they are said in holy scripture to cry to heaven for vengeance; and indeed are many times in most fearful manner punished by God in this life.

98. **How many are those sins that cry to heaven for vengeance?**
These four: willful murder; the sin of Sodom; oppression of the poor, widows, and orphans; and defrauding laborers of their wages.[84]

99. **In what things are we accessory to other men's sins?**
In those which indeed are done by others, but yet so as we are either the authors or helpers thereunto, or at least do not hinder them when we may; and therefore are they also imputed unto us.

100. **How many ways may other men's sins be imputed to us?**
These nine ways: by counsel, commanding, consent, provoking, praising or flattering, concealing others' faults, winking at or not taking notice thereof, partaking, and by unjust defending of another man's evil deed.

[83] Cf. Mt 12; Mk 3
[84] Cf. Gn 4; Ex 22; Jas 5

101. **Which are called the works of the flesh?**
Such as men living according to the flesh and degenerating from spiritual children of God are wont to commit.

102. **Which are those works of the flesh?**
St. Paul rehearseth them in this manner: "The works of the flesh are man-ifest, which are these: fornication, uncleanness, dishonesty, riotousness, worship of idols, sorceries, enmities, strifes, emulation, brawls, discords, sects, envy, manslaughters, drunkenness, commessations, and such like; which I foretell you, as I have foretold you, that whosoever do commit such things, shall not attain the kingdom of God."[85]

103. **Is it enough for a Christian to fly evil and decline from sin?**
In no wise; but it behooveth him also to do good, and practice virtues.[86] Otherwise, he "that knoweth what is good, and doth it not, doth sin."[87]

104. **What good must a Christian do?**
In general, he ought to do what good soever the law of nature, God, or man doth command, but in particular, everyone according to his vocation ought, with thanksgiving, to discharge his calling and to cooperate with the holy grace of God: "For every tree that bears not good fruit, shall be cut down and thrown into the fire."[88]

105. **Which are the principal kinds of good works?**
Those by which we live soberly, justly, and piously in this world; and by which the very just themselves become more and more just, and holy men become daily more holy.[89]

---

[85] Gal 5:19-21
[86] Cf. Ps 36; Rom 2
[87] Jas 4:17
[88] Mt 3:10; 7:19; Cf. 1 Cor 7; Eph 4
[89] Cf. Ti 2

106. **How manifold are these kinds of good works?**

Threefold, to wit: fasting, almsdeeds, and prayer; whereof we read thus: "Prayer is good, with fasting and almsdeeds."[90]

107. **What is the fruit of good works?**

They have the promise and rewards both of this and eternal life; they pacify God, conserve and augment grace, and finally, they make a Christian man's calling sure and perfect. "Brethren labor that by good works you make sure your vocation and election."[91]

108. **What is fasting?**

To abstain from eating of flesh upon certain days, according to the custom and prescript of the Church; and by making one meal a day, to live thereby more sparingly. But if we understand this word *fast* in a more general sort, it is every chastisement of the body piously undertaken, that either our flesh may become subject to the spirit, or obedience be exercised, or God's grace impetrated.

109. **What is prayer?**

Prayer is a raising up of the mind to God; whereby we either ask that we may be defended from evil, or that things necessary to our body and soul may be bestowed upon us and others, or lastly, praise and give thanks to God.[92]

110. **What is almsgiving or mercy?**

It is a good deed, whereby we have compassion of another body's misery, and succor him therein.[93]

---

[90] Tb 12:8
[91] 2 Pt 1:10
[92] Cf. John Damascene, *An Exposition of the Orthodox Faith*, Bk. 3, Ch. 24
[93] Cf. Mt 25

111. **How many sorts of almsdeeds or works of mercy are there?**

Two sorts, for some are corporal works of mercy, and other spiritual; because they belong to the relieving either of corporal or spiritual necessity.

112. **How many are the corporal works of mercy?**

Seven. To feed the hungry. To give drink to the thirsty. To clothe the naked. To ransom captives. To harbor the harborless. To visit the sick. To bury the dead.

113. **How many are the spiritual works of mercy?**

There are also seven. To admonish sinners. To instruct the ignorant. To give counsel to the doubtful. To pray to God for the quick and dead. To comfort the afflicted. To support patiently injuries. To pardon offenses.

114. **Which are the chiefest virtues of all others?**

Next to the three theological virtues, faith, hope, and charity, whereof we have already spoken, the chiefest which become Christians most of all are the cardinal virtues.

115. **Which are they you call cardinal virtues?**

Those that are, as it were, the fountains whence other virtues are derived, or as the *cardines*, that is, "hinges," whereon other virtues depending, a Christian's soul by holy life is opened to God, and shut to the world, the flesh, and the devil.

116. **How many are the cardinal virtues?**

Four: prudence, justice, temperance, and fortitude; whereby a man through Christ doth come to live prudently, uprightly, temperately, and courageously, and so please God.

117. Which are called the gifts of the Holy Ghost?
Those seven which rested, saith the prophet, upon our Savior, and from him, as fountain of all grace, are derived to others, to wit: the gift of wisdom, understanding, counsel, knowledge, fortitude, piety, and the fear of God.[94]

118. What are those things which are called the fruits of the Holy Ghost?
Those which people fearing God, and living according to his Spirit, do bring forth in their souls; and by which spiritual men are known from carnal.

119. Which are the fruits of the Holy Ghost?
St. Paul doth rehearse them in this manner: "Charity, joy, peace, patience, longanimity, bounty, meekness, faith, modesty, continency, chastity."[95]

120. Which are called evangelical beatitudes?
Those for which in the gospel even such people, as otherwise according to the world seem to be altogether wretched and unfortunate, are, notwithstanding, declared to be blessed and most happy.

121. How many are those evangelical beatitudes?
Eight, which our Savior Christ did thus deliver upon the mountain.[96]
1. Blessed are the poor in spirit, for theirs is the kingdom of heaven.
2. Blessed are the meek, for they shall possess the land (of the living).
3. Blessed are they that mourn, for they shall be comforted.
4. Blessed are they that hunger and thirst after justice, for they shall have their fill.
5. Blessed are the merciful, for they shall obtain mercy.
6. Blessed are the clean of heart, for they shall see God.
7. Blessed are the peacemakers, for they shall be called the children of God.
8. Blessed are they that suffer persecution for justice, for theirs is the kingdom of heaven.

[94] Cf. Is 11:1-3
[95] Gal 5:22-23
[96] Cf. Mt 5

122. Which are called evangelical counsels?

Those which in the gospel are propounded by Christ, not by way of commanding but counseling, as things not necessary for all to salvation, but more expedient and profitable for those that undergo them.

123. Which are called evangelical counsels?

These principally, to wit: voluntary poverty, perpetual chastity, and entire obedience, which, for God, is religiously yielded to man.

124. What be those things that are called the last things of man?

Those which last of all do happen to man, and are: death, judgment, hell, and heavenly glory. Whereof Solomon speaketh thus: "In all thy works remember thy last things, and thou wilt never sin."[97]

It is not absurd that they forgive sins which have the Holy Ghost, for when they remit or retain, the Holy Ghost remitteth or retaineth in them; and that they do two ways: first in baptism, and then in penance.[98]

"Let everyone, my brethren, I beseech you, confess his sin whiles he is yet alive, while his confession may be admitted, whiles satisfaction and remission made by the priest is acceptable before God."[99]

---

[97] Ecclus 7:40
[98] Cf. Cyril of Alexandria, *On the Gospel of John*, Bk. 12, on Jn 20:22-23
[99] Cyprian, *On the Lapsed*, n. 29

ABOUT THIS SERIES

Tradivox was first conceived as an international research endeavor to recover lost and otherwise little-known Catholic catechetical texts. As the research progressed over several years, the vision began to grow, along with the number of project contributors and a general desire to share these works with a broader audience.

Legally incorporated in 2019, Tradivox has begun the work of carefully remastering and republishing dozens of these catechisms which were once in common and official use in the Church around the world. That effort is embodied in this *Tradivox Catholic Catechism Index*, a multi-volume series restoring artifacts of traditional faith and praxis for a contemporary readership. More about this series and the work of Tradivox can be learned at www.Tradivox.com.

SOPHIA INSTITUTE

Sophia Institute is a nonprofit institution that seeks to nurture the spiritual, moral, and cultural life of souls and to spread the Gospel of Christ in conformity with the authentic teachings of the Roman Catholic Church.

Sophia Institute Press fulfills this mission by offering translations, reprints, and new publications that afford readers a rich source of the enduring wisdom of mankind.

Sophia Institute also operates the popular online resource Catholic Exchange.com. *Catholic Exchange* provides world news from a Catholic perspective as well as daily devotionals and articles that will help readers to grow in holiness and live a life consistent with the teachings of the Church.

In 2013, Sophia Institute launched Sophia Institute for Teachers to renew and rebuild Catholic culture through service to Catholic education. With the goal of nurturing the spiritual, moral, and cultural life of souls, and an abiding respect for the role and work of teachers, we strive to provide materials and programs that are at once enlightening to the mind and ennobling to the heart; faithful and complete, as well as useful and practical.

Sophia Institute gratefully recognizes the Solidarity Association for preserving and encouraging the growth of our apostolate over the course of many years. Without their generous and timely support, this book would not be in your hands.

www.SophiaInstitute.com
www.CatholicExchange.com
www.SophiaInstituteforTeachers.org

Sophia Institute Press® is a registered trademark of Sophia Institute. Sophia Institute is a tax-exempt institution as defined by the Internal Revenue Code, Section 501(c)(3). Tax ID 22-2548708.